LLOYD GEORGE

LLOYD
GEORGE

―――――

THOMAS JONES C.H. LL.D.

*'There is a path which no fowl knoweth and
which the eye of the vulture hath not seen'*
JOB 28: 7
Framed embroidered text above **L.G.'s**
bed in Downing Street

GEOFFREY CUMBERLEGE
OXFORD UNIVERSITY PRESS
LONDON
1951

Oxford University Press, Amen House, London E.C. 4

GLASGOW NEW YORK TORONTO MELBOURNE WELLINGTON
BOMBAY CALCUTTA MADRAS CAPE TOWN

Geoffrey Cumberlege, Publisher to the University

PRINTED IN GREAT BRITAIN

FOR
EIRENE AND TRISTAN

AUTHOR'S PREFACE

MANY years must pass before a definitive life of Lloyd George is published. This book is an interim, unofficial contribution, adapted to a particular series; the author is not a trained historian, but for some years was a civil servant and at that time saw much of Lloyd George. Very modern history, however, Harold Temperley tells us, has generally to be learned from books which are not histories and from writers who are not historians. This outline is drawn from sources available to the public, and from the author's personal knowledge. It traces the career of a significant political innovator who has been much lauded and decried and who has been the subject of violent controversy. For his part in the conduct of the First World War he has written his own defence in his remarkable *Memoirs*. Some disputed matters are dealt with in the following pages at perhaps disproportionate length in an attempt to clarify the issues involved. I have tried to rid myself of prejudice and partiality but I am not so foolish as to believe that I have succeeded.

My first and greatest obligation is to Mrs. Dorothy E. Forrester, M.A., for every sort of assistance in the preparation of this book. Herself a Welshwoman, she has helped me throughout in drafting, checking, and deleting material, and any merit the book may possess must be largely ascribed to her skill and devotion. I wish to thank her in the most whole-hearted fashion.

Next, I desire to thank the Council of the National Library of Wales for facilities placed at my disposal in the amplest manner, including access to the unpublished Papers of the late D. R. Daniel and Sir Herbert Lewis. The Librarian, Sir William Davies, and his staff never failed to respond to the demands made upon their kindness and knowledge. I am under obligations also to Mr. R. O. Roberts, M.A., and Mr. I. G. John, M.A.

Every writer on Lloyd George in relation to the War of 1914–18 and to the Conferences which followed must constantly turn, as I have gratefully done, to his *War Memoirs* and *Peace Treaties*.

To those who have written books or articles from which I have quoted, or have given me advice, I am indebted, and if I have failed to acknowledge them in the text I desire to do so in this place. To these I must add my old chief, Lord Hankey, who allowed me the rare privilege of reading his unpublished work on 'The Supreme Command'.

For invaluable guidance in the preparation of the text and their unfailing courtesy and forbearance I desire to thank Mr. T. J. Wilson, Director of the Harvard University Press and Professor Donald C. McKay, editor of the series, 'Makers of Modern Europe'.

T. J.

ABERYSTWYTH, WALES
  Christmas 1950

CONTENTS

ILLUSTRATIONS

MAP

I

PREPARATION

1863–89

WALES

THE greatest Welshman whom that unconquerable race has produced since the age of the Tudors—this was the verdict on Lloyd George pronounced in Parliament two days after his death by the Prime Minister, Winston Churchill. It was fitting that this tribute should have been paid in the Chamber where in former days Lloyd George's oratory had roused the Commons, stirring some to a frenzy of admiration, others to a frenzy of anger. Fitting also that it was paid by the only parliamentarian and leader of his day comparable to him in stature and achievement. They were lifelong friends; in turn they led the nation through a world war; both had seen their efforts crowned with victory. Contrasted in the circumstances of birth and education, each in the hour of need proved to be the saviour of his country.

It is in the direction of his ancestry and childhood that we may find some clue to the personality whose character and career we are about to trace through eighty-two years of ceaseless activity. Had Lloyd George remained in the populous city of his birth he would still have challenged his fate with courage and been as impatient of frustration as he later proved to be; but had he missed the rich intimacies of village life and the training of a remarkable uncle he might not have grown into the unmistakable Welshman, intolerant of injustice and oppression, famous throughout the world.

The parents of David Lloyd George spent three months in Manchester, and there he was born on 17 January 1863, at 5 New York Place. His father, William George, was the son of a well-to-do Pembrokeshire farmer, but, because of his intellectual bent, preferred the teaching profession to farming. He seems to have been of a roving, restless disposition, and before going to Manchester he had held posts in London, Liverpool, Haverfordwest, Pwllheli, and Newchurch. While at Pwllheli he had met and married Elizabeth Lloyd, whose home was in Llanystumdwy, seven miles away. A girl, Mary, was the first child of the marriage, and then came David. At this time the father's health broke down, so he gave up his teaching appointment and went back to his native county where he rented a small farm. After an illness lasting barely a week he died on 7 June 1864.

But Elizabeth George, widowed at the age of thirty-six, was not left friendless. Her brother, Richard Lloyd, six years her junior, hastened to her help. The affairs of the little farm were soon wound up and then, with few material relics of her married life except her husband's library, the widow and her little family set off with her brother for Llanystumdwy in Caernarvonshire; David was then about eighteen months old. A third child was born shortly afterwards who, in memory of his father, was called William.

The household at Llanystumdwy was ruled by Rebecca Lloyd, the mother of Richard and Elizabeth. Her husband, a shoemaker, had died twenty-five years before, when her only son was five years old and her daughters quite young girls. A good business woman, she retained and directed the two craftsmen who had been employed by her husband, while she herself bought the leather needed for the trade and saw to the accounts. When he grew up, Richard took his father's place in the workshop, but the mother held the reins in her capable hands until she died a few years after the widowed daughter had come back to her.

By the Welsh standards of that time it was a reasonably comfortable and prosperous home of its type and period to which Elizabeth George and her family returned. The house, 'Highgate', with its three rooms on the ground floor and two bedrooms above, stood on the main road from Llanystumdwy to Criccieth. Llanystumdwy is a pleasant village of stone cottages through which the River Dwyfor flows, the curving, upward sweep of the road carried over its waters by a long triple-arched bridge. Behind the village the rising ground gives promise of the distant heights of Snowdonia, while towards the river mouth and the sea, about a mile away, the country opens out into wide low-lying fields. Everywhere there are trees.

In the lower part of the village the episcopal church and school are situated. Here, too, is the village smithy. Nearer 'Highgate' were two Nonconformist chapels, but the Lloyd family were members of the Church of the Disciples of Christ, a sect which had hived off from the Baptist denomination because its founders wished to conform in creed, church government, and worship more closely to what, in their opinion, were the teachings of the New Testament. So the family attended Penymaes, the little chapel above Criccieth, about two miles away, where the Disciples met. Round about were the estates of the squires and landowners who were sharply divided by language, religion, and politics from most of the ordinary people.

The home in which David Lloyd (as he was called after the Welsh fashion) spent his early years represented what was best in the rural Wales of the period. It was a life far richer in cultural content than was imagined by its alien neighbours, who were shut out from all knowledge of it by ignorance of the language. There was a strong dual tradition: one of a national literature stretching back a thousand years and widely diffused; the other of the Christian religion, rekindled in the evangelical fervours of the eighteenth century—the Methodist Revival which, originating within the Established Church, had roused the nation from religious indifference, stung its conscience, quickened its mind.

The remote district in which the boy grew up was far less deeply penetrated by English and foreign influences than it has since become. Its centre was the chapel, its leaders were the Nonconformist ministers, sometimes men of exceptional natural ability and good education. The practice of inviting ministers from all over Wales to preaching festivals lasting two or three days meant that a Welsh boy in a small village such as Llanystumdwy could hear the ablest and most eloquent orators, speaking in the language of the people, once or twice a year—or oftener if he cared to walk a few miles from home. These men had a profound influence on aspiring youth. The Welsh literary tradition was also important in furnishing Lloyd George's mind and shaping his outlook on the world. The districts of Lleyn and Eifionydd in his native county were rich in minor and medium poets, the chief of whom were familiar and honoured names in his home, and throughout his life he was in the habit of quoting from them.

In Wales, when Lloyd George was young, there existed a sharp division between the common people and the upper classes, an estrangement which had a long history. During a period of 300 years the anglicizing policy instituted by the Welsh Tudors had succeeded in assimilating the Welsh landed gentry and nobility with the English ruling class. Deserted by the rich and great, neglected by many slack and perfunctory clergy of the Established Church of England, the daemon of Wales lay dormant, awaiting the appropriate stimulus to bring it to life again. It was the Methodist Revival of the eighteenth century which roused the sleeping nation. At first the reformers worked as 'shock troops' within the Established Church, but when they left it a great gulf was fixed between the common people who were predominantly Nonconformists and the gentry who were members of the English Church.

When the Welsh woke to new awareness of themselves they felt themselves foreigners in their own land. Two communities inhabited the country: one, strongly conservative, allied with and exerting the powers of government, ruled the destinies of the workers, controlling the security and well-being of farmer and peasant through ownership of the land and its resources. It was devoted to the maintenance of the English State Church and its schools and, in many overt or subtle ways, disparaged the national democratic sentiments of the people and their love for their language. This community had become so thoroughly attuned to English modes of thought that, to all intents and purposes, they were English people living in Wales, but holding by inheritance a highly privileged position.

The other community consisted of those who were not in sympathy with the governing class, but were Nonconformist, intellectual in their interests, Welsh-speaking, Liberal in politics, and openly or secretly resentful of the sway exerted over their lives by these renegades or intruders.

There could be no doubt to which group David Lloyd would belong. The squire, the vicar, the curate, the schoolmaster—for there was only the Church of England school—would belong to the other. Fortunately, in the daily give-and-take of life all but the doctrinaire learn to respect and rub along with their fellows. So the curate was a crony of Richard Lloyd the shoemaker, lent him weekly the *Guardian*, the church periodical, and frequented the informal debating society in the workshop where all things in heaven and earth were discussed; the schoolmaster, an enlightened, devoted teacher, got on well with his pupils—they with him and with their studies. But at times of crisis in the little world of school and the greater world outside the latent antagonism sprang to life.

4

Naturally a parliamentary election was such an occasion, and when David Lloyd was nearly six years old the contest of 1868 took place. The county of Caernarvon returned two Members; the boroughs' representation had varied, but the shire had been uncontested for seventy years and had always returned a Tory Member This time, however, to the ecstatic joy of Liberals and Nonconformists all over Wales, Caernarvonshire returned a Liberal.

Richard Lloyd was the only Liberal in his village who, openly, at any rate, professed the Liberal faith. His five-year-old nephew was the only child to wear the Liberal colour, but wear it he did, and proudly. There were humble families in his neighbourhood and in other Welsh counties, however, who possessed Richard Lloyd's courage, tenants of cottage and farm, and the general Liberal victory cost them dear. They were evicted from their homes for voting against their landlords and, with their belongings, turned out on to the roads. The effect of the intimate knowledge of such injustice and suffering upon a nature high-spirited, intolerant of opposition, and quick to take sides can be imagined.

In school, the storm-centre was religious teaching. With the exception of the bigots in their midst, the Welsh people had no objection to the Church of England as such but only to its privileged position, established and endowed, in a predominantly Nonconformist country like Wales. They objected to their children, who had to attend the church school when there was no other, being forced to learn and repeat the catechism, because this was for them insincere, and they disliked the pressure put upon them to be confirmed and to attend church on special occasions. Behind all this, embittering the relations between the two sections of the community, was the legal obligation of the Nonconformists to pay, to a church to which they did not belong, tithes on land held precariously and on unfair conditions. These were, primarily, matters for the parents, but they coloured the attitudes of the pupils, especially the more intelligent. Foremost amongst these was David Lloyd, who early showed the courage and independence which later marked the politician. His childhood, early manhood, and thirteen out of the first fifteen years of his parliamentary career were spent in opposition and in challenging authority. On his side, he felt, were the forces of justice and righteousness. In his intimate and affectionate home circle, and in the

5

village, as his exceptional gifts, his courage, and charm unfolded themselves, he enjoyed a position of privilege during those early years when such an environment fosters self-confidence and self-reliance. His beliefs were secure and he himself was secure.

He enjoyed to the full, until adolescence brought malaise and discontent with the restraints and limitations of village life, the delights which the country-side offered to this strong, intrepid boy, to whom natural beauty always appealed. Though David Lloyd never seems to have courted popularity, his personal attractiveness, the exciting games he devised, and his inborn distinction made him a natural leader of marauding expeditions on the strictly preserved lands round about, in search of nuts or fruit or even the forbidden rabbit. These early experiences may have helped determine the bias against landowners which marked his career as lawyer and legislator.

Sometimes he cared only for reading. He read and re-read the Bible stories in Welsh. He also read English books, novels, histories such as Rollin's *Ancient History* and Macaulay's *History of England*, and before his middle teens he had read *Sartor Resartus*, *Sesame and Lilies*, and *The Crown of Wild Olive*. At an early period he became very fond of the works of Victor Hugo.

Then there was always good talk, which he soon came to appreciate, in his uncle's workshop. The whole village, and the poets and *littérateurs* of the country-side, came there for the exchange of ideas, for counsel and criticism, to read or recite poetry. He might hear what had been the theme of a striking sermon at the last preaching meeting and how the listeners had been spellbound. Someone might bring in a copy of one of the many Welsh journals which, besides dealing with all things Welsh, kept the nation up to date in the political news of the day and in happenings abroad. Richard Lloyd might read what Gladstone had said about Home Rule for Ireland, and David Lloyd might notice that Wales suffered from the same injustices as Ireland.

On Wednesday evening the family always walked to Criccieth to Penymaes chapel for the week-night service and on Sundays they went three times. The meetings, morning and evening, were conducted by Uncle Lloyd or his fellow pastor—both doing this work, in accordance with the tenets of the Disciples of Christ, entirely as a labour of love. In the afternoon there was Sunday School. When he was twelve David Lloyd was baptized in the stream beside the chapel and after that he partook of Communion which, in this denomination, was administered every Lord's Day. He soon began to lead the singing and read portions from the scriptures.

By the time Lloyd George was twelve a momentous decision had been taken. Neither Richard Lloyd nor Mrs. George, in spite of their narrow means, ever dreamt of any career but one of the learned professions for their two boys. The religious bias of his home seemed, in that era of great pulpit oratory, to mark out David Lloyd, with his special gifts, for a career as a Nonconformist minister. There was, however, no paid ministry among the Disciples. Schoolmastering was excluded, for he would have had to join the Established Church in order to become a teacher in the parish school; and his shrinking from disease and death prevented his falling in with his uncle's wish and embarking upon the medical profession. So the career favoured by his mother was chosen: he should be a solicitor, a calling recommended to her by the kindness shown by a Liverpool lawyer during her early widowhood.

This was a course strewn with difficulties for, besides putting off for years the day when the boy would begin to earn a living, it involved spending a large sum on fees. The uncle and mother decided to use their savings to meet these expenses. But the passing of even the preliminary examination presented a serious obstacle because it included French, for which there was no teacher within reach. So Uncle Lloyd tackled it himself. No doubt this venture on the part of the shoemaker in his forties was taken entirely as a matter of course, so varied and unusual were his gifts.

Cassell's *Popular Educator* gave form to the lessons and a second-hand dictionary and grammar supplied the substance. At night, by candlelight, with these aids, the uncle and nephew picked their way through La Fontaine's fables and mastered the construction of French sentences.

One day in November 1877, David Lloyd and his uncle went away without telling anyone where they were going. When the news that their favourite had passed the preliminary examination of the Law Society reached the village on 8 December the secret of the mysterious journey was revealed.

In January 1879 he was articled at the office of Messrs. Breese, Jones & Casson, of Portmadoc, and a firm better suited to prepare

7

him for his future career could not have been found. The character of the principals was such that any boy was fortunate to be trained by them. Mr. Breese was Clerk of the Peace for Merioneth, Clerk to the Magistrates in two petty sessional divisions, and a Liberal agent. In such a varied country practice a clerk would obtain an insight into the affairs of landed estates and learn much about assessments, rating, electioneering, the franchise, and the poor laws—all valuable for later life.

Lloyd George became increasingly aware of the wide world and of his possible place in it. Of the widespread grief at the death of President Garfield (1881) William George in his biography of Richard Lloyd says he wrote in his diary: 'There never was anything similar. For myself I could not feel as much for any public man. Such is the influence of a good man. Is there not a hint of success here? Can he not be emulated? It is worth trying at any rate.' And after visiting the House of Commons in November 1881, when in London for an examination, he writes, and Du Parcq records: 'I will not say but that I eyed the Assembly in a spirit similar to that in which William the Conqueror eyed England on his visit to Edward the Confessor, as the region of his future domain. Oh, vanity!'

When he was nineteen he began to give addresses at Penymaes chapel, where the Disciples worshipped. Richard Lloyd notes the night, 17 July 1882, when he first spoke: 'A splendid meeting. D. Ll. G. speaking for the first time. O! my dear boy, he did speak so well! Never was anything more striking and profitable. May Thy support be his, O Lord, to prolong his life and strength with Thy blessing, to do good in reality to his age, through Christ. *Never* did I feel so deeply.' This address was the prelude to others in the home church and in the district. But never, apparently, did he lead the congregation in prayer.

Some years later his friend Sir Herbert Lewis recorded in his diary:

> Dec. 22nd, 1904.
> S.S. 'Ormuz'.

At breakfast this morning Lloyd George said he regretted that he had not become a preacher. The pulpit, dealing as it did with every phase of human life, offered infinite opportunities for influence, and it dealt with matters of eternal consequence. Politics, after all, belong to a lower plane; they are concerned with material things. 'That', he said, 'is why I have gone in to such an extent for persiflage—it is the only way in which one can let one's imagination have free rein.'

Of one thing I feel pretty sure. If G. had gone into the pulpit he would have started a new sect.[1]

Soon after his survey of the House of Commons as the 'region of his future domain', he had joined the Portmadoc Debating Society. The members of this society included his employers and other professional men. Lloyd George frequently took part in the debates, and his first reported speech on 'Should Irish landlords be compensated on account of the working of the Land Act?' is referred to by the *North Wales Express* (3 February 1882) as 'argumentative and nervous', and as 'shaking the very foundations of the Irish landlords' claim'.

He had been writing, too, in these years. The first article he sent to a newspaper—the *North Wales Express* (5 November 1880)—was accepted. He was then seventeen. It was an attack on Lord Salisbury and a justification of the Liberal Government. In it the methods of the future debater are foreshadowed. The war is carried into the enemy's camp. Generalities are not depended on, but facts are marshalled for the confounding of the opponent and, though the style shows some signs of pedantry and ornateness, the composition is vivid, strong, and effective. The same can be said of his two open letters to Mr. Ellis Nanney, his village squire, during the by-election of November 1880, in which he attacked the claims of the candidate and the foreign and domestic policy of the party he stood for with fierce but reasoned invective. At this election he had taken an active part, accompanying the Liberal candidate, Mr. William Rathbone, to meetings, entering with all the fervour of his impressionable, responsive nature into the excitement and carrying out faithfully duties as committee man.

Meanwhile, ill health had forced Richard Lloyd to give up his shoemaking business—and this at a time when the boys were costing the family a great deal, for William soon followed his brother's footsteps as a student of law. The family moved to Criccieth where it was possible to make money by taking in summer visitors; but in spite of their efforts the expenses incurred for the boys, which had used up their small capital, and the shortness of the season for letting rooms made it difficult to make both ends meet. On 9 May 1884, however, part of the long struggle was over for the devoted

[1] Sir Herbert Lewis, Papers in the National Library of Wales.

family: a telegram announced that David Lloyd had passed the final law examination.

The end of the period of apprenticeship brought the necessity for a new decision. Lloyd George severed his connexion with Messrs. Breese, Jones & Casson, though his brother remained articled to them, and opened an office of his own at Criccieth in the back parlour of his home. Since there was far too little work for a lawyer in this small town, he started practices also at Pwllheli, Festiniog, and Portmadoc. His uncle acted as managing clerk, keeping the Criccieth headquarters open while Lloyd George was absent. Before very long William George qualified, and then the burden was further lightened for Richard Lloyd.

Lloyd George immediately made his mark in the lower law courts. He was a wise counsellor and refused to take cases to court unless he was convinced that there was a good chance of winning them; in this his judgement rarely led him astray. As a pleader he displayed sound knowledge, careful preparation, skill in cross-examination, and, when the presiding justices considered cases on their merit, due respect to authority. When, however, he thought that the Bench was serving the interests of privilege—ecclesiastical or temporal—rather than the law, he used all his audacity and his ample and apposite vocabulary of invective.

The years between 1884 and 1890, when he first entered Parliament, were filled with legal work and other widening interests. His personal life broadened, for he left home and started a family of his own. On 24 January 1888 he married Margaret Owen, the daughter of Richard Owen, of Mynydd Ednyfed, a substantial farm about a mile from Criccieth, having overcome through her loyalty and his growing reputation the opposition of her parents to what they were inclined to consider a misalliance for their daughter. He was indeed fortunate in gaining the affection and companionship of this serene, steadfast, wise, and large-hearted woman.

His public life became increasingly crowded. He was in continual demand for addresses on temperance and foreign missions; he took an active part in organizing the farmers' union and in anti-tithe agitation, addressing meetings up and down his area. He was of the people, one of them, and he had emancipated himself from all the fears of landlord, law, and parson which restricted their lives. In him there was promise for them.

During the years immediately preceding his election to Westminster, the Welsh people were showing a quickened interest in politics, world affairs, and especially in their own national identity. This strongly nationalist trend was strengthened by the election to Parliament, in 1886, of Tom Ellis, the son of a peasant farmer in Merionethshire. The election was a milestone on the road to national self-respect. 'The Wales of the past, *Cymru Fu*, used to be all-in-all to us. From now on it must be the Wales of the future, *Cymru Fydd*.' This phrase became the motto of many societies in Wales which, growing into a National League, came into conflict with the less nationalist Liberal Federations of North and South Wales. Lloyd George eagerly threw himself into this new crusade.

Ever since July 1869, when the bill to disestablish the Irish Church became law, the disestablishment and disendowment of the Church had been the dominant subject of political controversy in Wales, with Irish Home Rule in the second place, and social and economic questions only slowly coming to the front. The merits of the controversy need not be examined in detail. The relation between the spiritual and secular power is one of the permanent problems of human society, and raises issues of the deepest import to all citizens. But though these were at the root of the Welsh controversy, the battle was largely fought on nationalist and sectarian rather than on philosophical and religious issues. At Cardiff, in February 1890, Lloyd George demanded 'as complete a measure of Home Rule as the one to be granted to Ireland'. Later, in Merthyr Tydfil (November 1890), he condensed his ideal into the words: 'A free religion and a free people in a free land.'

He was always aware of the political defects of his countrymen, with whose nature his experience in a lawyer's office had made him thoroughly familiar. In October 1894, when he had had some experience of Parliament, he stressed the Welshman's tendency to shy at 'the unpleasant truth' that only a concentration of energy and self-sacrifice would bring to Wales the measures which Ireland had taken so long to wrench from England. 'There is but one way of curing him [the Welshman] of his fault, and that is by adopting a method used by trainers when a spirited horse starts at an object in the roadway—turn his head towards it and compel him, whether he will or not, to stare at it. . . . Let us pursue the same strategy with the Welsh spirit. . . . The amount of pressure brought to bear on Parliament must be increased.'

The attempt to translate the nationalist sentiments into policy had led to conferences and conflicts. Some thought the Liberal Government should not be harassed; others demanded the formation of an independent Welsh party on the lines made familiar by the Irish. Some thought that Welsh members should pledge themselves not to take office under a Liberal Government unless their demands were acceded to; others saw in the appointment of Welshmen the opportunity to further Welsh causes.

The political life of the Principality had greatly changed during the eighties. Progressive leaders, strengthened by the widening of the franchise in 1885 which made Liberal representation dominant, had been quick to seize the opportunity provided by the Local Government Act of 1888, for this meant the substitution of the power of a popularly elected assembly, a county council, for rule by the justices hitherto representative of the privileged classes. The elections early in 1889 resulted in a sweeping victory for the Liberal cause. The people's trust in Lloyd George was shown at the first meeting of the new Caernarvon County Council by his election as alderman—an honour which he retained throughout his life—and by his nomination as Liberal candidate for Caernarvon Boroughs.

That his political ambition developed early is indicated by his comment, already quoted, after his first visit to the House of Commons when he eyed it as the region of his future domain. His subsequent activities were in line with this ambition, while his ever-increasing reputation as an eloquent, effective protagonist of popular causes and as a dangerous enemy of privilege and vested interest marked him out in the public eye as a promising candidate. Though older Liberals were inclined to distrust the young rebel, ardent, enterprising spirits regarded him as the only suitable candidate for Caernarvon Boroughs; the southern boroughs— Nevin, Pwllheli, Criccieth—nominated him, and the northern boroughs followed suit. Linked with his insight and shrewdness went a forceful personality, an impatience of obstruction, and a lack of respect for established institutions and the attachment men feel for them—these qualities had made him a storm-centre by the time he fought and won his first election.

II

MEMBER OF PARLIAMENT
1890–1906

As a result of the sudden death of Mr. Edmund Swetenham, Q.C., Conservative Member for Caernarvon Boroughs, Lloyd George found himself, at the age of twenty-seven, fighting his first election. His opponent was Mr. Ellis Nanney, the local squire in Llanystumdwy, who had opposed the Liberal candidate in the by-election of 1880, a personally acceptable and good-hearted man.

As Liberal candidate, Lloyd George pledged himself to a comprehensive programme: justice for Ireland; religious equality in Wales; various measures of land reform; direct local veto on the granting of licences for the sale of intoxicants; a liberal extension of the principle of decentralization; and the promotion of various other reforms, such as the abolition of plural voting, graduated taxation, a free breakfast table (that is, free from foreign duties on food), and the freeing of fisheries from irksome restrictions. He was elected by the narrow majority of eighteen, and continued to represent the Caernarvon Boroughs for fifty-five years.

The result was hailed with delight by the more radical elements in Wales. Other Liberals welcomed it as a victory for their cause, but some contended that the narrow majority was due to the record of the new member. In the May number of the newspaper *Cymru Fydd* this comment was made: 'He appeared before the constituency under serious disadvantages. He was young and unproved, he had his fortune to make in every sense. He had also unhappily brought himself to disfavour by some violent speeches, and the extreme views he had advocated more than once.'

NATIONALISM AND DISESTABLISHMENT

On 17 April 1890 Lloyd George took his seat in the House of Commons—as R. C. K. Ensor says: 'On the back benches appeared another man of destiny. . . . Black-haired, blue-eyed, Welsh-speaking, addicted to picture-phrases, using English with great wit and fluency, but with the air of a foreign language, this young man seemed then an incarnation of the Celtic spirit.'

The Conservatives, strengthened by the Liberal Unionists who had left Gladstone in 1886 on the issue of Home Rule for Ireland, were in power, with Lord Salisbury as Prime Minister. Gladstone, aged eighty, was in Opposition. Joseph Chamberlain sat on the Government benches, and it must have been strange for Lloyd George, who had written in the *North Wales Observer* (17 October 1884), 'Mr. Chamberlain is unquestionably the future leader of the people. . . . He is a Radical and doesn't care who knows it as long as the people do', to see his former hero sitting on the opposite side. There was only one Socialist Member, Cunninghame Graham, a picturesque Scottish laird.

During his two and a quarter years' experience of this Ministry (1890–92) Lloyd George's Welsh nationalism was confirmed. He was inured to discord within the Liberal party on nationalist issues, and, with the example of Ireland's record before him, he had learned the utility of successful obstruction. The ignorant opposition shown by the Tory rank and file, and even by the leaders, to questions affecting his country inflamed his zeal for her cause. Accordingly, Lloyd George took every opportunity of acquiring and practising the technique of parliamentary procedure in promoting legislation and obstructing it. His resourcefulness, industry, courage, and the quality of his oratory soon earned him a prominent place in the House and in the country.

His daily letter home described his doings and the political situation and asked for advice or criticism on notes of speeches submitted to the judgement of his uncle and his brother. This advice he sincerely valued. His letters home also show his complete objectivity in his unaffected appraisal of his successes. The directness of these utterances presents a striking picture of a completely detached, self-controlled agent ordering his activities to a certain end, and expressing without conceit or offence a fair estimate of his achievements.

On 13 June 1890 he delivered his maiden speech. The reception accorded to the speech by the House was very cordial. He wrote home: 'It has already made a great difference in the reception I get among the members of the House.'

The end of the year introduced Lloyd George to Wales in a new character. He had, on occasion, written anonymous political articles for newspapers in Wales. Now the *Genedl Gymreig* ('The Welsh Nation'), in the purchase of which he was supposed to have

14

been interested, proudly advertised on 19 November that the 'popular and talented' young Member was to write a weekly parliamentary letter and that with this authorship it was sure to be 'readable, interesting and edifying'. Never did parliamentary correspondent start his career at a more dramatic moment. Parnell was falling from power, and the House could think of nothing else. Parnell's stubborn defiance appealed strongly to Lloyd George's instinct for drama. On 10 December 1890, he wrote:

Mr. Parnell has proved to the world the kind of leader the Irish nation is on the point of losing. He is a man of iron determination, inflexible will, matchless courage and audacity and of peerless skill as a leader, but a man who will not allow even the demands of conscience and honour to stand in the way of his purposes, 'who neither fears God nor respects man'.... Who can withhold his meed of admiration from the old fallen commander and who can help feeling compassion at the ruin of such grandeur![1]

The main lines of policy which Lloyd George pursued during the first ten years of his parliamentary career were already implicit in the accounts he gives to the readers of the Welsh weekly during his first ten weeks as its correspondent. He was a Welsh nationalist who was also a radical of an advanced type. His tactics were strongly affected by his observations of what he considered to be the successful methods of the Irish. He did not feel that loyalty to a party, whether that of the Welsh members or of the official Liberals, should debar him from criticism or opposition if he thought that the party was not acting in a way likely to promote the causes he had at heart.

During the life of his first Parliament (until June 1892), Lloyd George took a prominent part in the debates on the Liquor Traffic Local Veto (Wales) Bill and the Elementary Education Bill; he also opposed the Clergy Discipline Bill which Gladstone, though in Opposition, was supporting. The veteran statesman actually replied himself (28 April 1892) to a speech by the young Member: 'I ask my honourable friend not to interpose unnecessarily, not to search with something of a feverish heat for arguments of all kinds in order to put this bill away.' But Gladstone asked in vain. Neither Lloyd George nor his companions (Tom Ellis and S. T. Evans) gave any quarter and, seeing that his replies to their objec-

[1] *Genedl Gymreig*, 10 December 1890.

15

tions merely played into their hands and prolonged the discussions, the old man ceased to speak and merely glared.

Parliament was dissolved in June and Lord Salisbury's Government, without resigning, appealed to the country; so, after a little over two years, Lloyd George had to fight his second election.

In the meantime he with his family—there were now three children, Richard, Mair, and Olwen—had settled in London, and, besides the practice in Portmadoc which he shared with his brother, William—who, in fact, bore most of the burden of it—he had established a practice in London. The meeting of the demands of his profession, on which he was financially dependent, his indefatigable attendance at the House and his speeches there and all over England and Wales, were only possible to a man possessed of great powers of physical endurance and mental concentration.

At the general election of July 1892, Lloyd George encountered a new opponent. This was Sir John Puleston, a Welshman who had helped Welsh cultural causes but whose career and views classed him as of the anglicized variety. Lloyd George's electoral policy was the same as it had been in 1890, so the points at issue between the two parties were unchanged. Polling day brought him victory again and an increased majority: George 2,154, Puleston 1,958.

Gladstone had gained a victory in the country, but a very narrow one, his majority of forty depending on the support of the Celtic fringe. The Irish group on whose support he could count numbered fifty; Wales returned thirty-one Liberals and only three Conservatives. This constituted a strong argument in support of Welsh claims. Moreover, on the Newcastle Programme, adopted by the Liberal party in October 1891 and confirmed in a speech by Gladstone immediately afterwards, disestablishment in Wales had been placed second only to Home Rule for Ireland.

After his election Lloyd George made a triumphal entry into Conway, and there in a speech made clear what was to be expected if the Liberal party did not honour its pledge to Wales.

Why had Wales made sacrifices in the face of unexampled difficulties and intimidation from squires and agents? It was not to install one statesman in power. It was not to deprive one party of power in order to put another party in power. It was not to transfer the emoluments of office from one statesman to another. No; it was done because

Wales had by an overwhelming majority demonstrated its determination to secure its own progress.... Welsh members wanted nothing for
themselves but something for their country, and I do not think they
would support a Liberal Ministry, I do not care how illustrious the
Minister might be who led it, unless it pledged itself to concede to
Wales those great measures of reform on which Wales had set its
heart.[2]

Possibly it was thought that the appointment of Tom Ellis, the
favourite and leader of Young Wales, to the office of Junior Lord
of the Treasury and Second Whip would serve as guarantee for
the tractability of the Welsh party. Tom Ellis had given the matter
much consideration and decided to accept the post. This decision
disappointed many people in Wales because it muzzled him as a
Welsh party leader by making him a Liberal watchdog. Lloyd
George's view was that having all Wales behind him if he took
office at all he should have demanded higher office—at least a seat
in the Cabinet.

It was an interesting group of Welshmen who now went to
Westminster. Some of them were later to hold important offices—
S. T. Evans, D. A. Thomas, and Herbert Lewis—but at this stage
they were attached to the 'ginger group', led by Lloyd George,
who, now that Tom Ellis had official ties, became the moving spirit
in Young Wales.

The defeat of the Conservative Government in the House in
August cleared the way for a new administration with Gladstone
at its head. Sir William Harcourt became Chancellor of the Exchequer; John Morley, Irish Secretary; Lord Rosebery, Foreign
Secretary; Campbell-Bannerman, Secretary for War; and Asquith,
Home Secretary. Its course was a difficult one, its majority small
and uncertain, and its legislation frustrated by the veto of the
House of Lords. The measures which the Government succeeded
in piloting through the Commons before this long session of Parliament came to an end were of a type to delight Lloyd George:
Home Rule for Ireland, the Parish Councils Bill, an Employers
Liability Bill. It is true that the Lords threw out the first, seriously
amended the second, and so mutilated the third that the Cabinet
abandoned it, but that was not the fault of the Government.

On 23 February 1893 Mr. Asquith moved the Suspensory Bill,
a measure intended to clear the way for a Disestablishment Bill

[2] *North Wales Observer and Express*, 29 July 1892.

by preventing 'for a limited time the creation of new interests in Church of England bishoprics, dignities and benefices in Wales and Monmouthshire'. The pressure brought to bear by the Welsh members to secure attention to their claims is illustrated by an interpolation in Parliament on the same day by Randolph Churchill: 'We have not been perfectly unobservant of the meetings of the Welsh Party and of the negotiations which passed between that Party and H. M. Government, and I venture to say that we are not ignorant of the ultimatum the Welsh Party gave.'

There was ample justification for Lord Randolph's view. 'Cost what it may', said Lloyd George in the *Genedl Gymreig* (14 February 1893), 'we shall force the Government to expedite the passage of the Suspensory Bill through the House of Commons this Session and we shall not permit the Administration to give precedence before it to anything but Home Rule and a simple Registration Bill.' Gladstone's fidelity to the principle that a nation had a right to autonomy had decided him, very much against the grain as a Churchman, to support Welsh disestablishment, but in spite of the official support of the bill it did not become law.

Through the long summer days when the Home Rule Bill was being debated, Lloyd George was mainly thinking out ways of securing the introduction of a Disestablishment Bill for Wales. Yet he writes with great sympathy of the Irish debate, and to Gladstone's exhortation to patience he responded with, 'I shall be perfectly content if we get Disestablishment next year' (*Genedl Gymreig*, 20 June 1893). There was a conflict in his mind between his loyalty to, and admiration of, the gallant, aged statesman and his eagerness to carry the Welsh Bill. At any rate, he did not move to actual rebellion until the Grand Old Man had resigned. His regard for Gladstone and delight in Gladstone's mastery of the House and of the art of oratory were then, and throughout his life, unbounded.

While the House of Lords was occupied in filling its cup of iniquity, by rejecting or mangling almost all of the Government's important bills passed by the Commons, the Liberal majority with its many factions and cliques played its part in wearing down the old statesman's endurance. Gladstone resigned on 1 March 1894, his last speech in the House being a vigorous assault upon the House of Lords. The Queen sent for Lord Rosebery. The interest of the Welsh members was now directed to the Queen's forthcoming speech. When it was read in the middle of the month in the Lords, the question of the ecclesiastical establishments in Wales and Scotland had precedence over all matters except the Eviction of Tenants Bill (Ireland) and a bill to amend registration and abolish plural voting. In the Commons, Asquith gave notice of the Bill for the Disestablishment of the Church in Wales, and on 26 April he introduced the bill.

The intervening five or six weeks had not been uneventful. Four members of the Welsh party, Lloyd George, D. A. Thomas, Herbert Lewis, and Frank Edwards, observing that time was being earmarked for other bills, believed that the Government did not mean to redeem its pledge to them and decided to withhold their support from it on all questions except the budget and registration. A meeting of Lloyd George's constituents at Caernarvon, on hearing his explanation, endorsed his action, with only one dissentient, while the executive of the North Wales Liberal Federation decided to support 'Welsh members in any course they might deem necessary in order to secure the passing of the Disestablishment Bill through the Commons during the session' (*Cambrian News*, 20 April 1894). It should be remembered, however, that twenty-seven of the Welsh members were not in the rebel camp with the Four.

Nearly all the newspapers of Wales, Welsh and English, supported the rebels, with the exception of the *Goleuad* and *Cymro*. Various bodies, religious and secular, when meeting to transact their own business, passed resolutions in favour of the action of the Four. On 23 May, speaking in Birmingham, Lord Rosebery declared: 'I hope before we meet the country, that we shall meet it with a measure of Welsh Disestablishment passed through the House of Commons. . . . I cannot control its fate after it leaves the House of Commons. I say if they (the Welsh members) don't believe in our honour and our honesty, the sooner they carry their threats into effect the better I shall be pleased.' This declaration satisfied the rebels, who undertook to support the Government so long as the Prime Minister's promise was kept.

On Monday, 28 May 1894, the Welsh Disestablishment Bill occupied a place upon the order paper immediately after the Budget. It passed its second reading with a majority of forty-four on 1 April 1895. The Government, however, was defeated while the bill was in committee on 21 June 1895.

The defeat was on a minor issue and the opposition majority was only seven. If several Welsh members had not been at Llandrindod at a meeting of the North and South Wales Liberal Federations, the defeat would probably not have occurred, but the position of the Government seems to have been so precarious that it might have happened in some other incalculable way. The result of the appeal to the country, which followed the fall of the Government, was a sweeping victory for the Conservatives.

It is perhaps idle to speculate about what would have happened if the Liberal administration could have lived out the span then allotted to governments and remained in office until 1899; for in spite of Lloyd George's hustling and driving, the Welsh Church Bill did not become law for twenty years, and then not until after the Parliament Act had nullified the power of the House of Lords. It is at least arguable that Wales would have done better if Lloyd George had turned his talents to keeping the Liberals in instead of undermining their position for his own ends and, doubtless, sapping the vigour and enthusiasm of the leaders. There were people in Wales who took this view. As it was, the Liberal party now went into Opposition for ten years.

The election which resulted in a Liberal defeat was the third which Lloyd George had fought in little over five years. This was a very serious matter for a poor man. In 1892 his constituents had presented him with a testimonial as an expression of their regard; in 1894 he told them that unless his expenses were paid, he could not stand again. This they agreed to do.

These early years entailed constant struggle and strain. Members of Parliament were not paid; there were two homes and two law practices to be kept up, one at Criccieth and one in London; continual travelling meant perpetual spending. What work, planning, and economies this occasioned Mrs. Lloyd George, now the mother of four children, can well be imagined.

Lloyd George's friends bear witness to the fact that he was not a lover of money as such. There were opportunities for Members of Parliament to feather their nests, quite legitimate ones, but these he did not take. Mrs. Lloyd George, with the housekeeping to manage, may have wished that he had done so. Sir Herbert Lewis, in his reminiscences, writes:

He was never a mammon worshipper. When he first came into Parliament he was living with his wife and children in a tiny flat under very uncomfortable and straitened conditions, just making both ends meet. He was offered the chairmanship of one of the Hardwood Companies that were coming on the market, at a salary of £500 a year, which at that time would have meant all the difference to his family between poverty and comfort; to himself the contrast mattered little. I believe that it was a perfectly sound proposition from the business point of view. . . . The head of a large organization . . . that was not paying came to him for legal advice, and was led to ask for counsel of a more practical kind. . . . The offer of a company directorship with a substantial salary was, having regard to his means at the time, a great temptation to him, probably the greatest and most insidious of its kind that ever came to him, but he wisely chose the narrow way. There are many members of Parliament who add to their income quite legitimately by accepting directorships of companies, but he exercised a wise discretion in refusing invariably the many offers of this kind that he received.[3]

Fortunately, the vitality and buoyancy necessary to stand up to a life of this kind were among nature's rich gifts to this much-favoured son. He writes to Sir Herbert Lewis during the autumn recess—the fact that in those days there was no autumn session did allow some opportunity for members to attend to their own concerns: 'I am really and seriously in a prostrate state. The doctor ordered absolute rest and physic a fortnight ago. I followed his precepts by addressing eight meetings in South Wales and going to bed at three o'clock in the morning and leaving his medicine at home. I have three or four meetings to face in the coming week with a heavy police court thrown in.' When Lloyd George's strong, deep, and lively interest was aroused, an almost inexhaustible fund of nervous energy was available in its service. This was to be still more clearly proved in the course of many a test of endurance in the lifetime of the next Parliament.

The actions and speeches of Lloyd George and his friends had not met with the approval of all Welsh Liberals, and in some quarters the fall of the Government was attributed to the persistent hostility of his 'small, self-advertising clique'. In addition to doubt about the political wisdom and loyalty of Lloyd George, there was disapproval of the campaign to capture the country for the *Cymru Fydd* League. This society was intended to unify Wales, but its opponents regarded it as an additional source of

[3] Sir Herbert Lewis, Papers in the National Library of Wales; see also E. T. Raymond, *Mr. Lloyd George*, p. 34.

division. Consequently, there were cross-currents to be navigated when he embarked upon his third election. Mr. Ellis Nanney was again his opponent, and though the differences within the Liberal camp may have made for a little awkwardness, they were not likely to induce many of its members to vote for the Tory, and Lloyd George was returned by a majority of 194. He returned to a Parliament, however, in which the Liberal party had been eclipsed, even Harcourt and Morley having failed to retain their seats. The Welsh members did much during the next few years to keep up the spirits of the Liberal Opposition, and it was not in vain that Lloyd George promised that the Government should suffer from 'Welsh earache'.

The Welsh press continued to criticize the action of Lloyd George and his friends. The *Goleuad* lashed out on 25 September 1895 with an article entitled '*Cleon*', in which that demagogue is contrasted with the wise Pericles, and Lloyd George is reminded that hundreds of Liberals voted for him, not because they believed in the kind of 'noise' he made, but because they were faithful to their party, and expected that he would do as much harm to the Tories as he had done to his friends.

He remained quite unmoved by these criticisms. He was convinced that he had acted rightly and that his tactics had nothing to do with the fall of the Ministry. No one ever wasted less time on barren regrets for the 'might have been' than Lloyd George. The Liberals were out, the Tories were in and likely to remain in for years. He therefore turned his forward-looking mind to the finding of a policy which would unite Liberals and give them a good chance of victory at the next election.

In order that justice should be done to the peoples of the Celtic fringe, and also in the interests of the efficient conduct of public affairs, Lloyd George considered that federal Home-Rule-All-Round should now be the leading item in the Liberal programme. It would be an issue on which Liberals would unite, and one which would stir the country.

In Wales this programme met with a mixed reception. One critic in the *Goleuad* (20 November 1895) compared Lloyd George to a dog, always after a new quarry: 'The day before yesterday it was the Land Bill, yesterday Disestablishment, today Home-Rule-All-Round, and tomorrow who knows what will crop up.' But Lloyd George held that he did not urge the relegation of Welsh disestablishment to a second place. Welsh Liberals should not bind themselves to any priority of items but should recognize the necessity of adapting themselves to the demands of political warfare and expediency.

In March 1896 he organized a meeting of Members of Parliament at which he proposed that this policy should be recognized as the chief item in the party programme. The meeting, which ended without any vote being taken, showed no very wide gulf between supporters and opponents. The cause, however, declined with the general atrophy of Liberalism that had set in, and two years later when Mr. Herbert Roberts (now Lord Clwyd) introduced a Home-Rule-All-Round resolution in the House of Commons, the House was counted out.

Lord Salisbury's triumphant party passed its time in practising the languid arts of braking and soft-pedalling. The Conservatives alone could out-vote the whole Opposition. The usual consequences of this situation followed: apathy and indifference spread and deepened, sittings became fewer, attendances smaller, the House not infrequently being counted out. And all this despite menaces to British interests abroad and the urgency of social questions at home. Lloyd George must often have mused over the uses to which he would have put this great majority, neglectful of its power and opportunity, if it had been ranged on his side. Meanwhile, he kept unremitting watch in the House, securing what he could by a well-considered policy of persuasion, stalling, and attack. Sir Herbert Lewis bears witness to the success of these tactics: 'The supineness of the crushed and dispirited opposition, small in numbers and divided in leadership, brought our own activity into bold relief and we quickly made ourselves a force to be reckoned with.'

An interesting comment on the skill and enterprise of Lloyd George is noted by Llewelyn Williams, who calls him the

finest Parliamentarian Wales has yet sent to the House of Commons. Mr. Lloyd George not only has shown an intimate knowledge of the rules of the House, a readiness in debate, and a keen perception of the weak points of the Tory case, but he has been able, by his pluck and resolution, to do more than any other man to infuse a new courage into the Liberal ranks and to discredit the methods and the policy of an overbearing majority.[4]

[4] Llewelyn Williams, in *Young Wales*, August 1896, p. 192.

While it is true that the causes for which Lloyd George now wrestled had in the first place been taken up because of their connexion with, or origin in, conditions in Wales, they had, with certain exceptions, a wider reference. A change of attitude became perceptible after the 1895 election. This change took the form of a widening of Lloyd George's political outlook. As Watkin Davies says: 'His unerring political instinct told him that the interests of Wales could best be served by identifying them with those of the rising English democracy.... It was only slowly that Lloyd George freed himself from the bonds of a narrow nationalism, but the process of emancipation began in 1895, to the great advantage of Wales as well as England.'

As one of the foremost Liberal speakers he travelled over the length and breadth of Britain. Always alive to the tragedy of human frustration and distress, he felt the urgency of the social needs of the time and the stirring in the ranks of labour to which they were giving rise. Welsh and English social problems, he saw, were identical.

Journeys abroad which Lloyd George now took contributed to a wider patriotism than that which had marked his earlier life, though nothing can have been more alien to his attitude than the Jingo imperialism which prevailed in certain circles in England, as distinct from the rest of the kingdom. In August 1896 he went for a tour in South America. The end of 1897 brought a visit to Italy, and in January 1899 he went for a short cruise in the Mediterranean, while the autumn of that year found him on a semi-official visit to Canada to study the opportunities it offered to emigrants.

It may have been this change in outlook which partly, at least, accounted for the form which Lloyd George's agitation for Home Rule took at this time, that is, devolution all round. He had seen the machinery of Parliament clogged by too much business, and now he saw how the imperialistic trend of popular feeling in England clouded the thinking of the electorate so that even where local governing bodies were Liberal, anti-progressive members were returned to Parliament. His efforts to secure the adoption of Home-Rule-All-Round as a main plank in the Liberal party platform were reinforced by speeches in the country. In Bangor he said:

The best-managed concern is the one that keeps abreast of its work. Parliament which is the pride of the greatest commercial community in the world is at least thirty years in arrears. The verse I would inscribe on every Parliament House is this: 'The cause which I knew not, I searched it out.' I would make these local Parliaments so many searchlights to flash into all the dark places of the land, so as to shame oppression, wretchedness and wrong out of their lurking-places.[5]

A two-way movement was going on in Lloyd George's mind. He took Britain as a whole into the scope of his thinking, and he saw the value for England of those benefits which he had desired for his own people.

Lloyd George and his friends in the House of Commons engaged in rough-and-tumble, day-by-day fighting which heartened the Liberal Opposition, dispirited by differences of opinion, lack of policy, and changes in leadership. The *Westminster Gazette* commented on 2 July 1896:

It is doubtful if a private member has ever done greater service to his Party in Parliament. He started . . . a little suspect with the majority of Liberals, but it is generally recognised now that, primarily on the [Agricultural] Rating Bill, but also on the Education Bill, no words of praise could be too strong for what Mr. Lloyd George has done.[6]

The Education Bill, which was brought forward in 1896, was withdrawn, but on 8 April, in the following year, the Voluntary Schools Act was passed. It provided for grant aid to voluntary schools and for exemption from rates of voluntary elementary schools. This act, therefore, extended the subsidizing of sectarian teaching, for these schools were almost always run by the Established Church and, in strengthening the position of these schools, accentuated the injustice felt by Nonconformist parents of having to send their children to them when there was no other in their district. Moreover, the act increased the amount of money paid to managing bodies which were not under public control. These features in the act led to constant opposition from the Liberals, and especially from the Welsh members, during the debates on the abortive bill of 1896, the act of 1897, and the Education Act of 1902.

[5] Speech by Lloyd George at Bangor; reported in the *North Wales Observer and Express*, 18 December 1895.
[6] *Westminster Gazette*, 2 July 1896; quoted in H. Du Parcq, *Life of David Lloyd George*, p. 171.

Other interventions by Lloyd George in debate are too numerous to detail: his support of his friend William Jones's defence of the Penrhyn quarrymen during their strike in the late nineties; his 'pregnant, rattling sentences' in favour of the Welsh Land Bill; his protest at the earmarking of time for the Voluntary Schools Bill at the expense of the consideration of regulations for the safety of the miners, may be cited as examples.

The year 1899, which, before the fall of the leaf, plunged Britain into war, brought, in the spring, grief to Wales. Tom Ellis died at Cannes on 5 April. There survives an undated note in Welsh written in pencil by Lloyd George to D. R. Daniel bidding him come to Criccieth to talk over their common loss: 'I feel paralysed.'

These events helped to shape Lloyd George's life during its next phase.

BOER WAR

News of Dr. Jameson's raid into the Transvaal, on his way to Johannesburg to bring relief to the wives and children of Englishmen alleged to be in danger, reached London on New Year's Day, 1896. The raid failed; Kruger handed Jameson and his small force over to Great Britain for trial and they were duly sentenced. But popular enthusiasm in London for the ringleaders served to increase the bitterness against England felt by the Boers.

After the raid grievances grew apace, and so did preparations for hostilities on both sides. In October 1899 Kruger precipitated war by issuing an ultimatum demanding sharply that no British troops on the high seas be landed at any South African port, and that those already in the country be withdrawn. In the House of Commons on 27 October a Member summed up the views of the majority by saying: 'I believe the war will be brief and that we shall be victorious and that such a result will be to the advantage of the Boers, the blacks, and the British alike.'

The fighting qualities of the Boers were grossly underestimated, and the series of British reverses and disasters with which the war opened came as a severe and sobering shock to a people who had entered upon it light-heartedly and had no notion that it would last thirty-two months and cost much life and treasure.

The Liberal party, already divided on Home Rule, was no less divided on the Boer War, between Liberal Imperialists and pro-Boers, or Little Englanders, as they were variously dubbed.

Opinion amongst the Welsh members reflected this cleavage, but Lloyd George ranged himself unwaveringly with the opponents of the war. His attitude was compounded of sympathy for a small nation, Gladstonian humanitarianism, and hatred of the renegade hero of his youth, Joseph Chamberlain who, with Alfred Milner, had charge of negotiations on behalf of England. His views were pronounced from the start. On 18 September, when he realized war was approaching, he wrote: 'If I have the courage I shall protest with all the vehemence at my command against the outrage which is perpetrated in the name of human freedom.' After war was declared, he wrote to his Welsh friend, D. R. Daniel: 'This war is a damnable, even worse perhaps, a senseless war.' But he was not a pacifist; military heroes were ardently admired by him, and speeches of this period support and advocate the use of force. If belief in the British Empire made him an imperialist then he was one, but he demanded an Empire founded on and sustained in righteousness. He saw the problem of the Boers through the sympathetic eyes of a fighter for the rights of his own small country. He praised the courage and tenacity of the Boers; the government of the Orange Free State, perhaps the best in the world; the Liberal elements in the Transvaal. He held that loyal subjects had been converted into rebels, and that fifty million Britishers were fighting a few thousand farmers who were holding their own with desperate courage—this was conquest, military occupation. We had set out to obtain the franchise for everybody, we would end it with the franchise for nobody. Bad statesmanship had blundered into the war; bad management was continuing it. He indulged in bitter personal attacks on Chamberlain and the Chamberlain family—at one point hurling charges against them of profiting by armament contracts, charges which were to recoil upon him later when he himself was entangled in the 'Marconi Affair'.

In the House of Commons he deliberately and persistently continued to attack Chamberlain, one of the greatest debaters in the whole history of Parliament. Had it not been for his solid argument, his dexterity, his virulence, his humour, and his sincerity, his quixotry might have been merely ridiculous; as it was, all these things combined to exasperate the domineering Colonial Secretary. One of Lloyd George's biographers, E. T. Raymond, had the good fortune to light upon 'a daring comparison between

Mr. Chamberlain and the man who is seen by the crowd as his antithesis' in a *Daily Mail* of this period; it is worth quoting, both for its insight and its foresight:

The same clear, low-pitched cruel voice; the same keen, incisive phrases; the same mordant bitterness; the same caustic sneer; the same sardonic humour; the same personal enmity. It is the very re-incarnation of the present Colonial Secretary in his younger days —a spectre of his dead self arisen to haunt him. . . . Will time that has had so mellowing an influence on the great Imperialist work a similar change in the virulent Little Englander? Will he a score of years hence be the tower of strength of the Imperial or the Parochial party? None can say now, but that he will be by then one of the fore-most men in the nation's Parliament is beyond question.[7]

Lloyd George made innumerable speeches in Parliament and in the country by which he sought to put an end to 'methods of barbarism', to secure an early and generous peace, and to dis-credit Chamberlain. The thought of Gladstone's Britain losing the esteem of freedom-loving peoples all over the world enraged him, and the prospect of the nation becoming military-minded, with incalculable effects upon peace abroad and social reform at home, filled him with dark foreboding.

The nineties in Britain were marked by aggressive national feeling and a widespread desire for expansion and domination. The war was undoubtedly popular. 'I am depressed about this war', wrote Sir Edward Grey; 'I admit the necessity of it, and that it must be carried through, but it has no business to be popu-lar.' The stand which Lloyd George took made him conspicuous. He risked his life at the hands of infuriated mobs, especially in Birmingham and even in his own constituency; he also risked his livelihood for principles in which he profoundly believed, and in doing so with endless courage and endurance he became the most hated public man in the kingdom.

The Khaki Election in the autumn of 1900 resulted in the return of 402 Unionists, 186 Liberals, and 82 Nationalists, a Unionist majority of 134. Lloyd George, who was opposed by a Colonel Platt, fought with his usual skill and vigour. He was returned with his majority increased to 296.

Parliament met in December, and Lloyd George renewed his relentless attacks on the Colonial Secretary, especially for the

[7] E. T. Raymond, *Mr. Lloyd George*, p. 69.

treatment of Boer women and children in concentration camps. At this time it looked as if the war was drawing to a close. The Boers asked for peace and on 26 February 1901 Botha and Kitchener met at Middleburg. The negotiations broke down. The war entered its remarkable guerrilla phase and was fought desperately by the elusive foe for another year. At last, in March 1902, the Boers sued for peace, and at Vereeniging on 31 May Kitchener made generous terms with the dour enemy.

EDUCATION ACT

On Monday, 24 March 1902, the day after the Boers sued for peace, Balfour introduced an Education Bill which aimed at systematizing the administration of the schools throughout the country. From this point of view it was an excellently conceived and constructive measure, but it contained proposals which were abhorrent to radicals and dissenters. Lloyd George had started his parliamentary fight on education measures in 1896, when the Voluntary Schools Act was passed. His opposition to the Boer War had made him notorious; his fight against this new Education Bill brought him influence and fame. By the time that the Liberals took office in December 1905 he was marked out by friend and foe for a place in the Cabinet.

Lloyd George was not a secularist in education. He had an ardent belief in the value of the Bible as an instrument of literary, moral, social, and religious training, and was strongly opposed to its exclusion from the schools. He spoke of it as

the most democratic book in the world. Its heroes are David the Shepherd and Jesus the Carpenter. Indeed it is extraordinary that respectable people can tolerate it: its terrible condemnation of oppression and riches, its magnification of poverty. Think who the evangelists were: one, a fisherman, another an exciseman (the most respectable of them all, perhaps) and the other just a simple follower of the man of the people who started the movement.[8]

But the bill by its treatment of denominational schools perpetuated two things which were anathema to him as dissenter and democrat: it forced sectarian teaching upon unwilling pupils and permitted the use of public money without full public control.

[8] D. R. Daniel, Papers in the National Library of Wales.

It was not only to the contents of the measure that Lloyd George took exception, but also to its introduction by a Ministry which had assured the electorate during the contest of 1900 that the South African war was the only question at issue. He wrongly held Joseph Chamberlain as especially responsible for this breach of faith, the very man who, in his early days, had been the most bitter assailant of sectarian teaching.

The objects to which Lloyd George addressed himself were three in number: while the bill was being debated he tried on the floor of the House and by organizing public opinion in the country to secure the emendation of offending clauses; when the passing of the act made further protest useless he set himself to obstructing its administration without actually breaking the law; and in the third place, he used all his resources to support the local authorities in their campaign against the act. His efforts only ceased with the formation of the Liberal Government in December 1905.

During the eight strenuous, crowded months of 1902 from March until the Education Bill received the Royal Assent on 18 December, Lloyd George was constant in his attendance at the House, directing his criticisms with all the force that an unerring command of detail could supply. Alert, diplomatic, blunt, fierce, as occasion demanded, he won the admiring gratitude of his friends and the respect of his foes as the unofficial leader of the Liberal Opposition to the measure.

But Lloyd George was sincerely interested in education, so his criticisms were not all destructive. His experience of the inestimable benefits of the opening of secondary schools throughout Wales, after the Welsh Intermediate Act of 1889, led him to urge the Government to make it compulsory and not merely permissible for the English local authorities to make adequate provision for secondary education.

It is not true to say that the fight against the measure was engineered by the politicians or forced upon them by the Nonconformists. The disturbance was spontaneous and caused by the introduction into the body politic of radical and Nonconformist England and Wales of something to which it was sensitively and violently allergic.

While the bill was being fought in the House, obstruction was being mobilized in the country. In Wales, which was predominantly Nonconformist, it was confidently expected that the Opposition would have the support of the local authorities to be set up to carry out its provisions. Not so in England. A passive resistance movement was therefore organized among individuals under leaders, such as Dr. Clifford, who refused to pay the education rate.

Lloyd George threw himself into the campaign in Wales. When the bill became law, concrete planning and definite action were needed. A general election which might transform the whole situation was possible and the Welsh county council elections, due in March 1904, certainly would give the ratepayers a chance to express their opinion. In January 1903, therefore, he advised the local authorities, set up by the act, to administer it, but to use every loophole it provided to carry it out with strict respect for civil and religious equality and so, in fact, to circumvent it. Lloyd George satisfied himself that his tactics were legal, and he deprecated the action of Carmarthen, for example, which refused to administer the act at all.

In the county council elections of March 1904, the Liberals, following the advice of their leader, voted only for those candidates who pledged themselves to secure religious equality in the schools and to refuse rate aid to schools not under full public control. These candidates swept the polls. Nevertheless, the new year brought its anxieties. The Government countered his moves by a one-clause measure, quite frankly levelled at Wales. This was the Defaulting Authorities Bill, permitting the managers of schools, if forced to spend money because of the refusal of the local authority to finance them, to be paid direct from the national exchequer, which would then be reimbursed by the deduction of the sum so advanced from the grant due to the authority in question.

Naturally, Lloyd George and his group fought the bill fiercely and doggedly. It was, however, rushed through the House, and by devices so unfair that Asquith led the Liberals out of the Chamber as an expression of sympathy with the protest of the Welsh party. This was only one of the many signs of solidarity within the Liberal ranks which had been brought about by opposition to the obnoxious act of 1902. The bill passed its third reading without a word or a division.

The Welsh Coercion Act, as it was called, received Royal Assent on 15 August 1904. Lloyd George forthwith framed a plan of resistance. A campaign fund was started, the money to be used for the establishment of revolt schools. Indeed, several were actually opened. At a great convention in Cardiff, in October 1904, it was decided that if the Coercion Act were applied to any authority it was to divest itself of all responsibility for the elementary schools in its area. Nonconformist parents were to withdraw their children from church schools, and new schools were to be opened for them. The English Free Churches promised help, Welshmen in the great cities subscribed, the chapels in Wales, even the weakest ones, gave generously, and door-to-door collections were taken. This period of education revolt coincided with a religious revival in Wales. Lloyd George's meetings were changed at times into revival meetings. This mixture of spiritual exaltation, hero-worship, and national feeling reinforced the determination of the people.

It is impossible to say what would have happened if the coming into power of the Liberals at the end of 1905 had not ended the protest movement. It was expected that following the Liberal victory at the polls the hated act of 1902 would be amended. Attempts to do so were made, but the power of sectarianism and the House of Lords was too strong. Anglican and Roman Catholic churches are still rate-aided. The revolt, organized and led by Lloyd George in Opposition, petered out when he took office.

Not even Lloyd George's resilient health could stand the strain he put upon it during his first years in Parliament. Following an operation for tonsillitis, he had to give up public speaking and, in November 1905, went to Italy with his brother. The resignation of the Balfour Ministry recalled him, and a few days after his return he became a member of Sir Henry Campbell-Bannerman's Cabinet.

III

CABINET MINISTER

1906–14

THE general election held in January 1906, which followed on the resignation of Balfour and the accession of Campbell-Bannerman, resulted in the rout of the Unionists and the return of a vast Liberal majority. In the new Cabinet, Lloyd George was President of the Board of Trade. He was forty-two when he became a Cabinet Minister for the first time; Asquith, Chancellor of the Exchequer, was eleven years his senior, and Winston Churchill, Under-Secretary for the Colonies, was eleven years his junior. Churchill had earlier broken with the Tories on tariff reform. These were to be the Big Three of their generation in shaping and guiding the destinies of Great Britain and Ireland.

SOCIAL REFORMER

From the outset of his career, as we have seen, Lloyd George was an ardent advocate of disestablishment of the Welsh Church, and had often embarrassed the tepid Liberal administration with his vehemence. When he took office in 1905, pledges were given that disestablishment would remain an integral part of the legislative programme of the Liberal party, but the immediate passing of any Welsh Church bill was overshadowed by larger issues involving not Wales alone, but the whole of Britain.

Throughout the eighties and nineties, at an increasing rate, the nation's awareness of what was comprehensively called 'the social problem' had grown in width and depth. Charles Booth's *Life and Labour of the People in London* (1889–1903) converted a vague, emotional impression of metropolitan misery into facts and figures. A Royal Commission on Labour had traced the features of trade unionism, old and new, and shown the class cleavage between the ranks of skilled and unskilled. A Select Committee of the House of Lords on the Sweating System (1888) had uncovered shocking conditions prevailing for workers in the slums. In 1905 Balfour appointed the Poor Law Commission; its Majority and Minority Reports, published in 1909, extended Booth's limited picture to the whole kingdom, and described the defective dealings of local authorities with children, adults, and the aged; with the destitute and diseased, the ignorant and insane, with unemployed and un-employable. The publication of the reports was followed by a large-scale agitation, led by the Fabian Society, to reorganize the existing administration of the Poor Laws.

This fermenting background of unrest and inquiry must be kept in mind as we go on to observe Lloyd George exchanging the role of demagogic agitator for that of responsible Minister. The change was made, but it was not complete—it was never quite complete. His revolutionary Budget, his unprecedented Insurance Act, his insolent attack on the House of Lords, attracted and absorbed public attention, extinguished the campaign of the Fabians, and postponed the break-up of the Poor Law for twenty years. In effect what he did was to spike the Socialist guns with essentially Conservative social measures derived from the Liberal arsenal.

One so impressionable as Lloyd George could not have been indifferent to the new currents of social thought, but he brought to his new office no economic system to which he was firmly anchored. He had probably read the immensely popular *Political Economy* (1848) of John Stuart Mill which discussed the social application of economic doctrine. We may be certain that he had not studied Marx's *Capital*, the first volume of which had appeared in English in 1886. What we do know is that the young lawyer and Member of Parliament never went anywhere without putting in his bag a shilling paper-cover translation of *Les Misé-rables* published by Routledge. This classic of rich humanity was for years his Bible; he read it over and over again. His early speeches had been those of a young and fiery Welsh radical who could not but be moved by the violent social contrasts of incal-culable wealth and indescribable poverty found side by side. Speaking in Bangor in January 1906, he observed: 'I believe there is a new order coming for the people of this country. It is a quiet but certain revolution.' This was his belief in early manhood; and as Cabinet Minister his policies were to reflect this belief.

This social faith was in the tradition of the early Chamberlain, whose dominant purpose had now become the consolidation of the British Empire by means of Protection. The Tariff Reform movement, led by Chamberlain, and hotly debated in the years

1903–6, interested Lloyd George, as it did the whole of Britain. In his public speeches Lloyd George spoke as an uncompromising Free Trader; with Asquith and Churchill he had pursued Chamberlain from platform to platform during the Tariff Reform campaign. But at the Board of Trade the new President, when promoting the Merchant Shipping Act and the Patents and Designs Act, was not quite such a Free Trade purist as on the platform—a fact which pleased his Tory critics. 'Free Trade may be the alpha, but it is not the omega, of Liberal policy', he said at Manchester on 21 April 1908.

The new President of the Board of Trade surprised the country not only by his ability in dealing with big business but also by his skill in removing the railwaymen's threat of a general strike on 6 November 1907. Campbell-Bannerman wrote to King Edward: 'The country was largely indebted for so blessed a conclusion . . . to the knowledge, skill, astuteness and tact of the President of the Board of Trade.'

This signal success was immediately followed by a devastating personal grief. His eldest daughter, Mair Eluned, died on 29 November 1907, after an operation for appendicitis. She was seventeen years old, a girl of exceptional talent and attractive personality, gentle, modest, and strong.

Lloyd George's efforts at mediation did not slacken. He proceeded to deal successfully with trade disputes in the cotton, engineering, and shipbuilding industries, surprising all by his unexpected patience in negotiating each settlement. No court painter or Harley Street physician ever displayed greater professional blandness. He began to outline the tasks of the new Liberalism in a series of speeches remarkable for their positive handling of social problems and their rare humanity. His influence grew rapidly and his opponents realized that here was a formidable enemy.

Campbell-Bannerman died on 22 April 1908, Asquith had become Prime Minister on 7 April. Lloyd George took his place as Chancellor of the Exchequer, and was himself succeeded at the Board of Trade by Winston Churchill. The new Chancellor was not versed, far less trained, in public finance, but he could be counted on to find a way of circumventing the Lords who had torpedoed so many radical measures introduced by Liberal governments. Lloyd George at the Treasury and Churchill at the Board of Trade were close friends, colleagues, and rivals in framing a programme of positive state action. In March 1908 Churchill published in the *Nation* 'The Untrodden Field in Politics', a manifesto stating the aims of the programme. This, in fact, advanced the Fabian doctrine of the National Minimum in health, education, and efficiency, and demanded labour exchanges, wages boards, and other buttresses of the standard of life with which we have since become familiar.

In the late summer of 1908 Lloyd George went to Germany, Austria, and Belgium, to study social legislation. Belgium had her successful 'Ghent scheme' of insurance against unemployment; Germany had an excellent network of labour registries to show him; but it was the contributory aspect of German national insurance against ill health and old age that impressed him most.

The Budget of 1909 was his main preoccupation during 1908, and he discussed it with Charles Masterman who was helping him with the difficult and novel land clauses—for the money he wished to raise for his programme of social legislation was to come mainly from a revolutionary tax on the landowners and the hereditarily rich. Nearly all his colleagues were against him on the taxation of land values. Sir Herbert Lewis notes his saying: 'I have had to fight and bully and badger my way against everybody. I drove the Lord Chancellor [Loreburn] out of the Cabinet Committee by taunting him: "You are concerned for your friends the Dukes", and the Attorney-General with: "You are concerned for the slum-owners."' During the months of preparation of the Budget, Lloyd George spoke jocularly to his intimate friends of tumbrels and guillotines, and seriously expressed his view, recorded by Mrs. Masterman, that 'all down history nine-tenths of mankind have been grinding corn for the remaining tenth and been paid with the husks and bidden to thank God they had the husk'.[1]

In the Cabinet, Lloyd George had the loyal support of Asquith and of Grey for his drastic proposals; he was not helped by John Burns, the first Labour representative in the Cabinet, who had become President of the Local Government Board in 1906. Among civil servants, Sir Robert Chalmers was his mainstay.

On 29 April 1909 the Chancellor of the Exchequer introduced the new Budget in a four-hour speech. The performance was a parliamentary failure. The speech was read, and was diffuse; but

[1] Lucy Masterman, *C. F. G. Masterman*, p. 150.

it was momentous, not only because it ranged over new fields of revenue but because it openly resorted to taxation as an instrument of social regeneration.

There were two main categories of new expenditure for which the Chancellor had to provide: the navy and social reform. Whilst he was not going to jeopardize the country's naval supremacy, he was not going to squander money 'on building gigantic flotillas to encounter mythical armadas'. He explained the principles of his compulsory and contributory health-insurance scheme. He told of the Development Fund—which was to be set up to consolidate the increased grants for afforestation, agriculture, railways, harbours—and of the plan to raise an autonomous fund from motorists for road development.

To obtain the necessary revenue, the Chancellor imposed a moderate increase on the income-tax, heavy increases on death duties, a super-tax of 6d. in the pound on incomes above £5,000 on the amount by which they exceeded £3,000 per annum, and an addition to the duties on liquor. These increases might perhaps have been accepted by the Opposition had he not coupled with them a comprehensive system of land taxes on the future unearned increment of land values, on undeveloped land, on the realization of leases, and on mineral rights. This complicated legislation accentuated the decline in house-building, which had already begun, by discouraging the small speculative builder who worked on narrow margins of profit.

The Finance Bill was under discussion for seventy-two days, and several all-night sessions. Lloyd George had a hard time during this period. E. T. Raymond says: 'For weeks a victim of neuritis he appeared night after night with his arm in a sling. It was no uncommon thing for him to speak twenty times in a single sitting.' His insecure acquaintance with the minutiae of his own bill meant that he often skated over a very thin sheet of knowledge, but it thickened as the debate continued. The bill passed the House of Commons on 4 November 1909, by 379 to 149 votes, and on 30 November was rejected in the House of Lords by 350 votes to 75. After its defeat, budget leagues, *pro* and *anti*, were formed to continue the debate in the constituencies. The Opposition was diverted from pure finance to discussing land royalties and the distribution of wealth. Nothing could have been more to Lloyd George's advantage.

Referring in 1912 to Lloyd George's position in 1909, Massingham, the Liberal editor, commented:

> Those who knew Mr. George's mind in those days knew also that he foresaw and planned a first rejection by the Lords, an endorsement by the country, and a following attack on the veto, in which the peers were bound, whatever their tactics, to succumb. All went well as this simple, though far from shallow, generalship foresaw. But while nothing miscarried the resulting situation was a difficult one.[2]

Lloyd George campaigned for his Budget in a series of vituperative speeches throughout 1909–10, and by them he roused the ire of the Lords. These speeches were conversational in style, incisive, and metaphorical. The most famous was delivered at Limehouse on 30 July 1909, to an audience of 4,000 poor folk in east London, to whom he talked of the rapacity of parasitic landowners, living on the unearned increase in land value.

> Who created these increments? Who made that golden swamp? Was it the landlord? Was it his energy? His brains? . . . It is rather hard that an old workman should have to find his way to the gates of the tomb bleeding and footsore, through the brambles and thorns of poverty. We cut a new path for him, an easier one, a pleasanter one, through fields of waving corn.[3]

This and similar speeches were printed by the *Daily News* in a penny pamphlet, and reached many thousands of readers in working- and middle-class homes.

Rejection of the Budget by the House of Lords precipitated a constitutional struggle—one which had been developing over a long period of years—between the Lords and Liberal majorities in the Commons. The Administration appealed to the country on the Budget, using it as the focal point of the wider issue of the perpetual thwarting of the people's will by the Lords whenever that will was expressed through a Liberal Government. In January 1910 Asquith was returned, but his working majority now depended on the support of Irish and Labour Members. The Budget of the previous April then passed through the two Houses, the Lords passing it without a division on 28 April 1910.

The fight against the House of Lords was not yet over; the Parliament Bill, which had been introduced by the Prime Minister on

[2] H. W. Massingham, in the *Nation*, 6 January 1912.
[3] Speech by Lloyd George at Limehouse, 30 July 1909; reprinted by the *Daily News*, with other speeches, in a pamphlet.

ORATOR, 1929

14 April 1910, providing in part that a measure passed three times by the Commons must be accepted by the Lords, was hotly contested by the Upper House in spite of a threat to create enough Peers to secure its passage.

The death of Edward VII on 6 May brought a truce, followed by a conference on the constitutional issue summoned on the initiative of the new King, George V. The Prime Minister, Lloyd George, Augustine Birrell, and Lord Crewe were the Liberal, and Arthur Balfour, Austen Chamberlain, Lord Lansdowne, and Lord Cawdor the Conservative representatives. After twenty-one sittings it failed, owing to pressure from Tory die-hards. To secure an agreed programme Lloyd George had proposed a Coalition, thus early revealing his pragmatic political temper.

The persistent obstinacy of the Peers brought about the second general election of 1910, which again resulted in the return of the Asquith Ministry. The struggle with the Lords was resumed, but this time a definite pledge to create about 250 Peers, a detailed list of whom was prepared, had been secured from the King in the event of the Lords throwing out the Parliament Bill again. They passed it on 10 August 1911 by 131 votes to 114.

Thus what R. C. K. Ensor calls 'the most decisive step in British constitutional development since the franchise extension of 1867', the Parliament Act which destroyed the absolute veto of the House of Lords, was the victorious outcome of the fight begun when Lloyd George flung down the gage of battle in his Budget of 1909.

The acts passed by Liberals in power since the end of 1905 were moderate experiments in social legislation, but they gave a decisive impulse to state intervention and may perhaps be regarded as the foundations of the Welfare State. They were all widely extended in the following forty years: Education (Provision of Meals) Act, 1906; Medical Inspection of School Children Act, 1907; Employment of School Children outside School Hours Act, 1908; Non-contributory Old Age Pensions Act, 1908; Housing and Town Planning Act, 1909; Labour Exchanges Act, 1909.

By 1911 Lloyd George was moving towards the fashioning of the National Health and Unemployment Bills. Anticipating the Beveridge plan of 1943, he believed that it would be wise to deal with all kinds of social insurance as a dovetailed entity, but at that time such a thing was not possible. To tackle the problems of social insurance at any time would have been a formidable enterprise, but to do so in the spring of 1911 was a Herculean venture. The Government was awaiting the issue of the constitutional struggle before dealing with Home Rule and Welsh Disestablishment, on top of the normal work of estimates and Budget. There was, however, an urgency about national insurance, for many of the Friendly Societies were heading for bankruptcy, and the principal trade unions were crippled with the burden of sickness, unemployment, and superannuation benefits. Fearing lest his pet bill might be framed in too technical language by parliamentary counsel, Lloyd George commissioned a young barrister of twenty-seven to draft the health part of the Insurance Bill. Wilfrid Greene (now Lord Greene and former Master of the Rolls) often worked through the night in order to have ready by next morning a set of draft clauses to be served up at the Chancellor's breakfast table.

The new National Insurance Bill was divided into two parts: Part I provided that nearly all manual workers between the ages of sixteen and seventy earning less than £160 a year were to be insured against ill health by the joint contributions of themselves, their employers, and the state. The aim was to work through such Friendly Societies and trade unions as became 'Approved Societies' for the administration of the act. The unemployment provisions, contained in Part II, were more experimental: ship-building, engineering, building, and a few other trades were selected to organize some two and a quarter million workers into a contributory scheme of insurance against unemployment, with benefit at seven shillings a week. These were vast measures without precedent in the country; and the organization necessary to get them into law and then into action was a tremendous problem. Masterman, Rufus Isaacs, Sir Robert Morant, and the Treasury officials, Bradbury and Braithwaite, were entrusted with the job, under Lloyd George's supervision. 'The German Insurance Scheme', Masterman and Morant groaned, 'had taken twenty-five years to complete. We were asked to complete a far more complicated and comprehensive scheme in six months. There was no office, no staff, no address, no telephone.' But Lloyd George would not be daunted, and he gave Morant the pick of the Civil Service to see the programme through.

The Northcliffe press attacked the bill with fury, and promoted a bitter opposition to it. We have the authority of the Chief Liberal

Whip (Alexander Murray, the Master of Elibank) for saying that had an election taken place at the end of 1911 the Liberal party would have been defeated. Two wars have made the British public familiar with identity cards and ration books, but the stamped insurance card, made in Germany, was unknown in 1911. Meetings of protest denounced the Chancellor as 'a tyrant, gagger, guillotine'. But he himself said the Insurance Act was 'doing the work of the Man of Nazareth' (*The Times*, 11 August 1913).

Thus, in the National Insurance Act of 1911, was launched a direct challenge to poverty which in the years from 1909 to 1922 Lloyd George was to follow up with a great series of social measures dealing with health, housing, education, wages, and employment. These had the combined result not only of improving industrial conditions for the workers, but of transferring a considerable portion of the national income from the rich to the poor. He was not a Socialist, nor did he see eye to eye with the Labour party, but there was no doubt where his sympathies lay.

Conceived as a vast democratic insurance system, to be administered by thousands of approved societies and scores of insurance committees, the National Insurance Act in its development has been bureaucratic—inevitably so, as its regulations are uniformly applicable to large numbers, are controlled by the state, and operated by salaried officials. The range of social service has greatly expanded since 1912; the biggest expansion—accepted by all parties and embracing full employment, children's allowances, and a national health service—took place in 1945 under James Griffiths and Aneurin Bevan, two of Lloyd George's countrymen, the one Minister of National Insurance and the other Minister of Health in a Labour Government. Their debt to the pioneering labours of Lloyd George is immense. They inherited a stable fabric of central and local government capable of undertaking the administration of their own comprehensive socialist measures.

From 1925 to 1935, as subsequent chapters will show, Lloyd George continued to prescribe radical remedies for the economic ills and miseries of his day, and from his pharmacopoeia later practitioners have borrowed freely.

MARCONI EPISODE

In 1912 Lloyd George had set up a Land Inquiry Committee to investigate rural conditions and the ownership, tenancy, taxation,

41

and rating of land and buildings in urban districts. The Rural Report appeared in 1913 and the Cabinet approved Lloyd George's land policy. He launched a campaign for 'the regeneration of rural life and the emancipation of the land from the paralysing grip of a rusty, effete and unprofitable system'. Unionists were divided in their attitude to it. 'The Liberal Party', declared Bonar Law, 'is blessed—from the party point of view it is a blessing—with one of the greatest demagogues who has ever existed in any country.'

The Liberal Government was hated by the privileged classes because of the land taxes, the death duties, the Parliament Act, and the Insurance Act passed under their administrations; and Lloyd George was held mainly responsible for these iniquities. His deeds were the whips, his words the scorpions with which they had been chastised. In the City he was profoundly distrusted for, under his influence, all finance had become 'a matter of political social reform, vindictive taxation and pseudo-philanthropy'. Moreover, his continued fight for Welsh disestablishment, and his renewed attacks on the Established Church had infuriated its champions. It is in the suspicious and embittered atmosphere of the time that the history of the so-called 'Marconi Scandal' must be placed in order to be understood.

In June 1911 the Imperial Defence Committee declared that the uniting of Britain and the Empire by wireless communication was a matter of supreme urgency. Following on this declaration, the Postmaster-General, Mr. Herbert Samuel, began negotiations with the English Marconi Company for a network of wireless stations. The managing director of the company was Godfrey Isaacs, a brother of the Attorney-General, Sir Rufus. On 7 March 1912 Samuel accepted the tender of the company subject to ratification by the House of Commons.

Ever since the beginning of 1912, or even earlier, rumours had been current in the City that Ministers were profiting from inside knowledge of these negotiations and were speculating in shares. The fact that these shares had risen sensationally in the year between the start of negotiations and the parliamentary acceptance of the tender did not help the situation. In addition to the rumours of profitable speculation, there were insinuations that the agreement with the Government had been corruptly obtained by Rufus Isaacs's influence over Samuel.

On 17 April 1912 Lloyd George and the Master of Elibank had

each purchased, in good faith, 1,000 shares in the American Marconi Company from their friend Sir Rufus Isaacs who had himself purchased 10,000 shares from his brother Godfrey—these shares not as yet being on the open market. The shares rose, and on 20 May Lloyd George sold most of his holding for a profit of £743. Two days later he bought 3,000 more shares for himself and the Master of Elibank. He retained these, against the advice of his broker, because he thought them a good investment. None of these shares was actually paid for by him owing, so he said, to carelessness, for he had the money. Many anxious and humiliating days were to pass before he sold all his shares in 1913, having lost over £500 in all and risked his career and his reputation.

These purchases were made in utter ignorance of the whispering campaign that was going on. Even had Lloyd George and the Master of Elibank been aware of it, it might have made no difference, for Sir Rufus had satisfied himself and assured his two colleagues that no connexion existed between the English and the American Marconi Companies which need make them hesitate to buy shares in the latter while the former was negotiating with the British Government. It cannot be denied, however, that though technically there was no link between the two companies, there must have been a very strong community of interest; indeed, the English company owned the majority of shares in the American company. If all the facts about the holdings of the English company in the American company were known to Sir Rufus, he should have seen the red light and realized how dubious the transactions would appear.

On 19 July 1912 the copy of the agreement between Marconi's Wireless Telegraph Company, Ltd., Marconi, and the Posmaster-General was ordered to be printed and to lie upon the table of the House of Commons. On 1 August questions were asked about the identity of the shareholders in the company and the rise in its shares. On 7 August feeling in the House during the debate was so uncertain that it was adjourned.

Rumours had by now found their way into certain periodicals, and at the beginning of the recess Herbert Samuel chanced to read an attack in the *Eye-Witness* (8 August) as he stood by a railway bookstall. He at once communicated with Sir Rufus, who with Lloyd George was at Marienbad, on the advisability of taking legal action. The Attorney-General wrote to the Prime Minister asking what ought to be done. Asquith, who knew the background from the Master of Elibank, replied that no notice should be taken of the scurrilous attack.

Parliament reassembled on 7 October and, in view of the atmosphere of hostility which had been fomented, the Postmaster-General moved that a select committee should be appointed to inquire into the circumstances relating to his agreement with the Marconi Company, and also into the desirability of a contract with the company. In the debate which followed, the Attorney-General took the opportunity to deny, on behalf of himself, the Chancellor of the Exchequer, and the Postmaster-General, the purchase at any time of shares in the *English* company, but neglected to acknowledge the purchase of *American* shares.

The legal training of the men involved probably served them ill at this juncture. The bare accusation alone was refuted. But it was not legal guilt which needed to be disproved; it was the confidence of the House and the nation in their integrity which had to be maintained or restored. To the plain man 'Marconis' were 'Marconis', whether English or American, and a complete statement on 11 October 1912 on the occasion of the debate in the House would have prevented much grief. The buying of the shares was an error of judgement, the failure to acknowledge publicly at the time of the inquiry the purchase of the American shares savoured of disingenuousness, though Lloyd George in the House on 18 June 1913 said the reason for this reticence was that 'the Committee afforded the better opportunity for presenting the whole of the facts'.

Unfortunately, the select committee (set up on 23 October) was a body of fifteen members chosen on party lines; its proceedings were not always efficient or dignified, and they were very protracted. It was not until the spring of 1913 that the by now longed-for chance to 'tell all' came, and by then the virtue had been taken out of the confession because the facts had already been told in the course of a lawsuit brought by Sir Rufus Isaacs and Mr. Herbert Samuel against *Le Matin*, which had repeated the charges of profitable speculation by the two Ministers.

An advisory committee, set up by the select committee to report on the technical advisability of the contract, at length reported, on 1 May, approving the plan in general, though guardedly. The main committee, dealing with the charges levelled against the members of the Government, presented its report on 13 June 1913 to the Commons; it was in four parts: a majority report, two draft reports, and a severe report by Lord Robert Cecil. The majority report was the one finally adopted. It affirmed that there was no foundation for the charges of corruption in connexion with the negotiations between the Postmaster-General and the Marconi Company, or for the rumours of improper dealings by Ministers in English Marconi shares. With regard to the dealings with the American company, it affirmed that 'in these transactions there is no ground for any charge of corruption or unfaithfulness to public duty, or any reflection upon the honour of the Ministers concerned'.

The report having been presented to the House, there followed a debate on a vote of censure on 18 and 19 June. Sir Rufus Isaacs and Lloyd George both made personal statements. The Chancellor made a clean breast of the whole affair. He said on the first day of the debate: 'I am conscious of having done nothing which brings a stain upon the honour of a Minister of the Crown. If you will, I acted thoughtlessly, I acted carelessly, I acted mistakenly, but I acted innocently, I acted openly and I acted honestly.'

The debate was on party lines, and the vote of censure was lost by 346 votes to 268, the division also being almost entirely on party lines. Lloyd George was cleared, but as he himself said in his statement during the debate: 'Although it is indiscretion [of which he was accused] on paper and impropriety on paper, in the background it is corruption, which you will hear of for months when it cannot be refuted. The charge has been exploded, but the deadly afterdamp remains.'

The Land Inquiry Committee's Report on urban problems was not published until April 1914, but its main features dealing with land, housing, and rating had been forecast by Lloyd George in pungent speeches late in 1913. 'Labourers had diminished, game had tripled. The landlord was no more necessary to agriculture than a gold chain to a watch.'

The summer of 1914, however, brought not a successful land campaign but first the prospect of civil war in Ireland and then the reality of the First World War.

IV

CABINET MINISTER IN WAR
1914–16

AT the outbreak of war in August 1914, Lloyd George was half-way through his fifty-second year and had been for nearly nine years a Cabinet Minister. What did he know of foreign affairs? What did he know of war or preparations for war?

In 1908 he had visited Germany, and in that same year had, with Grey, twice met the German Ambassador, Count Metternich, and discussed naval relations (for Britain regarded the great expansion of the German navy as ominous). But of actual foreign affairs he knew very little—in his *Memoirs* he blames this ignorance both on his preoccupation with domestic affairs and on the practice of the Foreign Office in withholding information from Ministers. The Boer War was his only experience in that field, and it was an experience which was on such a small scale that it could really have no bearing on the conduct of the new conflict.

Lloyd George was never a pacifist, but his views were normally near the old Liberal watchwords Peace and Reform, if hardly Retrenchment. He had been nursed in a community which hated all war, and as Chancellor of the Exchequer he deplored the waste of millions on it which could be more fruitfully spent on measures for the betterment of the poor—in 1910 he had scoffed at the building of Dreadnoughts 'against nightmares'.

But he had some hint of an impending crisis in June 1911, when the German gunboat *Panther* suddenly appeared in the French Moroccan harbour of Agadir. Morocco held a position on the Atlantic seaboard which made it of great strategic importance to Britain, as well as to France which protested against the German move. At the Mansion House on 21 July, the Chancellor, on his own initiative, sounded a warning note, in masterful language, which caused violent excitement in Germany. In the course of his speech he said: 'If a situation were to be forced upon us in which peace could only be preserved by . . . allowing Britain to be treated where her interests were vitally affected as if she were of no account in the Cabinet of nations, then I say emphatically that peace at any price would be a humiliation intolerable for a great country like ours to endure.' Germany took the hint, slightly modified her claims for the moment, the tension relaxed, and there was three years' respite for the preparation of defences.

By the winter of 1913–14 Churchill was at the head of the Admiralty and was putting up a tremendous fight with the Treasury for increased naval estimates to meet not only an expanding building programme but the cost of erecting oil tanks for oil reserves, it having been decided to apply this new motive power to the most vital units of the fleet. But Churchill met the determined resistance of the Chancellor.

Intimate peace-loving friends in Wales had been urging Lloyd George to stand for isolation and keep the country free from foreign entanglement, and he was aware that his own strong distaste for armaments was shared by many Liberals. But at this late hour, preoccupation with domestic affairs, even though they included painful events in Ireland, hardly explains the strange misreading of the international situation shown by Lloyd George up to the very moment of war. On 3 January 1914 he gave to the *Daily Chronicle* a heedless interview, as Asquith called it, which set all Europe by the ears. In it he argued for economy in the naval estimates because of the improvement of Anglo-German relations and because he saw, or thought he saw, a revolt against military oppression throughout the whole of western Europe. This declaration encouraged in Liberal circles a campaign throughout the country for a reduction of armaments.

More astonishing than the newspaper interview in January were a speech on 9 July, eleven days after the murder of Franz Ferdinand at Sarajevo, to a group of bankers at Guildhall, in which he stated: 'In the matter of external affairs the sky has never been more perfectly blue', and his reference on 23 July, the very day of Austria's bullying ultimatum to Serbia, when, dealing in Parliament with the possibility of economy of armaments, he said of Germany: 'Take a neighbour of ours. Our relations are very much better than they were a few years ago. There is none of that snarling which we used to see, more especially in the Press of these two great, I will not say rival nations, but two great Empires. The feeling is better altogether between them.'

Certain disputes between the two countries were in these months in process of settlement, and perhaps the friendly attitude of the

Chancellor contributed to Germany's belief that the moment was favourable for war and that Britain would stand aside.

During the opening stages of the immediate crisis leading to war, Lloyd George was clearly with the non-intervention group, but on 27 July he admitted to C. P. Scott of the *Manchester Guardian* (a man who was probably Lloyd George's closest political confidant) that a difficult situation would arise if the German fleet were to attack French towns on the other side of the Channel; that he was willing to go a certain distance with France and Russia in putting diplomatic pressure on Austria; and that 'if war broke out we might make it easy for Italy to keep out by, as it were, pairing with her'. At one point he proposed that steps should be taken to strengthen the army and equipment so that when it was judged the moment had come we could intervene effectively. On 31 July he was 'fighting hard for peace'. On 1 August Asquith noted: 'L. G. all for peace, is more sensible and statesmanlike for keeping the position still open.'

But the Chancellor was unsettled. Walter Runciman described him to Arthur Murray at this time:

When the crisis came it found Lloyd George vacillating. Right up to tea-time on Sunday, August 2, he . . . was doubtful of the action he would take. In course of conversation with about one half of our Ministerial colleagues in No. 11 on the afternoon of that day, he told us that he would not oppose the war, but he would take no part in it, and would retire for the time being to Criccieth. He would not repeat his experience of 1899–1902. I remember him saying that he had had enough of 'standing out against a war-inflamed populace'. Right up to the moment that we received the news that the Germans had crossed the Belgian frontier he left us in doubt as to what was his view and what action he would take.[1]

He had pleaded with his colleagues that if Germany did no more than trespass on a small corner of Belgium it might be overlooked, but the ruthless thrust of German armed might into the body of Belgium swept aside all doubts and hesitations. The issue settled, no one was more resolute in the prosecution of the war than the Chancellor of the Exchequer. Before he was again to set eyes on a world at peace he was to be Minister of Munitions, Secretary for War, and Prime Minister. Now on the outbreak of war,

---

[1] A. C. Murray, *Master and Brother*, p. 120, quoting Walter Runciman.

Asquith, with the enthusiastic approval of the whole country, sent Lord Kitchener to the War Office.

WAR FINANCE

When the United Kingdom declared war on Germany on 4 August 1914, Lloyd George had been Chancellor of the Exchequer for seven years and had presented six budget statements to Parliament and the country. As we have seen, one of these statements, that of April 1909, a strong expression of radical policy, had forced a constitutional crisis. From that date until 1914 large social reform and rearmament expenditures had conditioned measures in other spheres of British public finance. The trade boom of the years 1910–14, however, swelled the revenue from existing taxes and provided surpluses for the reduction of the national debt. Lloyd George's budgets from 1910 to 1914 had, therefore, almost perforce been uneventful, judged by 1909 standards, though their author did rouse opposition by his encroachments on the fixed provision for the reduction of the debt.

It was inevitable that Lloyd George should be criticized for diverting sinking funds, old and new, to objects of popular favour. More general criticisms were levelled against his methods; Charles Mallet says:

At the Exchequer Mr. Lloyd George's work was not so successful as at the Board of Trade. The truth is he did not always master very thoroughly the financial problems with which he had to deal. There are stories, well authenticated, of Treasury officials who saw with dismay important papers tossed aside, while the Minister invited them to talk to him instead.[2]

The truth was, that he preferred to master memoranda by compelling their authors to summarize the contents clearly and submit to cross-examination on every step in their exposition. In this way Lloyd George acquired much knowledge which was to serve him and the country in good stead at the outbreak of war. Much of his work, however, was not directly in the tradition of his office as Chancellor: social security, education, the constitutional struggle, the launching of national insurance, and the land campaign, for the discussion of these he was accessible to Ministers and civil servants, and all of them kept his name in the public eye.

[2] Charles Mallet, *Mr. Lloyd George: a Study*, p. 33.

The long-term task of British finance from 1914 to 1918 was to mobilize half the national income for the prosecution of the war. The problem did not thus appear in August 1914, nor could it have so appeared since the extent and duration of the conflict were not then known. At the Treasury during the first ten months of war, Lloyd George had the task of providing for large but unknown increases of Government expenditure and of keeping in operation as much as possible of the intricate machinery of the London money market.

With the advent of war the Treasury immediately became the centre for the determination of urgent questions of monetary policy, of which neither the Chancellor nor his able staff, with Sir John Bradbury at its head, had any previous experience. The Chancellor had to learn in the midst of a raging world financial crisis. It was the London money market which moved commodities around the world through the medium of bills of exchange. The Chancellor had never seen a bill of exchange and knew little or nothing of the delicate and complicated mechanism by which international trade is regulated. Lloyd George sought guidance from the Governor of the Bank of England and other financial experts to help him through the maze.

The City was not only excited by the advent of war, it was much alarmed; and the gravest panic was only narrowly averted. The Bank Holiday (which luckily had fallen on 3 August) was extended for three days, to give time for organization and the introduction of measures to prevent the country's financial collapse. 'These three holidays were some of the busiest and most anxious days I ever spent', Lloyd George wrote in his *Memoirs*. He was chairman at the Treasury of a series of meetings of Ministers, civil servants, and representatives of the financial and business communities. Decisions had to be hastily improvised with little reference to ideal or long-term solutions. The Stock Exchange was closed, the Bank Charter Act suspended, and a general moratorium declared.

The Cabinet was so preoccupied with the political and economic problems of the home front that it had to let Sir Edward Grey manage foreign affairs. The pressure of these problems did not, however, keep Lloyd George away from the House of Commons, and he took a remarkably large share, in view of the other claims upon his time, in the debates of the week beginning 2 August.

The Treasury conferences to which he summoned his experts met in the mornings and afternoons of 4–6 August. Amongst his advisers were Lord Revelstoke of Baring's Bank, Sir John (later Lord) Bradbury, Permanent Under-Secretary to the Treasury, Lord Reading, then Chief Justice, and Sir George Paish, economist and statistician. He also took the unconventional, if not unprecedented step, of inviting to the conferences Austen Chamberlain, the Chancellor of the Exchequer in the last Unionist Government. Among the notable representatives of the financial community were Lord Cunliffe, Governor of the Bank of England, Sir Edward Holden, Chairman of the London City and Midland Bank, Mr. Huth Jackson, and Lord St. Aldwyn, who, as Sir Michael Hicks-Beach, had been a violent parliamentary opponent of Lloyd George. On 5 August the Chancellor went down to the House of Commons to reassure the country and describe what measures had been taken to maintain 'business as usual'.

By the afternoon of 6 August the conference had completed its discussions, the banks had been reopened—'and as the responsible Minister', writes Lloyd George in his *Memoirs*, 'I awaited with great anxiety the moment when business should again start, to learn the outcome of our experiments'. When, on the evening of 7 August, Lloyd George announced in Parliament that the reports of banks throughout the country were perfectly satisfactory, Austen Chamberlain offered the Chancellor 'congratulations on the success of the measures taken by him and the heads of the Bank of England and other great interests with which he has been conferring'. Lloyd George was so far satisfied with the week's achievements as to join in a consideration of the artistic demerits of the new pound and ten shilling treasury notes.

In November 1914 Lloyd George was able to turn from rehabilitating the money markets to the problem of raising for the Exchequer the money needed for prosecuting the war. The United Kingdom's participation in the war was financed by a combination of taxation, borrowing, and monetary inflation, and the method adopted was based less upon budget estimates than upon periodic votes of credit, for it was impossible to arrive at precise estimates of future expenditure in a war of such unprecedented magnitude. The first vote of credit (for £100 million) was obtained by Asquith in the House of Commons on the second day after the declaration of war. On 19–26 August treasury bills were issued. There was an almost continuous stream of borrowing for short-term by means of five War Loans which tapped the ever-swelling stream of wages and profits.

Lloyd George advocated a relatively high ratio of taxation to borrowing for war purposes; as he said in Parliament (17 November 1914): 'Every twenty millions raised annually by taxation during this period means four or five millions taken off the permanent burdens thereafter imposed on the country.' Speakers at the 1915 meeting of the economic section of the British Association upheld his conclusion that the nation could bear greater taxes during the war, but they stipulated that the taxation would have to be 'intelligently applied so as to hit those who were benefiting financially from the War'.[3]

Lloyd George's Budget for 1915 doubled income-tax and super-tax; but the new rates were to apply only to the remaining four months of the financial year, and concessions were made to those whose incomes had fallen as a result of the war; the duty on beer was raised to an amount which he hoped would give £20 million by April 1916; and avoiding Pitt's paradox of borrowing to maintain a statutory sinking fund, he proposed the suspension of the existing sinking fund. Despite these proposed new sources of revenue he was still faced with a deficit of three-fifths of the year's expenditure, which had to be met from borrowed funds—including a £350 million war loan. A main criticism, recorded by U. K. Hicks in the *Review of Economic Studies*, of the finance of the early stages of the war is that greater and earlier additions to taxation should have been made 'before private budgeting had adjusted itself to the new incomes'. Criticism of the Budget was, however, extremely lenient, and after a swift passage through the House of Commons it was entered on the statute book on 27 November 1914.

On 4 May 1915 Lloyd George introduced his financial statement. With the cost of the war increasing every day, proposals for much higher taxes were to be expected, but he explained that the Government wished to know the issue of the summer campaign before making final proposals. In the meantime he submitted two alternative estimates, one based on the assumption that the war would last another five months, the other on the assumption that it would last until the end of the financial year (though he

---

[3] *Economic Journal*, March 1916.

told his friend Riddell at this time that he believed it might last another three years). The only significant change in taxation that he proposed was a large addition to the alcohol duties, designed rather to restrict consumption than to provide revenue. The time was one of renewed political division; the second war Budget was therefore criticized more sharply than its predecessor. It is true that this Budget, Lloyd George's last as Chancellor of the Exchequer, must be reckoned the weakest link in the series, for he failed to impose the increased taxation for which the country was prepared; but its weakness was largely determined by the demands on time and thought created by military operations, and it was generally understood that the real Budget would follow later in the year.

Lloyd George left the Treasury for the new Ministry of Munitions at the formation of the Coalition Government on 25 May 1915. The Budget was still being debated, and it fell to Reginald McKenna to steer the Finance Bill through Parliament. It became law on 29 July.

Lord Cunliffe 'was in tears' at Lloyd George's departure from the Treasury—a departure which the Chancellor regarded as temporary, and which took place against the wishes of his uncle, Richard Lloyd, but he never went back, and spoke rarely in the later budget debates, though he took a natural interest in financial affairs for the rest of the war period.

STRATEGY AND SUPPLY

In the opening months of the war Lloyd George had brilliantly mastered the financial crisis and carried through, with the quick support of public opinion, drastic measures for the provision of the cash required to keep the wheels of industry and commerce revolving faster than ever before. He then turned his omnivorous attention to the higher strategy of the war.

'Lloyd George had in him the makings of a greater soldier than anyone engaged on either side, with the possible exceptions of Foch and Ludendorff. Born under other social conditions, he might well have been in the army, and in that case the British Army would have thrown up another Marlborough'—so wrote Herbert Sidebotham, an able student of war. Side by side with this judgement we may place that of John Buchan, who had made special studies of the careers of Augustus Caesar, Oliver Cromwell, and Robert E. Lee: 'Of all the civilians I have known, Lloyd George seems to have possessed in the highest degree the capacity for becoming a great soldier. But he might have lost several armies while he was learning his trade.'

Statesmen and soldiers alike had to learn, line upon line, defeat upon defeat, how to run a world war. Naturally the soldiers enjoyed the greater prestige; they were at least professional students of war, and some had fought in South Africa. But this war was like no other, and text-books and precedents were not very helpful. A layman's handicap was, therefore, less than it might have been, especially if the layman had the restless, probing, rebellious mind of Lloyd George. He never was much impressed by rank or authority, by dukes or field-marshals. Five months of war had convinced him that military leaders were not overcharged with brains, and he did not enjoy being treated by them as an amateur. Like Churchill, and unlike Grey, he was intensely interested in military operations. His curiosity was insatiable, he had few fixed presuppositions, and he was unhampered by excessive knowledge of technical detail.

By the end of 1914 the Germans had been beaten on the Marne, 'the greatest battle ever fought in the world'. The invasion of France was halted and the Germans were back on the Aisne, but large areas of France, with their rich coalfields and industries, were still under German occupation. Costly offensives against 'sand-bags, wire and concrete' had only driven the enemy back a mile or two, while, of the Fatherland, not a yard was in Allied hands.

In August 1914 it was widely believed that the war would be over by Christmas; in January 1915 responsible opinion placed the end in the autumn of that year; in February Kitchener judged that about the beginning of 1917 Germany must sue for peace. It was increasingly accepted that the only way to certain victory was to hurl astronomical masses of men, guns, shells, and tanks at the enemy in France. At the opening of 1915 there was no other ruling policy, but not everyone was content with it, least of all Lloyd George.

On the last day of 1914, in a letter to Asquith, Lloyd George protested against the prevailing policy, or lack of one, and asked that a series of meetings of the War Committee of the Committee of Imperial Defence should be summoned to study the situation.

On 1 January 1915 he circulated the first of several important memoranda he was to write at crucial moments in the war. These memoranda are not the casual exercises of an arm-chair strategist: their chief characteristic is their sense of urgency, of time as everything in war. They were wrought out of one challenging assertion after another in an argumentative chain, leading to an entirely unambiguous policy of immediate action. The January memorandum pleaded for unorthodox measures to overcome the stalemate in France. It raised sharply the issue whether victory was to be sought in eastern or western campaigns or in some combination of both. Half a million newly trained Britishers would be ready in March. What real difference would it make to hurl them at the entrenched enemy in the West? He wanted, instead, to launch an attack on the Central Powers through the Balkans. If successful, this would divert part of the enemy forces to another field of action and thus weaken the resistance in France. He suggested two independent operations: first, the weakest part of the enemy's front, Austria, should be attacked with the co-operation of Serbians, Rumanians, and Greeks; divisions of Regulars should be sent to Salonika, and their place in France taken by Territorials from Britain. The second operation should be aimed at Turkey, which had declared war on the Allies. The Turks had collected troops in Syria, and whilst they were engaged in attacking the British on the Suez Canal a force should be landed in Syria to cut them off.

We now know that at the very time of Lloyd George's memorandum, proposals similar to those voiced by his 'raw amateur mind' were being discussed in Paris and were favoured by soldiers like Galliéni, Castlenau, and Franchet d'Espérey and by politicians like Briand and Viviani. French and Joffre were against operations in the Near East. Joffre, indeed, saw victory in the West almost within sight. 'A week, a couple of months, six months, a year, nobody can say exactly when, but the result is sure as soon as the crucial questions of munitions is answered', wrote Poincaré in his *Memoirs*. The influence of Joffre was decisive at this time, not only on French but also on British strategy.

On 8 January 1915, at a meeting of the War Council, Lloyd George put his case for an attack on Austria. He was confronted with the weighty arguments of the Westerners but backed up by Churchill who was a convinced Easterner. The debate was continued on 13 January and 'at the end of a long day Churchill suddenly revealed his well-kept secret of a naval attack on the Dardanelles. . . . Fatigue was forgotten. . . . Mr. Lloyd George liked it. Lord Kitchener thought it worth trying. Mr. Lloyd George's thesis had won favour to the point that, if stalemate was admitted in the spring, troops could be dispatched to another theatre which was to be studied.' Churchill and Lloyd George had each won approval for his policy in principle. But forceful as these exceptional Ministers were, the strategy of the war on land in its first years was fixed in Paris by Joffre and in Whitehall by Kitchener. Expert military opinion could always pile up real and serious objections to every proposal advanced by mere laymen; on the other hand, without a change of strategy, Lloyd George saw nothing but an eternal and expensive stalemate in the West.

A decision in favour of Lloyd George's policy might have been right in January or February 1915, and even then right only if whole-heartedly and immediately set in motion, militarily and diplomatically; it might even have been right a few months later on the same conditions. But the failure of the naval effort at the Dardanelles, the fluctuating policy pursued throughout the summer in London and Paris, the disastrous course of the war on the Russian front, were all excellent reasons why the Balkan States should continue to 'wait and see'.

Throughout 1915 Grey had, by a number of secret treaties, been doing what he could to solidify the Allies' position in the East, but, as his biographer, Trevelyan, says: '[His] failure to unite the Balkan States was the greatest defeat of his diplomacy during the war.' Grey later defended himself before the Dardanelles Commission by saying: 'Diplomacy was perfectly useless without military success'; but it depends on the diplomat. If Lloyd George had been at the Foreign Office and Grey on the other side of Downing Street, for better or for worse we should have had a different story to tell. Was it 'a time and a place to be respectable?' Trevelyan asks. Grey himself had to resort to bribes and secret treaties. Lloyd George would not have been more scrupulous. As Chancellor of the Exchequer he gave Noel-Buxton a letter which Grey would not allow him to use. It ran:

Any Balkan State that decides to throw in its lot with the Triple Entente in this struggle may depend upon the support of British credit in raising the necessary funds to equip and maintain its army. I autho-

56

rise you to make such arrangements on my behalf as you may deem desirable to guarantee British financial assistance under these conditions.[4]

A million pounds to Enver Pasha at the right moment, it has been said, might have changed the policy of Turkey.

The failure of the bombardment of the Dardanelles, on 18 March 1915, was followed by many months of confused and irresolute action. The formation of the first Coalition Government in May had multiplied counsellors without increasing wisdom. Its members never really coalesced. Nor was the team-work between the Cabinets in London and Paris any better. They went on wrangling and exchanging one compromise for another. 'The Allies never pulled their weight because they never tried to pull it all together at the same time and in the same place', this is the verdict of Sir Valentine Chirol, who was charged at the time with a mission to the Balkans.

Had the policy urged by Lloyd George in his memorandum of 1 January 1915 been promptly carried out it could hardly have produced more inglorious results than were actually achieved in the course of this disastrous year. At its close there was still a deadlock in France; Russia had not been equipped with arms, and her ignominious retreat had not been prevented; Bulgaria had joined the enemy; Rumania and Greece were neutral; Serbia was knocked out, and Germany free to make her way to Turkey and the East; the one attempt to give effect to the views of the Easteners, at Gallipoli, had failed, and the battle losses on the Western Front were enormous; 'They gained no territory worth mentioning, and no strategic advantages of any kind', summed up Churchill in *World Crisis*.

In the early months of the war, Lloyd George had become in turn, aware, concerned, and alarmed at the failure of adequate supplies of ammunition to reach the soldiers in France. No withholding of money or excess of supervision by the Treasury had caused this scarcity; he had given the War Office complete freedom to order what it wanted, and contracts were to be concluded without prior approval. But such freedom was so novel as to prove embarrassing. In Lloyd George's *War Memoirs*, the Master General of Ordnance and his staff appear as having neither the

[4] T. P. Conwell-Evans, *Foreign Politics from a Back Bench*, p. 88.

conception of, nor the imagination to grasp, the gigantic quantities of ammunition which would be needed to meet an unending succession of terrific German attacks. It took months and months of precious time, one futile committee of Ministers after another, innumerable telegrams, private letters, messages from France, and, at last, articles in the press, before any effective impression was registered on the mind and will of the War Office. It was not only that it thought in the outworn terms of the Boer War, but that it could only think in terms of the armament firms with which it had been accustomed to do business; it lacked the foresight and urgency to provide for the arming of the million men, sanctioned by Parliament, now flocking into the recruiting offices in thousands daily. Nor did it commandeer the country's vast engineering and chemical resources, or restrain and divert the key mechanics now joining up indiscriminately. Furthermore, the gravity of the position in France was not fully grasped even by the Cabinet because important communications were concealed from it.

That Lloyd George from October onwards sought to rouse his colleagues is clear from the letters he prints. In the *Memoirs*, he describes Kitchener as secretive, a blend of sagacity and opacity, a revolving lighthouse which radiated light far into the surrounding gloom and then suddenly relapsed into complete darkness. In contrast, his biographer, Sir George Arthur, tells us Kitchener's mind was as infinitely broad as it was accurately precise, and that nothing was too small, too large, too distant for him. Where others saw a short, sharp war he foretold in August 1914 a three years' campaign, and he sometimes spoke of five years. We must assume that the light flashed on manpower and left gunpower in darkness. It is clear today that Kitchener's towering prestige, which was an immense asset with the public, was a hindrance in Cabinet, that he was overworked and ill at ease with politicians, manufacturers, and labour leaders. 'Did they remember when they went headlong into a war like this, that they were without an army, and without any preparation to equip one?' he groaned at the end of a wearing day. There was no precedent for this sort of trench warfare stretching from the Belgian coast to Switzerland; there was no plan for the production of guns, mortars, projectiles, for years of fighting on a hundred-mile front.

The fact that the nation was unready in an unforeseen war was to Lloyd George a clarion call to extraordinary effort. His mind was now as full of war as it had earlier been of peace, and the complacency of easy-going colleagues galled him. This is the impression he made on Poincaré some months after the beginning of the war when he met the French President in Paris: 'Just as in the days immediately before the War the Welsh Minister showed little favour for the Triple Entente, so to-day he is heart and soul for it. He has adapted himself to the happenings of the hour with a mental agility which is extraordinary.'

On 15 April Asquith set up the Munitions of War Committee with Lloyd George as chairman. Shortly after his appointment he was told by secret messengers from Lord French of the shortage of shells, and soon after (14 May) Colonel Repington published the same facts in *The Times*. Lloyd George wrote (19 May) the substance of what he had learnt to the Prime Minister, and declared that he could not continue to preside over a Munitions Committee from which vital information was withheld, or deal with a Cabinet which would not recognize the immediate necessities: 'It is now eight months since I ventured to call the attention of the Cabinet to the importance of mobilising all our engineering resources for the production of munitions and equipments of war', yet nothing had been done.

In a little more than a month after the creation of the Munitions of War Committee the Government was faced with a crisis. On 17 May 1915 Asquith invited his colleagues to hand in their resignations. Immediately before this decision was taken, Bonar Law, Leader of the Tory party, and Lloyd George had agreed—first among themselves, and then, when they went together to see Asquith, with him—that if grave parliamentary conflict were to be avoided, the Government must be reconstructed on a broad and non-party basis. In less than a quarter of an hour the Liberal Government, which had assumed office in December 1905, had come to an end, and the first Coalition Government came into existence. The new Coalition included several Conservative leaders in high office: Balfour, Curzon, Austen Chamberlain, Carson, and Bonar Law.

The agitation over the shortage of shells was but one of several factors which brought about the fall of the Government; its immediate occasion was the conflict over operations in the Dardanelles between Churchill and Lord Fisher (First Lord of the Admiralty and the First Sea Lord respectively), which had culminated in the resignation of the latter and the exile of the former to the shades of the Duchy of Lancaster, where, as he said in *Thoughts and Adventures*, 'he knew everything and could do nothing'. There was also disappointment with the setbacks in France and with Asquith's handling of the war. He had the qualities of a judge or chairman, combining admirable temper with great dexterity—qualities of value in composing the quarrels of such clashing temperaments as Kitchener, Lloyd George, and Churchill—but there was a half-and-halfness, a lack of complete concentration on the prosecution of the war, and weeks would go by without the War Council being summoned. The need for an active supervisor and stimulator of the national effort was widely felt, and Lloyd George's fitness for the Prime Ministership was now being freely canvassed at least seven months before his elevation to it took place. Early in the crisis Bonar Law had urged him to accept the top place, but Lloyd George had refused to enter into competition with Asquith.

The new association of Ministers in the Coalition Cabinet, after years of bitter controversy, caused some to fly apart and some to fly together. They were never a team. On intellectual grounds Asquith was more naturally drawn to the Oxford and Cambridge scholars, Crewe, Curzon, and McKenna, than to the non-academic, middle-class minds of Lloyd George and Bonar Law. Nor did Lloyd George's enthusiastic devotion to the manufacture of munitions and to the forcing of conscription commend him to old associates in the Liberal party, who in general were against this measure.

The whole problem of conscription had nearly split the country, for Britain had never before been in a position where war had to be regarded as an unlimited affair which would seriously upset the everyday life of the ordinary citizen. The subject was one which deeply divided political, industrial, and religious opinion. Roughly, Conservatives were for conscription, Liberals and Labour against, and the Cabinet itself was as deeply divided as the country. It was not until 25 May 1916 that universal military service became law. Lloyd George would have supported a much earlier recourse to compulsion. So would Churchill, Curzon, and Carson. As far back as the Constitutional Conference of 1910, in a secret memorandum proposing a party truce, Lloyd George had asked that the question of compulsory training should not be shirked.

Asquith's first suggestion on the formation of the new Government was that Lloyd George should go to the War Office, but on 26 May it was announced in the press that he was to take charge of a new department to be called the Ministry of Munitions. On the previous day he said to Riddell: 'I had to do it. They all wanted me to, and the King was anxious that I should. It will be a temporary arrangement only. I shall go back to the Treasury and shall retain my house at Downing Street, which I shall probably use as the offices of my department.'

The Prime Minister's residence, No. 10 Downing Street, stands between the Treasury and No. 11, and all three intercommunicate. When Chancellor of the Exchequer, Lloyd George saw Asquith almost daily after breakfast. This was no longer possible when as Minister of Munitions his working day began at nine o'clock, and the change had important results. His place at No. 10 after breakfast was taken by Reginald McKenna, who had succeeded him at the Treasury. This led to jealousy and friction and to efforts by Asquith and Lord Reading to reconcile the two Ministers. Politicians are an ambitious and a jealous tribe, and self-abnegation is a rare virtue amongst them. To Lloyd George, McKenna was merely a ready reckoner, a competent arithmetician, a banker in blinkers, whereas Lloyd George, as Lewis Harcourt once said, used figures as adjectives. It is agreed that with all his ability McKenna was donnish and peevish and, whatever else he may have been, he was a disintegrating force in the Asquith Coalition.

The new Government, and Lloyd George's place in it, were not helped by attacks on Asquith in the Unionist press and articles in his defence in the Liberal press. Lloyd George was on intimate terms with many editors, and such relationships are delicate and dangerous. On 15 March 1915 an article appeared in the *Daily Chronicle*, headed 'The Intrigue against the Prime Minister', which mentioned Lloyd George as one of the candidates likely, in the minds of Unionist editors, to displace the Prime Minister. This article angered Lloyd George because the paper was known over long periods to voice his own views—he played golf with its editor, Robert Donald, and went to the theatre with him. But the editor was also acquainted with McKenna, whom Lloyd

George accused of having inspired the offending article. The two Ministers appeared before Asquith, 'fighting like fishwives'. Asquith, says Lloyd George, was in tears. On the previous day it was Lloyd George who, according to Asquith, had been in tears protesting his utter loyalty to his chief.

Ever since his entry into public life Lloyd George had valued the help of the press, and he had been well repaid for his assiduous cultivation of it. He never underrated a pressman however humble his rank; he lightened the task of reporters by dictating in advance what he proposed to say or correcting proofs of a speech after its delivery; when speaking Welsh he would supply an authorized English translation. He was never for many days together out of the news through all the years of his parliamentary life. To be ignored, he held, was the worst fate which could befall a politician; far better to be attacked. Before launching a legislative measure he would canvass the opinions of newspaper men who knew what the country would stand. In his years of office there were no public relations officers, as there are now, attached to Ministers and departments, but there was usually a private secretary who dealt discreetly with journalists in a shadowy back room.

Lloyd George's most constant adviser in the years of war and peace-making was Lord Riddell, a leading figure in the world of newspapers. Riddell was not only a shrewd, prosperous solicitor, a director of the Sunday newspaper with the largest circulation and of other papers and periodicals, but he was a man of wit and charm and great sagacity who kept any company happy and amused with his kindly humorous wisdom. He was attached to no party, and his impartiality could be relied on. He was intensely interested in successful persons in any walk of life, and in tracing and comparing reasons for their success; by bringing together important persons at decisive moments he participated in great affairs, and this gave him satisfaction—he handsomely filled the role of a rich parliamentary private secretary. He was constantly in and out of 10 Downing Street when Lloyd George became Prime Minister: if Northcliffe wanted to see Lloyd George he rang up Riddell; if a notable personage visited London whom Riddell thought the Prime Minister ought to meet, he would have a luncheon; if an important interview could better take place over a game of golf, Riddell would arrange to have it conducted on the golf-course at Walton Heath—a machine-gun from a Walton

Heath bunker on a Saturday morning, it has been said with truth, might have changed the course of history both in Downing Street and in Fleet Street. Riddell became the chief intermediary between the Government and the press both during the war and afterwards.

Lloyd George did not, of course, dictate to great editors; he could, when he wished, be definite in expounding a policy or proposal, but he preferred to use what Riddell happily called the art of subtle indirection, of which he was a master: 'No one is more facile in the use of hints, slight changes in manner and inflections of voice.' With this technique his secretaries were only too familiar, and they had perforce to guess the wishes of their chief and bear the consequences of a failure to read them aright.

MINISTRY OF MUNITIONS

For thirteen months the Ministry of Munitions gave full scope to Lloyd George's ardent but practical imagination and to his consuming activity. Beginning with a table, a chair, and two private secretaries, the Ministry spread itself until its headquarters staff numbered over 25,000 and filled a hundred hotels, clubs, and bungalows in Whitehall, Westminster, and Kingsway. Big ideas, of which Lloyd George always had a profusion, were let loose over the country and the traditional character of a civil service department was transformed. This was to be a business organization and there was to be no red tape. Finance was subordinated to policy and limits of cost were not to be allowed to interfere with programmes of production. 'What we stint in materials we squander in life. . . . What you spare in money you spill in blood', said Lloyd George in Parliament on 20 December 1915. There was to be one supreme aim: to provide the armaments needed for victory.

The new Minister took care to equip himself with legislative powers which would leave him unhampered when he wished to take direct and drastic action in dealing with masters or men or materials. He short-circuited Parliament by the device of Orders in Council, and assumed responsibilities, as the clause set forth, 'to ensure such supply of munitions for the present war as may be required by the Army Council or the Admiralty, *or may otherwise be found necessary*'. This last clause, as he interpreted it, enabled him to lay the foundations of the Ministry's productive capacity on a scale so vast that it was almost sufficient—so far as guns, ammunition, rifles, machine-guns, and trench-warfare supplies were concerned—to carry the country to the end of the war.

As we have seen, in the opening winter of the war Lloyd George was much alarmed at the slowness of the War Office in adapting its manufacturing programme to the unprecedented needs of the army in France, to say nothing of the starved Russian ally who was daily clamouring for supplies. In his *Memoirs* he attacks the War Office with an array of statistical and epistolary evidence. It is a wearisome tale, this gibing and sniping of two departments with appeals to the Prime Minister and the Cabinet to arbitrate. One example after another is given of the rigidity of the military mind and its antipathy to new ideas and new weapons. The official *History of the Great War* concedes that the habits of economy ingrained in peace time in the War Office were only slowly and unwillingly discarded. The whole spirit of the country, it rightly claims, had been opposed to preparations for a great war. This had been true of Lloyd George himself. But he now put that far behind him—this 'strategic elasticity', to use a phrase of his, was what made him such a great War Minister. It can be argued on behalf of the Ordnance Department that it had not, any more than had the Committee of Imperial Defence or the Cabinet Ministers or the generals, foreseen a war of positions, whereas Germany had prepared for such a war with heavy guns and high explosives for attack and with machine-guns for defence. The prodigious demand for ammunition was one of the major surprises of the war. It took months to realize that trench warfare was not a passing but a permanent phase. Lloyd George was one of the first to grasp the new facts and to act on them. 'Please tell your gallant husband', he promised an officer's wife, 'that I am piling up for the gunners mountains of shell, high as Ben Nevis, hot as Vesuvius.'

When the Ministry of Munitions was created there were in being the Munitions Supply Organization and the Armaments Output Committee. The latter was a central organization with twenty-five local armaments committees scattered through the provinces. These local committees had been set up in part because of increasing difficulties with labour. Industrial unrest had spread with the rising cost of food, and demands for increases of wages led to scores of labour disputes in the early months of 1915. In February the Committee on Production was set up, and on 9 March the Government obtained powers under the Defence of the Realm (Consolidation) Act to commandeer the output or plant of any factory or workshop, to direct the work done or the engagement or employment of workmen. A few days later Lloyd George presided over conferences of labour leaders which concluded what became known as the Treasury Agreement, by which the unions agreed temporarily to suspend certain restrictions and permit dilution by semi-skilled and women's labour in return for the limitation of the profits of all the chief War Office and Admiralty contractors. The Government undertook that any departure during the war from the practices ruling in workshops, ship-yards, and other industries prior to the war, should only be for the period of the war and should not prejudice the position of the work-people concerned.

It was one thing to accept these proposals at the Treasury and another to make them effective in the workshops. The unions delayed the removal of restrictions, and the Government let three months pass before putting into force its pledge to limit profits. The workmen felt that to sacrifice their hard-won rules would only swell the profits of private contractors. Legal effect was, therefore, given to the voluntary agreement of March by passing the Munitions of War Act in July.

Lloyd George realized that his success in raising the output of munitions would depend on the degree to which he secured the co-operation of employers and workmen alike, so he set out to obtain it by a personal tour of the chief engineering centres. He delivered a series of rousing speeches: 'Plant the flag on your work-shops. Every lathe you have, recruit it. Convert your machinery into battalions . . . and liberty will be once more enthroned in Europe', he said at Manchester on 3 June 1915. He justified the action of the Government in taking over the control of workshops, insisted on priority over all civil work and the subordination of labour to the direction of the state.

The enlisted workman cannot choose his locality of action. He cannot say, 'I am quite prepared to fight at Neuve-Chapelle, but I won't fight at Festubert, and I am not going near the place they call "Wipers".' He cannot say 'I have been in the trenches eight hours and a half and my trade union won't allow me to work more than eight hours.'[5]

[5] Speech by Lloyd George at Cardiff, 11 June 1915.

This tour, with its emphasis on the grim realities facing the ill-armed soldiers in France, did something to correct the optimistic accounts of the war daily displayed in the newspaper head-lines, but its defence of industrial conscription went too far for much Labour and Liberal opinion.

Returning to headquarters at 6 Whitehall Gardens, the Minister continued to recruit his staff. He needed, he proclaimed aloud, men of push and go, hustlers; and by the end of July he was able to tell the House of Commons that ninety men of first-class business experience had placed their services at the disposal of the Ministry, the vast majority of them without any remuneration at all. To place these captains of industry in executive posts within the department and not merely to appoint them as members of advisory committees was the first of many departures from ortho-dox practice. These men brought with them a dislike of bureau-cratic routine, of files and records; they were given a free hand, and there was clashing and confusion, to the delight of the critics. Some compromise had to be struck between business freedom and bureaucratic responsibility to Parliament, between central super-vision and untrammelled local decisions. These frictions were not completely smoothed out in Lloyd George's period as Minister, but the rival activities of the great improvisors were not a serious handicap to the economical use of the country's resources, for in 1915 it was almost impossible for any department to over-produce.

The introduction of hosts of women into munition factories led Lloyd George in September 1915 to institute an inquiry into the health of the workers and to set up, under B. Seebohm Rowntree, a welfare department, the first enterprise of this kind on a large scale. 'It was', writes Lloyd George in his *Memoirs*, 'a strange irony ... that the making of weapons of destruction should afford the occasion to humanise industry.'

Another notable reform, the indirect result of their war service, was the granting of votes to women. Before the war this issue had deeply divided political parties, and the denial or postponement of legislation had led to scenes of shocking violence on the part of suffragettes who were contrasted in this with the law-abiding suffragists.

Now the leaders of the movement promoted the employment of women in munitions, where they gained a mastery of technical operations. Lloyd George pays high tribute in his speeches not only to their skill but to their courage and devotion in danger and difficulty. Though not a crusader for women's suffrage he had always believed in it strongly and now affirmed that their 'heroic patriotism' had made their claim 'irresistible'. The Representation of the People Act (6 February 1918) included provision for extending the suffrage to women, and a one-clause act (21 November 1918) permitted them to sit in Parliament. The first woman to do so was Nancy Astor from Virginia. At the Coupon Election of 1918 six million women were qualified to vote.

The task before the Minister was enormous: he had not only to harness the entire engineering resources of the country to the making of munitions of war, but he also had to convince his colleagues and the country of the necessity of doing this at once if lives were to be saved and the war to be won. Into both tasks, day by day from 9 a.m. to 8 p.m., he threw his unrivalled executive energy, and in the shortest possible time he achieved both objects.

Lloyd George never under-estimated the staying power of Germany; he planned for a long war, and budgeted not for fifty or seventy but for a hundred divisions and for surpluses beyond the quantities ordered by the authorities. He repelled with passion the charge that he was over-ordering, over-building, over-producing. The Cabinet appointed a committee to investigate these charges; it met, and when the meeting was over Lloyd George's secretary observed: 'I suppose, sir, that means the end of your programme.' 'No,' was the reply, 'it means the end of the Committee.'

Great Britain had a big load to carry. She had to equip the navy, keep the seas, maintain a continental army, and provide money and munitions for Allies who became more and more dependent upon her productive power. All these demands had to be harmonized with the maintenance of her export trade at the highest point possible. Lloyd George refused to be dominated by financial limitations, and insisted that dilution of labour should be pushed to greater and greater lengths, that luxury trades should be discouraged by taxation and a simpler style of living adopted. He was obsessed with the needs of Russia's unarmed millions, and did his utmost to persuade the Allies to pool their resources and help one another. To this end he attended one conference after another—in Paris, Boulogne, Calais, London. He established cordial relations with M. Albert Thomas, the French Minister of Munitions, and at Boulogne they forced such a close scrutiny of the gun programme on the High Command that it revolutionized the scale and character of the programme. Together they planned a central munitions office for the Allied states, to regulate purchases and prevent competition among the Allies themselves, but the opposition of the military authorities blocked its establishment. Some co-operation was secured by means of special missions and agencies, such as those later associated with the names of Lord Rhondda and Lionel Hichens. But the complete confidence in each other which French and British statesmen desired for the General Staffs was only attained in the last months of the war, and by then Russia had left the Allied Powers and the United States had joined them.

The abuse of alcohol was a major cause of broken time and lessened output in the workshops and shipyards, a deadlier foe than Germany, Lloyd George declared. In March 1915 he had laid before the Cabinet proposals for total prohibition during the war. Russia had prohibited vodka and France absinthe, but no British government had dared to cut off whisky. King George, however, set a personal example of abstinence which became known as 'The King's Pledge'.

When Lloyd George became Minister of Munitions a Central Liquor Control Board with far-reaching powers was set up: drinking hours and facilities were reduced drastically; to economize grain, beer and spirits were diluted; taxation was increased. In Carlisle 'the trade' was acquired by the state, and this arrangement continues today. So successful were these regulations that excessive drinking ceased to be a glaring social scandal. Although the Lloyd George Cabinet accepted a recommendation of the Control Board that 'the trade' should be purchased—and Milner with Waldorf Astor and others had a bill drafted—it was not introduced. In 1917, yielding to pressure from two Tory brewers and politicians, Younger and Gretton, Lloyd George dropped the bill. The policy had ceased to be a war-time necessity and had become one of post-war reconstruction.

After the war all Lloyd George could do was to persuade Parliament to make permanent some of the war regulations, and he has to his credit beneficial and lasting changes in the drinking habits of the country.

Difficulties with labour continued to prove the greatest hindrance to production. Lloyd George travelled around the country imparting counsel and stimulus to the workshops, everywhere striking the patriotic note. His relations with trade unionists were always apt to be civil and correct rather than cordial and trustful; they repelled his blandishments, and while his swift and smart repartee amused them they did not give him their complete confidence. At times the civil and correct relationship broke down, as it did in December of 1916 at Glasgow, where shop stewards were strongly entrenched and were resisting the Munitions of War Act. At noon on Christmas Day Lloyd George addressed a meeting of between 3,000 and 4,000 workmen at the St. Andrew's Hall or, more accurately, confronted an audience who greeted him with yells and catcalls. 'For no less than 45 minutes Lloyd George stood there unheard. That Christmas Day speech was never made, though he dictated an appropriate one for the reporters in the train afterwards', writes Sir Ronald Davison in the *Manchester Guardian* (12 May 1945). The Glasgow Labour paper *Forward* was, a few days after the affair, suppressed—it was alleged for publishing a full account of the meeting. Lloyd George denied that the suppression had anything to do with the report and argued that *Forward* had committed offences under the Defence of the Realm Act by discouraging recruiting and the making of munitions. Similar difficulties occurred in Sheffield, Coventry, and other centres. It was not an easy or quick process to convince the rank and file of the necessity for a revolution in production. There followed the arrest and imprisonment of several unofficial Clyde leaders, and the situation became greatly worsened by strikes and by the deportation of labour leaders.

By the spring of 1916 Lloyd George had broken the back of the munitions problem, and supplies to France were more or less satisfactory. But at the same time the War Committee was troubled about the situation in Russia, where German propaganda was making great headway and where supplies of munitions and army equipment were being badly held up. The munitions for Russia which Kitchener had ordered earlier from America and Japan were not due for some months, and were now intended for a projected offensive in the summer of 1917. The French Government sent M. Viviani and M. Albert Thomas to examine the situation on the spot. At the end of April M. Thomas saw Lloyd George and other Ministers in London and impressed them with the gravity of the position. Asquith thought Lloyd George should go to

Russia. Early in May the Czar made it known that he had long wanted Kitchener to pay a visit to Russia to advise on the prosecution of the war. For some days the composition of the mission was in doubt, until Asquith decided the matter by announcing in the House of Commons on 25 May that the Minister of Munitions had agreed to devote his energies to the promotion of an Irish settlement, which had been newly bedevilled by the Easter Rebellion and its suppression. Kitchener and his staff left London on 4 June for Scapa Flow, where he was received at noon of the 5th by Admiral Sir John Jellicoe. At five o'clock the *Hampshire*, bound for Archangel, steamed at full speed from the Grand Fleet to her doom. Kitchener and his staff were drowned, of the crew only twelve survived. On the 6th Lloyd George walked into the Cabinet room and found the War Council 'sitting at the table all looking stunned by the tragedy'.

There was now an empty place at the War Office, and Asquith asked the Minister of Munitions to occupy it. Lloyd George, as was his custom, summoned his counsellors. On 15 June he dined at Riddell's with Christopher Addison and Robertson Nicoll. He also saw Reading, Bonar Law, Beaverbrook, and Sir Edward Russell of the *Liverpool Post*. On the 17th he drafted a letter to Asquith full of gloomy forebodings. (Though the letter was never sent, he later published it in his *Memoirs*.) He was completely out of sympathy with the way the war was being run and seriously considered resigning in order to form and lead a 'ginger' opposition. He and Sir William Robertson were at cross-purposes. Lloyd George wanted active co-operation with Russia and a major attack launched from Salonika. He was haunted by the nightmare of the Somme offensive. It was impossible for a person of his habitual joy in life to conceal his deep misgivings about the course of the war from his colleagues and intimates. A black pessimism was his prevailing mood in these autumn months of 1916.

In October 1915 he had complained to Reading and Riddell that Asquith was hopeless. He had remonstrated with him without effect; he told Riddell: 'And so I left the room. I could not stand it any longer.' Six months later he thought Asquith was the best man for Premier but wished he would make him (Lloyd George) 'a sort of executive officer ... exercising general supervision ...', but by this time, he told Riddell, he had given up seeing Asquith privately to discuss matters. More and more he had found it impossible to co-operate with his Liberal colleagues and easier to work with the Conservatives, with Bonar Law and Carson especially; also, in the background, with the two newspaper magnates Beaverbrook and—on and off—Northcliffe. For two days in April 1916 he had been on the brink of resignation over the problem of getting more troops; he got them and the crisis passed. At the end of April Riddell thought he was contemplating a new party, but the time was not yet ripe. He was, with all his genuine admiration of Asquith's gifts of intellect and loyalty, dismayed at his detachment, his lack of stable resolution and any sense of urgency.

The keynote to the actions and reactions, open and secret, of Lloyd George in the period before he became Prime Minister may be given in three quotations, one from a man of business, the other from an eminent civil servant, the third from the Archbishop of Canterbury, Cosmo Gordon Lang.

On 4 March 1915 F. S. Oliver in his weekly letter to his brother in Canada wrote:

> The only two men who really seem to understand that we are at war are Winston and Lloyd George. Both have faults which disgust one peculiarly at the present time, but there is a reality about them and they are in earnest, which the others aren't. I have hopes that the Government will burst from rottenness somewhere about midsummer. In that case there will be a Coalition Government—probably with Lloyd George as Prime Minister.[6]

Sir William Beveridge in the *Economic Journal* (March 1946), quotes Sir Hubert Llewellyn Smith as saying that in the troublous times of 1916 'Lloyd George had a passion to win the war which none of the other members of the Cabinet seemed even to understand'. And Archbishop Lang recorded in August 1915: 'Only Mr. Lloyd George had "that glow in the soul" so necessary for victory.'

We must assume that Lloyd George's colleagues were desirous of victory, and according to their lights and gifts were labouring to achieve it; but of none of them could it be said that he was possessed as was Lloyd George by Chatham's arrogant conviction: 'I know that I can save this nation and that no one else can.' This at once explains and justifies Lloyd George's moods of frustration and depression, the manœuvrings and conspirings of 1916. And not only was this seething ferment within himself fed by an imagination which never ceased to remind him of the awful ravages

---

[6] F. S. Oliver, *The Anvil of War*, p. 92.

of the war, and the strength and skill of the enemy, but he was being repeatedly assured, and not only by flatterers and place-seekers, that he was the man of destiny, the only man who could pull the country through. In an oft-quoted conversation between Bonar Law and John Redmond on 15 March 1916, Law, who was then said to be hypnotized by Asquith, indicated that Asquith would probably go and be succeeded by Lloyd George. In the Conservative circles which he now frequented the Government was more and more discredited by its vacillation over conscription, and he was more and more mixing himself up with groups and individuals who were hostile to the retention of Asquith as Premier. Carson, especially, was now in the ascendant with Lloyd George, dining with him at Lord Lee's sometimes twice a week. In his newspapers, Northcliffe, without openly supporting, was paving the way for Lloyd George's elevation to the Premiership by his unmeasured attacks on Asquith; but at the same time he was warning the Minister to leave strategy to the soldiers.

Not even the titanic events of the war could subdue the rivalries and antagonisms, the vanities and intrigues of the leaders, charged though they were with the nation's destiny.

It is plain from the published diaries of the time that in the spring and summer months of 1916 Lloyd George was engaged in conversations with persons who were as critical of Asquith as he himself was and even more openly determined to dethrone him. On 11 June he told Riddell: 'If I went out I should at once form a great Party organisation. I have promises of all the money necessary.' These entries show that the crisis of the first week of December 1916, which elevated Lloyd George to the Premiership, was neither sudden nor unexpected. It was the culmination of widespread discontent freely expressed in clubs, coteries, and cabals throughout the year, most of it provoked by a desire for a more energetic prosecution of the war.

The tunnelling went on, but the explosion was postponed. On 6 July 1916 Lloyd George accepted the post of Secretary of State for War. On this same day the perceptive Mrs. Asquith wrote in her diary: 'We are out, it is only a question of time when we shall have to leave Downing Street.' She was right.

WAR OFFICE

The result of the tremendous drive which Lloyd George had put into his work as Minister of Munitions became evident in 1916, reaching its peak at the Battle of the Somme, which opened on 1 July. During his period in this office, ninety-five new factories—filling, shell, projectile, explosive, cartridge, and so forth—were built. The output of every sort of weapon and munition was multiplied, many, many fold. The Ministry's activities penetrated far beyond the factories to the control of raw materials and machinery in non-munition factories. On the day on which Lloyd George left the Ministry to become Secretary of State for War, Sir Walter Layton handed his chief a remarkable certificate of results which showed that various types of munitions which took a year to produce at the outbreak of war could now be manufactured some in a few weeks and others in a few days.

Truth demands that we should add an important point, that quality was not always as good as quantity. From August 1915 onwards there was never a time when some type of ammunition was not under suspicion and requiring adjustment. The penalty of hurried design, hurried production, and unskilled inspection was that at the beginning of the Battle of the Somme the official historian says 'wholesale and terrible defects of guns, ammunition and fuses were reported';[7] but still, at the close, the Minister was able to claim that 'after four months of incessant bombardment night and day, there were more guns and there was more ammunition than on the first day the battle began'.

Lloyd George was succeeded at the Ministry by Edwin Montagu, who, in the House of Commons on 15 August 1916, paid this tribute to the first Minister of Munitions:

> Everything I have said of our success is a tribute to him. He chose the great leaders of industry who formed the pivots of our machine. He formulated the needs of the moment to labour and persuaded them to agree to meet our necessities. He realised the scope which our operations should embrace in all the essentials of the production of munitions, and his tireless energy and vigorous personality were the inspiration of the whole vast fabric.[8]

Sir William Robertson, in *Soldiers and Statesmen*, gives his biased estimate of Lloyd George's brief five-month reign at the War Office in a sentence: 'There is nothing of much interest to record, for he was connected with no measure having any special

---

[7] Official History of the War, *Military Operations, France and Belgium 1916*, i, 124.　　　　[8] Hansard, fifth series, vol. lxxxv, 15 August 1916.

influence on the course of the war.' On the other hand, the Minister himself claimed that he tidied up the appalling muddle in Mesopotamia and reconstructed the transport system on the Western Front. Of the former he gives a gruesome account in his *Memoirs*. He himself had opposed the initiation of the campaign, and its divided control and amazing incompetence were later to be uncovered by the commission appointed in August. Lloyd George called upon Sir John Cowans, 'a born organizer', to clear up the muddle—'a man whom I have always considered to be the most capable soldier thrown up by the War in our Army'—and 'no more was heard of scandals of Mesopotamia'. Much of this tribute to Cowans should be passed on to Major-General S. S. Long, C.B., Director of Supplies and Transport.

To deal with the traffic congestion in France, arising from an army expanding from six to sixty divisions and the failure and refusal of the French to provide the required railway facilities, Lloyd George chose another 'born organizer' in the person of Sir Eric Geddes, who had been one of his chief assistants at the Ministry of Munitions. Geddes commended himself to the War Minister as not afraid to 'think big' and, in a world war, megalomania, as Churchill has said, is a positive virtue. The obstacles hitherto placed in the way of railway supplies to the armies in France were instantly eliminated: 'What soldiers had been denied was freely accorded to a civilian.' He knew how 'to add a nought, or a couple of noughts to almost any requisition' for supplies, and he proceeded to order hundreds of locomotives, thousands of wagons, tens of thousands of tons of steel with which to build thousands of miles of light railways behind the lines. He was clearly a man after Lloyd George's own heart.

The year 1916 saw the Battle of Verdun, Germany's extended submarine campaign, the confused and unspectacular Battle of Jutland. It also saw the co-ordinated offensives in the three principal theatres of war agreed on at the Inter-Allied Conference at Chantilly in 1915: Brusilov's successful Russian offensive, the counter-offensive of the Italians in the Trentino, and, starting on 1 July, the Battle of the Somme.

In all the six volumes of Lloyd George's *Memoirs* there are no more bitter or scathing chapters than those in which the battlefields of Verdun, Somme, and Passchendaele are described. All

his rage against the stubborn unbending strategy of the Westerners is poured into these scornful pages. No one can read
them today without being tormented by the doubt whether the
enormous sacrifice might not have been avoided by less bull-
headed, more flexible, more original generalship. Lloyd George
and Churchill remained impenitent Easterners, when both sides
of the account lay open before them.

The voluntary and sacrificial armies who died on the Somme
were composed of 'the finest manhood of the United Kingdom
and Ireland', says the official historian; 'never again was the spirit
or the quality of the officers and men so high'. At the end of the
first day of the fighting the British killed and wounded reached
the unparalleled figure of 57,000. On two-thirds of the front the
gallantry of the troops had proved of little avail, and one gathers
from the official history that this want of success, on the first day,
had shaken the confidence of the authorities in the possibility of
a rupture of the German Front in 1916. Lloyd George says in the
Memoirs that he protested against 'the unintelligent hammering
against the impenetrable barrier', and urged Asquith and Sir
William Robertson to stop the useless slaughter, but without
avail. It is not correct to say, as he does, that our losses were twice
as great as those we inflicted; they were not in fact widely different.
But they were sufficiently terrible for Churchill's epitaph in *World
Crisis* to be true: 'The battlefields of the Somme were the grave-
yards of Kitchener's Army.' The British losses in these four and a
half months were equal to the whole of their losses in the Second
World War—armed forces, merchant navy, and civilians combined.

In the autumn of 1916 German agents were busy sowing
rumours in neutral countries of a possible negotiated peace. The
optimism with which our generals had launched the Somme offensive had cooled considerably, but the public, devouring headlines
which announced 'Great Gains at Small Cost', knew only half the
story and thought victory was in sight. Lloyd George, 'looking
white and feeble', was frequently depressed. He went for a few
days to Brighton, and the fruit of his resilience and refreshment
was a sensational interview with Mr. Roy Howard, president of
the United Press of America. The British Minister declared:
'Britain has only begun to fight. The British Empire has invested
thousands of its best lives to purchase future immunity for civilisa-

tion. This investment is too great to be thrown away.... The fight must be to a finish—to a knock-out.' 'But how long do you figure this can and must go on', asked the journalist. 'There is neither clock nor calendar in the British Army to-day' was the quick reply.[9] The report of this interview appeared in America on 28 September and resounded throughout the world. On 11 October in the House of Commons and on 9 November at Guildhall, Asquith in less strident but in no less firm tones repeated 'Never again!' and denounced a 'patched-up, precarious, dishonouring compromise, masquerading under the name of Peace'. On 13 November, however, Lord Lansdowne circulated to the Cabinet a courageous and careful memorandum in which he threw doubts on the possibility of victory and reflected the uneasiness caused by the 'knock-out' interview. Lloyd George, it was true, had said in that interview: 'The world must know that there can be no outside interference *at this stage*'—a very momentous limitation comments Lord Lansdowne, and adds: 'Let our naval, military and economic advisers tell us frankly whether they are satisfied that the knock-out blow can and will be delivered. The Secretary of State's formula holds the field and will do so until something else is put in its place.' In response to Lansdowne's request, Haig and Robertson pronounced the prospects for 1917, given ample troops and munitions, to be very favourable.

The upshot of the Cabinet discussion was that without admission of defeat by the enemy, peace overtures should not be encouraged. Lloyd George was quite certain that if hostilities were once suspended, for whatever reason, they would not be renewed. 'In the meantine', write Asquith's biographers, 'the idea that there was an atmosphere of "defeatism" in the Cabinet was subtly exploited by certain newspapers to discredit the Prime Minister.'

Encouraged by the unexpected successes of Brusilov in June 1916, Rumania now actively prepared, after two years' delay, to join the Allies, but wasted two more precious months in obtaining pledges of support and reward from Russia, France, and Britain before declaring war on 27 August. During the following days, Germany, Turkey, and Bulgaria declared war on Rumania, and Italy now formally declared war on Germany. But Rumania's delay had given the Central Powers time to recover from the Russian assault.

Lloyd George at the War Office was deeply disturbed by these

[9] *The Times*, 29 September 1916.

swift events. On 4 September he sent a note to the Director of Military Operations calling for joint Allied action to relieve the pressure on Rumania, a project which, the Chief of the Imperial General Staff acidly remarks, had been under consideration for months past. The relations of Russia and Rumania were not of the friendliest; consignments of ammunition destined for the latter were side-tracked by the former; Russia was short of skilled men to serve the big guns and, as Churchill points out, there was a gap of twenty miles between the Russian and Rumanian railheads making speedy succour impossible. But these trifling details did not trouble Lloyd George.

On 20 October he crossed with Asquith, Grey, and Balfour to Boulogne for a conference with the French. Rumania was counting on British and French troops immobilizing those of Bulgaria, and Lloyd George, opposing his colleagues, supported the French demand for reinforcements for Salonika. He wanted eight divisions sent out, 'quite ignoring the fact that some three months must elapse before the divisions could be got into the country and made ready to go on', says Robertson, who as usual argued that the best help to Rumania could be given on the Somme. Meanwhile the famous German commanders Falkenhayn and Mackensen were busy sweeping through Rumania and securing her granaries and oilfields. Her fall at the end of 1916 helped still further to depress the stock of Asquith and his administration.

Lloyd George was convinced of the importance of closer co-operation with Russia, and wanted Robertson, Joffre, and Cadorna from the West to meet their opposite numbers in conference in Russia. Robertson saw in this a plot to be rid of him from the War Office and refused to budge. Asquith and Balfour both pressed him to go, but he merely reiterated his blunt refusal. Lloyd George offered to go himself, but withdrew his offer on hearing that if Rumania fell the French Government would fall. So the project, which had been agreed on in principle and which might have had most important consequences, came to nought.

Lloyd George extracted from Robertson a cheerless memorandum on how the war was to be brought to a successful end, and on 3 November invited half a dozen of his more important Cabinet colleagues to dine at No. 11 and discuss the seriousness of the situation. He followed this up with a long and gloomy memorandum intended for a joint Allied conference in Paris in mid-

77

November, which Hankey took to Asquith, who refused to adopt
it and insisted on severely condensing it. In its truncated form,
turned into French, it was taken to Paris. Asquith, Lloyd George,
Robertson, Sir Frederick Maurice, and Hankey crossed to France
on 14 November, 'an extraordinary harmonious and almost hilarious party'. But there was neither harmony nor hilarity in the conference. The generals met separately at Chantilly and outflanked
the politicians by, themselves, framing the programme for the
winter of 1916–17 and for 1917—a programme which, observes
Lloyd George, was to repeat 'the bloody stupidities of 1915 and
1916'.

On 9 November he had remarked to Hankey: 'We are going to
lose this War', and before crossing to Paris he had talked of throwing
up his War Office post; he would not desert the sinking ship,
but would take some post like that of Food Minister. After the
conference he was so disappointed with its farcical results that he
was inclined to immediate resignation and told Hankey so. It
was at this crucial point that Hankey made a not entirely novel
suggestion: he proposed the substitution of a smaller War Committee, as the present one 'wastes a tremendous amount of time'.
Asquith was to remain Prime Minister, so Hankey saw 'no disloyalty in discussing it if a change is urgently necessary'. Later
Hankey wrote: 'The Prime Minister however quite properly says
that if he is not fit to run the War Committee he is not fit to be
Prime Minister. The obvious compromise is for the Prime Minister to retain the Presidency of the War Committee with Lloyd
George as Chairman and to give Lloyd George a fairly free run
for his money.'[10]

This idea struck Lloyd George with the same force as the light
from Heaven struck Saint Paul on the road to Damascus—which
was odd, for the notion of a small executive, with or without autocratic power, had been repeatedly canvassed. Both agreed that
Asquith should continue to be Prime Minister. But before submitting the plan to Asquith, Lloyd George thought it best to
sound Bonar Law, so a telegram was sent to Lord Beaverbrook
asking him to arrange a meeting between Law and Lloyd George
on the following evening. The crisis had begun or, rather, was
developing; the issue turned on whether the control of the war
should be in the hands of five Ministers or twenty.

[10] Lord Hankey, *The Supreme Command 1914–1918* (unpublished).

Ever since the early days of the war Asquith had been aware that a root difficulty in its conduct was the reconciliation of rapid executive action with Cabinet responsibility. His own bias was strongly for traditional procedure, and such radical changes as were to be brought about by Lloyd George in his first week as Premier were repellent to him. His old-fashioned prejudice was rooted in his dislike of publicity and his disdain for the vulgar and noisy press. But he himself had been driven to have recourse to various devices for curtailing debate and expediting decision.

The peace-time Cabinet of twenty or more Ministers had no agenda, no order of business, no secretary, no minutes. No note was kept of the proceedings by anybody except the Prime Minister who, in his own handwriting, reported to the King what had taken place. Side by side with the Cabinet there had, in recent years, grown up the Committee of Imperial Defence, presided over by the Prime Minister, with no rigid membership and no executive authority. From 4 August 1914 until the end of November the peace-time Cabinet had charge of the war; then a War Council was formed to overcome the defects which were already appearing in the larger body. It was superseded after the formation of the first Coalition Cabinet by the Dardanelles Committee of ten Ministers, which had its first meeting on 7 June 1915. In September of that year Asquith proposed the appointment of two small committees, one to deal with the conduct of the war and its problems, the other to concern itself with the financial outlook. But the pressure of the numbers desiring to be members and the clash of their temperaments brought the plan to nought. However, on 2 November 1915, Asquith announced to the Commons that he proposed to limit still further the size of the body charged with the strategic conduct of the war; it was to consist of not less than three and perhaps not more than five members, with the proviso that it could summon to its assistance any Minister whose special knowledge was needed. In this same debate Carson anticipated the plan Lloyd George was to adopt when he came into power:

What is wanted for carrying on a war is a small number . . . of competent men sitting, not once a week, but from day to day, with the best expert advisers they can get, working out the problems that arise in the course of the War from day to day. . . . I would much prefer to see the right hon. Gentleman exercise the right he has of cutting his

Cabinet down to five or six from twenty-two, placing upon those five or six the whole burden of responsibility.[11]

On the day following this debate the new War Committee met. It consisted of Asquith, Kitchener, and Balfour; then Grey and Lloyd George were added, then Bonar Law and McKenna; Curzon and Austen Chamberlain were usually present. Secretaries attended, conclusions were recorded and circulated to the Cabinet, which continued to meet and to preserve its unbusinesslike procedure. This War Committee functioned until the break-up of the Government in December 1916. It then consisted of seven Ministers. Under the new régime it was transformed into a War Cabinet of five.

IRELAND

While primarily concerned during 1915–16 with his duties, first as Minister of Munitions and then as Secretary of State for War, Lloyd George was far from being completely absorbed by them. The whole problem of Ireland and its relations to Great Britain had become more and more pressing, and its importance was increased by the influence which Irish-American opinion could have on the possible participation of America in the war; of this Lloyd George was well aware. Discontent and disloyalty had been fermenting in Ireland for years, and had taken on a militant aspect with the formation of secret and revolutionary societies like the Irish Republican Brotherhood. While Cabinet Ministers had constant dealings with the Irish Parliamentary Party, under the leadership of John Redmond, they had no first-hand knowledge or, or insight into, the extent to which it was being undermined by the revolutionary nationalists. The founding of the Ulster Volunteer Force, under the leadership of Sir Edward Carson, to resist the Home Rule Bill of 1912 was followed in the south by the founding of the Irish National Volunteers. Although gun-running and drilling went on openly and unchecked in both areas, Redmond underestimated the determination behind the two movements.

The outbreak of war brought 50,000 Irish, Protestant and Catholic alike, flocking to the colours, but the patriotic outburst of the south was quenched by the 'stupidities which almost look like

[11] Hansard, fifth series, vol. lxxv, 2 November 1915.

malignancy' of the British War Office. Lord Kitchener, records the *Memoirs*, 'approved the embroidery of the Red Hand of Ulster on the banner of the northern division but banned the South Irish Harp on the southern'. Lloyd George had to oppose Kitchener in the Cabinet in a similar attempt to stamp on Welsh national sentiment.

A small and resolute Irish minority in the south saw in England's preoccupation with the war an opportunity to strike for independence, so an insurrection was planned for Easter 1916. The rebellion broke out and a Provisional Government announced the establishment of the Irish Republic with P. H. Pearse as President. For six days there was much fighting and destruction of property in Dublin, though there was little in the rest of the country. On the 29th Pearse agreed to unconditional surrender. John Redmond expressed his 'horror and detestation' of the Rising, but wrote to Asquith appealing for leniency: 'The precedent of Botha's treatment of the Rebels in South Africa is the only wise and safe one to follow.' Instead of leniency, fourteen of the leaders were shot—thereby joining the roll of Ireland's martyrs and heroes.

On 11 May Asquith crossed to Dublin, and visited Belfast and Cork. On 26 May, after his return, he announced that the Cabinet had asked Lloyd George to negotiate for a settlement of the Irish question.

A conversation on 30 May between Carson and Lloyd George has been recorded which shows Lloyd George's grasp of the situation's possible repercussions. It had been urged that the next six months should be spent in mollifying the present bitterness:

L.G. (with sudden energy)—'In six months the war will be lost.'
Carson (throwing up his arms)—'If the war is lost we are all lost.'
L.G.—'The Irish-American vote will go over to the German side. They will break our blockade and force an ignominious peace on us, unless something is done, even provisionally, to satisfy America.'[12]

The numerous executions had made a profound impression on the Irish in America and were exploited there to the full. T. M. Healy says: 'A Requiem Mass was said in every Church, by order of the Bishops, for the men shot. The "funerals" got up for the Dublin dead in April were attended by millions in the U.S.A.'

[12] William O'Brien, *The Irish Revolution*, p. 273.

Lloyd George, after private interviews with John Redmond and Sir Edward Carson, submitted certain 'Headings of Agreement' which were taken to Ireland by the two leaders. Both were loyal patriots and put the winning of the war before national troubles. After hours of appeal and persuasion, and threats of resignation, they obtained the approval of their followers.

For a brief moment it looked as if the age-long conflict was about to end. But this was not to be. The settlement, according to Lloyd George, in the *Memoirs*, 'was thereafter deliberately smashed by extremists on both sides'. But was he, as negotiator-in-chief, entirely without blame? The Cabinet had unanimously agreed to request him to seek a solution; they had not defined in any way its nature or limitations. When agreement was reached his colleagues were astonished; they had never expected it. Some were alarmed at the prospect it opened up and others were annoyed that he should have succeeded in an impossible task. Bonar Law and Balfour supported him. Lloyd George had assured Redmond that he had 'placed his life upon the table and would stand or fall by the agreement come to'. When resistance to the agreement hardened, he wavered; he had for months been canvassing grounds for resignation; why did he not take the one now presented to him? And finally, the agreement, when publicly analysed, revealed a fundamental ambiguity or misunderstanding. The southern leaders had told the Belfast Nationalists that under the agreement six of the Ulster counties were to be left under the Imperial Government, but that the exclusion would be only a temporary war-time measure. Carson had told the Belfast Unionists it was to be *permanent*. On 13 July 1916 a letter from Lord Midleton appeared in *The Times* confirming, on behalf of the southern Unionists, Redmond's interpretation: 'A conference took place, at which he [Lloyd George] informed us that his proposals involved (1) a temporary settlement during the War, with the establishment of a Home Rule Parliament; (2) the reconsideration of the whole Irish question after the War with that of the Empire at large.' But on 29 May, two months previously, Lloyd George had sent Carson a private letter (printed by Gwynn in his book on Redmond) in which he stated: 'We must make it clear that at the end of the provisional period Ulster does not, whether she wills it or not, merge in the rest of Ireland.' It was not until 14 December 1921, in the debate on the Irish Treaty in his first speech in the

House of Lords, that Carson referred to this letter. 'I went over [to Ulster], and I had as a guarantee a letter from the present Prime Minister, which I shall always keep as a precious possession, guaranteeing me that the Six Counties would be left out, and that they never could be put back again without an Act of Parliament'.

In the face of growing opposition from both sides the Government abandoned Lloyd George's scheme, as revised by the Cabinet; but the negotiations, spread out over two months, served to convince America that a genuine effort at a settlement was being made, and the 'Headings of Agreement' became the indisputable Magna Charta of Carson's Six Counties and the political grave of John Redmond.

CABINET CRISIS

The events which immediately preceded Lloyd George's elevation to the Premiership have been recorded by participants and chroniclers in detail and have been the subject of embittered controversy. Lord Beaverbrook, 'the weaver behind the Gobelin tapestry', as Garvin, editor of the *Observer*, described him, has written the fullest and most reliable account; of it Lloyd George has said: 'I am prepared on the main facts to accept his narrative.' This must be a little modified by Austen Chamberlain's objection: 'He has, however, completely failed to understand the position of the Unionist Ministers with whom I co-operated.' There are, in addition to Beaverbrook's *Politicians and the War*, the biographies —to name the chief—of Asquith, Balfour, Carson, Churchill, Curzon, and Grey; Austen Chamberlain's letter to Chelmsford, Viceroy of India, dated 8 December 1916; the diaries of Riddell and Dr. Addison, the notes of conversations with the chief actors preserved by Sir Robert Donald, and the memorandum written by Lord Crewe, dated 20 December. No adequate life of Bonar Law has appeared, but Lord Beaverbrook has used his papers, and does his utmost to stress Bonar Law's influence on the course of events. Lloyd George devotes a chapter (xxxv) of the *Memoirs* to the crisis, and states categorically: 'I neither sought nor desired the Premiership', and this is borne out with emphasis by Beaverbrook. It is not proposed here to attempt to harmonize the divergent records, but only to select and summarize the facts and opinions which seem to be most widely supported.

The first and major fact is that Lloyd George was determined to get the direction of the war into his own hands, either as chairman of a small executive council of three or four, or by resigning as Secretary of State for War and, if necessary, forcing a general election.

Lloyd George would have preferred—but not for long, we may be certain—that Asquith should remain President of the Cabinet and Leader of the House of Commons. Bonar Law who, no more than Asquith, fully trusted Lloyd George, was for retaining Asquith as Prime Minister, while Carson would have welcomed his exclusion. Bonar Law, who sought to keep up relations of loyalty and frankness with Asquith, was being half pushed along by Beaverbrook and half towed along by Carson in wavering support of Lloyd George. His Unionist colleagues had small confidence in Asquith, but had no wish to make Lloyd George chairman of the new council. Balfour was in favour of separating the functions of Prime Minister and Leader of the House from those of chairman of the War Council. He wanted Asquith's retirement from the Government averted if possible, but deemed the possible loss of Lloyd George to be the greater disaster. The suggestion that he himself should be Prime Minister was mooted, but Asquith would not have this and it is certain Balfour did not press it.

On Friday, 1 December, Lloyd George saw Asquith and put forward, formally, his scheme for a small executive body to run the war; Asquith replied the same day with unsatisfactory counter-proposals. On Sunday, 3 December, Bonar Law met his Unionist colleagues, who passed a resolution of an ambiguous character, the purport but not the text of which he conveyed to Asquith that afternoon. Asquith got the impression that the Unionists would not support him in resisting Lloyd George's demands. Under this impression when he saw Lloyd George, and later Bonar Law, on the same day, he agreed to the proposed functions and number of the new War Council, while reserving for further consideration the question of personnel. Lloyd George telephoned to his home in Walton Heath that the interview had been satisfactory. Asquith felt warranted in informing the King that the Government must be *reconstructed*, but this did not involve his *resignation*. At 11.45 p.m. he issued a press notice to that effect. Next morning, Monday, 4 December, Lloyd George and Carson breakfasted with Lord Derby—whose support they had secured—and discussed the new administration. Later in the morning Lloyd George was so much under the impression that his scheme was accepted that he asked Hankey to draft rules for the new War Committee.

In the meantime, Asquith had been upset by a leading article in *The Times* of that morning which displayed intimate knowledge of Sunday's negotiations and stressed the fact that he was not to be a member of the new War Committee. He wrote to Lloyd George: 'Unless the impression is at once corrected that I am being relegated to the position of an irresponsible spectator of the War, I cannot possibly go on.'

For months past, Northcliffe's papers, including *The Times*, had remorselessly attacked Asquith, but they had also been hostile to Lloyd George. Now the offending article came out with a eulogy of the latter, and Asquith naturally thought that Lloyd George had inspired it. Lloyd George denied this but he was probably not believed, though it is now known that he had nothing to do with it. The article was written by Geoffrey Dawson, the editor of *The Times*, who had seen Carson on Sunday. The newspapers were naturally kept informed during the crisis by their parliamentary correspondents, as well as by Lloyd George himself, his secretaries, and his partisans.

During Monday, Liberal Ministers visited Asquith and gave him contradictory advice. 'Rigidity', thumped McKenna and Harcourt; 'Elasticity', whispered Montagu and Reading. Asquith stiffened, and that evening wrote to Lloyd George: 'I have come decidedly to the conclusion that it is not possible that such a Committee could be made workable and effective without the Prime Minister as its Chairman.' This was to deny the understanding reached on Sunday. To this Lloyd George replied on the following day with a virtual resignation: 'I place my office without further parley at your disposal.'

That Tuesday afternoon Asquith saw Curzon, Robert Cecil, and Austen Chamberlain. He asked them whether they would be prepared to go on with him whilst Lloyd George and Bonar Law resigned. They answered with a perfectly definite negative, and held themselves free to serve in a Lloyd George administration. They withdrew, joined their Unionist colleagues, and presently sent Curzon with a message to Asquith urging him to resign or to accept their resignations. He informed Curzon and the Liberal

Ministers who were assembled that he had decided to tender his resignation. He did so at seven o'clock that evening.

At 9.30 p.m. the King summoned Bonar Law to the Palace as the leader of the largest single party in the House of Commons and asked him to form a Ministry. This proposal had been anticipated, and Lord Beaverbrook says it had been agreed between Lloyd George and Law 'that while Lloyd George's Premiership should be aimed at as the ideal, Bonar Law's should be accepted as the practical solution if all else failed'. Law asked for time. A meeting at Buckingham Palace was suggested by the King, and this took place on the following afternoon with Asquith, Bonar Law, Lloyd George, Balfour, and Arthur Henderson present. In the meantime, Bonar Law had seen Asquith and Balfour. Asquith, following his own inclinations, confirmed later by the advice of his Liberal friends, refused to serve in an administration formed by Bonar Law, or Balfour, or Lloyd George. Bonar Law returned later to the Palace and advised His Majesty to call in Lloyd George, who was then entrusted with the task.

On Thursday, 7 December 1916, Lloyd George kissed hands on appointment as Prime Minister, being within five weeks of his fifty-fourth birthday, and having been a Member of Parliament for half that period.

In the House of Commons, two days after Lloyd George's death, Churchill summed up these events: 'Presently, Lloyd George seized the main power in the State and the Leadership of the Government.' (Hon. Members, 'Seized?') 'Seized.' ('Hear, hear.') 'I think it was Carlyle who said of Oliver Cromwell: "He coveted the place; perhaps the place was his."' (Cheers.)

Asquith and Lloyd George, the two protagonists who had thus clashed and separated, had worked well together for years in neighbouring offices and dwellings, and had been jointly responsible for large measures of social reform. Both were great parliamentarians; one was intellectually massive, judicial, serene, the other energetic, emotional, swift, subtle, resourceful. Both had courage in plenty. One was more suited to lead in peace, the other to lead in war. As the war proceeded, Lloyd George had forged his way to an unrivalled position in the eyes of his countrymen, the Empire, the Allies, and the enemy, by his union of emotional earnestness, oratorical power, and driving force. On Monday, 4 December, the Conservative *Daily Telegraph* committed itself to this view: 'We are unable to think of any statesman now in power in any of the combatant countries whose withdrawal from office would have such an effect of discouragement upon associated nations as would be caused by that of the War Minister.'

Had Asquith allowed Lloyd George the exceptional war powers he had demanded it might have concentrated on his head the furious criticism for failures that had been hurled at the Prime Minister—for failures did not suddenly cease—and this might have sapped Lloyd George's influence in the country; but, more likely, he would have felt himself hampered by Asquith and a large Cabinet and would have staged another crisis. Asquith's refusal to co-operate with or work under the Liberal party's most dynamic leader doomed that party to a future of divided counsels, quarrels, and futilities.

Not only had the two leaders of the one party grown apart, but the strains and stresses of the Cabinet had failed to produce a sound Coalition. Kipling's ship found herself in the storms she encountered. Not so the Cabinet, whose members continued to be of such diverse parties and temperaments as never to be braced or fused by controversy. Some pulled lengthways, some shoved crossways, and the skipper's orders were neither heard nor heeded. 'I'm going to pull out', said a rivet in one of the forward plates. 'If you go, others will follow', hissed the Steam. 'There's nothing so contagious in a boat as rivets going.'

V
PRIME MINISTER IN WAR
1916–18

As you enter Canterbury Cathedral your eye is at once arrested by a tablet naming in order all the Archbishops from St. Augustine to Cosmo Gordon Lang and William Temple. No such comparable list of Prime Ministers is visible as you enter Westminster Hall. If we select, somewhat arbitrarily, Walpole as the first of the line, and if we count from 1721 to Lloyd George in 1921, there are thirty-six names in the two centuries. Within that period the nature of the office and the men holding it varied greatly. There had never before, Lloyd George tells us, been a 'ranker' raised to the Premiership, 'certainly not one except Disraeli who had not passed through the Staff College of the old Universities'. Most Prime Ministers had been born of ruling families in affluent circumstances, and were conscious of an aptitude for high affairs. They inherited traditional policies and controversies and modified or extended them, here a little and there a little, with a gradualness which was never successfully menaced by catastrophic change. Many were great orators, and others usually had debating gifts above the average. They were at least as interesting to meet as bankers or field-marshals or millionaires, though a modern novelist has dismissed the lot as dull. 'For my part', sums up Somerset Maugham, 'I would much sooner spend a month on a desert island with a veterinary surgeon than with a Prime Minister.'

When criticizing Asquith in the *Memoirs* and describing the qualities essential to the Chief Minister of the Crown in a great war, Lloyd George drew his own self-portrait. Asquith, he grants, had courage, composure, and judgement in a superlative degree:

But a War Minister must also have vision, imagination, and initiative—he must show untiring assiduity, must exercise constant oversight and supervision of every sphere of war activity, must possess driving force to energise this activity, must be in continuous consultation with experts, official and unofficial, as to the best means of utilising the resources of the country in conjunction with Allies for the

88

achievement of victory. If to this can be added a flair for conducting a great fight, then you have an ideal War Minister.[1]

Such a combination of qualities constitutes leadership. The leadership which a Prime Minister must possess has sometimes been compared to that needed by a managing director of a vast commercial and international enterprise, but the responsibility of the politician to the public is far more immediate and exposed than that of a manager to his shareholders; he cannot escape close and constant observation, and this evokes an answering behaviour, a public posturing, a studied showmanship—modest, dignified, vulgar, flamboyant—according to the inmost nature of the man.

When Lloyd George assumed the reins of government he was not a comparative stranger to the public, as was Campbell-Bannerman before and Stanley Baldwin after him. He was, in fact, the most widely known and discussed of all Cabinet Ministers. Self-advertisement was hateful to a 'classical' statesman like Asquith, who found himself in the position of a democratic leader. Democracy is not a cloistral but a vulgar creed, and Lloyd George had breathed nothing else from his cradle upwards. He had learnt the arts of leadership on the election platform, on the floor of the House, and as a Minister of the Crown in major offices. He had already practised the arts of management on millions of voters in the country, on hundreds of Members of Parliament in the Commons, and on a handful of colleagues in the Cabinet. In all three spheres he displayed consummate gifts of leadership.

The source of his leadership lay in the fire and zeal which burned within him; in his active, agile, planning, and executive brain; besides, he radiated authority and force not only to a commanding but to a dominating degree. He had a musician's eye for the large and rapidly turning pages of an operatic score, while conducting chorus and orchestra. He was an artist, but he was not an academician. He 'was born fresh every morning'. He arrived in the Cabinet room with his batteries fully charged, with ideas which he wished discussed and, brushing aside irrelevant secretarial programmes, he issued a whirl of lightning instructions. Waking early, he had read the official memoranda and telegrams in the red boxes at his bedside, and had devoured the newspapers of all colours. At breakfast he began the innumerable interviews

[1] Lloyd George, *Memoirs*, i. 602.

which filled his days, cross-examined Ministers, experts, friends, visitors from the Front or on missions from abroad. He had a retentive memory for essentials, though he was apt to be inaccurate in detail, and there was no limit to his curiosity within the field of politics and war. Asquith said of Lloyd George and Churchill that they thought with their mouths. Lloyd George was the better listener; he listened with both ears and was always ready to learn from persons of knowledge and experience whatever their rank or status. This sometimes led to specious and spurious second-raters gaining access to and influence over him until they were found out, and they were not always found out. He was the most punctual of Ministers. When crossed or badly served he could flash impatience and censure with savage bluntness; but modern Prime Ministers have been so long in training that they have their tempers well in hand.

He first won fame as a skilful negotiator in disputes, and lubricator at the Board of Trade. He was always confident of his ability to find a solution, however fleeting it might prove. He avoided breaking on small points which would appear absurd when made public. His mind had few deep grooves and was endlessly adjustable and accommodating. He handled deputations 'without side or swank', entering the room briskly, exchanging a nod of recognition with any member known to him, preparing the atmosphere with welcoming warmth. He listened with patience, flattered the speaker by the attentive alacrity with which he seized a point, sharpened it, and conceded inessentials. He never haggled over details. He was acutely observant as the negotiations proceeded, divining much more than he knew, pouncing on any weakness in the deputation's case, brushing aside as of no importance what he did not want to hear. He had always been briefed by the experts and had ascertained in advance the currents of public opinion, not only by a perusal of the press but by circuitous and subterranean inquiries. And he knew when to touch the tender chords. When Minister of Munitions and desperately short of guns in France he found their makers reluctant to divulge their trade secrets to one another. He told them: 'The great offensive in France begins this afternoon at three o'clock. How many of you have sons there? Will they have enough guns? How many of you put your secrets before your sons?'

The account given here of Lloyd George's activities during

1916, when he was treading the winding stair to the Premiership, has sometimes shown him in an unflattering light, oppressed 'by a sense of frustration and tangled impotence' and engaged in open and secret agitation for the change of leadership which he had at last brought about by placing himself on top. 'Why', asked Lord Morley, 'do people always talk as if a politician has to be so much better than other men in other professions?' It would be a gross misreading of Lloyd George to think of him as merely ambitious and athirst for power. With the desire to be first was mingled the noble aim of serving the state to the uttermost, and a passionate desire to win the war. His accession to the highest office, with the baser arts and stratagems of the ascent left behind and below, was accompanied by a cleansing of the air he breathed. Responsibility elevated his character, as it has done with other rulers of men from Agrippa to Lincoln. His mind widened, his patience increased, and, generally, his demeanour was appropriate to the great place he now occupied.

Science had not yet but would soon make it possible for the modern Prime Minister to enter every home and talk to every voter at his own fireside. This means of awakening the half-conscious electorate coincided with a decline or dilution of the sort of political earnestness which prevailed among Victorian voters—voters who were fed on serious metropolitan and provincial journals fully reporting the proceedings of Parliament. This gravity was largely a reflection of the depth and wealth and force of Gladstone's voluminous speeches which moulded the mind and morals of the nation. Lloyd George's conversational idiom, on the other hand, was more intelligible to the new audience, which could be quickly reached by his *Slings and Arrows*—his felicitous images, his raillery, his invective, and his humorous sallies. His critics have accused him of conscious cynicism in the composition of his politically idealistic public speeches, whereas his real fault was his desire to please his audience—his weakness was an extreme responsiveness to atmosphere and in place of an immovable candour a too adroit opportunism.

At the moment of becoming Prime Minister Lloyd George described himself as 'the most miserable man on earth', but this was but the mood of a moment. A private diary records on 8 December: 'I saw Lloyd George first thing this a.m. for about ten minutes at his flat, just before Ellis Griffith arrived for breakfast.

Lloyd George was in fine fettle—said he put a month's work into yesterday and that the King was "amazed" at his making a Cabinet so swiftly.' Later the strain of the crisis told on him and for a few days he was ill, but, like Gladstone, he was endowed with 'an untiring body subject to an unfailing will'. Another and a different comparison suggests itself, not for the first time. Lloyd George had the self-mastery, self-confidence, inexhaustible energy, the intensely practical comprehensive genius attributed to Julius Caesar. He had in his prime the lucidity of judgement which intuitively grasped the line of safety, the gift of fitting means to ends, of attracting ability, of using the arts which flatter and conciliate—not the simple and the ignorant only—by recalling names and circumstances and services.

With the unsleeping concentration and speed which were his second nature, as they were Caesar's, he brought all these gifts into full play on the decisive day when he bent all his strength to the task of securing Conservative, Liberal, and Labour support for the new Cabinet. His scouts had found out that 136 Liberals out of 260 were ready to follow him. Of the support of Balfour, Bonar Law, and Carson he was already assured. On 7 December he saw four other Tory leaders—Curzon, Austen Chamberlain, Robert Cecil, and Walter Long—and he satisfied them. On this same day he received a deputation of Labour and Socialist leaders at the War Office. It was a crucial interview: he had to win or perish. 'I made the best speech I have ever made', he told Riddell, and he made it without preparation. The speech was an excellent example of Lloyd George's power of skilfully navigating the shoals and shifting sands, the cross-currents running through a meeting where one slip would mean shipwreck.

In years to come, his speech at this 'celebrated doping seance' was to give rise to much recrimination. He was charged with having promised to nationalize mines, railways, and shipping. He had not done so, though he grazed the edges of a promise. He himself favoured such a policy in war time 'as far as possible . . . however, I shall have to discuss details further with my colleagues'. Among his hearers were such connoisseurs of terminological inexactitude as MacDonald, Snowden, Henderson, and J. H. Thomas, and it is inconceivable that any of them was misled. Lloyd George states he secured the support of Labour by a majority of one, Snowden says by 17 to 12. Confident that he could form a Coalition Government, he had an audience of the King that same evening and accepted the post of Prime Minister.

The country, in the main, was relieved at the fall of Asquith and, as Curzon told the Lords, was not only willing to be led, but was almost calling to be driven. There was widespread unease at the prevailing extravagance and lack of discipline at home at a time when news was arriving daily of thousands giving up their lives for their country. The new Premier felt this contrast deeply. On 6 December, the day before his official installation, a group of friends and advisers had urged Lloyd George to give unmistakable evidence to the country that he was as much a democrat as ever; to deal generously with Labour (the most difficult element in the situation, for their leaders did not lead but followed); and to deliver a speech in the high moral tone of 1914—'endure to the end'— so as to wipe out the memory of the American interview and to rise above the level of club gossip and the less reputable papers.

This advice, which betrays the current anxieties of his counsellors, he heeded when constructing his Government and when making his first speech in Parliament as Prime Minister on 19 December. He opened that speech with these solemn words: 'I appear before the House of Commons to-day, with the most terrible responsibility that can fall on the shoulders of any living man.' He then, characteristically, went at once to the point of danger, the German peace proposals which had reached the Cabinet on the previous day, and he made it plain to the world that only a peace which offered complete restitution, full reparation, and effectual guarantees against repetition would be entertained by Great Britain. He went on to ask for the mobilization of all the national resources, painting, as he put it, not a gloomy but a stern picture. Sacrifices should be real and should be equal. Let the nation place its comforts, its luxuries, its indulgences, its elegances on the altar as the men were doing who were in daily communion with death: 'Let us proclaim during the War a National Lent.'

In his own home he set an example of plain living, of sober, even abstemious habits. It was not necessary to urge the hostess of No. 10 to give evidence of a simple democratic way of life— from first to last she knew no other, either at Criccieth or in London. There was never any discrimination between high and low at that warm Welsh hearth in the heart of the metropolis.

CABINET AND SECRETARIAT

The Premiership is the most difficult office to fill; for its holder has the most miscellaneous matters to handle, the most numerous masters to please, the most momentous decisions to take, and he is always liable to be dismissed at short notice. Daily he has to maintain responsible relationships with Crown and Cabinet, with Parliament, party, press, and public, by means of letters and speeches and secretaries—and of secretaries Lloyd George never could have enough.

On settling into No. 10 he brought his personal secretariat with him from the Treasury—John T. Davies, William Sutherland, and Miss Frances Stevenson. Davies was charged with the optimum allocation of the Prime Minister's time. Sutherland saw to the press, and was reputed to be uncommonly skilful in the politics of the corridors. This staff was now extended to the basement and the garden—the Garden Suburb, as it was christened—where were installed men of the calibre of Waldorf Astor, Philip Kerr, W. G. S. Adams, David Davies, Sir Joseph Davies, Cecil Harmsworth, and later, Edward Grigg. At the same time the staff of the Committee of Imperial Defence under Colonel Hankey became the new War Cabinet secretariat with assistant secretaries including Sir Ernest Swinton and Sir Mark Sykes and men who were themselves to become Cabinet Ministers, Amery and Ormsby Gore, now Lord Harlech.

By 1916 practically every question of higher civil and military policy concerning the war had been concentrated in the War Committee of seven, with, above it, the traditional Cabinet of twenty-three. Lloyd George swept both away—'You cannot run a war with a sanhedrim', he told the Commons (19 December 1916)—and substituted a War Cabinet of five members, shut out the heads of the great departments of state, brought Hankey and his assistants inside the Cabinet room and bade them record the proceedings and become the connecting links between the War Cabinet and the departments.

The War Cabinet consisted of five members: Prime Minister and First Lord of the Treasury, D. Lloyd George; Lord President of the Council and Leader of the House of Lords, Lord Curzon; Chancellor of the Exchequer and Leader of the House of Commons, A. Bonar Law; Ministers without Portfolio, Lord Milner and Arthur Henderson. These five persons were specially charged with responsibility for the conduct of the war, and with the exception of the Chancellor they were free from departmental duties. The Cabinet met for the first time on the morning of 9 December at the War Office, and on the evening of 10 December the official list of about thirty Ministers comprising the new Government was issued to the public, and a similar list of thirty under-secretaries soon followed. Some Asquithians of repute gave the new Government three months in office and then a general election. 'Kicking and biting mules are not in it, I should say, with them', wrote Sir Henry Jones. The concentration of the War Cabinet into a very few hands, the choosing of heads of departments for their administrative and business rather than for their parliamentary experience, the fuller recognition of the partnership of Labour; these were the main departures from precedent, apart from the setting-up of a Cabinet secretariat.

The new secretariat saw to it that agenda were prepared and submitted for the Prime Minister's personal approval; that Ministers and experts were summoned for items with which they were concerned; that minutes were circulated within a few hours of a meeting; and that conclusions and decisions were communicated to the heads of the chief departments and followed up by the assistant secretaries, who also acted as secretaries to the numerous Cabinet committees. A large clerical staff was engaged at the Cabinet office to deal expeditiously with the typing, printing, indexing, and filing of papers. This was the secret of the speed with which Hankey could produce any minute or memorandum required in Cabinet or conference, at home or abroad.

The superior efficiency of the new system over the old in discussing major policy, reaching decisions, running the war generally, and working the institutions of the country was undoubted. One of the defects of the large Cabinet was that it hardly ever considered general policy, for pressure of detailed departmental business was apt to squeeze it out. 'I think only of the present twenty-four hours', Joseph Chamberlain used to say. Lloyd George also lived intensely in the present moment, unhampered by the past, untroubled by petty inconsistencies, but, as Churchill has pointed out, 'without taking short views'. The War Cabinet, composed of Ministers unhampered by departmental ties, assisted by an efficient secretariat, met daily, free to concentrate on the larger problems of the war. In its first 146 days, including Sundays, there were 146 meetings; in its first eighteen months there were 525 meetings of the War and Imperial Cabinets and thirty conferences with the Allies, or 555 meetings in 474 working days.

The proceedings always opened with reports on the military, naval, and air situation by the representatives of these departments, which were usually followed by a survey of the political situation by the Foreign Secretary. This meant that only rarely did the five members sit alone. On an average, there would be half a dozen others present and when a highly controversial issue was at stake an extra twenty might attend, but these visitors withdrew when the item for which they were summoned had been dealt with. Usually disputes between departments were referred for settlement to *ad hoc* committees of the contestants, at which Curzon, Milner, or Smuts presided, arbitrated, and promulgated a decision in the name of the War Cabinet. General Smuts, in London for the Imperial Cabinet, had remained on at Lloyd George's request to serve in the War Cabinet.

The new system had the advantage over the old of creating a body whose decision was final and was more rapidly reached. The smaller numbers promoted greater frankness, and if the utmost secrecy was required a written record would be made and kept by the secretary only. It ensured the presence of Ministers concerned in each question and eliminated them from discussions in which they were not interested. By means of the secretariat, the preparation of subjects for the agenda and their preliminary discussion with the departments could be advanced or even short-circuited without troubling the War Cabinet.

A major drawback to the system was the withdrawal of the Prime Minister from daily and direct contact with the House of Commons. This gradual estrangement was to contribute, after the war, to the downfall of Lloyd George. Fortunately, during the war he had in Bonar Law a deputy highly skilled in managing the House, and as they were neighbours in Downing Street they were in constant touch. They were not rival but complementary personalities: Bonar Law was stronger in tactics than in strategy. Baldwin once described their partnership as the most perfect in political history. It lasted for five years and then weakened; while it lasted it was of the first importance. Lloyd George had complete confidence in Bonar Law's practical judgement and was in the daily habit of ventilating in his presence all his plans and problems before submitting them to the War Cabinet. His friend's uniformly critical attitude was a source of endless delight to him.[2]

Nothing human was alien to Lloyd George, and he quickly became part of all he saw and felt. Great sorrows had deepened Bonar Law's native pessimism. The loss of a devoted wife and of two sons in the war had chilled the hearth at No. 11 and quenched the desires of its 'meekly ambitious' occupant. Lloyd George describes in the *Memoirs* a drive together on a sunny day at Cannes, when he tried to rally his companion with his own enthusiasms. '"Will you tell me", I said, exasperated at all his disdain for the attractions of life, "what is it that you do care for? Scenery—music—women—none of them has any meaning for you. What is it that you do like?" "I like bridge", was the reply.' And, he might have added, chess.

The other members of the War Cabinet, Curzon, Milner, Henderson (for a short period), and later George Barnes, Carson, and General Smuts, were all strong and able men whose knowledge and counsel were invaluable to the 'constitutional dictator' who now presided over them.

Curzon was a patrician, 'reared in another planet', Balliol scholar, Chancellor of Oxford University, ex-Viceroy of India, who had served his country 'in divers offices in many lands'. Equipped with vast stores of information, especially on Asiatic questions, he displayed them with vice-regal impressiveness at the Cabinet table, and excelled in exposition. He was less well furnished when decisions were required of him; Winston Churchill, in *World Crisis*, says that 'in deeds he rarely dinted the surface of events'.

Milner was partly German in origin, with the temperament of a German bureaucrat, a Liberal imperialist with Labour leanings on domestic issues, simple and straight and resolute. Neither a demagogue nor a diplomatist, he was an efficient administrator who made a perfect chairman of a contentious committee on which agreement had to be imposed.

Henderson and Barnes were trade-union leaders, with Liberal antecedents, who had played important pioneering parts in building up the Labour party. Each had lost a son in the war. Neither

[2] Ibid. i. 612.

was a doctrinaire Socialist, but both were good internationalists; Barnes was to represent his country at the Paris Conference, and Henderson to preside over the League of Nations in Geneva.

Lloyd George's Liberal followers found it hard to understand his partiality for Carson, the champion of Ulster's resistance to Home Rule; gentle and selfless in private life, he was in public obstinate, fearless, and uncompromising. On the other hand, Smuts personified the triumph of Liberal policy in South Africa and was enthusiastically welcomed for that reason as well as for his own great qualities. He possessed the art of timing his decisive interventions so as to produce their maximum effect.

PROBLEMS OF WAR 1916–17

Having radically changed the machinery of Cabinet government at the centre, Lloyd George as supreme director of major policies addressed himself afresh to the problems of the war. The chief of these in his view were: to defeat the submarine, to secure unity of command on the Western Front, and to secure unity in the direction of the total war effort of the Allies and the Empire. To the progressive achievement of all three aims he made a greater contribution than any other political or military leader. These were to be his dominant interests while the war lasted, but they were far from exhausting his energies.

SUBMARINE WARFARE

At the end of 1916 and early in 1917 von Bethmann-Hollweg, the German Chancellor, and President Wilson both put forth peace feelers. Replies to the two independent peace notes were immediately prepared after consultation among the Allies. A point-blank refusal to negotiate with the enemy would have offended public opinion at home and abroad, while to enter into conference without a firm outline of terms in advance would be suicidal. Germany's approach was couched in the terms of a belligerent conscious of victory at a moment when, as we now know, her generals had pronounced her military position hopeless. The note was mainly meant for domestic and neutral consumption, and as a justification in advance for the impending intensified submarine campaign; it did nothing to shake Lloyd George's resolution.

The purpose of President Wilson's inquiry was to take soundings among the belligerents in order 'to call out . . . an avowal of their respective views as to the terms upon which the war might be concluded' (*The Times*, 22 December 1916). The replies to both notes, agreed to by all the Allies, did substantially set out the peace terms which were afterwards formulated at Versailles. These replies together with the outline of Germany's penal terms communicated to Colonel House by Bernstorff (31 January 1917) combined to stiffen American opinion and to hasten America's entry into the war.

On 1 February Germany announced her inauguration of unrestricted submarine warfare, a move which had been threatened two years earlier. Henceforward all merchant shipping was to be sunk at sight without warning. The method of frightfulness was to be tried out with ruthless resolution. 'Humanity', 'popularity', 'liberality' were, as Fichte had said a century earlier, 'three infamous neo-Latin words' for which there were no German equivalents. It was really a gambler's last throw on the part of Germany. It might win them the war before American participation became effective. If it did not, the war was lost anyway, America or no America. On 6 April 1917 America declared war on Germany.

The early submarine had been of limited range; but Germany had lately been concentrating on building the cruiser type which could cross the Atlantic. One had, in fact, done so in June 1916, and had sunk five American vessels in territorial waters—'a characteristic sample of Prussian psychology', says Lloyd George in the *Memoirs*, 'meant to intimidate America into complacence'. Britain was unprepared for vessels which could traverse these vast distances, far beyond the range of her patrols. She was short of destroyers and her mining had proved useless. Day by day the First Sea Lord retailed to the Cabinet a gloomy tale of sinkings without hope of effective counter-measures. So utterly unrelieved was the tale of woe that Lloyd George would sometimes rally and chaff the Admiral across the table and bid him sweep the seas with his telescope to discover, if he could, some dove of hope or promise above the waves, some gleam of sunshine in the pitiless storm— but this banter only shocked Jellicoe.

Throughout the first half of 1917 Lloyd George was haunted by this growing menace, and well knew what it meant if it was not checked. He was determined to combat it by every known method, and sought information on the subject from all sources that might help him to this end. At this time Hankey and his assistants had learnt that the views of the senior admirals on the impracticability of the convoy system were not shared by some of the younger officers, 'the Young Turks' as they were called, and this was brought to the notice of the Prime Minister. By 11 February Hankey had gathered the fruit of many conversations into an impressive memorandum packed with argument in favour of trying out the convoy system, and two days later Lloyd George left it with Carson, Jellicoe, and Admiral Duff. On 25 April the Cabinet took the unusual step of asking the Prime Minister to visit the Admiralty in person and investigate its anti-submarine policy. When he arrived on the 30th he found 'the Board in a chastened mood', and the official attitude towards the convoy system changed. Not only had America entered the war and increased the number of escorts available, but certain experiments in the Channel with the French coal convoy had proved highly successful. The Admiralty had at last reached the stage of being willing to extend these experiments from the Channel and the Mediterranean to the Atlantic. Lloyd George and the 'Young Turks' had won.

In a grave memorandum signed on 27 April, immediately before the Prime Minister's visit to the Admiralty, Jellicoe had urged a withdrawal from the Balkans in order to release ships for the importation of food necessary to prevent a state of siege. Lloyd George took Jellicoe with him to an Anglo-French conference in Paris (4 May) where this withdrawal was agreed upon. But it proved unnecessary, as an alternative policy put up by the Ministry of Shipping provided the transport by inducing the United States Government to give the Allies absolute priority over all other countries in drawing supplies of foodstuffs, minerals, and fuel from the North American continent. The double policy of concentrating supplies in Allied ships for the Allies only and protecting them by convoy delivered Britain from the submarine peril. The gross tonnage sunk by the enemy showed a marked decline from September onwards until the end of the war. In 1917 and 1918, at the same time that Germany increased its building of cruiser sub-marines, the British increased their building of merchant vessels, and organized British food supplies by means of foreign purchase, increasing home production, and rationing. Over the whole of this field of war activity, devised to counter the submarine and to protect Britain from blockade, Lloyd George kept an intimate and directing control, lending his personal backing to Maclay, Devonport, Rhondda, Lee, and Ernle, to mention the chief Ministers on whom he relied to execute the programmes. Through this long and doubtful and decisive struggle his indomitable spirit upheld his less buoyant colleagues, and in the end brought victory.

UNITY OF COMMAND

Unity of command, equally with the defeat of the submarine menace, was a major objective of the new Prime Minister's policy from the moment he rose to the highest place. He was not so unrealistic as to propose a single commander for all the Allied armies; neither Russia nor Italy would have listened for an instant to such a plan. His proposal was confined to the Western Front, and it was 1918 before it was acted upon. Briand supported him with perorations, but Lloyd George did not confuse or identify speech and action. Words were important, but deeds were more important. To attain his end he used all means: public and persuasive speeches, negotiations within conferences, intrigue without. His project, sound and sensible in itself, was opposed in part because of his known contempt for British generals, his partiality for campaigns outside France, and his doubt of the Allies ever breaking through 'the impenetrable barrier in the West'. It was not until the last year of the war that machinery was created to co-ordinate or to attempt to co-ordinate the effort of the Allied Governments in all its phases—political, diplomatic, economic, military, naval— under a supreme War Council.

Lloyd George often pours scorn on the bondage to professional etiquette which hampered discussion with the military authorities and obstructed his aims. In the field of domestic politics he had not allowed himself to be restrained by etiquette; there he was essentially a coalitionist. This lack of rigid attachment to party had been the cause from time to time of charges of disloyalty. His impatience with any hard-and-fast code was akin to his impatience of rules and regulations. Routine also bored him, and he rebelled and broke loose in ways his secretaries could not anticipate. He could always be counted on to be punctual in keeping appointments, but pomp and ceremony had little attraction for him.

He did not dress up, fold his arms, and glare in the manner of a Mussolini.

Lloyd George thought of the war as a single gigantic struggle to defeat the enemy. All fronts were one battle-front across the world; there should be one strategy, not six strategies; all resources —armies, guns, ships—should be in one Allied pool. That is how he felt and argued and planned and schemed.

The obstacles to such an overriding conception were manifold and real and lasted through the war. The chief of these was the chronic strife between the Easterners and the Westerners. Lloyd George was never convinced that to concentrate attention on the West was right. He was confident that the Turk could have been overthrown in 1916, and that in 1917 a reinforced Italy could have defeated the half-starved and unreliable Austrians. Generals would never willingly spare a battalion for another front and should be compelled where persuasion failed. They underrated Britain's ever-growing superiority to the enemy in guns, ammunition, and aeroplanes. The necessary depletion of Allied strength on the West would still, he argued, have left forces superior to those of the enemy. But the inflexible Allied generals were too strong for an amateur who was accused of fighting battles without maps and with always seeking for the chink in the enemy's armour.

Politicians and generals were not only patriots—English, French, Italian—they were human, all too human. In a chapter of the *Memoirs* headed 'Psychology and Strategy', Lloyd George diverges from his main narrative to stress the mixture of motives, good and bad, which ferment in the same breast at the same time, and he illustrates the effect of personal ambition in deflecting decisions of high military policy in the discussions in which he participated. Not only the generals, 'fearfully and wonderfully made', to whom throughout his book are imputed a double dose of selfishness and more than their share of stupidity, but statesmen, even his friends Briand and Albert Thomas, were not immune from excessive partiality for their own country. Briand's idea of the one front was the French Front; he would not spare a single gun for Italy. Lloyd George rarely quotes the poets, but in this context he cannot resist the well-known lines from Burns:

> Where Self the wavering balance shakes
> 'Tis rarely right adjusted.

It is only fair to say that in the role of War Minister he himself displayed a remarkable freedom from narrow personal motives and patriotic prejudice, whether he was dealing with France, Italy, or Russia. His supreme concern was that Britain should do her utmost to achieve, rather than to be credited with, victory.

RUSSIA

In the opening months of the war Lloyd George had fully realized the enormous part Russia was playing and might play in it, and in February 1915 he had put his views on the deplorable absence of co-ordination between East and West bluntly before Asquith. Disturbing reports of the lack of ammunition on the Russian Front reached the War Office only to be ignored. The manufacturing resources of France and Britain, had they been drawn upon earlier, might have prevented the slaughter of many thousands of Russian soldiers—men who had courage in their hearts but were without weapons in their hands—and might have postponed if not prevented the Revolution. In 1915 and 1916 the engineering backwardness and managerial incompetence of that peasant country were only slowly and partially overcome with the aid of the factories of the West.

In September 1915 Lloyd George published *Through Terror to Triumph*, the speeches in which he had striven to disturb the complacency induced by official reports of the progress of the war. In one of his appeals he said: 'Russian fortresses, deemed impregnable, are falling like sand-castles before the resistless tide of Teutonic invasion. When will the tide recede? When will it be stemmed? As soon as the Allies are supplied with abundance of war material.'

From May 1915 onwards the Germans had swept the half-armed, half-trained hordes of Russia across the passes and marshes until by September their wavering line was 200 miles beyond War-saw. The amazing fact was that it had been possible to stabilize a line at all with a threadbare army in face of the great German guns; the price paid in Russian lives was terrific.

To this critical situation was added the Czar's failure, in September 1915, to turn himself into a constitutional monarch and the Duma into a democratic instrument. 'The axle of the nation's life' was neither the ruthless nor the stupid autocrat of popular caricature. Guided by the protective, energetic, mystical Empress and the clever, debauched, hypnotic monk Rasputin, the Czar repelled the advances of the progressive *bloc* in the Duma. Defeatism infected soldiers and civilians and slowly festered and burst into unplanned revolution.

Lloyd George had, since the beginning of the war, pressed for closer co-operation with Russia, and as has been told he was to have gone to Russia in 1916 (perhaps with Kitchener on the ill-fated *Hampshire*) had he not been diverted to Irish affairs by the Prime Minister. 'This escape, at least,' he wrote, 'I owe to Ireland.' More than once he had urged that Allied statesmen and generals should meet on Russian soil. It was not surprising, therefore, that within a week of succeeding Asquith he revived the proposal for a conference in Petrograd. The conference, with Lord Milner representing the War Cabinet and Sir Henry Wilson the army, met from 1 to 20 February 1917, and reviewed matters military, political, and financial. On 12 March the Revolution broke out and the deliberations of the conference, all the talk of pooling resources and supplying Russia's urgent needs, went for nought. Once more the Allies were too late.

Neither Milner nor Wilson sensed its proximity, nor did any member of the mission register in advance the impending explosion—with one exception. A junior member of the group, David Davies, a mighty hunter, visiting a country landowner in the vicinity of Petrograd to inspect a pack of hounds, had scented the truth and wrote a report to the British Prime Minister foretelling the immediate collapse of the Czarist régime.

Lloyd George did not know all but he knew more than his colleagues of what was happening in Russia. The correspondents of a Prime Minister are many and various and it was characteristic of Lloyd George that he paid heed to them, regardless of party or rank. He was always listening, learning, pouncing on what was significant in a letter or interview, and he expected his secretaries to do the same and to keep him informed. In his day No. 10 had an ever-open door.

Among experts on Russia he had been in touch with Sir Bernard Pares, General Sir Alfred Knox, Harold Williams, and Bruce Lockhart, to mention well-known names. As early as 26 July 1915 Pares had discussed with him at breakfast the political bearing of supplies of Russian munitions. Less than a fortnight later (5 August) this matutinal conversation was transmuted at the

Bangor National Eisteddfod into this passage of prophetic eloquence:

> The Eastern sky is dark and lowering. The stars have been clouded over. I regard that stormy horizon with anxiety, but with no dread. To-day I can see the colour of a new hope beginning to empurple the sky. The enemy in their victorious march know not what they are doing. Let them beware for they are unshackling Russia.[3]

In November 1915 he was being told by Sir Ian Malcolm, who was touring Russia for the Red Cross: 'The Emperor and family and Court have not a single friend. It is said they have made every possible mistake.'

The rumblings of the coming storm could be clearly heard, and when in 1917 the strange names of Kerensky, Lenin, and Trotsky sounded for the first time across the green table of No. 10 Downing Street, Lloyd George knew better than his colleagues, better than his Foreign Secretary, how to assess them. The prevailing opinion was that all three were either corrupt traitors or crazy visionaries. Lloyd George had a premonition that the romantic and rhetorical Kerensky would not long remain in power, and that Lenin with his inflexible purpose, his cold and concentrated will, his elastic tactics would endure. When he met Kerensky in 1918 he found him vague, over-estimating 'the chattering conventicles' he represented, and his paper resolutions of little value against the machine-guns of the Bolsheviks. Later he was to describe Lenin as one of the greatest leaders of men ever known in any epoch.

The origins and course of the Revolution are described by Lloyd George in some of the most vivid chapters of the *Memoirs*, and the subject is briefly and brilliantly handled in Churchill's *World Crisis*. If one statesman morbidly detested the Revolution, painting Czarism in the glittering rhetoric of a great colour artist, the other saw it sympathetically through the eyes of a radical, always and everywhere the friend of the underdog; and he saw it as a student of the earlier revolution in France. Of all historic upheavals the French Revolution was the one in knowledge of which Lloyd George was most deeply steeped, and he was always ready to discuss its leading figures and parties. 'Lloyd George qui se croit Napoléon', joked Clemenceau.

The divergent attitudes toward the Russian convulsion exhi-

---

[3] Speech by Lloyd George at Bangor, 5 August 1915.

bited by Churchill and Lloyd George were characteristic of the British Ministers in general, but during the eight months of the Russian provisional government, April–November 1917, all were eager to use any and every means to keep Russia in the war as a fighting force. As the triumph of the Bolsheviks became certain, some Ministers shuddered at the thought of direct dealings with them and feared that their subversive doctrines might injuriously affect Britain. These fears were not shared by Lloyd George, nor was he concerned to overthrow the Bolshevik Government. What he did fear was that the Bolsheviks might merely be ploughing 'a field in readiness for planting with Prussianism'. He feared that the Germans might penetrate deeply enough into Russia so that they could secure military stores, gain access to wheat, cattle, coal, and oil, and, finally, perhaps be able to train Russian man-power for use in the war against the Allies. Had not Napoleon enrolled conquered races in his *Grande Armée*?

These fears provided the original motive for Lloyd George's support of limited intervention, and it was inevitable, in giving effect to it, that Allied support of non-Bolshevik administrations and factions should not only wear the appearance of hostility but in fact be hostile to the revolutionary rulers in Petrograd and Moscow. And later this was to explain if not to justify the suspicion and bad faith which prevailed in the coming years between the Soviet régime and the Western Powers.

UNITY OF COMMAND 1917–18

It was with the French that Lloyd George had most to do during the war, for it was upon them in the early years that the main burden rested, and his conferences with their leaders were frequent. Britain entered the war, as Smuts put it, not as a principal combatant but rather as an auxiliary to France. It was a modest role, and although the situation was radically transformed in the first two years and British participation in every arm—financial, military, naval—enormously increased, her subordination continued. It was the soil of France which was being defended, and this naturally tended to put the supreme military direction in French hands. The English Channel can be as wide and estranging as the Atlantic Ocean. British generals had often to press their claim to control their own forces.

When war broke out in 1914 the British Cabinet had no comprehensive plan of campaign agreed upon with the French, and throughout 1915 no common direction existed. Sir John French was dominated by Joffre, and Joffre not only towered over his own armies but enjoyed unchallenged prestige with political circles in Paris. His official ascendancy was justified at a time when the number of French and British in the line was as four to one, and when the casualties bore a similar proportion. But during 1916 the relative strength of the armies profoundly changed, for in the first eighteen months of the war Britain had recruited over two and a half million men.

The need for concerted effort was admitted but not faced at the first Inter-Allied Military Conference held at Joffre's headquarters in July 1915. In December the French Government made Joffre Commander-in-Chief of the French armies instead merely of armies in the north-east. When, at the end of 1915, Haig succeeded French, Haig's relative position had remained essentially un-altered, but the scale of his effort on the Somme, in the following summer, was bound to make a difference. In that grim struggle the British army, in Liddell-Hart's phrase, 'came of age'. The rela-tions of the great commanders continued nevertheless studiously vague and undefined. Though there were strained occasions when Haig had to register protests at French General Headquarters, his unvarying practice was to meet the wishes of Joffre whenever pos-sible.

In the course of 1916 the prestige of Joffre declined. Lloyd George compares his waning influence with that of Kitchener. Both enjoyed a reputation with the public long after their close colleagues had encountered their limitations and had wished to remove them from their pedestals. Dissatisfaction with Joffre's failure on the Somme and his unfriendly relations with Sarrail who was in charge at Salonika made him unpopular with the politicians, so in December he was superseded and consoled with the dignity of Marshal of France.

Less than a month earlier, 15 and 16 November, Joffre had pre-sided at a conference of Allied commanders at Chantilly and had settled the military plan of campaign for 1917. It had been agreed that the Allies should be ready to undertake continued offensives on all fronts from the first fortnight of February 1917, with a view to a decision. During the winter Franco-British pressure was to be maintained, and in the spring the main weight of the attack was to be undertaken by the British in view of the earlier strain endured by the French, especially at Verdun. It was a plan based on the idea that 'wisdom demanded continuous hammering of the weakening vital spot', giving the enemy no breathing-space. Both Joffre and Haig were convinced that the Germans, with their interior lines and excellent communications, could quickly transfer German troops to confront British and French troops should they attempt 'a way round'. Therefore, when Lloyd George became Prime Minister within a few days of the Chantilly conference, he found the plans for the 1917 campaign settled and settled in a way which could not be agreeable to him either as an Easterner or as a believer in unity of command.

His first attempt in his new position to secure unity resulted in failure and humiliation. He was bent on helping Russia and Italy and was dreaming of a military *coup* in Syria. He was only restrained from campaigns in the Balkans by the shortage of shipping to carry reinforcements and by the unyielding opposition of Robertson. His ministerial colleagues were torn between loyalty to their mobile chief and to the stubborn general. So Lloyd George had recourse to his favourite device of a conference, first in Rome and then in Petrograd.

The Rome conference met on 5, 6, and 7 January 1917, the venue being chosen as most convenient for the generals and diplomats. Lloyd George prepared for the meetings with his usual thoroughness. Reports were requisitioned from all the departments concerned. Sir Rennell Rodd was summoned to London for consultation. Milner, Henry Wilson (destined for Petrograd later), Robertson, and Hankey accompanied the Prime Minister to Rome; Albert Thomas, Lyautey, and Berthelot went with Briand. Generals Cadorna, Sarrail, and Milne were in attendance.

Lloyd George circulated an elaborate memorandum to the conference in which he surveyed the military, shipping, and political situation, stressed the lack of any comprehensive Allied plan of campaign—'except for each general to continue punching on his own front'—and appealed again for the establishment of a common front and the pooling of resources.

The conference, opening with 'a whole Duma present', was quickly reduced to a workable size which could be accommodated in a small room at a round table. Lloyd George's persuasive powers had full play for his first speech as Prime Minister to a European conference:

He alluded to the possibility that Russia might prove unable to hold up the Central Powers. . . . If Russia went under there were several courses open to the Central Powers. They might exploit their successes in Russia itself, advancing to Petrograd and Odessa. Or they might concentrate on the Balkans and drive us into the sea. Greece would then fall under their control, and their submarine campaign in the Mediterranean would be intensified to threaten the essential communications of the Allies in the Mediterranean, including those of Italy, who was so critically dependent on overseas supplies for the means of carrying on the War and for existence itself. Yet a third course was that the enemy might turn on Italy itself, where, as General Cadorna had pointed out, the left flank was threatened from the Trentino. How was all this to be met and countered? asked Mr. Lloyd George. . . . He made an impassioned appeal to the Italians, the descendants of the greatest road-makers in history, who had themselves accomplished some great road-making feats on the Alpine front, to re-create the old Roman road to the Balkans. He also pressed that plans should be worked out for reinforcing the Italian front by British and French troops. . . . In Italy we should be attacking where Austrians and not Germans predominated, where the front was weak . . . instead of where it was strongest. . . . With an unerring instinct he put his finger on Russia as the weak point. . . . The Balkan theatre attracted him but he was obliged to reject it for the present owing to shipping considerations.[4]

This brief summary illustrates Lloyd George's argumentative gifts, his concrete speculations about alternative emergencies, and the boldness of his policy. This method of reasoning and argument he displayed on many subsequent and sometimes critical occasions. He did not always succeed—he did not now in Rome—in his attempt at a fundamental reconstruction of Allied strategy. Several reasons are easily suggested for this failure. He proposed to divert the Allied effort from the agreed Chantilly plan and to provide Anglo-French troops and guns for an offensive through the Julian Alps, with Laibach as early, and Vienna as ultimate, objective. Cadorna showed only a tepid interest in Lloyd George's strategic conception, partly because he had been quick to discover from Robertson that Lloyd George had neither informed his own military advisers of his new plan, nor convinced them of its wis-

[4] Lord Hankey, *The Supreme Command 1914–1918* (unpublished).

dom. The French in the meantime were in process of changing the Chantilly plan at the bidding of Nivelle, Joffre's successor, and did not wish to imperil the offensive in the West. The British Prime Minister therefore met with the resistance of Briand and Albert Thomas, as well as that of his own generals.

NIVELLE OFFENSIVE

Nivelle was a new arrival at French Headquarters; he shot up like a rocket and fell like the stick. He attracted Lloyd George at once, partly because he spoke English fluently, partly because he had the gift of confident and lucid exposition. He was certain he could smash the German Front, having available behind the French Front a powerful mass which could be flung suddenly on the enemy from an unexpected part of the French line. Reversing the Chantilly plan, the French were now responsible for the main burden of the attack; the role of the British was to be subordinate. Secrecy and surprise were vital to success and the whole operation was to be carried through within from twenty-four to forty-eight hours.

Painlevé and Pétain among the French, Haig and Robertson among the English, were sceptical of the results promised by Nivelle. Lloyd George learned of the plan on Christmas Day, and at a conference in London on the 26th with M. Ribot he insisted on Haig being consulted, especially as the British were being asked to take over twenty-five miles of the line in order to release French troops for the projected army of manœuvre. Subject to this proviso, the Cabinet desired Haig 'to conform to the wishes of the French Government in this matter to the utmost possible extent'. Failing agreement, the matter was to be brought up again by the French Government.

Shortly after, when at the Rome Conference Lloyd George's proposal for an offensive on the Italian Front was turned down by French resistance and Italian indifference, he swung round to support the Nivelle plan and did his utmost to make it a success in transport, material, and men.

On 15 February Lloyd George saw Commandant Bertier de Sauvigny, a French military attaché accredited to Robertson. On the 16th Sauvigny telegraphed to Nivelle that the British Prime Minister held it to be necessary for Nivelle to have the disposition of all the forces on the Western Front; that though the prestige of

Haig was too high to permit of his being openly subordinated to the French command, yet, if the War Committee considered the measure necessary, Lloyd George would not hesitate to give secret orders to that end to the British Commander-in-Chief; and that a conference should take place as soon as possible. On 24 February Robertson was told that unless he had any special question to bring forward he need not attend the Cabinet meeting that day—a very unusual occurrence. Two days later, at Calais, the French put forward a proposal for the organization of unified command on the Western Front under Nivelle, who from 1 March was to have authority over the British forces operating on this front and to have a British Chief of the General Staff who would transmit orders to the British Commander-in-Chief. This proposal took Haig and Robertson completely by surprise; they were now told that at the War Cabinet on the 24th it had been decided to place the British armies under Nivelle. The French document was lacking neither in clarity nor precision and went further than Lloyd George had intended, so far that it took Hankey's breath away, though he had been at the decisive Cabinet meeting. He sat up half the night drafting a reconciling formula to suit all parties. The new formula restricted the subordination of the British to the French Commander-in-Chief to the impending battle only, which was reckoned to last not more than a fortnight. To make the formula work, two further conferences in London were necessary. Nivelle was tactlessly straining the Calais agreement and dictating instructions in peremptory language. Haig was hurt and Robertson was furious. Lloyd George saw Haig and Nivelle separately and together, and then sent both to Robertson to draw up a fresh formula. Henry Wilson was to be liaison officer and Nivelle could call on British reserves in the event of his breaking through the enemy lines.

The execution of the new offensive was precipitately timed for the middle of February, but owing to a series of delays it did not take place until two months later, by which time all hopes of secrecy and surprise had vanished. The Germans knew all, and had not only massed ample divisions and guns to meet the main attack but had secretly completed a remarkable withdrawal of forces to the Hindenburg Line, a system of fortified entrenchments along a stretch of over seventy miles, which completely upset Allied strategy. Nivelle, incredulous and obstinate, persisted in his plan and changed nothing, though he knew that his detailed plans had fallen into the hands of the enemy. On 6 April he appeared before a council of war in Paris, where he offered his resignation, but the politicians could not face such a change of leadership with the British already engaged in the preparatory bombardment for the Battle of Arras and with the French Battle of the Aisne about to begin. The first opened on 9 April and had much initial success, in the course of which the Canadians took Vimy Ridge; the second was later reported to be 'a success but not a breaking through'. Whether a victory or a defeat, it was a disappointment; so Nivelle was superseded by Pétain, and the new Commander-in-Chief had the disagreeable task of repressing the mutinies which were now rife in the French army. To complete the contemporary picture it should be added that on 12 March the Russian Revolution began, on 6 April the United States declared war on Germany, and on 9 April the Russian provisional government issued a proclamation in favour of peace. As one giant stepped off, the other stepped on to, the arena.

This brief summary of the Nivelle offensive has been necessary because of its bearing on the question of unity of command. Had the original time-table been observed, Lloyd George believed Nivelle would have scored an immense success, and he blamed the delays which proved fatal on the divided command. Three conferences had to be held, one in Calais and two in London, to compose the differences which arose in co-ordinating the direction of the offensive.

Not only were the politicians in Paris and in London critical of their generals, but the Commanders-in-Chief were themselves not in agreement and Ministers had to arbitrate between them. Lloyd George had no great opinion of Haig and Robertson as strategists, but was careful in his procedure in the Cabinet not to overstep the line dividing the responsibility of statesman and soldier. Nevertheless, he chafed at having to defer to their 'costly and inefficient platitudes in action'. 'Epauletted egoism impenetrable to ideas', he summed it up in his *Memoirs*. But did he reflect that his own indirect methods of assault contributed to the defeat of his own admirable ideas? Why did he fail at the Calais Conference? He claims in the *Memoirs* to tell the story 'without variation or varnish to suit anybody', but he does not quite succeed. He blames Haig and Robertson for viciously delaying and destroying the

Nivelle plan, but to them it was amazing that the new British armies with vast stocks of war material were to be handed over within forty-eight hours and for an indefinite period to a newly promoted foreign general without experience of high command, whose optimistic views were shared by no responsible soldier in the British army and by few or none in the French. Reviewing all that had happened, Lloyd George concluded that 'had the two Allied Armies been as completely under the control of one *Generalissimo* as they became . . . in April, 1918, the Nivelle strategy . . . would have secured a notable success'. But that had not been the proposal in 1917, as is pointed out in the official history.

It is plain from memoirs of this time (those of Ribot, Cambon, Robertson, and so on) that Lloyd George would have been glad to remove Haig but was unable to do so. His justifiable desire to secure unified command failed at Rome and at Calais in part because of his own tactics. Whether complete candour in advance with Haig and Robertson would have secured better results we cannot say. What we can say is that the clandestine methods used by the Prime Minister intensified distrust of him in and out of office now and in the years to come.

These reflections do not conflict with the contention that unity of command was not a matter of strategy or tactics but of organization, in which Lloyd George could claim to be as much an expert as his generals. And it is quite true that Lloyd George knew when and whom to bully and when and whom to persuade. He was always a supreme actor, and we are not surprised to learn that after the crisis over Nivelle the Prime Minister's relations with Haig improved for some time to come; and that within a few days he was hotly defending the conduct of the Field-Marshal at a new conference, held once more in London.

The Chantilly programme had been scrapped; Lloyd George's proposals for combined operations on the Italian Front pushed aside; the Nivelle campaign was petering out; there was hesitation about whether or not the initial success on the Arras Front should be followed up, Lloyd George at first in favour, then doubtful, as the casualties increased. What was to be the military programme for the remainder of 1917? The situation was once more fluid.

The proper organization of the Empire's effort in the war was one of Lloyd George's major objectives on becoming Prime Minister. No sooner had he taken office than he told the House of Commons that he proposed to summon to London representatives of the Dominions and of India to take counsel together on the progress of the war. The meetings took the concurrent forms of the Imperial War Cabinet and the Imperial War Conference.

The Imperial War Cabinet, presided over by the British Prime Minister, was the first of its kind in the Empire's history with power to make decisions and give effect to them. At the opening session, the first of fourteen between 20 March and 2 May 1917, Lloyd George dealt with the course of the war and with the essential requisites of peace. He laid down that the Germans must be driven out of the territories they had invaded, that Europe must be democratized, that the Turkish Empire must be disrupted, and that the British economic and industrial fabric ought to be reconstructed in order to improve the standards of living. He did not hope to see the Germans defeated in 1917. They still possessed enormous resources. The failure of the Nivelle offensive, the dejection of the French troops, the enemy's ruthless submarine campaign, the Russian Revolution, weighed increasingly upon him as well as upon the other Ministers.

The gloom was diminished if not dissipated by the entry of America into the war on 6 April. This opened up visions of certain victory in the long, if not in the short, run. It had been part of President Wilson's deliberate policy to preserve a strict neutrality and to avoid openly planning for war. America was unwarlike, especially in the Middle West, and though in 1916 Congress passed appropriation bills for expenditure on defence, the country in the spring of 1917 was unprepared. But America was an immense reservoir of food, munitions, money, and men, and she could build ships even if she found it not easy to run them remuneratively. Reading between the lines of the *Memoirs* it is plain that Lloyd George chafed at the slowness with which American help materialized. Missions led by Balfour, Northcliffe, and Reading were dispatched to Washington to expedite matters. Wilson presumably knew his own public, whose homelands and folk in Europe were involved in the conflict, better than Lloyd George could know it, and the pace at which it was wise to lead his people into war. 'But Wilson was not Lincoln', commented Lloyd

George. America's main military contribution was not to be made until 1918.

The meetings of the Imperial War Cabinet ended early in May. A month later a War Policy Committee was set up, presided over by Lloyd George with Curzon, Milner, and Smuts as members. The War Cabinet, overwhelmed with business, concerned itself with day-to-day detail along the whole political, administrative, and operational fronts. The new committee investigated policy, studied memoranda, examined witnesses of the highest standing. It confronted once more the major issue which divided Lloyd George from expert military opinion, that of Eastern Front versus Western.

Lloyd George was often charged (for example, by Viscount Esher) with possessing too active an intelligence, an intelligence which made him rush from one solution of a problem to another, in contrast, for example, to the 'continuous' mind of Milner. Robertson complained to Riddell that when a plan did not turn out well Lloyd George 'wants to try something else too quickly'. But Lloyd George never varied in his belief that the enemy's weakest point should be attacked, and that it was to be found in the East. There was no period in the first three years of the war, Lloyd George maintained, when the vulnerable Turk could not have been overthrown and the road opened to Russia and Rumania. An early concerted and determined attack by the Russians from the Caucasus and by the British from Egypt might have crumpled up the Turkish armies in a single campaign.

'When I became Prime Minister at the end of 1916, we were still maintaining a defensive attitude on all the Turkish fronts although we had overwhelming forces at our disposal in these areas', he says in the *Memoirs*. Lawrence of Arabia had demonstrated what mobile cavalry divisions, wasted against barbed entrenchments on the Western Front, could have done in Palestine. Early in the year General Maude had driven the Turks out of Kut and had taken Baghdad. This victorious advance might have continued had a junction been made with the Russians of the Caucasus, but by this time the Bolshevik Revolution had spread among the Russian troops a yearning for peace. Circumstances had changed, and it was a year too late.

Smuts was sent to uncover the intentions of the French, and in a Cabinet memorandum he surveyed the battle-fronts. He was disturbed by the leanings of the French towards a defensive policy which, if adopted, would discourage the Allies—a rot, once it set in, would be difficult to stop. He was therefore in favour of reviving the earlier project, supported by the Admiralty, of a Flanders offensive which should endeavour to recover the northern coast of Belgium and deprive the enemy of its submarine bases in that area.

Haig and Robertson held it to be essential to continue offensive operations on the Western Front. It was no longer a question of aiming at breaking through the enemy's front, but of wearing down and exhausting the enemy's resistance. This was the policy of Pétain, who was eager to protect his forces from further wastage until the arrival of the Americans, and to confine his efforts to local operations for the rest of 1917. This fitted in with Lloyd George's preference for operations on the side rather than at the centre, using surplus strength in Palestine, Syria, Turkey, Bulgaria, and even Austria. He pressed for a campaign in Palestine and the capture of Jerusalem. The War Office delayed, hampered, resisted. Smuts who, also, looked to the Palestine campaign to defeat the Turks, was offered the command in Palestine, but refused it because he was convinced, after consulting Robertson, that he would not be supported by the War Office. In June Allenby was appointed Commander-in-Chief of the British Forces in Egypt, and before the end of the year he had captured Beersheba and Gaza and on 9 December 1917, Jerusalem surrendered.

Throughout this controversy Lloyd George was acutely conscious of the narrow limits of British man-power, especially in executing the vast shipbuilding programme which had to outpace the ravages of the submarines. To produce the three million gross tonnage required Britain was almost driven to recall men from the forces. Against the defensive policy in the West could be urged—and the British generals did urge—the danger of the Germans withdrawing their reserves in order to launch attacks on Russia and Italy.

The Cabinet, which had to weigh these contradictory considerations, decided to press the French to continue the offensive. Accordingly, at the conference in Paris on 4 and 5 May where Lloyd George met Ribot, Painlevé, Nivelle, and Pétain, he made an impassioned appeal of great power, putting new life and hope into the Frenchmen.

The Allies must assemble all their resources. We shall certainly suffer very serious losses; but since we are at war we cannot help having losses. What is above all else essential is tenacity and endurance. The plan worked out by the Generals is excellent; it is important that to it should be added a common agreement regarding the intensity of the operations which we are to conduct throughout the summer. That is what I wanted to say to our French colleagues in the name of the British Government.[5]

The fact that at this very moment subversive sentiments were spreading from one French army corps to another and that soldiers were refusing to march was kept from the knowledge of both Germany and Britain by extraordinary measures of organization and discipline. On 15 May Pétain became Commander-in-Chief and immediately began the work of healing, and, by means no less extraordinary, in two months restored what Churchill in *World Crisis* calls 'the morale and discipline of that sorely-tried, glorious Army upon whose sacrifices the liberties of Europe had through three fearful campaigns mainly depended'.

FLANDERS OFFENSIVE

The main and by far the gravest issue before the Cabinet Committee on War Policy (8 June to 20 July 1917) was Haig's proposal for a British offensive in Flanders. There were three schools of thought about the future direction of the war after the failure of the Nivelle campaign, said Henry Wilson in his clear, black-board fashion:

1. Somme—i.e. wearing down the Boches.
2. Verdun—i.e. whirlwind attack.
3. Pétain—i.e. do nothing.

We have tried 2 (Verdun), which has been a complete failure. There remains Somme and Pétain. To my mind the Pétain plan is one to be avoided, and a Somme, with intelligence, is our only chance.[6]

At the Paris Conference (4 and 5 May) the Ministers, including Lloyd George, had endorsed the programme of the generals to wage a war of attrition, attacking the enemy with all available resources. Lloyd George demanded that the enemy must not be left in peace for one moment: 'We must go on hitting and hitting

---

[5] Gabriel Terrail (Mermeix), *Nivelle et Painlevé*, p. 129.
[6] Major-General Sir C. E. Callwell, *Sir Henry Wilson*, i. 340.

with all our strength until the German ended as he always did, by cracking.'[7] The war of attrition was not, as Lloyd George afterwards claimed, an afterthought of beaten generals to explain away their defeat.

The preparations for the Flanders campaign had been maturing since early in 1916; Haig was completely wedded to it and was supported by Robertson. It was to be strongly pressed on the generals and on the Cabinet by Admiral Jellicoe, who declared in his melancholy fashion that unless the nests of submarines were destroyed and Ostend and Zeebrugge cleared of Germans before the winter the navy could not hold the Channel and the war was lost. The release of the coast was Haig's fixed objective, which, if successful, might end in sweeping the Germans out of Belgium; but the plans for achieving this were not laid before the British Ministers until June 1917, and by that time Haig's optimism was equalled only by Lloyd George's pessimism. He was filled with misgiving, resisted the project of the soldiers, predicted its failure, finally gave it his approval, and ever after carried with him, as he says in the *Memoirs*, 'his most painful regret' that on this crucial issue 'he did not interfere with the soldiers'.

The debate in the Policy Committee was conducted at the highest level and with becoming gravity—weighty memoranda were tabled and clashes averted by adjournments for further examination and reflection—but what was it that now destroyed the brief unity found at the Paris Conference? It is probable that Lloyd George's eloquent endorsement at that conference of the agreed policy (which impressed all who heard it) was due to his desire to hearten France in a moment of gloom, and that he had gone beyond his own sober belief. During June and July the submarine nightmare lifted somewhat and its menace paled. But defection in Russia was spreading, and discontent among the French troops grew more and more alarming. From these premisses the politicians and the soldiers drew opposite conclusions. Lloyd George was for changing Haig's programme into an attack on Austria *via* Italy and waiting in the West until the Americans arrived. For a moment he even thought of visiting President Wilson in Washington to exchange views. Haig and Robertson, on the other hand, argued that no time should be given to the enemy to reinforce his line in the West with divisions from Russia, as that

[7] Terrail, ibid.

would enable him to deal the Allies a smashing blow in the later part of 1917. Secondly, they argued that the offensive would put fresh heart into the French, exhausted by nearly three years of incessant fighting. A vigorous British campaign would pin the enemy to the ground, while the French were recovering. War-weariness, Russian and German propaganda, weak politicians, and divided counsels were combining to undermine the valour of France, and the possibility of her collapse at this moment could not be ruled out.

The Cabinet Policy Committee was divided. Milner and Bonar Law (who often attended) sided with Lloyd George, but Smuts, the member with most military prestige, was with the soldiers and so, less definitely, was Curzon. All felt unwilling to overrule the military and naval authorities and impose on them a strategy in which they did not believe. It was agreed that the generals should have 'a good try', and if progress was not up to expectations the operation should be called off and help sent to the Italians.

The melancholy sequel is well known. Three and a half months followed (31 July–10 November) in which eight battles were fought, small successes achieved, but no great victory won. The name 'Passchendaele' should be applied to the fighting of the last four weeks, when the rain and mud were appalling. Terrific bombardments had already churned the earth and destroyed the drainage system of the country; torrential rains filled every crater; guns were bogged, and man and beast, when shot off the duckboards, were engulfed. Haig held on tenaciously, with heavy losses, on the principle that 'the man who gives the last kick wins'. He is excused by his apologists on the ground that it is not always easy at the moment to decide whether an attack has failed or succeeded, and that the successes of 20, 25 September and 4 October might reasonably be expected to be followed by others. They were not, and at last on 10 November the campaign ended from sheer exhaustion. The name Passchendaele has become a synonym for military failure and useless slaughter.

Lloyd George christened the offensive 'The Campaign of the Mud: Passchendaele', the account of which fills 140 pages of the *Memoirs* and sums it up as 'one of the blackest horrors of history'. These pages constitute a powerful indictment of army strategy from the failure of Nivelle's attack, which Lloyd George had ardently supported, to the close of the second battle of

Passchendaele in mid-November. They are the vitriolic outpourings of a prosecuting counsel in a criminal court, outpourings in
which the most scornful, blistering epithets are hurled at the two
defendants, Haig and Robertson. These generals are condemned
for their inexhaustible vanity, their narrow and stubborn egotism,
their muddle-headedness, their misrepresentations, their lack of
flair and flexibility—these last, in Lloyd George's esteem, qualities
so much more valuable than military training. He had little
patience with the dull, stolid, and industrious; he was attracted
by the Nivelles and Henry Wilsons whose ways were his ways.

It is not possible to accept the Passchendaele chapters as they
stand; they must be modified and corrected if the roles of the
protagonists are to be fairly judged. Earlier critics, according to
their predilections, have apportioned the blame for 'the supreme
martyrdom of the War' between the British Prime Minister,
the Commander-in-Chief, and the Chief of the Imperial General
Staff, but today we have available not only the contributions of
later students of war but also the official histories of the fighting
countries.

The grave charges made by Lloyd George against the
Commander-in-Chief have serious and solid substance in them,
even though they are couched in unmeasured language and betray
no hint of defects in his own performance as Prime Minister.
Haig's confidence was excessive—to use no stronger term. His
biographer, Duff Cooper, admits that with him optimism was not
merely a sentiment but a policy. So it was with Wellington. Haig
lost good weather early in the year by giving way to Nivelle at
Lloyd George's behest. The blame for later delays in June and
July Haig must share with the French, who wanted a part in the
coming offensive but arrived late, and with British commanders
who secured from him postponements of the dates fixed for
attacks. It is true that Pétain preferred limited objectives to a
grand offensive, and preferred the defensive to both, at any rate
for the French, but it is also clear that in June, and later, he was
all for Haig's campaign. On 30 June he sent General Antoine to
say so, and his views had not changed in October according to
Haig's own statement later in The Times (14 November 1934):
'The mere suggestion of a pause in our attacks in the North
brought Pétain in his train to see me and beg me to put in another
effort against Passchendaele without delay.'

Lloyd George's account of the gigantic casualty figures of this campaign do not agree with those given by the official history, Lloyd George's being much larger. But whatever the correct figures were, they were very large. Were they justified? What was gained? The Germans sustained heavy losses and were prevented from seeking a decision elsewhere; the French were not seriously attacked and were given time to recover. The German official history of the war concludes its account of the campaign with these words: 'Germany had been brought near to certain destruction . . . the casualties were so great that they could no longer be covered.' The full effect of the enemy's exhaustion was to be felt in the failure of the Germans to achieve complete success in the spring of 1918. That is the answer to Lloyd George's contention in the *Memoirs* that although 'almost every effective German division on the Western Front was successfully engaged by the British . . . the German Front was never broken'.

Lloyd George's policy of a defensive on the Western Front and an attack in Italy was never properly tried out and cannot therefore be judged as he judged Passchendaele. The alternative hypothetical battles he fights on paper are always victorious. It is unlikely that the Germans would have remained inactive spectators in the West, and it is certain that they could transport help to Austria more easily and quickly than could the Allies to Italy, for their shrunken shipping was needed more and more to bring men and material from America.

There was no 'unity of command' as between the Prime Minister and the Commander-in-Chief. Neither made the best use of the great qualities of the other. The one was contemptuous of generals, the other distrusted politicians. Lloyd George was not lacking in courage, but it never fell lower than in these months. He was restless, capricious, agitated, wishing to close down the campaign in Flanders, haunted by the mounting casualties, harassed by domestic politics and press criticism. On 6 September he went for a fortnight to Criccieth, suffering from neuralgia. From there he fired conundrums at Robertson with a view to attacking Turkey. He would have liked to be rid of Haig, but could not face public opinion without an acceptable alternative.

Various rumours found currency at this time. Sir Herbert Plumer and his Chief of Staff, Sir Charles Harington, had made a good combination in winning the local battle of Messines, 'the most perfectly planned and successfully conducted operation in the whole war'. Plumer, it was whispered, was offered Robertson's post of Chief of the Imperial General Staff, and Sir H. Rawlinson that of Commander-in-Chief. Another alternative suggestion for Haig's place was Arthur Paget. But Lloyd George decided not to risk a change at the top. One army rumour credited him with fearing that Haig would be president of the new British republic! He went so far as to call in two soldiers to advise the Cabinet independently on the general military situation—not two of the most judicial minds where Haig was concerned—Lord French and Sir Henry Wilson. The experts differed, and neither clearly agreed with the Prime Minister's Eastern policy. But both favoured the appointment of a central *entente* body charged with the 'Supreme Direction' of the war. It was a defect not a merit in Lloyd George that having failed with Nivelle he did not thoroughly support Haig's policy when it was approved by the Cabinet, nor countermand it when it failed, nor finally dismiss him. But it was to his credit that out of this unhappy situation he did finally create the Supreme War Council and achieve unity of command under Foch.

HOME FRONT

However deeply Lloyd George was immersed in the major strategy of the war and however frequent his absences at conferences abroad, he watched the Home Front with a hundred eyes. The range, intensity, and speed of his activities had never been approached by any previous Prime Minister. The infinite variety of person and subject and scene suited his temperament. 'To have Ireland alone on your mind would be appalling', he remarked.

At breakfast, a simple meal at 10 Downing Street, he met an assortment of Ministers, fed their vanity, cheered their departmental efforts, composed their minor differences. At a weekly Wednesday breakfast with his Chief Whip he met Liberal and Labour Members and distributed the same judicious and discriminating attention. In speech after speech of great pictorial and inspirational power he kept before the men and women mobilized for war the supreme moral issues at stake and communicated to them his own buoyancy and faith in victory. In the opening months of 1917 his indomitable platform idealism brought him immense popularity in Britain and in France, while his fame spread to all parts of the world. But as the year wore on troubles multiplied, the prospect of triumph receded to 1918, and the outlook of the nation had to be painfully adjusted to the postponement of its hopes. The problems of shipping, food, rationing, recruiting, labour, and Ireland clamoured and contended for attention.

Lord Devonport, the Food Controller, trusted mainly to voluntary economy and set up local food committees. The production and sale of the principal foods were brought under control and profiteering was gradually eliminated. But prices rose with the scarcity of foods—over 100 per cent. above pre-war level—and in the towns queues formed outside the shops of grocers and butchers, women waiting wearily to be served often only to find supplies exhausted. Devonport resigned in June. Lord Rhondda, who succeeded him, faced a murmuring public. But he brought to the situation a skill greater than had his predecessor, for he knew how to manipulate the press and he had and used a brilliant team of civil servants: Wintour, Beveridge, Tallents, Frank Wise, and E. M. H. Lloyd. Gradually the situation was mastered. Purchasing organizations were set up abroad. Fifteen Food Commissioners covered Britain. Price fixing was applied at all stages from production to retailing, and with the adoption of systematic rationing the queues disappeared. In developing this vast machinery of minute control over the whole body of citizens, Lord Rhondda at the Food Ministry and Lord Ernle at the Ministry of Agriculture had the whole-hearted support of the Prime Minister. Their policies sometimes clashed, and Lloyd George took a malicious delight in the dialectics of the noble lords before he handed them over to the judicial and decisive mind of Lord Milner for the settlement of their disputes.

In the workshops of the country, especially those engaged in shipbuilding and engineering, there was much irritation. The outbreak of war was followed by a suspension of industrial strife and a high rate of recruitment. This concord did not last. Soon there was trouble over hours and pay and conditions. Anomalies were inevitable. Tradition prescribed a low wage and severe discipline for the soldier who faced danger and death, but for the civilian, freedom, an ever-ascending wage, and the right to strike. An immediate and complete conscription of wealth and labour in August 1914 was impracticable; what was possible and what happened was that the control of the state spread in all directions and was applied to farms and factories, mines and workshops, railways and shipyards. Wheat, sugar, coal, timber, petrol were placed under controllers. Alongside and beneath this socialistic supervision, private enterprise remained widely operative, working on Government account, with wages and profits as essential elements of the system. Profiteering, the source of chronic trouble in peace time, remained to poison relations in war. Compulsory arbitration had been substituted for strikes and lock-outs by the Munitions Act of 1915, and disputes declined in the year which followed. But in 1917 the red dawn in Russia, the machinations of shop stewards in the provinces, the bureaucratic weaving of red-tape in Whitehall, combined to produce a crop of grievances, genuine and imagined, which caused Lloyd George to take action. At the end of May he announced the Cabinet's decision to have the prevailing unrest examined by commissions of inquiry, consisting of a Labour representative, an employer, and an independent chairman for each of the eight areas into which the country was divided. The commissioners were well chosen and they reported, with unusual dispatch, within five weeks. They recommended, *inter alia*, an immediate reduction in the price of food through Government subsidies, and the increase of self-government in each trade by means of councils. But the sedative effect of the reports was perhaps even more important than any specific recommendations. They demonstrated that the overwhelming majority of the working class was determined to go through with the war.

In July Lloyd George made a number of ministerial changes. He brought Sir Edward Carson into the War Cabinet and put Sir Eric Geddes in his place at the Admiralty; Churchill, richly equipped with administrative gifts and imagination and boldness, came back to office as Minister of Munitions; Edwin Montagu became Secretary of State for India in place of Austen Chamberlain, and Dr. Addison was given the new post of Minister of Reconstruction. This committee had been set up early in the year with Lloyd George as chairman and Edwin Montagu as vice-chairman. At its first meeting, on 17 February, Lloyd George spoke impressively about the great task confronting the committee, his high hopes for it, the need of painting a new picture of Britain with fewer grey colours in it, the duty of the Government to be ready when the Armistice came with schemes for the reform

DAME MARGARET LLOYD GEORGE

of local government, land, health, and trade policy. On 10 July
Montagu went to the India Office, and was succeeded by Addison.
The members of the earlier body were politely thanked for their
services and discharged. The emphasis had shifted from projects
of social reform to the difficult and dangerous operation of con-
verting the industrial war machine into an instrument of peace.

At the end of July Riddell took a house, Great Walstead, Sussex,
for a month so that Lloyd George could get 'some short holidays
and at the same time keep in touch with his work'. Here the Prime
Minister received his colleagues and secretaries, French and Italian
Ministers, and the soldiers, Robertson, Maurice, Henry Wilson,
and Lord French. In October the problem of providing rest and
refreshment for Prime Ministers was handsomely solved by Sir
Arthur Lee (later Lord Lee of Fareham) who presented the estate
of Chequers to be their official country residence.

Chequers was a Tudor mansion with rich parliamentary associations and a name reaching back to the Keeper of the King's
Exchequer under Henry II. It is situated in the Chilterns, less than
forty miles from Downing Street, and the adjoining Coombe Hill,
to which Lloyd George was fond of walking, commands one of
the finest prospects in England. It is in Buckinghamshire, 'perhaps
the most political of English counties', the subject of one of Rosebery's finished orations, and the centre of a patch of country made
famous by John Hampden, Burke, George Canning, and Disraeli
(who took his title from the village of Beaconsfield). To this welcoming house with its long gallery, its Cromwellian relics, and its
art treasures, Lloyd George and—in a later war—Churchill were
to have constant recourse while Prime Ministers: both turned it
into a hive of activity at the week-ends. The only Prime Minister
to whom it made no appeal was Bonar Law; perhaps it was Neville
Chamberlain who both cared and did most for it, its trees and
shrubs and birds.

It was at the Chequers house-warming on 13 and 14 October,
when Painlevé, Franklin Bouillon, and Foch were of the party with
Smuts, Balfour, and Hankey, that Lloyd George first ventilated to
the Frenchmen his notion of an Inter-Allied Supreme Council at
Versailles. It was on this occasion that Foch commented in the
visitors' book: 'Les affaires de l'Angleterre iront encore mieux
quand son Premier Ministre pourra se reposer à Chequers.'

It was on 2 November of this year (1917) that Balfour, then

Foreign Secretary, in a letter to Lord Rothschild, made on behalf
of the Government the famous declaration in favour of the establishment in Palestine of a national home for the Jewish people, 'it
being clearly understood that nothing shall be done which may
prejudice the civil and religious rights of the existing non-Jewish
communities in Palestine or the rights and political status enjoyed by Jews in any other country'. Lloyd George in the *Memoirs*
makes the origin of the declaration turn on the services of Dr.
Weizmann as chemist, but Lord Samuel has qualified this in his
own *Memoirs*.

Long before he [Lloyd George] had to cope with a shortage of
acetone he had taken a close interest in the Palestine question and
had shown a full understanding of its significance. From the beginning he had been unwavering in his support of the policy that was
ultimately embodied in the Balfour Declaration. As Prime Minister
his approval ensured its adoption. Afterwards, at the Peace Conference in Paris and subsequently, his tenacity was to carry it through
many difficulties and over many obstacles. And it was Weizmann the
enthusiast, Weizmann the diplomatist who is entitled to high credit
whenever the story is told; Weizmann the chemist only in a very
minor degree.[8]

Indeed, as early as 1915, when Samuel had circulated a memorandum in which he advocated encouragement for Jewish settlement and a British Protectorate for Palestine, Reading had written
to him (5 February 1915): 'I had a talk to Lloyd George about the
matter before his departure for Paris. He is certainly inclined to
the sympathetic side. Your proposal appeals to the poetic and
imaginative as well as to the romantic and religious qualities of
his mind.'[8]

Throughout this first year of his Premiership, Lloyd George
did not minimize the importance of keeping his Liberal followers
together in some sort of party organization and of providing it
with an ambitious programme of radical reform. Post-war political
strategy was frequently discussed with intimate advisers like
Riddell, Christopher (now Lord) Addison, and Sir Frederick
Guest, and with less intimate groups of Liberal Ministers and
Peers. Lloyd George was increasingly conscious of his dependence

[8] Viscount Samuel, *Memoirs*, pp. 143, 147.

on his Tory supporters, and disposed to conciliate them perhaps more than was necessary in view of his strong position in the country. He thought Asquith was playing a 'deep game', and he was determined that should an election come he would demand of his own followers unqualified support against Asquith. Churchill, on the other hand, at this time thought an attempt should be made to bring Asquith back into the fold. He was not encouraged; neither was Lord Derby when later in the year he proposed Asquith as Ambassador to Paris. The Liberal rift continued.

PEACE OVERTURES

At intervals throughout 1917 the enemy had made furtive attempts to discover on what terms the Allies would make peace. Austria, Turkey, and Bulgaria became more and more desirous of peace and less and less sure of Germany's invincibility. On 24 March 1917 the Emperor Charles of Austria addressed a very secret letter to his brother-in-law, Prince Sixte of Bourbon, an officer in the Belgian army, for transmission of its contents to Poincaré.

Lloyd George was brought into the talks about peace initiated by this communication in April, but is at pains to stress that their direction remained in French hands. Such was the weariness of the combatants on both sides that the utmost care had to be taken to prevent leakages which would weaken the people's will to war and might imperil the life of the Austrian Emperor. Sixte asked M. Paul Cambon, the French Ambassador in London, for some information about Lloyd George, as his discretion was doubted, and got this reply:

He is a Welshman, not an Englishman. In fact, he is the reverse of an Englishman: enthusiastic, bright, quick-witted, and unsettled. An Englishman never goes back on what he has once said; Lloyd George is apt to perform evolutions, his words have not always the weight of a Balfour's or a Bonar Law's. On the other hand, he has some qualities of priceless value at the moment; among others that of not being obsessed by the fetish of Constitutionalism. Mr. Asquith would never have consented to discuss a matter of this sort without telling his Cabinet, whereas Mr. Lloyd George has solemnly promised not to mention it to any of his colleagues. He will say a few words only to the King, and get his promise of secrecy also.[9]

[9] G. de Manteyer, *Austria's Peace Offer*, p. 105.

These promises were strictly kept. Lloyd George had several interviews with Sixte in Paris and London, and on 23 May accompanied the Prince to an audience accorded by King George.

The concessions suggested by Austria were chiefly at the expense of Germany, and included the restoration of Belgian independence and the return of Alsace-Lorraine to France, while other terms were not ruled out, such as the recognition of Serbia or a southern Slavonic state, so long as safeguards against terrorist societies were provided, and the ceding of the Trentino or, alternatively, Cilicia to Italy.

Lloyd George met Ribot at Folkestone on 11 April, and it was agreed that, without betraying Charles, Italy's attitude and claims must be ascertained. This was done on 19 April at St. Jean de Maurienne, where Ribot and Lloyd George met Sonnino. Under pretext of discussing rumoured Austrian peace moves in Switzerland, they found out the strong objections of the Italian Foreign Minister to such overtures. Next day Lloyd George told Sixte that the claims of Italy could not be set aside and that the *entente* could not, in honour, make peace without her. On 22 April M. Jules Cambon, on behalf of the French Government, saw Sixte and formally declined the Emperor's offer; but Sixte persevered and conversations continued until the end of June, when finding his efforts useless he returned to his regiment.

Meanwhile, it had been discovered that secret but abortive advances had been made to Austria by a faction on the Italian side. Lloyd George believed that those then in charge of French policy feared Italy would drop out of the war once peace was made with Austria. He had all along been keener than Ribot to conduct these secret negotiations, and was pursuing a double offensive, diplomatic and military. The French view that Italy 'could not be allowed to get the Trentino until France had secured possession of Alsace-Lorraine' plainly made any separate peace impossible. Lloyd George regretted the failure of Sixte's negotiations, for he believed the efforts of the Emperor Charles to have been sincere and a genuine attempt to safeguard his 'ramshackle' empire from vassalage to Germany, in the event of a Prussian, and dismemberment in the event of an Allied, victory.

In July the German Government fell into the hands of the Junkers, with Michaelis, the Prussian Food Commissioner, becoming Chancellor. On 19 July the Reichstag passed a Peace

Resolution vague in sentiment but concrete as to German aims. Michaelis by his interpretation of the resolution reserved his right to make any peace the Imperial Government liked. Lloyd George regarded his speech as ominous because it reaffirmed the supremacy of the Imperial power as against the Reichstag and the inviolability for all time of the frontiers of Germany. The first principle made it clear to the Allies that they would not be making peace with a democracy, the second recalled the pretext used in annexing Alsace-Lorraine in 1871 and in invading Belgium.

Lloyd George regarded all advances made directly or indirectly by Germany as suspect. He believed that those who made them had no real power in their own country; that the offers were only permitted in order to bring about division and confusion in Allied councils, and that the military would have welcomed an early, even if inconclusive, peace only in order to exploit the experience of the war for waging a future, decisive struggle.

The next move was made by the Pope. On 16 August he appealed to the belligerent nations to make peace, and he raised the question of Belgium. Michaelis did not disclose to his colleagues, nor even until 5 September to Kühlmann, his Foreign Secretary, the fact that a British inquiry about Germany's intentions with regard to Belgium had been received via the Vatican.

Next Kühlmann, through Brussels and Madrid, tried to establish contact with Britain. Balfour, British Foreign Secretary, told Lloyd George that he was inclined to think Kühlmann's approach, the first to be received through the orthodox channel of a neutral Foreign Office, a genuine one; and the Cabinet took his advice to refer the matter to a conference of ambassadors of the Great Allied Powers instead of acting alone. Lloyd George saw M. Painlevé, who on 8 September had succeeded Ribot as French Prime Minister, at Boulogne and was told that the German peace offer was serious. On this account, the British were in favour of meeting an exalted German emissary in Switzerland, as suggested, but the French were opposed on the ground that if it became known that an offer to restore Alsace-Lorraine to France and its independence to Belgium had been made, the French nation would not go on fighting and the war would end with the military power of Germany unbroken.

Meanwhile, in Berlin, the Kaiser had summoned a Crown Council on 11 September to discuss the Papal note and to resolve the question of Belgium. Soldiers and admirals favoured the retention of Liège and the Flanders coast. The discussion was indecisive. Michaelis and Kühlmann dispatched a courteous reply to the Pope on 19 September in which no mention was made of Belgium. Ludendorff's record of what passed between the Kaiser, Chancellor Michaelis, and the military chiefs at this time, from which Lloyd George quotes in his *Memoirs*, shows how far they had been from contemplating an independent Belgium or a lasting peace.

When the Allied ambassadors met in Paris on 8 October they approved the sending of a reply to the intermediaries simply to the effect that the British Government would be willing to receive any communication the German Government might desire to make and to discuss it with their Allies. No reply was received to this telegram. On 9 October Kühlmann said in the Reichstag that with the exception of the French demand for Alsace-Lorraine there was no absolute impediment to peace by negotiation. On 10 October Lloyd George commented that no statement could be more calculated to prolong the war. His own confidence in the ultimate victory of the Allies and his conviction that the satisfaction of their war aims was not in sight decided him to parley no further with the enemy.

On 29 November 1917 a letter appeared in the *Daily Telegraph* from Lord Lansdowne, a Conservative Peer who had been Foreign Secretary, advocating peace by negotiation. We have seen that he had privately circulated a similar document, prompted by Lloyd George's 'Knock-Out-Blow' interview. What made Lord Lansdowne imagine that at such a moment Germany would pay heed to terms acceptable to the Allies it is hard to say: Russia was on the point of making the peace, or rather the capitulation, of Brest-Litovsk, and German divisions from Russia were reaching the Western Front; the corn and oil of Rumania were at Germany's disposal; Italy was being defeated; the U-boat campaign had not been completely checked; there had been no breakthrough on the Flanders Front. Lansdowne's letter had a mixed but on the whole unfavourable press in Britain, and the Government hastened to dissociate itself from it.

Lloyd George replied to this letter on 14 December in a speech at Gray's Inn, and said that it had brought a group of persons into the open who believed in a half-way house between victory and defeat. To end a war, embarked upon to enforce a treaty, without reparation for the infringement of a treaty, merely by entering into a new, more sweeping treaty, would be indeed a farce in the setting of a tragedy.

Four days later, in response to an Austrian approach, General Smuts left on a secret mission to Switzerland where he discussed the making of peace with Count Albert Mensdorff, the former Austro-Hungarian Ambassador to London, who was acting on behalf of Count Czernin, the Foreign Minister. At the same time, and also in Switzerland, Philip Kerr saw Dr. Parodi, a leader of the minority party in Turkey which was favourable to the *entente*, but Parodi could not speak for the Turkish Government. Smuts soon realized that Mensdorff had no power or desire to negotiate a separate peace and wished merely to act as intermediary between Great Britain and Germany.

The series of secret conversations from March onwards had proved inconclusive, but all pointed, as did the Lansdowne letter, to the need for some fresh authoritative proclamation of the terms on which Germany could have peace. Lloyd George had been quite willing to meet peace advances half-way if business was meant, but he never let go his grip on the levers directing the engines of war. While ready to welcome any messenger with tidings of peace, he had to uphold the fighting spirit of the troops and the endurance of the toilers in field and factory; nor could he forget the tens of thousands of bereaved and sorrowing families.

He decided to tell the world anew what Britain was fighting for, and to make this all-important declaration to an audience of trade-union delegates attending a Labour conference at the Caxton Hall, London, on 5 January 1918. He prepared the speech with characteristic thoroughness, and obtained in advance the general approval not only of Cabinet and Dominion Ministers, but of Asquith and Grey.

He repudiated predatory aims. He dealt positively with Belgium, Poland, Turkey, and the German colonies. Referring to Alsace-Lorraine, and pointing to M. Albert Thomas in the audience, he cried out: 'We mean to stand by the French democracy to the death in the demand they make for a reconsideration of the great wrong of 1871'—a perfect example of his habit of mingling passion and caution. He concluded with three conditions which must be fulfilled: the re-establishment of sanctity of treaties; a territorial settlement based on the right of self-determination or the consent of the governed; and, finally, the setting up of an international organization to limit the burden of armaments and diminish the probability of war. This declaration, which in many respects was akin to President Wilson's later peace proposals, had an enthusiastic reception, especially in France. In Britain it united the nation behind the Prime Minister.

Three days later, and quite independently, President Wilson announced to Congress his famous Fourteen Points, which were animated by an even loftier idealism than had inspired the British Prime Minister.

Count Hertling, now German Imperial Chancellor, in Berlin and Count Czernin in Vienna both replied to the two speeches on the same day, 24 January. Hertling's reply, covering the Fourteen Points, was equivocal and governed by his view that the military situation would never be so favourable to the Central Powers as then. Count Czernin in a friendlier tone also went through the Fourteen Points in detail and expressed himself as in agreement with them in the main, but while more civil than Hertling he was actually no less adamant about terms. On 12 February Lloyd George declared in Parliament that the Government had examined the two statements with a real desire to come 'somewhere near a basis of agreement', but could find none.

Meanwhile, attempts at fresh secret negotiations were renewed by Austria, and Lloyd George learned that Czernin would be willing to meet him in Switzerland. The Prime Minister was still hankering after a separate peace with Austria and was eager to go, but he was restrained by the Foreign Office who doubted Czernin's sincerity. On 9 March, after many delays, General Smuts and Philip Kerr set out for Switzerland and met Skrzynski, the Austrian emissary. The envoys returned and reported their impression that Czernin had changed his mind, probably because of Russia's collapse and Germany's progress in the West, and that he now believed that it might pay better to treat with the American President. This final effort at a separate peace proved fruitless and no further meeting was held. On 21 March Germany advanced on the Western Front, not with buttered words but with guns and lethal gas, and staked everything on a last bid for victory.

Lloyd George attributed the military failures of 1915, 1916, and

1917 fundamentally to the lack of a single front and unity of command. Each Allied Commander-in-Chief was responsible for his own sector, while the statesmen were assumed to survey the struggle as a whole. In practice this meant the absence of anything that could be called united strategy. The hurried and swollen international conferences had done little more, and often less, than synchronize Allied operations. The effective unity of the Central Empires and Turkey, governed by a treaty which declared that the initiative should be in the hands of Germany, was opposed by four governments and four general staffs with no real coordination of effort. This contrast had long obsessed Lloyd George, and he was now determined on setting up an inter-Allied body with its own staff which should include not only military and naval advisers but civilian experts competent to speak on man-power, railways, shipping, finance, blockade, and diplomacy. He bent his great powers of persuasion and his manœuvring skill to this end. He was hampered by the recent discredited experiment of placing British armies temporarily under the French High Command in the Nivelle campaign, an arrangement which he had himself supported. He was also hindered at every step by Sir William Robertson, the official military adviser of the Cabinet, who saw in the new plan the emergence of a rival authority.

On 3 September 1917 Lloyd George addressed an important letter to President Wilson proposing an Allied Joint Council and touching delicately on American participation. He sounded Lord French and Sir Henry Wilson, both of whom supported the immediate formation of a Supreme Council for the superior direction of the war. Similar ideas were occurring at this time to French Ministers. On 30 October Lloyd George wrote to M. Painlevé, the French Premier, on the lines of his letter to President Wilson, proposing an inter-Allied general staff to advise their governments on how to win the war. Painlevé and Pétain approved the scheme, and the British War Cabinet accepted it in principle. The new—primarily political—body was to be composed of the Prime Minister of each country, a member of each Cabinet, and a military member.

Lloyd George then hurried away to a conference at Rapallo, taking Smuts and Sir Henry Wilson with him, to deal with the situation created by Germany's staggering blow which had sent Italy reeling—he remarked to his travelling companions that the Allies were 'within a shade of final disaster'. At the Rapallo

Conference he made the fullest use of the Italian disaster at Caporetto to obtain support for his inter-Allied council. Its constitution was there and then (7 November) agreed between the British, French, and Italian Governments. Cadorna was transferred from his Italian command and made a military representative on the new council, with Wilson for Britain, Foch (later Weygand) for France, and, later, Bliss for America. Versailles was chosen as the place of meeting.

On 12 November Painlevé invited a distinguished company to luncheon in the banqueting-hall of the Ministry of War in Paris. At his table sat Lloyd George and Winston Churchill. In solemn and sombre tones and with brutal and deliberate frankness Lloyd George delivered a speech in which he attacked Allied strategy and the lack of Allied unity. The speech, which was soundly critical in substance and which announced the establishment of the Supreme War Council, was highly provocative. He cast such aspersions on British generals that when it was published the immediate fall of the Government was not only desired but expected in some quarters.

A few days later, Colonel House and General Bliss were instructed by President Wilson to attend the Supreme War Council. All this instant and pervasive activity, public and private, was characteristic of Lloyd George once his mind was made up. No likely source of support or success was left unused directly by himself or indirectly by his colleagues and secretaries.

Meanwhile, Sir William Robertson and other opponents and critics had not been idle. Robertson had powerful friends in and out of the Cabinet, and Lloyd George had perforce to tread warily when launching a scheme to which his Chief-of-Staff was unalterably opposed. There was a motionless crocodile 'waiting and seeing' on the banks of the Thames for a chance to snap its jaws on the nimble goat, but 'the goat, leaping yards in the air, escaped as by a miracle', writes Ian Colvin in his *Life of Carson*.

On 19 November a full-dress debate was staged in the House of Commons, and was the scene of one of Lloyd George's great parliamentary triumphs. Floors and galleries were crowded. Asquith's lifeless attack, in which, according to *The Times*, he dealt with secondary points and minor pleas in cold, forensic fashion, contrasted sharply with the pugnacity of the Prime Minister who, beginning in slow and measured tones in the manner of the great

Welsh preachers, rose imperceptibly until he was 'playing with the whole gamut of human emotions', and the House 'rocked with joy'. He retracted nothing of his Paris speech, he softened nothing, he apologized for nothing. He had been deliberately disagreeable all round. He had made up his mind—no doubt not for the first time—that unless some change were effected he could 'no longer remain responsible for a war direction doomed to disaster for lack of unity'.

In the form agreed at Rapallo the Supreme Allied Council func-tioned for a few months, gathering a staff and preparing a series of notes on problems of strategy. 'Nine-tenths of the detailed work of the inter-Allied Staff was initiated and carried out in the British section', wrote L. S. Amery in *Blackwood's Magazine.* Two more conferences, one at Doullens and one at Beauvais, the supersession of Robertson, endless talk and, above all, the hammer blow of the German offensive in March 1918 were necessary before, on 14 April, Foch was acclaimed Commander-in-Chief of the Allied armies in France.

OUTLOOK FOR 1918

The final defection of Russia as a fighting factor in the war had to be accepted towards the end of 1917 and profoundly influenced the prospects and plans of the Allies for 1918. The enemy's Western Front would inevitably be reinforced by divisions brought from Russia faster than American troops could be brought across the Atlantic; this would incline Germany to seek a decision in 1918, while to defer a decision to 1919 would better suit the Allies. Ever since the previous autumn when the decisive failure in Flanders became clear, Lloyd George had desired to see an offensive staged against Turkey, but was opposed by his own generals. Nor were Haig and Pétain agreed during these months of dispersion of command. At first Haig favoured an offensive in France in the spring, but as the German preparations accumulated he seemed sometimes to veer towards Pétain's preference for limited objectives until the Americans arrived. Foch was opposed to both generals, and advocated combined forces in one general plan to prepare for and fight the expected offensive action. Robert-son supported a defensive policy in the distant theatres if only to save shipping, which should be used to the uttermost to bring American troops to France. The divergence of view of the Prime

Minister and his Chief-of-Staff was theoretically solved when Clemenceau, presiding at the meeting of the Supreme War Council on 1 December 1917, invited the permanent military advisers to study the whole situation and make recommendations. They did in fact—much to Lloyd George's gratification—give their support to an attack on Turkey by Allied forces in Palestine and Mesopotamia, but on the understanding that the British Government had 'no intention of diverting forces from the Western Front or in any way relaxing its efforts to maintain the safety of that front . . . '.[10] On the Western Front the permanent military advisers were inclined to compromise between a defensive policy in 1918 and victory in 1919. It was these hesitations which stung Foch, the official historian reports, into urging 'a concerted offensive aiming at a decision'.

A prolonged cause of friction between the Allied commanders during the winter 1917–18 arose from the demand of the French for an extension of the line held by the British. For this there were sound political and military reasons. Men up to fifty years of age had been called up in France. The French losses in the earlier phases of the war had greatly outnumbered those of the British. They were holding a line roughly stretching for 350 miles, against about 100 miles held by the British; but 'activity' or 'quiescence' rather than length of front were the criteria which should be applied. The British Government in September 1917 accepted the French claim in principle, and it was left to Haig and Pétain to fix the amount of the extension and the time at which it should take place. Haig agreed to extend his right some twenty-eight miles by the last week of November. Delays in giving effect to this arrangement led to a demand by Clemenceau for a still further extension, and brought about threats of resignation from both Haig and Clemenceau. The matter was referred to Versailles. The permanent military advisers reported in favour of an extension to about half-way between the two points. At the end of January, Smuts, who had visited the Western Front, reported to Lloyd George against any extension beyond the point Haig had agreed to. To go beyond, urged Smuts, would be straining the army too far, would imperil the preparation of defence works and the provision of much needed rest for the troops. Primed with the views

[10] Official History of the War, *Military Operations, France and Belgium, 1918,* i. 75.

of Smuts, Lloyd George at the meeting of the Supreme War Council on 1 February came to the aid of Haig in a speech of great argumentative force. Haig finally accepted the compromise proposed by the permanent military advisers, subject to his agreement with Pétain on the method of carrying it out; but this conference never took place, and Barisis, Haig's original point, remained the junction of the armies until the great German offensive in March.

The Supreme War Council met at Versailles on 30 January 1918, and accepted in principle the treatment of the whole Allied forces in France as a single strategic field of action and the creation of an Allied Mobile Central or General Reserve, as it was variously called. Implied in this, if at first covered up, was the creation of a single Commander-in-Chief.

The creation of an Allied Central Reserve and the appointment of a generalissimo on the Western Front were sound and proper aims which the Prime Minister had long pursued. He was opposed by Robertson, his Chief-of-Staff, who had the support of Haig and Plumer and of Asquith. In the Cabinet, Lloyd George's strongest backing came from Milner. Derby was resigning 'twice a day' on the Robertson issue. Haig had not approved of the new system, but his constitutional objection had been satisfied by making the British military member at Versailles a member of the Army Council and his instructions 'lawful commands' within the meaning of the Army Act. Robertson would only accept a Versailles council which was composed of or was subordinate to the Chiefs-of-Staff. Lloyd George thought of several alternative plans: (1) to send Robertson to a Home Command and replace him by Plumer; or (2) to replace Robertson by Haig, and Haig by Plumer; or (3) to send Robertson to Versailles and make Henry Wilson C.I.G.S. Robertson was offered the third choice and refused it; and as the official historian of the war records:

On the 16th February, without his knowledge, the Official Press Bureau issued a notice that the Government had accepted Sir William Robertson's resignation as C.I.G.S.; on the 18th, General Wilson was ordered to assume the duties of C.I.G.S., and General Robertson to take over from him the Eastern Command, which had been vacant since the former had gone to Rapallo.[11]

Thus ended the triangular conflict. It had long been evident

[11] Ibid., i. 88.

that Lloyd George preferred to work with the sparkling and opti-mistic Wilson rather than with the gruff and grunting Robertson. Robertson belonged, with Haig and Jellicoe, to the inarticulate. All three were alike incapable of instructing a Cabinet in the prin-ciples of strategy, displayed no magic or brilliance in exposition or creative imagination in planning. These were gifts to which Henry Wilson had a better claim. He had an engaging *bonhomie*, a trenchant vocabulary, and a power of surmounting friction with badinage of a tonic quality which commended him to Lloyd George. But Wilson's reputation as a consummate intriguer made his choice for the position at Versailles and then as C.I.G.S. un-popular with the soldiers. If Wilson was a river, Robertson was a rock. Lacking originality, he believed in a few simple and clear ideas: the concentration of force on one Front, a war of attrition, and no side-shows. He excelled in organization and staff work. Lloyd George and Robertson parted 'with expressions of great kindliness'. Years later they met for the last time at a great peace meeting presided over by Robertson at which Lloyd George spoke. Lloyd George had often complained of the failure of the army authorities to promote talent from the ranks; his stoutest oppo-nent in this war was the one and only British soldier who had ever risen through all the ranks from trooper to Field-Marshal.

In these opening months of 1918 Haig, apt to take too optimistic a view of the deterioration of German soldiers and civilians, held that the enemy would attempt a knock-out blow and would not be 'able to continue the War if he failed to gain a decision in 1918'. And the supreme question in the minds of statesmen and generals at this time was: Would the 'magical operation' of the transfusion of (American) blood take place in time to reanimate the exhausted troops of the Allies? It did.

National suspicions and jealousies were rife in the early months of 1918, and Clemenceau was suspected sometimes of desiring to act as generalissimo himself—French generals were less indepen-dent than British, and it was thought that Clemenceau would impose his will at Versailles on Foch through Weygand. Lloyd George now proposed that Foch be Chairman of a War Board, and he did this in a speech which brought tears into the eyes of his audience and left Foch dumb. By this attempt to unify the General Reserves and place them under a single direction he thought he avoided the drawbacks and obtained the advantages of a generalissimo. In fact he did neither. The unmoved British Field-Marshal put an awkward question in constitutional procedure. Haig wanted to know, and that in writing, 'by what channel' he was to receive orders from the new body. Lloyd George replied that he and Milner were acting on behalf of the British Government. Haig's intervention foreshadowed his later refusal (4 March) to contribute divisions (other than those in Italy) to the Versailles Reserve. In the meantime he made with Pétain a vague and loose pact of mutual assistance. For Haig it must be said that his own divisions were seriously below strength, and that at this same moment he was taking over several miles of the French line. Hence, when the Supreme War Council met in London on 14 March, Lloyd George had to admit: 'Though myself a warm advocate of the scheme of a General Reserve, I have come to the conclusion in view of the exceptional concentration against us that it would be very difficult for Field-Marshal Haig to spare the necessary reserves.' This tactful avoidance of a collision with Haig was due to Lloyd George's knowledge that not only Haig but Clemenceau and Pétain were now opposed to the General Reserve. Neither Frenchman was in favour of an army of manœuvre commanded by Foch, Gascon by birth and Catholic by faith. Lloyd George gave away all he had fought for—but only for a few days.

On 21 March the long-expected German offensive was launched near St. Quentin; the British line was overrun and the situation swiftly became critical. Milner hurried across to France on 24 March, and on 25 March agreed with Clemenceau that Haig and Pétain must throw in their reserves to stop the breach between the British and French armies—the decision which Foch had sought power to execute when he pleaded two months earlier for a single plan of action for the two armies. On the 24th in a message to the War Office Haig suggested that Foch should be given the Supreme Command. A conference of British and French representatives assembled at Doullens on the 26th, and an agreement initiated by Milner and supported by Haig was reached: Foch should co-ordinate the action of the Allied armies on the Western Front, and the British Commander-in-Chief would furnish him with all necessary information.

No American had taken part in this consultation, but Pershing later accepted the agreement signed by Clemenceau and Milner. Strictly interpreted, Foch could only consult and advise and persuade, he could not command. This halting compromise lasted just over a week, and on 3 April at Beauvais Foch was entrusted with the strategic direction of military operations, subject to each Commander-in-Chief having a right of appeal to his government. This was the nearest approach to unified command achieved in the war. That it was then accepted 'not for the purpose of winning victory but to prevent irretrievable defeat' is the verdict of General Bliss, who was present. And the British official historian, summing up the crisis, concludes: 'Thus the dangerous situation, mainly brought about, first, by the British Government consenting to the extension of the British front without providing the reinforcements necessary for the purpose; and, secondly, by General Pétain contemplating the separation of the French from the British Army, was in a fair way to be remedied.'

VICTORY

On New Year's Day the Prime Minister issued an appeal to the nation:

To every civilian I would say: 'Your firing line is the works or the office in which you do your bit; the shop or the kitchen in which you spend or save; the bank or the post-office in which you buy your bonds. To reach that firing line and to become an active combatant yourself there are no communication trenches to grope along, no barrage to face, no horrors, no wounds. The road of duty and patriotism is clear before you; follow it, and it will lead ere long to safety for our people and victory for our cause.' [12]

On 17 January Lloyd George made a speech on the Military Service Bill with great success. 'I really think I did fairly well', he told Riddell, 'they stood up when I left the House.' It was his fifty-fifth birthday.

It was this question of man-power which was one of the causes of the acute friction between the Prime Minister and Haig, his Commander-in-Chief. In December 1917 Lloyd George had presided over a Cabinet Man-power Committee which examined and compared the needs of army, navy, munitions, food, coal, shipping assistance to the Allies, and the maintenance of the export trade. This was a vastly wider field than was present in the minds of the generals when they made a gross demand for an additional million and a quarter men in 1918. The Prime Minister had to hold firmly

[12] 'Appeal to the Nation' speech by Lloyd George, New Year's Day, 1918.

in his mind at once and always these competing claims upon British resources and make the most provident use of them in organizing the total national effort. He was dealing with a country to which universal military service had long been repugnant, and he had to carry opinion with him at every turn of the recruiting screw. The calling up of thousands of young men under the Man-power Bill, men who had been hitherto exempt and many of whom were earning high wages, was very unpopular, but ultimately the trade unions concerned co-operated in making the act effective.

In examining the demands of the generals, Lloyd George was influenced by his settled conviction that the rate of wastage and the number of casualties on the British Front in France was un-justified and excessive. Riddell, in his *War Diary*, reports: 'He had asked Pétain how we could cut down our casualties. Pétain, who is a blunt sort of man, replied:"By getting better Generals!" Our casualties are 48 per cent. while those of the French are only 25 per cent.' The Cabinet Committee decided that after meeting the needs of navy, air force, and shipbuilding it would be possible to find a total less than one-third that of the number asked for. The Cabinet Committee further laid it down that the number of battalions in a division should be reduced from twelve to nine, which would increase the proportion of guns per thousand in-fantry. Foch favoured the Cabinet's policy. Haig was opposed to it and preferred the alternative of reducing the number of divi-sions. The Cabinet had its way; the battalions were disbanded and the reorganization was completed by 4 March. The energy devoted to it might have been better applied to fortifying the primitive and neglected defences of the Fifth Army, soon to be overwhelmed.

Lloyd George is charged by his critics with retaining an unduly large home-defence force because of his fear of invasion. But he never seriously entertained any such fear. He maintained that the men kept at home were required for essential services. An expert estimate was made, and it was decided that proper defen-sive precautions could still be maintained with the reduction of the home-defence force by four divisions and the release of about 40,000 men for employment in France. To the further charge that in fact half a million men were hurried across to France between March and August 1918 to counter the terrific German onset, Lloyd George replies in the *Memoirs* that the life-and-death crisis alone made this possible. 'We slashed desperately at some of our vital war industries . . . which nothing but the need for restoring confidence in a momentary panic created by a great defeat could have justified.'

On the other hand, he slurs over the fact that on 1 January 1918 there were almost a million men employed in theatres other than the Western Front, and that the movement of these troops from East to West would not be prevented by psychological complexes at home. In fact, during the critical months of 1918 about 100,000 of these men were brought to France, and could presumably have been brought before the opening of the German attack on 21 March had the Government so willed.

February 1918 was a troublous month for the British Prime Minister. The strain of solving numerous problems, personal and administrative, could not be evaded, and this lowered his vitality, deprived him even of sleep, and caused much vacillation and a momentary loss of nerve. The dark menace of the great German offensive was casting deepening shadows along the Front in France. The advocates of a negotiated peace were growing bolder. The convention which for six months had been attempting to make Irishmen agree was breaking down and bringing the dreaded conscription issue nearer. The scarcity of most foodstuffs continued, and food controls had to be extended. Churchill's loosely defined bonus of $12\frac{1}{2}$ per cent. to munition workers caused widespread demands for wage increases which were difficult to resist and led to some strikes. Priceless weeks were lost in disposing of Robertson and by the failure of Allied generals to pool their strategy and resources. Lloyd George himself, using methods which to him doubtless seemed simple and direct but to others complex and crooked, was not without blame. He neither sacked his C.I.G.S. nor trusted him. Strong as his position was in the country, he became the target of effective criticism because he was suspected of trespassing on the territory of the generals and of using the press to undermine their authority, for four press Lords held office in his Government—Beaverbrook, Northcliffe, Rhondda, and Rothermere.

GERMAN SPRING OFFENSIVES

On 21 March 1918 the long-expected German massed attack, which Churchill has described as the greatest onslaught in the history of the world, opened in darkness and fog at 4.40 in the morning. The bombardment lasted with varying intensity for five hours. The enemy had assembled over a million men, equipped with guns, mortars, corroding mustard gas, and smoke shells, with food supplies and medical services on a corresponding scale—'one of the most remarkable pieces of staff work that has ever been accomplished'. The supreme objective of the offensive was to 'roll up and smash the British and the Belgians'. Ludendorff's strategical adviser Wetzell (whom Lloyd George was to meet between the wars in 1936 at Heidelberg) warned him that methods which held good against Russians and Italians would not necessarily succeed against British and French. The Kaiser, with Ludendorff and Hindenburg, watched the mighty battle from the neighbourhood of St. Quentin.

The Versailles Council had expected the blow would fall simultaneously in Champagne—as Pétain thought—and against the Arras sector. Both were wrong. The enemy had taken elaborate and successful measures to mislead. The initial attack was directed against the whole front of the Fifth Army, the centre of the Third Army, and a short stretch of the First Army—altogether a line of sixty to seventy miles. Forty-three enemy divisions were massed against the thirteen and one-third divisions and three cavalry divisions of the Fifth Army, and nineteen against the eight divisions forming the centre of the Third Army. Pétain's tardiness in coming to Haig's active assistance in these opening days meant that the struggle was almost entirely between the British and Germans. The upshot of a fortnight's fighting (21 March to 5 April) was the penetration of the British Front to a maximum depth of forty miles. This penetration had the fortunate effect of shifting the weight of the attack from a point behind which the British were hemmed in by the coast, where elastic defence was impossible, to a space which was both nearer the French and afforded more room for manœuvre. It was this contrast in elbow-room which had been at the back of Haig's original distribution of his forces— a distribution severely criticized by Lloyd George in the *Memoirs*. Gough, the unlucky commander of the Fifth Army, has recorded his opinion that Haig's policy was absolutely sound, though he 'ran it a bit fine' in the number of divisions allotted for his task. Sir J. E. Edmonds sums up, in an article on the Fifth Army: 'Never in history has an Army come under such unmerited criticism—the deeds of the Fifth Army should have gone down to posterity as well sung as those of the Old Contemptibles of 1914.'

The second phase of the onslaught, the battles in the plain of the River Lys, opened on 9 April and continued for three weeks, during which the enemy achieved a maximum penetration of twelve miles, but failed to capture any one of three crucial towns —Arras or Béthune or Hazebrouck—and were finally repulsed in their attack on Kemmel Hill. These results against immense superiority of numbers were only achieved by the utmost bravery and steadfastness. Foch had decided that his supreme objective must be to preserve the union of the French and British armies, and to secure this he had to denude and imperil Haig's defensive forces in Flanders and thus conform to what Ludendorff desired. It was feared that the Germans would be in Calais in three weeks. On 11 April, in London, Sir William Robertson remarked to Colonel Repington that 'we *might* lose the war if we let go the Channel ports, but we *must* lose it if we are separated from the French'. On 12 April Henry Wilson in a telegram to Foch raised the question of flooding the country round Dunkirk. And on this same day Haig issued his famous Order of the Day: 'There is no other course open to us but to fight it out. Every position must be held to the last man. There must be no retirement. With our backs to the wall and believing in the justice of our cause, each one of us must fight on to the end.' His orders were faithfully obeyed. The enemy was halted, the Front did not break, the French and British armies were not divided. Ludendorff failed, and was discouraged; his troops needed a month to rest and refit. This meant not only a respite for the exhausted soldiers of the Allies but precious time in which to bring thousands of American troops across the ocean.

The total British losses in the two spring offensives came to about 236,000. When the French losses are added the total for the Allies was around 330,000; the German casualties are given as 348,300 by the British official historian, who comments: 'It is evident from these figures and rough calculations that, as in other great battles of the War, the losses on both sides were nearly the same.'

Such, in baldest summary, is what happened in those forty tremendous days in Picardy and Flanders. 'April 12th', Churchill wrote in *World Crisis*, 'is probably, after the Marne, the climax of the War.'

What was happening in Whitehall? At its usual morning session on 21 March the Cabinet was informed that the bombardment had begun where expected, and on the following day no anxiety was expressed. On 23 March, however, reports were disturbing: casualties were high; the Third and Fifth Armies were in retreat; reserves were only slowly coming to their aid. Lloyd George was early astir on this Black Saturday. He postponed the Cabinet and went across to the War Office and took charge. His commanding presence and concentration were soon felt. He decided to throw all available reinforcements into France with the greatest possible speed, and this he did. By 20 April the number available for drafting to France rose to over 212,000.

On the evening of this same Black Saturday it was decided to send Milner to France to attempt to improve Allied co-operation in the field. This resulted in the conferences at Doullens, Beauvais, and, later, Abbeville, the three stages leading to the proclamation of Foch as General-in-Chief. On the next day, Sunday, Lloyd George went from Walton Heath to London in the afternoon and saw Lord French at Downing Street. He dined with Mr. and Mrs. Churchill at Eccleston Square, and we have Mr. Churchill's impressions of this day:

I never remember in the whole course of the War a more anxious evening. One of the great qualities in Mr. Lloyd George was his power of obliterating the past and concentrating his whole being upon meeting the new situation. . . . The resolution of the Prime Minister was unshaken under his truly awful responsibilities.[13]

He arrived back at Walton Heath at 10.30 p.m. looking very tired. 'Things look very bad', he told Riddell who was waiting for him, and Riddell recorded in his *Diary*:

Notwithstanding the news, the P.M. was firm and cheerful. Although very anxious and much worried, he did not fail to have a good laugh as usual. His courage is remarkable. His work and anxieties are always with him, but he mingles them with bright and amusing conversation which lightens the burden.[14]

On Monday, 25 March, the Cabinet decided to take drastic measures to comb more men for France from essential industries

---

[13] Winston Churchill, *World Crisis*, ii. 1291.
[14] Lord Riddell, *War Diary*, p. 320.

(munition-workers, coal-miners, transport-workers), to raise the age-limit of enlistment to fifty and higher in some cases, and to extend compulsory service to Ireland. The Prime Minister introduced the necessary legislation on 9 April and it was hurried through Parliament.

At the same time, Lloyd George turned to the other great reservoir. As far back as November he had discussed with Generals Pershing and Bliss and other Americans problems of man-power and tonnage and displayed his impatience with the slow and meagre arrival of soldiers from the United States. The situation in France precipitated a series of urgent appeals from the Prime Minister to the President and American public. To Reading, the British Ambassador, Wilson swore '. . . I will do my damnedest'.[15]

Lloyd George repeatedly stressed his preference for infantry and machine-gunners who could be put immediately into the French and British lines, as against the transport of fully equipped divisions. To this view Pershing was stubbornly opposed, desiring naturally, as did Pétain and Haig, to preserve the corporate identity of his own troops under his own command. On 28 March, however, in the grave emergency, Pershing put four American divisions into the line to relieve French divisions. On the same day Lloyd George telegraphed to Churchill, who was in Paris, to urge Clemenceau to appeal to President Wilson for more troops. This was done. Wilson sent a favourable reply but left the detailed disposal of the troops to Pershing. On 2 May at the conference at Abbeville the matter was again thrashed out and a compromise reached which avoided both a dead-lock with Pershing and an appeal over his head to higher authority. It was pointed out by General Bliss that the Americans had started with a plan which contemplated an independent army ready to play its part in a campaign in 1919. This orderly development was completely upset by the spring emergency of 1918.

Triangular altercations continued over men, munitions, and equipment, and compromises were patched up somehow; despite the interminable discussions, disputes, and delays, the loaded ships safely crossed the ocean in defiance of the submarines.

The end of April saw the close of the second spring offensive against the British. For the Prime Minister it had been a month of many cares and little relief. It opened with a hurried visit to

[15] R. S. Baker, *Woodrow Wilson: Life and Letters*, viii. 59.

France. He left London at 9 p.m., slept at Folkestone, crossed the Channel at 7 a.m., and was back at Downing Street at 4 a.m. next morning, 'the freshest of the lot', with a big and difficult House of Commons speech before him. This month saw the blocking raids of the British naval forces, the end of the battles of the Somme, and the beginning and end of the battles of the Lys—desperate struggles in which the Germans hurled ninety divisions against less than two-thirds that number in a vain attempt to destroy the British army. And not a day passed in this month that the Prime Minister was not harassed by some phase or other of the insoluble Irish problem. On the 14th the appointment of Foch as General-in-Chief was finally sealed with the title. On the 18th Derby became Ambassador Extraordinary to France, Milner took his place at the War Office, and Austen Chamberlain joined the War Cabinet.

Statesmen and generals continued to meet and dispute, usually somewhere in France. On 31 May, Lloyd George, Balfour, Milner, and Henry Wilson crossed to Paris, and hotly debated the use to be made of the American troops. Black depression, it is recorded by Woodrow Wilson's biographer, hung over these deliberations within sound of the guns of the enemy, and the French Government was packing up papers preparatory to possible removal from Paris. It was at these discussions that Foch charged Lloyd George with failing to sustain the strength of the British divisions in France and was pacified by being invited to send to London a man-power expert to examine the figures and produce more men if he could. In fact, by the end of June, replenished not only from home but from Italy, Egypt, and Salonika, the British forces in France were stronger than when the Germans attacked on 21 March.

MAURICE DEBATE

May started off with a serious threat to the Government and to the integrity of Lloyd George, for on 7 May 1918, 'the most dry, reserved, and punctilious man in the War Office', as the *Manchester Guardian* (8 May 1918) described him, Major-General Sir Frederick Maurice, committed a gross breach of the King's Regulations by writing a letter to the press charging Lloyd George and Bonar Law with making inaccurate statements in Parliament on military matters. In less than a week the Army Council placed him on retired pay. This was the penalty for acting on his conviction, 'fully realising the consequences to myself, that my duty as a citizen must override my duty as a soldier'; his reason being the expectation that his letter would force Parliament to order an investigation into his charges. It was a vain hope. He showed the letter before publication to his wife and mother only, and then disappeared into the country. Only a very simple soldier could expect by this strategy to get the better of two astute politicians.

The statements which General Maurice challenged were made by Lloyd George in the House of Commons on 9 April: first, that notwithstanding the heavy casualties in 1917, the army in France was considerably stronger on 1 January 1918 than on 1 January 1917, and second, that in Egypt and Palestine there was a very small proportion of British as compared with Indian troops; and by Bonar Law on 23 April that the extension of the British Front which took place before the battle of 21 March was an arrangement made solely by the military authorities.

The general inference drawn from these statements, taken together, was that the forces on the Western Front were adequate, and that if mistakes had been made, even in the extension of the line, General Headquarters was responsible for them and for the disaster to the Fifth Army. As the *Manchester Guardian* said (8 May): 'The statements went to the heart of the responsibility for our recent reverses.'

The Maurice letter appeared at a moment when the political atmosphere was tense and easily excited. There had been disasters at the Front, further German attacks were pending, while at home unrest was induced by the removal of exemptions from military service and by the decision to apply conscription to Ireland. Speeches by the Prime Minister and the Leader of the House appeared to be almost calculated to undermine public confidence in the supreme direction of the war, and might affect the morale of the troops. It was commonly held that Lloyd George and the new C.I.G.S., Sir Henry Wilson, would have liked to replace Sir Douglas Haig and were said to be plotting this, while the military caucus which supported the former C.I.G.S., Sir William Robertson, was supposed to be just as eager to get rid of Lloyd George. That part of the press which remained loyal to Asquith was openly advocating his return to the premiership. These were the conditions into which General Maurice flung his letter.

The letter was, indeed, a bomb-shell. But though it created much heat and confusion, its result was to strengthen rather than to damage the Government. Eighteen years later, Lloyd George wrote in his *Memoirs* contemptuously of 'the fizzling cracker that was chosen to blow up the Government'. Whether the turn events took was quite fair to General Maurice will later become apparent.

On the very day that the letter appeared, Bonar Law told the House that the allegations were to be inquired into by two judges who were to sit in private, to have access to secret documents, and to report as quickly as possible. But by that night, because of the feeling that the Government must clear itself in the eyes of the country in order to stay in power, it was decided to fight out the whole question on the floor of the House.

Lloyd George summoned all his own energies and those of his staff to prepare his case. On 8 May, the day before the debate, he rehearsed his speech to Milner and Chamberlain, a sure sign of the seriousness with which he took the challenge. On the next day the House was crowded, as were all the galleries; it was a great occasion, and Lloyd George rose to it triumphantly.

Asquith moved that a Select Committee be appointed to inquire into Maurice's charges. In a studiously moderate speech he explained why he preferred this to an investigation by judges. He reminded his listeners that never, since he had occupied a seat on the front Opposition bench, had he voted against a motion proceeding from the Government, and he deprecated reading more into his motion than was stated in it. But he must have been mesmerized by his own integrity if he imagined that the issue could possibly be limited as he wished. For the paper most identified with his own party (the *Westminster Gazette*) had flagrantly and unmistakably proclaimed that there was an alternative Government and that it was time it took the reins, and the Government had let it be known that it would regard Asquith's motion as a vote of censure. The House, its judgement clouded by the critical situation on the Western Front, had two issues before it, the challenge of the Maurice letter and the threat of an alternative Government.

The Prime Minister immediately rose to reply. His speech was accepted by the great majority as a complete answer to General Maurice's charges. It ended with an eloquent appeal for unity and loyalty at that critical period of the war. The effect it had may be

illustrated by press comments. *The Times* said: 'As for the question of fact, the Prime Minister's case was overwhelming'; and
of the General: 'All things considered, it is hardly surprising that
the House of Commons should have refused so decisively to hear
any more of him.' In short, Sir Frederick Maurice had, to most
people's satisfaction, been proved wrong without being heard.

No one on the front Opposition bench spoke after the Prime
Minister, not even Runciman whose name was associated with
Asquith's motion. Several Members spoke whose speeches re-
flected the confusion of their minds; some military Members
made clearer statements; Sir Edward Carson appealed to the
Opposition to withdraw the motion, while Lord Hugh Cecil
voiced the views of the Members who had called out during
Lloyd George's defence: 'We want to hear Maurice.' He said:

> Of all forms of enquiry, the least desirable seems to me that of the
> Prime Minister sitting alone in judgment upon himself, selecting the
> evidence, reviewing it, and ultimately proclaiming himself clear and
> acquitted from all blame. . . . It does not seem to me a very desirable
> thing to make an attack upon a man who is necessarily not present,
> while at the same time, you are refusing an enquiry.[16]

The division resulted in a majority for the Government of 293
votes to 106. This division, *The Times* pointed out, was 'the *début*
of an organised Opposition, the first step was taken towards what
may become a permanent cleavage'. Its effect became apparent
in the Coupon Election of December 1918. In fairness to Lloyd
George it should be remembered that he appealed earnestly to
Asquith, the Opposition Leader, not to press the matter to a
division.

The tactics of General Maurice were not well adapted to achieve
his end. In 1922 he wrote: 'It would have been easy for me to go
to the House of Commons and coach those who were ready to
attack Ministers. I stayed in the country.' This may have been
high-minded, but having started on his campaign he should have
seen it through. Most probably it did not for a moment occur to
him that the Ministers could altogether evade an inquiry, which
is exactly what happened. It may be, however, that his letter
achieved its underlying purpose, for he says that he had 'learned
that a scheme for removing Haig from the supreme command in

---

[16] Hansard, fifth series, vol. cv, 9 May 1918.

France was rapidly coming to a head'. This, at any rate, did not materialize.

In July 1922 Maurice dealt with the controversy in a pamphlet, *Intrigues of the War*, with a preface by the Marquis of Crewe, and addressed a letter to the Prime Minister asking him to admit that the information he used on 9 May 1918 was incorrect. A reply was sent through a secretary, in which the Prime Minister was content to leave the General's criticism 'to the unprejudiced judgment of posterity', but when he came to write his *Memoirs* (chapter lxxx) he reviewed the controversy, and 'using figures as epithets' he had no difficulty in making the General look ridiculous. The real points at issue were not faced. What had actually happened was this: on 9 April, making no distinction between combatants and non-combatants, the figures used by Lloyd George and taken from the official records show that Haig had more men in January 1918 than in January 1917. But included in the 1918 figures were 300,000 unarmed British labourers and Chinese coolies who did not appear in the 1917 figures. On 18 April, in reply to a parliamentary question, the Parliamentary Secretary of the War Office replied: 'The combatant strength of the British Army was stronger on the 1st January, 1918, than on the 1st January, 1917.' This reply turned out to be based on a mistaken return, supplied by the War Office when asked for it in a great hurry, which included the whole strength of the British forces in *Italy* as well as in France. The mistake was discovered shortly afterwards and was reported to Philip Kerr, of the Prime Minister's secretariat. On 9 May Lloyd George made use of the incorrect return of 18 April to justify his figures of 9 April, though in the meantime they had been corrected.

Actually, according to Sir James Edmonds the official historian:

At the beginning of 1918 the British Armies on the Western Front (including the detachment in Italy) were about 100,000 weaker in fighting troops, mostly infantry, than in January, 1917.[17] It is obvious that the British Armies in France could have been brought up to full establishment [by moving troops in from Egypt and Palestine] before 21st March without unduly weakening the forces elsewhere had the Government so willed.[18]

[17] *Journal*, Royal United Institution, February 1937, p. 19.
[18] Official History of the War, *Military Operations, France and Belgium, 1918*, i. 52 n.

Lloyd George accurately stated on 9 May that the divisions had been moved, but he did not say that the order was given *after* the disaster of 21 March.

The second of Maurice's charges related to the Prime Minister's statement that there were more Indian troops in the Near Eastern theatre than there were British. Lloyd George had said that there were three white divisions; in fact there were five, and there was not in these an appreciable mixture of Indian troops. The third charge, that Bonar Law was inaccurate about the genesis of the extension of the British Front, was substantially right. Law's statement was only technically correct, for the extension was due to pressure from Clemenceau and Pétain and was only reluctantly agreed to by Haig. The conclusion of the whole matter would appear to be that Maurice had, in the language of golf, a good lie for his ball, but that no one could have foozled his shot worse. He should have remembered the wise words of the first Lord Birkenhead: 'The man who enters into real and fierce controversy with Mr. Lloyd George must think clearly, think deeply, and think ahead. Otherwise he will think too late.'

END OF WAR

On 27 May the first of three new German offensives opened, this time against the French, in the Chemin des Dames sector; the Battle of the Matz followed on 9 June and on 15 July the Rheims–Soissons offensive, called the Second Battle of the Marne. In the first of these pushes the enemy created a record by advancing to a depth of twelve miles in the first day, which brought them within the alarming distance of forty miles from Paris. In the midst of the third offensive, which proved to be the last attack of the German armies on the Western Front, came Foch's counter-stroke of 18 July.

During these months of recoil and retreat which preceded Ludendorff's Black Day, 8 August, several major and compensatory factors turned the tide in favour of the Allies—factors whose importance is clearer now than it was then. There were three major ones. First, Ludendorff in attracting Allied reserves from the north to oppose his German offensives in the south did so with deliberate intent to ensure the success of his decisive blow against the British in Belgium. His succession of sweeping tactical victories, however, involved him in such costly casualties as to deflect him, now disillusioned, from the northern offensive until it was too late to undertake it. Second, Ludendorff was now at last confronted by a General-in-Chief of the Allied armies in the person of Foch, who displayed such restraint, patience, and skill in handling the Allied reserves as fully to justify his elevation to the supreme control. And, finally, Ludendorff was running a race with American reinforcements which were reaching France in ever-increasing numbers, thanks to the co-operation of the Ministry of Shipping, the British Admiralty, and the American navy —the equipment of these armies being accomplished by a co-operation so excellent that Mr. Churchill (who should know) could, in *World Crisis,* only compare it to two friends sharing a luncheon-basket.

Lloyd George on 11 June presided at the opening of the second Imperial War Cabinet. It continued to meet for over two months, during which time the Prime Minister and other representatives of the Empire examined the conduct of the war and the preparations for peace. Despite the series of disasters in France, or perhaps because of them, the resolution of the British was unshaken. No one entertained any thought but of ultimate victory. 'It is an undefeated people,' wrote Smuts, 'for better or worse they have never been defeated and they do not know defeat.' He himself assumed that nothing material would happen in 1918, and, with his colleagues, was considering whether the war could be ended in 1919 or would have to be prolonged into 1920.

On 15 July Ludendorff launched the last German offensive of the war, east and west of Rheims; its repulse in the days which followed marked the turn of the tide which led to final victory. The offensive was planned in part as a threat to Paris, in part to attract British divisions from Flanders. Early on the morning of the 18th an Allied counterstroke was delivered, to the astonishment of the enemy who had grown accustomed to his own uninterrupted initiative. Foch and Pétain had ordered the secret preparation of a striking force of twenty-two divisions—eighteen French, two British, and two large American divisions. The Americans distinguished themselves in this, their first battle. It opened not with the usual artillery preparation but with an advancing wave of small mobile tanks—the *moustiques*—emerging from the forest of Compiègne through morning mist. The surprise was complete and it was successful. The battle, the second battle of the Marne, was decisive only in the sense that it marked the first stage of the passing of the initiative from Ludendorff to Foch. This was confirmed at the second stage three weeks later: the battle of Amiens under Haig, on 8 August, 'the Black Day of the German Army'. The preceding three weeks had been a period of intense and secret concentration masked by deceptive movements of troops and misleading rumours, resulting in what has been described as 'perhaps the most complete surprise of the War'. A fortnight before the battle, Lloyd George had been 'inspecting' Cavan with a view to his replacing Haig, but Haig's great achievement on 8 August ended all such schemes.

From this time onwards, until the Armistice on 11 November, hope mounted among the Allies and declined among the Germans —and hope, say students of war, not loss of lives is what decides the issues of war. When on 14 August the Kaiser met his counsellors and the Emperor Charles of Austria at Spa a conviction of defeat prevailed, but no one was ready to ask at once for terms nor to order a retreat of the troops to a shortened line of defence. Neither course was adopted; fighting went on for weeks because of doubts and hesitations, and conferences continued in a vague search for the right moment and the right method to end the struggle.

On 4 September General Guillaumat, Sarrail's successor at Salonika, now Military Governor of Paris, crossed to London and persuaded Lloyd George against the advice of Henry Wilson, an ultra-Westerner, to launch a Balkan offensive under Franchet d'Espérey on 15 September. It was so successful that a fortnight later the Bulgars accepted drastic armistice terms. The first enemy prop had fallen.

These events in Europe were followed in Palestine by a short, swift, and decisive campaign, directed by General Allenby. The Arabs, under the Emir Feisal and Colonel Lawrence, interrupted communications by destroying telegraph and telephone offices. Within a week (19–25 September) the Turkish armies were annihilated in the battles of Megiddo. A month later, at Mudros, an armistice was signed between Turkey and the *entente* Powers. The second prop had fallen.

On 4 October the German and Austrian Governments addressed notes to President Wilson proposing an armistice. One sentence in the appeal of Prince Max of Baden, the new German Chancellor, should be specially noted in view of subsequent controversy: 'The German Government accepts the programme set forth by the President of the United States in his message to Congress on January 8, 1918, and in his later pronouncements, especially his speech on September 27th, as a basis for peace negotiations.' This declaration embraced what came to be known as the Fourteen Points, the Four Principles, and the Five Particulars. On 5 October the Allied statesmen were gathered at the Villa Romaine, Versailles, when they were told by Clemenceau that the Central Powers had asked for an armistice.

Not only up to this moment but throughout October the British and French military authorities failed to realize the weakness which now paralysed the enemy. Foch gave evasive answers when questioned on the duration of the war, and Henry Wilson was planning a supreme effort for July 1919. On 19 October Haig considered that the German army could retire on its own frontier and recuperate through the winter. Smuts did not foresee the early end of the war, but shared Haig's views.

What strikes most chroniclers of these months is the astonishing suddenness of Germany's collapse and surrender and the miracle by which the nightmare of war was lifted from the backs of the fighting nations. Historians will long continue to assign varying orders of importance to the factors which brought victory to pass: the stranglehold of the British Navy (about which our narrative has said far too little), the blockade, the tank, the Fifth Army, the propaganda or paper war, the breakdown of morale, the succession of costly German offensives in France in 1918, the failure of the Germans to fall back earlier on the defensive, the arrival of American reinforcements, the collapse of the Eastern props—none of these won the war, all of them won the war.

From July onwards Lloyd George intermittently spent the summer and autumn at Danny Park, in Sussex, a house rented by Riddell. On 4 August, the fourth anniversary of the outbreak of war, he addressed a message to the peoples of the British Empire: 'I say "Hold Fast", because our prospects of Victory have never been so bright as they are to-day.' This message was read in every theatre and cinema, in every Bank Holiday gathering. On 7 August he spoke for an hour, reviewing the course of the war

to a crowded House of Commons. He paid a notable tribute to
the untrumpeted work of the navy: 'In the month of June alone
British ships of the Navy steamed 8,000,000 miles. That was apart
from the efforts of the Mercantile Marine. No darkness arrests
it. The Navy never goes into winter quarters!' On the 8th he
travelled to Neath for the National Eisteddfod, and passing
through Cardiff in the afternoon told the crowds of a telegram
he had just received: 'We have won a great victory this morning.
We have driven them back at some points seven miles. It shows
the tide has turned. The enemy have done their worst, they can
do no more and if we only hold together we will have the greatest
triumph for liberty the world has ever seen.' Next morning he
received the freedom of Neath and spent the rest of the day singing Welsh hymns with thousands of his countrymen in the
Eisteddfod marquee. He then went off to Criccieth for a few
days' 'rest', where he was joined by Milner, Addison, his doctor
Bertrand Dawson (later Lord Dawson of Penn), two electioneering
experts, and several secretaries. There was a Red Cross fête, a village concert, a picnic during which Lloyd George climbed trees;
but there was also much talk of a general election, of the bartering
of seats with the Tories, of the need of improving the health services.

On 12 September he was in Manchester receiving the freedom
of his native city. In the evening he was taken ill with influenza
and laid up for several days in the Town Hall. He returned to
Danny Park, and from 5 to 9 October was at Versailles with
Clemenceau, Orlando, and the generals. He had crossed the
Channel in order to discuss the armistice terms proposed for
Bulgaria and Turkey, but the publication of the peace notes
from Germany and Austria raised the question of terms with
major enemy Powers. President Wilson had replied to the notes
without consulting the other Allies, and Lloyd George had to
point out that Britain would not concede the freedom of the
seas in war-time, which was included in the Fourteen Points. A
cautionary message was sent to Washington stressing the importance of consultation with the military experts and asking the
President for an American representative possessing the full confidence of his government to be sent to Europe for day-to-day discussion. Even while exchanging notes, the Germans continued to
sink ships without warning and wantonly to destroy the fruit-

orchards of France and Flanders as their soldiers retreated. Wilson hinted at the need for real change in the character of the government which permitted these atrocities. Ludendorff, who insisted that to cancel submarine warfare would be equivalent to capitulation, was dismissed by Prince Max on 26 October. On the following day the Chancellor reported to the American President the change wrought in the Constitution, and invited proposals for the peace of justice which had been proffered. The President had already communicated to the associated governments the proposals sent by him to Germany, and the British Cabinet had considered them in the light of the views of their own experts on 24 October.

Over Turkey a sharp dispute arose between Lloyd George and Clemenceau, because of the latter's desire to put a French admiral in charge of the Allied naval forces operating against Constantinople. This, Lloyd George insisted, would not be tolerated by British or Empire public opinion, but fortunately the Turks short-circuited the dispute by asking the British admiral at Mudros for an armistice. The French accepted this as a *fait accompli* and the trouble ended.

On 29 October Lloyd George was again in Paris, and there heard the news that Austria had surrendered. By 4 November Allied premiers and Colonel House (for the President) at the Supreme War Council had agreed on the text of the terms to be offered to Germany and the steps to be taken should she refuse them. Differences had arisen in Paris over the interpretation of Wilson's Points, Principles, and Particulars, especially over the freedom of the seas, on which Colonel House was strongly opposed to the British view. House went so far as to suggest that unless Britain relented America might have to conclude a separate peace. Lloyd George was adamant, and with the French and Italians he prepared a covering note to the President to accompany the draft of the armistice terms, in which the Allied governments reserved to themselves complete freedom on this subject when they entered the Peace Conference. The note also commented on another point laid down by the President on 8 January 1918, which dealt with the restoration of the invaded territories: 'By it they understand that compensation will be made by Germany for all damage done to the civilian population of the Allies and their property by the aggression of Germany by land, by sea and from the air.' Wilson forwarded the views of the associated governments to Germany, and stated that he was in agreement with this concluding paragraph; he added that Foch was authorized to deal with representatives of Germany.

Events moved rapidly. The German fleet mutinied, the Kaiser fled to Holland, all the seven German kings gave up their thrones, south Germany formed republics, workers' and soldiers' councils sprang up. On 8 November, in a railway carriage in the forest of Compiègne, Marshal Foch and Admiral Wemyss handed a German delegation, headed by Erzberger, the armistice terms which amounted to a demand for complete surrender. They were given until 11 a.m. on 11 November to sign them. On that day Lloyd George announced from 10 Downing Street: 'The Armistice was signed at 5 a.m. this morning, and hostilities are to cease on all fronts at 11 a.m. to-day.'

In the House of Commons that afternoon he received a great ovation, and moved, 'That this House do immediately adjourn, until this time to-morrow, and that we proceed, as a House of Commons, to St. Margaret's to give humble and reverent thanks for the deliverance of the world from its great peril.' Rejoicing crowds gathered before Buckingham Palace and paraded Whitehall. On the next day when the Prime Minister and his wife appeared outside No. 10 for a moment, the swarming throng instantly surrounded them and they had to be rescued by a posse of police from Scotland Yard and propelled indoors. One of a myriad messages of congratulation which reached him at this hour summed up the rest. It was from Colonel House: 'No one has done more to bring about this splendid victory than you.'

COUPON ELECTION

During the summer of 1918, and indeed earlier, Lloyd George was planning an election which would give him a mandate from a united nation not only to lead it to victory but to negotiate the peace and carry out a programme of reconstruction at home and abroad. Within a fortnight after the Armistice was signed Parliament had been dissolved. Polling took place on 14 December. Within another fortnight the results were available. The Prime Minister had secured the authority he sought, and resumed office and power backed by a huge majority.

For no action in his political career has Lloyd George been more

ąan for holding this election. War fever,
ɔops abroad and the difficulties of securing
... less of the electorate, were all argued against
...ce it may be said at once that the Parliament
w. ، ، old and a dissolution long overdue; that most of
the ، ، war and peace which he proclaimed were common
to men. ،rs of all parties; that the effects of the election on the
Treaty of Versailles have been exaggerated, and that he should
not be blamed for European events which were beyond his control.

There were in 1918 sound constitutional reasons for an appeal
to the country. Early in 1918 a Reform Act had been passed which
introduced universal adult male suffrage and extended the franchise to women over thirty. The electorate had changed profoundly, and a Prime Minister about to embark on peace-making
had every right to make sure that he was supported by a majority
of the nation.

Throughout this year, backed by the Northcliffe press, he went
on with preparations for an election, despite Liberal, Unionist,
and Labour opposition. A speech at Manchester in September
served to introduce the campaign and prepare the country for
continuing a coalition with Lloyd George at its head. On 2
November he wrote to Bonar Law expressing his conviction that
a coalition election ought to be held as soon as military considerations allowed, and that candidates officially recognized should be
pledged to support 'this Government' in the prosecution of the
war to its final end. He summarized the policy of the Manchester
speech, accepted Imperial Preference as defined by the Imperial
Conference, and the solution of the problem of Ireland on lines
which took into account that a Home Rule Act was on the statute
book and that Ulster must not be coerced—the settlement, however, to be postponed until the condition of Ireland made it possible to attempt it.

Before the letter to Law was read to the Unionist party on 12
November the war was at an end. On the day after the Armistice
the Unionists and the coalition Liberals, at separate meetings,
decided to maintain the coalition at the general election. On 14
November the Labour party decided to leave the coalition.

The Prime Minister's feelings in the first flush of triumph over
the enemy were expressed in his speech to the coalition Liberals on
12 November at 10 Downing Street:

Are we to lapse back into the old national rivalries and animosities and competitive armaments, or are we to initiate the reign on earth of the Prince of Peace? It is the duty of Liberalism to use its influence to ensure that it shall be the reign of peace. . . . We must not allow any sense of revenge, any spirit of greed, any grasping desire to override the fundamental principles of righteousness. Vigorous attempts will be made to hector and bully the Government in the endeavour to make them depart from the strict principles of right, and to satisfy some base, sordid, squalid ideas of vengeance and of avarice. We must relentlessly set our faces against that.

He concluded:

I was reared in Liberalism . . . I am too old now to change. I cannot leave Liberalism. . . . Now is the great opportunity of Liberalism! Let it rise to it! Don't let it sulk. If there are personal differences, in God's name what do they count compared with the vast issues and problems before us? Let us help to regenerate the people, the great people who have done more to save the world in this great crisis than any other nation.[19]

The campaign, which lasted barely three weeks, was not waged on these heights. The charge brought against the Prime Minister is that he did not peg public opinion at this ethical level. Could he have done so? His prestige as the architect of victory was at this supreme moment unparalleled in British political history, and had he been able to rely on a referendum his majority against any conceivable rival candidate would have been overwhelming. But he underrated his unique power to sway the country, of which his wife and some of his secretaries sought in vain to convince him. He argued that he was the Leader of a party half of which was opposed to him: he could not ignore the mechanics of party warfare, he had to provide a programme and to endorse candidatures.

There were two tests of the candidates: the first, a pledge to support 'this Government', the second, loyalty to the Government in the division of the Maurice debate. Those who had voted with the Opposition on that occasion were proscribed. A candidate who subscribed to Lloyd George's programme and passed these tests was given a certificate, or 'coupon'—hence the label 'The Coupon Election'. The Prime Minister refused to support anyone who had joined in the attempt 'to overthrow a Government that was in the midst of a crisis while wrestling for victory'. Those who

[19] Speech by Lloyd George at Downing Street, 12 November 1918.

had then opposed and were now willing to support the Government were likened to Germans crying 'Kamerad', after sniping, poisoning, machine-gunning. This was some distance from the spirit of the Downing Street speech of 12 November: 'I would quit this place to-morrow if I could not obtain the support of Liberals.' The result of this electoral trafficking proved most damaging to Liberal representation and in the long run to the Prime Minister's position. *The Times* rightly commented on 4 December: 'Nobody, we imagine, has any doubt that Mr. Lloyd George would have been wiser if he had frankly gone to the country on his own great war record and his own views of social reform without any attempt at securing pledges or making bargains over candidates.'

Statements issued to the press on the Prime Minister's authority on the eve of the election summarized the election issues. Their substance and order were as follows: (1) prosecution of the Kaiser and punishment of those responsible for atrocities; (2) the Central Powers to pay indemnities up to the limit of capacity; (3) enemy aliens to be expelled from Great Britain; (4) rehabilitation of those broken in the war; (5) domestic reform in all spheres.

It is charged against Lloyd George that he deliberately misled the electorate into believing that Germany could pay for the war or, at least, that colossal reparations could be obtained. As refutation, in *The Truth about the Peace Treaties*, he relies upon the speech which he delivered in Bristol on 11 December. Before making the speech he was armed with three official estimates; one from the Board of Trade fixed the total claims for reparation at not less than £2,000 million; a Treasury Committee reported that £3,000 million was recoverable; and an Imperial Committee appointed by Lloyd George, consisting of statesmen and bankers, concluded that

so far the direct cost of the War to the Allies had been £24,000,000,000; and the Committee have certainly no reason to suppose that the Enemy Powers could not provide £1,200,000,000 per annum as interest on the above amount when normal conditions are restored.
The Indemnity should be payable in cash, kind, securities and by means of a Funding loan.[20]

These were the facts in Lloyd George's mind when he delivered

[20] Speech by Lloyd George at Bristol, 11 December 1918.

the Bristol speech, the only one in which the subject was treated in any detail.

He had an excited audience; the interrupting voice was very active and elicited some encouraging responses. 'Who is to foot the bill?' asked the orator. A voice replied: 'Germany.' The speaker argued that it was a question of justice, not vengeance. The party that does the wrong and challenges a lawsuit to determine it must pay the costs. At this there were cheers, and a voice: 'In full?' In reply Lloyd George said: 'I am coming to that. Certainly in full, if they have got it.' Then he explained why he had always said that Germany should pay 'up to the limit of capacity'. It was because it was not right for the Government to raise false hopes on the eve of an election. 'If I were to say to you, "Not merely ought Germany to pay, but we can expect every penny", I should be doing so without the whole of the facts.'

He then told his hearers that the Government's financial advisers were doubtful about whether Germany could pay the bill, estimated at £24,000 million, and gave the reason in general terms. He said that a British Imperial Committee had met, and the night before he had received its report:

You will be glad to hear that they take a more favourable view of the capacity of Germany than do the officials of a Government Department. They think that the assets of Germany, the wealth of Germany have been underestimated in the past. . . . If that is so, you may find the capacity will go a pretty long way.

He then made two conditions: there must not be a large army of occupation keeping British men from industry, nor must the debt be paid by dumping German goods in England and so damaging her own trade. He summarized his conclusions as follows:

First, as far as justice is concerned, we have an absolute right to demand the whole cost of the War from Germany. The second point is that we propose to demand the whole cost of the War. The third point is that when you come to the exacting of it you must exact it in such a way that it does not do more harm to the country that received it than to the country which is paying it. The fourth point is that the Committee appointed by the British Cabinet believe that it can be done.[21]

Lloyd George himself was 'entirely sceptical' of receiving from

[21] Ibid.

the enemy substantial aid in liquidating the war burden of the Allies. It was, he thought then and wrote later, incredible that the Imperial Committee should have found that Germany could pay £1,200 million per annum for a long period of years. To describe this, as he did in Bristol, as a more favourable estimate than the figures of the Treasury and Board of Trade officials, *which he did not reveal during the election*, was indeed a triumph of understatement.

Lloyd George challenged anyone to find a single sentence in the Bristol speech which committed the Government to the recovery of vast sums from Germany. No one will be found to take up this simple challenge, for it is not by single sentences that the speech is to be judged but by its cumulative effect; the ordering of its arguments, the high-lights and the shadows. It is not unfair to say that he was inclined to shout the popular demands and to whisper the qualifications which diminished the chance of their fulfilment. For example, at an overflow meeting on the same day as the Bristol speech he demanded the payment of 'the uttermost farthing', and declared 'we shall search their pockets for it'. Such expressions were hardly becoming to the world's outstanding statesman and led to others even worse being fathered on him.

It is simply not true that he was 'a fire-brand scattering hate across England', as he was described by William Allen White, but he did too little to dispel illusion and dissipate hate. To secure a temporary advantage he played upon the baser passions of the electorate. He cannot be condemned by the standards of contemporary statesmen but, judged by standards set by himself, he is condemned because he did not lead, nor seriously try to lead, the nation along the path illumined by his own inner light—that light which sometimes shone through his utterances, as at Downing Street on 12 November.

The election resulted in a resounding success for Lloyd George but left him leaning heavily for support on the Unionists, who began to presume on their strength.

On 2 January, *The Times* reports, he stated that 'if the Government did not do their best to fulfil the promises made he would no longer be head of the Government, but would go back to the people and ask for the renewal of their confidence'; and two days later he referred to democracy, freedom, and right, with emotion and uplifted hand: 'If I betray these principles now,' he exclaimed, 'let my tongue cleave to the roof of my mouth.'

Years later Lloyd George contrasted his own policy with that of President Wilson who fought the November (1918) congressional elections as a party leader, urging voters to support Democrats only—and this although all parties in the United States had worked together under him for victory. It was, writes Lloyd George in *The Truth about the Peace Treaties*, 'a fatal error of judgment and of character which seriously impaired and finally destroyed the President's negotiating authority to conclude a peace in the name and on behalf of his own country'. The Democrats were defeated and the Democratic President who, contrary to precedent, left his country in order to carry on the peace negotiations had not the support of the Republican Congress. Nor did Wilson consent to strengthen his position by taking with him to Europe one or two well-disposed Republican leaders.

The elections in the United States and in Great Britain foreshadowed the political doom of both President and Prime Minister.

VI

PRIME MINISTER IN PEACE
1918–22

PEACE CONFERENCE AND TREATY

DURING the first half of 1919 Lloyd George was mainly occupied with the Paris Peace Conference and the preparation of the Treaty of Versailles—a conference, it has been said, which never met, and a treaty which was a myth. There is some basis for both statements. But the comprehensive term, conference, may be allowed to describe the 2,000 meetings, plenary and subsidiary, private and public, of some sixty commissions and committees, ranging from 200 or 300 persons to the diminishing councils of ten, five, four, and three, all seeking peace and pursuing it. The Treaty of Versailles may be regarded as a myth in the sense that it became customary to debit to it most if not all the miseries which have befallen Europe since its imposition.

President Wilson arrived in London from Paris on 26 December 1918, and was given a great public reception and a banquet of unusual splendour at Buckingham Palace. Lloyd George rather grudgingly concedes President Wilson's immense prestige at this moment. 'He did not make the same appeal' to 'the combative instincts' of the British as Clemenceau and Foch did, said Lloyd George in his book on the Peace Treaties, but there are other than combative instincts even in the British, and to the common conscience the American President spoke as the great voice of Humanity.

At Buckingham Palace President Wilson received Lloyd George and Balfour, who found him 'extremely pleasant', 'genial and friendly in his accost'. His special concern was that the League of Nations should be placed first on the Conference agenda. To this Lloyd George readily agreed.

In December thirty-two states had been invited to send delegates to Paris, but no one had settled what was to be their relation to the five Great Powers. Which meetings were they to attend? Which problems were they to discuss? How many treaties were there to be? How were these Powers of particular interests to transmit their views to the Powers of general interests and be made to feel that they mattered? Their presence in Paris tended to focus attention on minor problems to the neglect of the great issues of disarmament, reparations, the League of Nations, the Rhineland, German colonies, and the new states. Nor should it be forgotten that they met to shape the peace when armed conflicts were still raging in parts of Europe and Asia.

The Conference opened on 18 January, the representatives advised and assisted by hundreds of experts drawn especially from the foreign offices and universities of Britain, France, and the United States. Experts, for months past, had been engaged in shaping the outlines of a new world order, anticipating inquiries, and marshalling the answers in the departments of geography, history, law, economics, politics, and diplomacy. Charts and blueprints abounded. One of the most important experts on procedure was Sir Maurice (later Lord) Hankey, who arrived on the scene equipped with unique secretarial experience from the British War Cabinet. He was to prove a powerful catalytic agent in reducing to order the multitude of meetings and consultations. And after some three weeks of meetings, when the Council of Four decided that a secretary was necessary, Hankey became a regular attendant and kept the minutes. Count Aldrovandi was almost always present as secretary to the Italians. Philip Kerr acted as secretary to Lloyd George. He had not the technical detailed knowledge of a Foreign Office diplomat, but he had an elevation of mind, a gift of exposition, and a charm of manner which impressed all with whom he had to do, and his deep spiritual placidity influenced the British Prime Minister.

But if the tactics of the general secretariat were admirable, its strategy was defective. There was no grand plan to guide the Conference as a whole, no central focus or directing brain, no definition of the connexion between the preliminaries of peace and the contemplated Peace Congress, or which belligerent, neutral, and enemy states would attend it. No one had clearly grasped the relation of the Armistice to the Peace Treaty, or the problem of dovetailing immediate military and naval arrangements with ultimate political programmes. The Armistice itself had to be renewed on 16 January at Trèves, and again on 17 February at Spa. And the sudden cessation of the war had thrown up urgent executive problems, such as disarmament and feeding the starving populations of Europe. From the moment of the Armistice Lloyd George had been deeply concerned that Germany should be fed, and pressed this policy on the Council of Ten, especially in response to the urgent appeal of General Plumer in his telegram of 8 March 1919. Pressure of daily events largely determined agenda and procedure.

Lloyd George first arrived in Paris on 11 January, well in time for the opening meetings, and was housed in a palatial flat in the rue Nitot, with Balfour in the flat above and the British delegation in the Hotel Majestic. He was back in London from 8 February to 5 March, and again from 14 to 17 April. He finally left Paris on 28 June. During these months the diffused administrative elements took formal shape and functioned in turn or simultaneously as Supreme War Council, Inter-Allied Conference, Council of Ten (three premiers, three foreign secretaries, Wilson and his Secretary of State, two Japanese), Council of Four (Clemenceau, Lloyd George, Orlando, Wilson), Council of Three (with Orlando absent), Council of Five (foreign ministers), after 28 June Council of Heads of Delegations, and, as a final deposit, a Council of Ambassadors. It was on these bodies and their committees that the main task of preparing the German and Austrian treaties rested. The six plenary sessions held between 18 January and 6 May were mainly for window-dressing purposes. It was difficult to keep 500 newspaper correspondents healthily occupied.

During the preparation of the Treaty it proved as hard to unite the Allies in making peace as it had been in waging war. Traditions, principles, interests, tempers clashed. As happens in all such meetings, the initial task of central planning was delayed by purely personal considerations. Thus Lloyd George writes of this early period:

We were all feeling our way, and I had a sense that we were each of us trying to size up our colleagues, reconnoitring their respective positions, ascertaining their aims and how they stood in reference to the desiderata in which each of them was most deeply interested and involved.[1]

There were personal dislikes. Clemenceau hated President Poincaré and vice versa. Wilson and his Secretary of State, Lansing,

[1] Lloyd George, *Peace Treaties*, i. 214.

were not enamoured of each other, and even House became separated from his chief before they returned to America.

During the protracted proceedings there were days of acute crisis and moments of angry recrimination. Wilson opposed the French demands for annexation or pseudo-annexation in the Rhineland and Saar valley with such insistence that Clémenceau, in effect if not in words, called him a pro-German and abruptly left the conference room. A week later differences were so acute that the President threatened to take his delegation home and ordered the *George Washington* in readiness to sail for Brest. On another day Wilson published an appeal to the Italian people over the heads of Orlando and Sonnino, and they packed up and departed for Rome in a huff. Nor was Lloyd George himself always amiable. Stephen Bonsal tells a story—perhaps apocryphal—of an occasion when Wilson was compelled to intervene to prevent the fiery Welshman 'doubling his fists and squaring off' against the French Tiger.

At the meetings, Wilson was concerned primarily with self-determination, the Covenant, and the League of Nations; Clemenceau with French security and the disabling of Germany; Lloyd George with the balance of power in Europe and its restoration, and with the House of Commons which had resulted from the new election. Clemenceau and he were also hampered by secret treaties with Japan and Italy, concluded in the course of the war and ante-dating the Fourteen Points.

Though he was not the prophet of the League of Nations that Wilson was, Lloyd George supported the project more cordially than did Clemenceau, but without enthusiasm and without minimizing the difficulty of making the League an effective instrument. Actually, probably more thorough preliminary work in investigating its problems was done in Great Britain under his administration than in any other country. During the Peace Conference Lloyd George chose as his representatives on the League of Nations Drafting Committee two able and enthusiastic advocates of the League, Lord (Robert) Cecil and General Smuts. The Covenant of the League was on the whole the joint product of Anglo-American co-operation, in which the British contribution was by no means negligible. Lloyd George himself never attended a meeting of the League.

The relation of peace-making to democratic foreign policy came sharply to the front at the Conference. One of Wilson's Points had declared for 'open covenants openly arrived at'. Was the process as well as the result of negotiation to be subjected to complete publicity? Yes, Wilson seemed at first to say; but, argued Lloyd George, if at every stage of the discussion public and parliamentary agitation had to be pacified, the discussion might be prolonged *ad infinitum*. What he wished to avoid was a peace settled by public clamour. Eventually Wilson and Lloyd George agreed to a statement on publicity issued by the Council of Ten to the press (17 January 1919), which expressed the basic principle as follows: 'The essence of democratic method is not that deliberations of a government should be conducted in public, but that its conclusions should be subject to the consideration of a popular Chamber and to free open discussion in the Press.'[2] Ray Stannard Baker complains that Lloyd George was always thinking of the political aspects of every publicity question. Of course he was, and also of the publicity aspects of every political question.

Eighteen months elapsed between the promulgation of the Fourteen Points and the signing of the Treaty of Versailles. It was hardly to be expected that none of the Points would be blunted in the interval; what is remarkable is the degree to which the expressed war aims of the Allies were retained without serious change.

Lloyd George had formally and firmly objected at the conversations preceding the Armistice to Point II (freedom of the seas). He told House: 'The English people will not look at it.' He could not give up the one power which had enabled the American troops to be brought to Europe. He also extracted from the President the Lansing Note defining Points VII and VIII ('restoration of the invaded territories' as covering 'damage done to the civilian population of Allies and their property'). After the Armistice one fresh condition had been introduced: the demand for the trial and punishment of the Kaiser as an act of international justice. This was done at the instance of Clemenceau, who was supported by Lloyd George. Their decision was embodied in Article 227 of the Treaty, but was never put into effect because Holland would only surrender the Kaiser under pressure; the discussion marked a stage in the evolution of international morality and foreshadowed the great development in theory and practice registered at Nuremberg in 1946.

[2] Foreign Relations of the United States, *Paris Peace Conference 1919*, iii. 621.

Apart from the Kaiser's fate and reparations (the latter will be dealt with later)—two subjects which had been canvassed in the Coupon Election—the questions which bothered Lloyd George most as he had set out for Paris were the representation of the British Empire and the future of the German colonies. It was agreed that the Dominions and India should be on an equal footing with Belgium and other smaller Allied states. On the second question, after some consideration, it was finally agreed that the territories could not effectively be administered as mandates by an international authority, and that they were to be administered as part of the Dominion most closely concerned.

Involved in the Versailles debates on European security were the questions of conscription and disarmament—two issues important to Lloyd George in retaining public approval in Britain. President Wilson was perhaps as eager to abolish compulsory military service as Lloyd George. The Prime Minister opposed conscription, although he approved of resort to it as a war emergency. In the future, he held, the League should make conscription in any country unnecessary.

On the second issue, the British Liberal Minister shared the view which became popular in the inter-war years that disarmament would lead to security. He supported Wilson's proposal to disarm Germany as a preparation for a general reduction of armaments, and wanted an immediate drastic reduction of enemy forces and a consequent reduction of British troops abroad; later, in the League Covenant, provision for a general and permanent limitation of the armaments of all nations. But, as Clemenceau objected, if the military terms were signed and the Allied armies demobilized what force would be left to enforce the economic and political terms on Germany?

The subject of French security largely dominated the Conference and was uppermost in Clemenceau's mind. As he told Wilson, where it was concerned he, the springing Tiger, was as cautious as an elephant about to cross a bamboo bridge. The question occupied the forefront of the discussions of German disarmament, the Rhineland, the Saar, and the military guarantees.

It was at a critical period of the Conference, the last week in March and the first week in April, when feelings were running high, that Lloyd George retired with his counsellors to the forest of Fontainebleau to review the situation in comparative seclusion.

'I am going to Fontainebleau for the week-end', he told Riddell, 'and mean to put in the hardest forty-eight hours' thinking I have ever done.' The result was the notable memorandum entitled: 'Some Considerations for the Peace Conference Before They Finally Draft Their Terms, March 25th, 1919.'

The cumulative demands of France for excessive reparations, her desire to dismember Germany and to deprive her of the Rhineland and the Saar valley, of Upper Silesia, Danzig, and areas in East Prussia had alarmed the British Prime Minister, who had fears that when presented with the Treaty the Germans might refuse to sign it. He pleaded for a peace based on justice, but also one the Germans could carry out and which would not be provocative of future wars. 'We cannot both cripple her and expect her to pay.' He stressed the importance of not throwing the organizing might of Germany on the side of Bolshevism, the new European peril. The peace should offer Germany an acceptable alternative to Bolshevism. The League of Nations should be the effective guardian of international right and should strive to abolish competitive fleets and armies.

The Fontainebleau Memorandum was a most statesmanlike document. It would have made a striking manifesto to the electors of Great Britain in December 1918 and produced a better House of Commons. But critics complain that while Lloyd George wrote as a statesman he negotiated as a politician; to them an answer may be given in words once used by Clemenceau in the French Chamber: 'men retain their virtues and their faults together'.

On the occasion of the memorandum, Clemenceau's reply, that while Lloyd George objected to the territorial exactions in Europe proposed by France at the expense of Germany he did not himself offer to appease Germany with colonial or naval or commercial satisfactions at the expense of the British Empire, met with a sharp rejoinder:

M. Clemenceau suggests that the peace we propose is one which is entirely in the interests of Britain. I claim nothing for Britain which France would not equally get . . . and if my proposals seem to M. Clemenceau to favour Britain, it is because I was, until I read his document, under the delusion that France also attached importance to colonies, to ships, to compensation, to disarmament, to Syria and to a British guarantee to stand by France with all her strength if she were attacked. I regret my error and shall be careful not to repeat it.[3]

In the light of the years and the events which have followed, one paragraph in the French reply to the Memorandum may be worth recalling:

Mr. Lloyd George's note lays stress—and the French Government is in agreement with it—on the necessity of making a peace which will appear to Germany to be a just peace ... in view of German mentality, it is not certain that the Germans have the same conception of justice as have the Allies.[4]

It is impossible to attempt an analysis of all the many matters which occupied the Council of Four—such important subjects as the territorial settlements of Poland and Italy, in which Lloyd George played an important part as negotiator—but some account may be given of one of the major Conference issues: reparations. Lloyd George's part in these negotiations has been much criticized; a full examination of it would require too much statistical and other detail. We have already recounted Lloyd George's ambiguous handling of the problem at the general election, and the pledges he gave during his campaign. His actions in Paris were governed by these pledges, and he usually, but not always, tried to interpret them in Germany's favour. It was left to the ingenuity of the American delegates to draft the compromise which finally found its place in the Treaty as Articles 231 and 232. 'Instead of asserting the *right* of the Allies to the reimbursement of war costs, the Treaty affirmed the *responsibility of Germany* for causing the damage they had suffered as a consequence of the War.' As Keynes, in *The Economic Consequences of the Peace*, said: 'The President could read it as a statement of admission on Germany's part of moral responsibility, while the Prime Minister could explain it as an admission of financial liability for the general costs of the War.'

The fact that Lloyd George's moderation in Paris had been suspected and denounced by the Northcliffe press and in the House of Commons made it difficult for him to follow the dictates of his intelligence. The Government had refused to make Northcliffe a peace delegate or to entrust him with propaganda arrangements at the Conference, and this had enraged him. 'He flared up at me

[3] 'Papers respecting Negotiations for an Anglo-French Pact.' Cmd. 2169 (1924), p. 91. [4] Ibid., p. 90.

like Vesuvius in eruption.' Telegrams of protest reached Paris from Coalition Members on a scale that forced Lloyd George to return to London (14-17 April) to explain and defend his policy. This he did with supreme skill and success, using the unwelcome threat of another appeal to the electorate and diverting much attention to Russia. He seemed not merely a man, but a thunder-storm—wrote Garvin in the *Observer* on 20 April—rarely had there been such clearing of the air: 'In direct audacity, mastery of manoeuvre, vital perception, in all the fighting craft of politics, it was Mr. Lloyd George's oratorical Austerlitz.'

Clemenceau was similarly being watched in the French parliament and press, and if he had been overthrown his successor would have made still more extreme demands for payment. French policy on reparations was not inspired mainly by economic considerations but by fear and the political desire to weaken Germany by any and every means. Wilson was guided by righteous principle and resisted the demand for punitive damages and war costs. Lloyd George was stable in aim, if opportunist and variable in method. He wished to fulfil his pledges, but in a sensible, practical way.

The French were persuaded that it would be better for them to forgo war costs in favour of civilian damage because their percentage of the latter was higher. The British, because their percentage was low, overcame the handicap by including war pensions and separation allowances in the definition of civilian damage.

Wilson's surrender to these provisions was regretted but not taken too tragically by the American experts at the time because it was hoped by them that the Reparation Commission would have discretion 'to modify, suspend, extend and possibly even cancel payments'. This conception of the Reparation Commission as an impartial and independent body was originally shared by Lloyd George, but was blocked by the French, who insisted that the Commission add the total figures of German indebtedness and collect the entire bill even if it took fifty years. The upshot was that the Commission had to determine Germany's obligations within two years and might extend the date or modify the form of payment but could not cancel any part without the specific authority of the several governments represented upon the Commission.

On 7 May 1919 the text of the Treaty was presented to the

German delegates at the Trianon Palace Hotel, Versailles, and their observations invited. Their counter-proposals were received on 29 May; and on 1 June, at his flat, Lloyd George considered these with nine British Ministers and the Dominion Premiers present. It was a remarkable gathering. General Botha reminded Lord Milner that it was the seventeenth anniversary of the peace of Vereeniging, when moderation saved South Africa for the British Empire. Churchill had come over with the views of the Imperial General Staff. Smuts was there to plead for moderate terms. In this way Lloyd George collected opinions. He was neither a continental dictator nor a trade-union delegate, but a democratic leader working within the limits of a parliamentary system: he listened to his colleagues, read the newspapers, and made up his mind. This process might modify or annul the effects of his own intuitions.

The result of two days' deliberation was to authorize the British Prime Minister to press for concessions to Germany under four heads: her eastern frontiers, the period of military occupation, her admission to League membership, and a modification of the reparation clauses in the direction of fixing a definite amount.

Neither Wilson nor Clemenceau welcomed Lloyd George's change of front after months of debate and ultimate agreement, though he could retort that it had been Wilson's original view to hear the Germans before reaching a final decision. A fresh crisis arose. On 3 June Wilson summoned the American delegation to consider the suggestions for revision. He was annoyed and angry. Were the terms unjust or merely hard? 'For they are hard—but the Germans earned that.' To alter, at Germany's dictation, the delicate compromises would throw the whole Treaty into the melting-pot again. Lloyd George was alarmed, and feared the Germans would not sign. He seemed prepared for any concession which would bring immediate peace. 'We know the Germans better than you,' said Clemenceau, 'it is not for us to ask pardon for our victory.'

In the end, Lloyd George secured a reduction in the size of the army of occupation and in the contribution to be made by Germany to its cost. A plebiscite for Upper Silesia was accepted, and Germany, if well-behaved, might join the League 'in the near future'. Another outcome of this last-minute attempt at revision was an invitation to Germany to offer within four months of the signature of the Treaty a lump sum in settlement of her whole liability.

The revised terms, with a memorable covering letter drafted by Philip Kerr, was finally handed to the Germans on 16 June. The first German note in reply ran to about 65,000 words, and it took Lloyd George all day to read it. On 22 June the Weimar National Assembly voted for acceptance with reservations concerning Articles 227 to 231; on the same day the Allies rejected the reservations, and fixed 7 p.m. on the 23rd for unconditional signature, otherwise the Allied armies would march to Berlin and the blockade would be reimposed. Acceptance was announced at Versailles at 5.30 p.m. The ceremonial signing followed on Saturday, 28 June 1919, in the Hall of Mirrors.

To sum up on procedure: despite some work on the treaties, the first eight weeks were largely wasted in confusion; the next four saw the absence of Wilson in Washington and Lloyd George in London, and coincided with the attempt on Clemenceau's life which left him with a bullet in his lung; the final weeks witnessed a hurried concentration on the text of the treaty to be presented to the German plenipotentiaries at Versailles on 7 May. In the words of Harold Nicolson: 'It is the way of every conference to begin like a tortoise and to end like a greyhound.' The American blue-print which had allowed for German representatives and a negotiated peace never reached the agenda; the vanquished were invited to receive the ceremonious communication of terms at the hands of the victors. A written discussion with the Germans followed, in consequence of which some alterations were made in the Treaty, but in substance the Versailles Peace was imposed upon the Germans much as the Germans had imposed the treaties of Brest-Litovsk and Bucharest on Russians and Rumanians.

The treaty which had emerged was a compromise between French and British conceptions of European stability, with America leaning to the British views; and with Wilson and Lloyd George promising to bind their respective countries to come to the aid of France if she were wantonly attacked—a contingency not then seriously apprehended by the guarantors.

Other facts were hidden in the womb of the future: the large post-war loans made by Britain and the United States to foster German recovery; the currency policy which ruined the German middle class; the great sale by Germany of worthless paper marks which later stirred 'the greatest compassion' in the breast of Dr. Schacht. Between 1920 and 1931 Germany had received from abroad some thirty-seven milliard marks and had paid twenty-one milliards in reparations. At the Lausanne Conference in July 1932 reparations were finally cancelled. Concealed also in the dark impenetrable future was the astounding truth that a defeated and bankrupt Germany would rise from the ruins and so indoctrinate her people and reconstruct her industry as to be able in 1939 to challenge the victorious powers of 1919 to a fresh and terrifying Armageddon.

On Sunday, 29 June 1919, Lloyd George left Paris. He remarked to Riddell on the way to Boulogne: 'We do not quite appreciate the importance and magnitude of the events in which we have been taking part.' He was met at Victoria Station by the King and given a great reception on the drive to Buckingham Palace. On 3 July he addressed the Commons on the Peace Treaty and defended it as satisfying the highest demands of justice and fair play. The final guarantee of future peace would be the League of Nations, provided it had behind it the sanction of strong nations prepared at a moment's notice to stop aggression. He begged the nation to think, act, and work together and not to demobilize the spirit of patriotism too soon. On 5 August the King conferred the Order of Merit on Lloyd George in recognition of his pre-eminent services 'both in carrying the War to a victorious end and in securing an honourable peace'.

These were great events, and their grand objective had been the destruction of German militarism and the prevention of another world war. In this the architects of peace completely failed: in effect Germany paid no reparations. In the war-guilt clauses and in the clauses dealing with the Eastern frontiers and with Silesia Hitler was to find abundant fuel for the kindling of the Second World War. There were moments when the League of Nations, with its defective composition, seemed as likely to provoke war as to preserve peace. Was the Treaty to blame? Many verdicts have been passed upon it.

The popular view of the Treaty, especially in Britain as its terms became known, was that it was unduly lenient to the Germans. This view had forced Lloyd George in the middle of April to face his critics in the Commons. The popular impression, however, was most effectively removed in December by the publication of the brilliantly written and immensely influential *Economic Consequences of the Peace* by John Maynard Keynes, which almost overnight transformed an unknown Treasury official into a world figure of seemingly unchallenged authority. Keynes had been in Paris from January onwards as the representative of the Chancellor of the Exchequer; he had fought hard for easier terms, and in June, having failed, he had resigned. It is too much to claim that the book was responsible for the defeat of President Wilson and the withdrawal of the United States from the peace treaties and the League, for much had happened in America between the return of the President in July and the publication of the book in December, but in the opening months of 1920, in the thick of the fight before the final voting in the Senate, the exaggerations of the book and its caricatures of the peacemakers greatly contributed to the immediate decision of Americans to keep out of Europe, and coloured the isolationist views of the next twenty years. The mischief wrought by Keynes's extravagant ill-founded strictures was not confined to Washington. It fanned at once German nationalism and sense of injustice and the British love of leniency.

Keynes's sensational pamphlet may be compared in the world of economics, not unfairly, with Lloyd George's demagogic Bristol speech in the world of politics. 'His statistics were anything but invariably accurate, but his public did not want exact accuracy and would not have been grateful for it.' This was written of Keynes, not of Lloyd George, by the editor of *Lloyds Bank Review* (January 1947). It is worth stating, to off-set Keynes, three contemporary judgements of the Treaty by men who helped to fashion it. Professor Shotwell put his finger on one of its weaknesses: more than a dozen different commissions worked independently, and when their demands were added together the whole was greater than the sum of the parts. The Englishman behind his walls of water, declared M. Tardieu, could not grasp the view of the French with a frontier thrice violated in fifty years. Lord (Robert) Cecil summed up: 'We are prepared to say with the utmost confidence that the broad lines of the Treaty are right.' And, having regard to the circumstances of 1919, many today would endorse his view. The later matured judgement of one of the participating experts (Isaiah Bowman in 1946, in *Foreign Affairs*) is that 'probably no major peace settlement came nearer the mark of principle than the European territorial settlements of 1919'.

The evils of the period between the wars must be assigned not to the Treaty alone or mainly but to the first war itself and to the fact that the Treaty was never enforced. It was unfairly made the scapegoat by active organized German propaganda and the passive concurrence of British public opinion. The attempt initiated by Wilson to democratize Germany under the Weimar régime failed through American abstention and French lack of co-operation. Had Lloyd George supported whole-heartedly the maximum demands of the French in 1919 could we have escaped 1939? No confident answer to this question is possible, and popular opinion today cannot avoid importing into its verdict on his policy knowledge not available to him at the time. It is plain today that Poincaré had a clearer understanding of the dangers of a resurgent Germany than had Lloyd George. Even before the Second World War had broken out there were many who must have wished that Lloyd George had either yielded to the extreme demands of France or supported the full enforcement of the agreed Treaty in which, by achieving a rough average of justice and security, he had faithfully reflected the contemporary views of his countrymen.

CONFERENCE ERA 1920–22

The Treaty of Versailles was signed on 28 June 1919, and when it was ratified in Paris on 10 January 1920 the world felt that the Great War was at last ended. There followed the treaties with Austria, Bulgaria, and Hungary, and a little later, in August 1920, the Treaty of Sèvres was signed in favour of Greece—only to be revised in favour of a victorious Turkey in the Treaty of Lausanne, July 1923. Balfour and Curzon, successively Foreign Secretaries, had more to do with the making of these agreements than had Lloyd George. They were advised by two distinguished civil servants, very different in type, Sir Eyre Crowe and Sir William Tyrrell, the one industrious, precise, and proper, the other intuitive and personal. Lloyd George devoted himself to the general settlement of European problems in a series of international conferences, nine of which were held in 1920, seven in 1921, and seven in 1922, ranging in length from one day at Hythe to six weeks at Genoa. In most of these, as the sole survivor of the Big Four, he was the central and dominating figure.

The framers of the Treaty of Versailles had provided for its execution numerous agencies which would function after the dispersal of the Supreme War Council: the reparations and other commissions instructed to deal with Germany, the Ambassadors' Conference acting as a consultative body in Paris, the League of Nations, and the International Labour Office in Geneva.

But all this elaborate machinery could not overcome the exhaustion, the antipathies, and the rivalries of the nations of Europe, or achieve their permanent pacification. The passions of war could not be extinguished overnight; the delirious enthusiasm which had accompanied the signing of the Treaty dissolved into disenchantment. Frontiers had been drawn and nationalities defined for peoples who had not served the long apprenticeship which self-government exacts. Western democracy is a way of life which calls for the exercise of rights and duties in an atmosphere of liberty and normally steers clear of revolutionary extremes. The war had been won by the great peoples of France, America, and the British Empire, and it was natural to suppose that the democratic system for which they had fought would be widely extended. It turned out quite otherwise.

In the first three post-war years Lloyd George was actually the Prime Minister of Europe in a way without parallel in the long roll of British Premiers. He was transported in special trains and special steamers from one meeting to another accompanied by ministerial colleagues, secretaries, attendants, and journalists, the accommodation provided for him eclipsing that which royalty enjoyed when journeying abroad. He popularized and dramatized foreign affairs for the newly enfranchised millions.

Economic forces were more and more clamouring for attention, turning themselves into political issues, both binding the world into one and dividing it into competing entities. Trotsky at Brest-Litovsk and President Wilson with his Fourteen Points had endeavoured to launch mass diplomacy upon the nations of Europe. Lloyd George more than any other British statesman wrought the transition from the Old to the New Diplomacy, and brought into the foreground of international debate the condition of the poor and the oppressed.

Apart from its spectacular attractions, Lloyd George was drawn to diplomacy through conference by his well-justified belief in his own powers around a table. He could be light-handed and graceful and most cautious withal when addressing the assembled delegates or the press; he was not shy with foreigners as many Englishmen are; with journalists he was at home. But the large numbers which followed in his train shrank to half a dozen or less when it came to doing business, and from the most intimate negotiations even the professional diplomats of the local embassies were excluded. During each conference there would be numerous unfettered, unrecorded, confidential conversations, and these would control the subsequent debate in open session. Lloyd George knew that his gifts lay in his power of rapid assimilation, his sense of atmosphere, his persuasiveness, his ability to pick out weak points and enforce strong ones. Failure to reach agreement or to do no more than expose divergencies to the world could, as a rule and for the moment, be veiled in intentional obscurity by drafting a dextrous formula, an art in which his secretaries became proficient.

Lloyd George did not so much learn the arts of diplomacy in war as apply the gifts with which he was already endowed, gifts which had made him a formidable negotiator in his first post at the Board of Trade. His native intuition and power of foreseeing several moves ahead were valuable assets, but they could not always compete with the ripe experience of the trained diplomat, experience acquired by years of residence in foreign courts. His gifts did not protect him from falling under the spell of men of the exceptional quality of a Venizelos, and to this liability some of his worst mistakes, Smyrna, for example, were attributable.

Many instances could be adduced of the extreme informality with which he transacted business of the highest importance. Here is one for which we have the testimony of Lord Hardinge of Penshurst. The quotation refers to the period of the Paris Conference.

Sometimes he did not even consult his own Foreign Secretary, Mr. Balfour, on the most weighty and important matters. For instance, I went one morning at the usual hour of 11 a.m. to see Mr. Balfour, and while discussing with him various matters connected with the work of the Delegation, Mr. Philip Kerr, Lloyd George's Private Secretary, entered the room. He handed Mr. Balfour a paper saying it was a draft Treaty of Guarantee by England and America of French territory in the event of German aggression. Mr. Balfour asked who had drawn it up and by whose orders. Kerr explained that Sir C. Hurst, the Legal Adviser of the Foreign Office, had been called up out of bed at midnight by Lloyd George and received his instructions to draft a Treaty of Guarantee. He had done so and the text of the Treaty had been already submitted to President Wilson and M. Clemenceau, both of whom had approved it. . . . The sequel to that morning's incident was that at a plenary meeting of the Conference held at 3 p.m. that afternoon I saw the treaty in question receive the signatures of President Wilson, Lloyd George and Mr. Balfour.[5]

Here is another example, which Baldwin was fond of telling. Lloyd George on one occasion asked Balfour to go to Paris on a diplomatic mission:

'I am to persuade the French to reduce their battle-fleet in comparison with that of the U.S.A.; to reduce their submarine fleet as it is inconceivable that France will go to war with England; to let us build a bigger air force than France so that we may repel any attack by them. For this mission', said Balfour, 'I think a trained diplomatist is required.'[6]

If Lloyd George was comparatively ignorant of foreign countries and sometimes light-hearted in his treatment of them, he had a knowledge, wide and deep, of his own country, and he was as firmly anchored to the fundamentals of local and imperial patriotism as Pitt or Palmerston. It is this which explains why he was a daring social reformer at home, and a cautious statesman abroad. 'The limiting factor was not so much what he thought right as what . . . he thought it safe to put before the House of Commons and the public.' His objectives in the series of conferences were not only moderate and conciliatory but stable. Contrary to the popular impression, he was steadfast in pursuing them.

When the war ended Germany's navy was at the bottom of the sea, her overseas possessions were in the hands of the Allies, and France was established as the chief land power on the Continent. The European ascendancy which Germany had enjoyed for fifty years before 1914 had passed, with the help of her Allies, to France. Her body had been battered and bruised as theirs had not been, and she counted on their healing help to restore her. This help was promised to her and then withdrawn. Revolution had alienated her former Eastern ally and debtor, Russia. She was torn by the wish for large reparation payments and the fear of a recuperated and mighty Germany. This dualism in Allied councils provides

[5] Lord Hardinge of Penshurst, *The Old Diplomacy*, p. 241.   [6] Author's diary.

the key to the clashing policies of the conference era. Broadly, France was for the strict fulfilment of the Treaty and Lloyd George for conciliation and concession: scale down reparations, resume co-operation in the economic field, draw Germany away from Russia and Communism into the ambit of Western civilization. It was a policy which finds a parallel today, with this difference: that the condition of Germany is now more difficult than it was in 1919. The conferences were concerned with these opposing policies in relation to reparations, disarmament, and efforts to stop hostilities between Greece and Turkey, Poland and Russia.

In December 1921 Lloyd George and Briand, who both favoured a policy of reconciliation so far as public opinion would permit, had agreed that the Supreme Council should meet at Cannes in January to discuss a Pact of Security with France and to draw up a skeleton agenda for a European Conference at Genoa, to which Germany and Russia should be invited. Rathenau was brought to Cannes to discuss reparations.

Briand was suspected in Paris of being too subservient to the British Prime Minister. Illustrated papers showed him learning to play golf with Lloyd George as coach; such levity was too much for President Millerand, and Briand, 'with the perpetual smile and the perpetual cigarette', was recalled; he resigned and made room for Poincaré, a stern, unbending legalist who was determined to enforce every jot and tittle of the Treaty of Versailles. The fall of Briand and the rise of Poincaré to power had most important and unfavourable repercussions on the policies of Lloyd George.

On 14 January Poincaré and Lloyd George met at the British Embassy in Paris. Acting boldly, without previous Cabinet sanction, Lloyd George renewed the offer of the pact which he had made to Briand, but Poincaré stipulated for a Military Convention with specific undertakings about the number of troops Great Britain would furnish and other details. Lloyd George offered to support France 'with all our force', but Poincaré was not content with this. 'I must say', comments Lord Hardinge, 'that Lloyd George acted with great dignity and firmness under provocation and impressed me most favourably....'

At the Imperial Conference in June 1921, the first to be held since the war, Lloyd George, in his survey of the international situation, welcomed any approach the United States might care to make towards the reduction of armaments. He had in mind naval competition, Pacific and Far East problems, particularly the Anglo-Japanese Alliance. In August the American President issued formal invitations to Great Britain, France, Italy, and Japan to meet at Washington on Armistice Day, 11 November. Charles Evans Hughes, then Secretary of State in the Harding Cabinet, and the real originator of the Conference, was elected chairman. Balfour was present as the chief British delegate, a position which the Prime Minister would naturally have been glad to occupy had it been possible for him to leave London at that time. Great Britain desired to stand well with Japan and with the United States. The possibilities of two misunderstandings were avoided and the Anglo-Japanese Alliance was superseded by a four-power treaty (Great Britain, France, United States, Japan)—an achievement which owed much to Balfour's statesmanship. Speaking in London on 21 January Lloyd George said: 'The Washington Conference is establishing peace in the great West, and I am looking to the Genoa Conference to establish peace in the East. They will be like two wings of the Angel of Peace hovering over the world.'

GENOA CONFERENCE

The Genoa Conference was the next stage in Lloyd George's persistent attempt to arrest the economic decay of Europe, to discuss the problem of Russia, and to bring French policy into line with his own.

In the very first week of the meeting of the Paris Conference in January 1919 Lloyd George had brought up the question of relations with Russia, which had been outlawed since the Revolution of November 1917. He outlined three possible policies: military intervention; a *cordon sanitaire* or iron curtain between Russia and the rest of Europe; or a meeting with Russian representatives, a meeting which never took place. His next important step was to encourage trade relations with Russian co-operative organizations at San Remo in April and with the Russian Trade Mission led by M. Krassin in London from June to November 1920. This ultimately led to the signing of a trade agreement in March 1921 by Sir Robert Horne, Chancellor of the Exchequer, and M. Krassin. It was declared to be merely preliminary to political and economic relations between the two countries. It fitted in with Lenin's temporizing policy and his readiness to conclude trade agreements with capitalist countries. 'We go to Genoa', he said, 'not as Bolsheviks but as merchants.'

Lloyd George gathered on 10 April 1922 the leading representatives of thirty-four nations within the palaces of Genoa in the most ambitious, most heroic enterprise of his life. One is reminded of the earlier project of his countryman, Robert Owen, to emancipate the human race from ignorance, poverty, division, sin, and misery. But Lloyd George was far more opportunist than perfectionist on the voyage to Utopia. 'I want dreams, but dreams that are realizable.'

The odds against him at Genoa were overwhelming. The Conference held the hopes of the world for six weeks, and failed or succeeded according to the tests applied. Its results were inconclusive, and confessed failure was avoided by the expedient of adjourning to a gathering of experts at The Hague, where no satisfactory agreement was reached with the Russians on the vexed issue of the restitution of nationalized private property. This postponement provided a face-saving truce for a few months, and when it failed left each power free to take its own line. This meant that France would continue to exclude Russia from Europe, to isolate Germany, to threaten the occupation of the Ruhr in order to secure not only Ruhr coal but Lorraine ore and the output of Poland, Silesia, and Czechoslovakia. To this policy Lloyd George was opposed: he sought not only, as France did, security against Germany, but security against war.

Genoa, according to Lord D'Abernon, was a conflict of three vanities: Lloyd George, Rathenau, and Poincaré—and perhaps if we knew more of Russian human nature we should add a fourth, the Russian representative Tchitcherin, who was surprised to find in Lloyd George not so much a lyrical Welshman as a stubborn Britisher. Poincaré absented himself, and his representative Barthou was instructed to write *Verboten!* across any discussion of burning topics like reparations, disarmament, and the peace treaties. Earlier attempts to overcome these objections at a meeting of Lloyd George and Poincaré at Boulogne had only deepened their dislike for each other, and Rathenau had unwisely commented on what he called the defeat of Lloyd George at this encounter. This was resented by Lloyd George, who at Cannes had got on well with Rathenau and had supported a moratorium on German cash payments immediately due. At Genoa Lloyd George avoided Rathenau. This led to suspicions that Germany was being isolated, and this in turn brought about the signing secretly on Sunday, 16 April, of the treaty of Rapallo by which Germany and Russia renounced mutual claims and undertook to assist each other 'in the alleviation of their economic difficulties in the most benevolent spirit'.

The storm caused by this 'act of sabotage' threatened to shipwreck the Conference, but it passed; the four commissions continued with their tasks, political, financial, economic, and transport, and after the usual crises they duly presented their reports.

At the Paris Peace Conference Lloyd George had expressed his fear of the organizing brains of Germany being put at the disposal of the revolutionary fanaticism of Russia, and at Genoa he spoke of a hungry Russia being equipped by an angry Germany. He did not wish to force them into a 'fierce friendship'. Why, Lord Grey asked, not make use of the League of Nations? Neither Russia nor Germany would be there, was the reply. Why, others asked, have dealings at all with Russia? Lloyd George quoted the precedent of Pitt who endeavoured to make peace with the French revolutionaries in 1796 and failed. In 1797 Pitt made the same attempt and again failed. Lloyd George was prepared to make peace with a government whose principles were just as odious and whose actions were just as loathsome as those of the French terrorists of the 1790's.

Critics whispered in the clubs that the Conference, if successful, would be used as an electioneering cry which might give the Prime Minister a new lease of office. If that thought crossed his mind, which was not unlikely or entirely unworthy, the postulate was success. He wanted trade restored and an end put to the suffering of the workless and wageless millions in western Europe and to the famine and pestilence in the East. The most cynical electioneer could not be indifferent to such facts, and Lloyd George was not a cynic. He put forth the most valiant exertions at Genoa to secure a pact of non-aggression. He got its simulacrum not its substance, mainly because the French insisted on several reservations, especially one exempting the Little Entente from any obligation of disarmament. Also, in 1922 as in our own day, it proved difficult to penetrate the Bolshevik mentality and to secure a final statement on any subject whatever. Tchitcherin wished to add items to the agenda, and proposed a universal conference. The Prime Minister retorted:

> The Conference has already got as large a cargo as it can carry. Every civilized country marked a load line on their merchant ships in order to show how heavily they could be laden. M. Tchitcherin must not remove the load line. If he does he may sink the ship and perhaps find himself among the drowned.[7]

Lloyd George made heavy draughts on his undefeatable spirit, his inexhaustible good humour, resilient temperament, amazing patience, to hold the remarkable Conference together. He could claim that all the right questions had been put, some of them had been answered, all had been ventilated in the face of the sun and in the eye of light.

The Conference came to an end on 19 May in the Palazzo di San Giorgio. In his farewell speech Lloyd George echoed an evangelical hymn of his boyhood:

> At Cannes we threw out the life-line. We have not yet drawn it in as I thought we might; neither has it been snapped; neither has it been let go; it is still there. We would like to draw all the distressed, all the hungry, all the suffering in the East of Europe back to life with all the health that the accumulated energy and skill of other lands can give.[8]

The Prime Minister reached London on the 20th, and Victoria Station was thronged with a welcoming crowd. 'Russia has been brought back into the world,' he told the press. If Poincaré had imagined that Britain would drop Lloyd George after Genoa as France had dropped Briand after Cannes the hope was premature.

IRELAND

The Irish Nationalist party had provided Lloyd George in his youth with a model and an inspiration for Welsh political action. When at the head of affairs he was to find his course continually obstructed and deflected by the feuds of Irishmen. To these we must now turn from the complications of the foreign scene.

Lloyd George was a federalist and in favour of separate legislatures for England, Scotland, and Wales as well as for Ireland. He

[7] *Manchester Guardian*, 12 April 1922.
[8] *The Times*, 20 May 1922.

had taken up this position at the outset of his public career and he
retained it consistently thereafter. Devolution was to reappear in
his election address in 1929. He was against making concessions to
Ireland which could not be made to other parts of the United
Kingdom. The key to his Irish policy, however, is to be found not
in this belief in Home-Rule-All-Round but in his unwillingness to
coerce the Protestant minority in Ulster. As he had said to Parliament on 7 March 1917, he would not put under Nationalist rule
the people who were

As alien in blood, in religious faith, in traditions, in outlook—as alien
from the rest of Ireland in this respect as the inhabitants of Fife or
Aberdeen. . . . To place them under national rule against their will
would be as glaring an outrage on the principles of liberty and self-
government, as the denial of self-government would be for the rest of
Ireland.[9]

He was never, as Gladstone was, a crusader for Home Rule.

During the agony of the war, the importance of propitiating
Irish-American opinion had weighed heavily on him. Cecil Spring-
Rice from Washington and Walter Hines Page in London pressed
him hard for some solution of the age-long controversy. In May
1917 the Prime Minister offered either the immediate application
of the Home Rule Act to Ireland minus the six counties, or a convention of Irishmen of all parties who should be asked to hammer
out an instrument for their own government. Hitherto, said the
Premier, Britain had done all the construction and Ireland all the
criticism. Let them reach 'substantial agreement' and he would
give legislative effect to it. The first choice, involving partition,
was unacceptable to the Nationalists, so in June the Prime Minister set up a convention of 101 members, with Sir Horace Plunkett
as chairman.

The convention was composed of Ulster Unionists, Southern
Unionists, Nationalists, Labour, and Government nominees. Sinn
Feiners refused to serve. Ulster had entered the convention with a
guarantee obtained by Carson from Lloyd George 'that there
should be no coercion of Ulster'. Redmond, who was a sick man,
did his utmost to unite Nationalists, Southern Unionists, and
Labour. Lord Midleton, a Southern Unionist, very nearly succeeded in doing this by means of a compromise on the fiscal

[9] Hansard, fifth series, vol. xci, 7 March 1917.

question and an agreed constitution, but he and Redmond were effectively thwarted not only by Ulster's stolid 'No!' but by a few of the Catholic Bishops, who played an ambiguous role between Nationalists and Sinn Fein.

For months vain efforts to secure unanimity persisted, only to be finally blocked by the extremists of both sides. Meanwhile disaffection had been spreading for months past, especially in the south-west where there was an organized conspiracy against law and order. In March 1918 Redmond died, broken-hearted; the National Volunteers numbering tens of thousands then went over to Sinn Fein. The war had put a stop to emigration, so Ireland abounded in young men steeped in idealism but with minds poisoned against England, whose every act was judged in the light of ancient wrongs and malicious history. 'The fight for Irish freedom', Dorothy Macardle reports Dr. Fogarty, Bishop of Killaloe, as saying, 'has passed into the hands of the young men of Ireland . . . and when the young men of Ireland hit back at their oppressors it is not for an old man like me to cry "Foul".' In April conscription was extended to Ireland—an act which Lord Midleton described as one of the most foolish experiments ever attempted in that country. This decision caused Lloyd George far more heart-searching than is reflected in the *Memoirs* and was pressed upon him by the Unionist colleagues by whom he was then surrounded. Conscription had to be given up in June.

The general election which followed the Armistice secured a great victory for Sinn Fein over the Nationalist party, and Sinn Fein, repudiating Westminster, set up its own system of government and proclaimed Irish independence. A guerrilla war raged between the Irish Republican Army and the police, known as the Royal Irish Constabulary. This Service suffered such severe losses that recruiting for it had to be transferred to London. This was the origin of the force clad in khaki and black caps nicknamed Black-and-Tans, and extended to include Auxiliaries, a body of ex-officers who were more mobile than members of the regular army and more able to cope with the secret bands of roving militant Republicans. Throughout 1919, 1920, and the first half of 1921 the history of Ireland is a history of ambush, murder, and outrage by gunmen on both sides, of hunger-striking in prisons, of a reign of crime and terror, 'the methods of beasts'. It was not at once that Lloyd George fully realized the fact that, in southern

Ireland, British constitutional rule was over, that civil and legal administration had passed to Sinn Fein, with a republic as its firm objective. He was much occupied with conferences on foreign affairs abroad, and with industrial strife at home. The strain on him was such that friends advised him, but in vain, to resign and take a long holiday. He still thought in terms of Gladstonian Home Rule with self-determination for Ulster, and he scoffed at Asquith's proposal (January 1920) to place Ireland on a Dominion basis.

In March 1919 the Government had brought in a bill which offered Ireland two parliaments, one for the South and one for the Six Counties, linked together by a joint council and with certain powers reserved for the Imperial Parliament. It was not until 23 December 1920 that the bill was passed into law. Thus was brought into existence the Parliament which now functions in Belfast. Partition was made definite, and a new basis secured for an attempt to bridge the moral dualism of Ireland.

Pursuing in Parliament a policy of mediation with his gloved right hand, Lloyd George used his gauntleted left to enforce martial law, announced on 10 December 1920, in the south-west of Ireland, and planned, it was hinted, its extension to the whole country. Confronted with what was indistinguishable from civil war, his policy had hardened. The task of Dublin Castle was one of infinite difficulty and danger, and Lord French and the Irish Executive in discharging it were loyally supported by the Prime Minister in the belief that a few months of resolute government would bring the anarchy to an end and enable peace to be made with the moderates. Lloyd George 'thanked God for Sir Hamar Greenwood and General Tudor'. He should have included in his thanksgiving two distinguished civil servants whose contributions to a peaceful solution were of the first importance: they were Sir John Anderson and Sir Alfred Cope, under-secretaries to the Lord Lieutenant.

Britishers grew increasingly ashamed, as the facts became known, of the deeds done in their name. Day after day C. P. Scott in the *Manchester Guardian* insisted that Englishmen wished to do justice to Ireland and were 'resolved in the process to keep their hands decently clean and their reputation in the world unsullied. That is where Mr. George is failing us.' But there were also Sinn Feiners who were ashamed. Father O'Flanagan, Acting-President during Mr. de Valera's absence in America, and Arthur Griffith got into touch with Lloyd George and there were proposals for a Christmas truce.

All these efforts came to nothing and it began to look as if the pacification of Ireland would be a matter not of months but years, when relief came from an unexpected quarter. The King went to Belfast to open the Ulster Parliament on 22 June 1921, and made a moving appeal for forbearance and conciliation. Its effect was immediate, and on 24 June Lloyd George addressed letters to Mr. de Valera and Sir James Craig inviting them to a conference in London. In July the British Prime Minister had four interviews with Mr. de Valera in Downing Street and on the 20th the British proposals for an Irish settlement were handed to him. They included Irish Dominion status subject to conditions dealing with defence, trade, and debt: proposals already put privately to the Irish leaders by General Smuts in Dublin. The agreement, if reached, was to take the form of a treaty—in itself this marked a great change in procedure. The Irish reply on 10 August refused Dominion status as illusory, and offered instead a 'treaty of free association with the British Commonwealth group'. This formula or a near variant persisted almost to the last hour of the negotiations. The Prime Minister claimed allegiance to the Crown as fundamental to any agreement.

From the middle of August to the end of September the Prime Minister and the President of Eire fired letters and telegrams and messages at each other from London and Dublin, from Gairloch where Lloyd George was on holiday, and from Inverness where he gathered together his colleagues for a meeting of the Cabinet in the town hall—a characteristic action not welcomed by Ministers, who thought he might have travelled to Edinburgh to meet them. The position was finally adjusted by an invitation to a conference in London, and Mr. de Valera's agreement to send delegates 'to explore every possibility of settlement by personal discussion'.

Mr. de Valera remained in Dublin. On the Irish side two men came quickly to the fore: Arthur Griffith and Michael Collins, two strongly contrasted types. Arthur Griffith, the creator of Sinn Fein, for sixteen years had been telling his countrymen to look to themselves and not to England for salvation. He preached to the generation made intellectually receptive by the Gaelic League and economically independent by the revolution in landholding begun in 1881, 'the first well-fed generation of young Irishmen'. Quite unlike the popular conception of an Irish leader, he used the fewest possible words to express his meaning and answered the questions of others rather than make speeches of his own. All too familiar with his country's sad story, he strained every nerve to make impossible a renewal of hostilities.

Michael Collins had the qualities which make the popular hero; he arrived at the conference with a romantic legend already gathered around him—stories of his daring adventures and magical escapes. Broad-shouldered, black-haired, the early picture of the smiling young Irishman as a brutal assassin had softened into that of an honourable foe driven to guerrilla warfare as the only way by which a little country could stand up to the biggest empire the world had ever seen. His irrepressible gaiety of spirit, picturesque speech, dislike for petty detail, concentration on main issues, willingness to admit blunders and worse on his own side, his avoidance of self-advertisement, captivated everybody at once from the Prime Minister, who had to do business with him, to the girls who pursued him for favours.

The conference had its first session on 11 October, when seven British Ministers met the Irish five. Lionel Curtis, author of an important article in volume xi of the *Round Table* outlining suggestions for a settlement with Ireland, was one of the British secretaries. His opposite number on the Irish side was a former school-fellow, Erskine Childers, doctrinaire and irreconcilable. Full-dress debates with twelve plenipotentiaries present were found unsuitable when the most vital issues were joined, and the Prime Minister, usually with Austen Chamberlain or Lord Birkenhead, met with Griffith and Collins alone. Die-hards in Parliament became so restive and suspicious that the Prime Minister challenged them to open debate, and on the last day of October he defeated them by ten to one after one of the most skilful speeches he ever delivered, where he had to preserve the most delicate equilibrium between the conflicting forces. On the night before he had secured from Arthur Griffith a personal pledge of participation in the Commonwealth and allegiance to the Crown in return for the recognition of the essential unity of Ireland.

During the final stages of the conference Lloyd George had taken measures to keep Bonar Law and Carson informed of the proceedings, using Sir Robert Bruce, editor of the *Glasgow Herald*, as his secret intermediary. Bruce reports a dinner with the two Unionists in which matters were brought to a head:

To end I said: 'The issue lies in the hands of you two men. If there is to be a failure and all that that will mean, do not let the onus for the failure lie on Ulster's shoulders.' Carson would not move. 'The Little Man', so he called the P.M., 'has betrayed Ulster and I'll have nothing to do with him.' A servant announced that my taxi was at the door. I said 'Goodnight' to Carson. Bonar had kept silent. He came with me to the door. . . . 'You have Carson's answer?' 'Yes, but what is yours?' . . . 'You can now tell the Little Man that in my own way and time I shall work for a Settlement.' . . . In about three weeks Bonar rose in the House and made his statement which ensured the settlement.[10]

The Government gave Ulster the choice: either to come into an All-Ireland Parliament with safeguards against oppression by the South, or to retain her present Parliament, share all imperial burdens, and submit to a commission which would redraw her boundary as nearly as possible on sectarian lines.

The last fortnight of the negotiations was filled with rumours and denials of deadlocks and breakdowns. The fact daily repeated that Ireland was a mother country stirred no filial emotion in Downing Street. 'Ireland is two nations', snapped Bonar Law, 'and two religions.' There were divergencies on the oath of allegiance and on the meaning of external association. The Cabinet of Dail Eireann, after a meeting which lasted seven hours, turned down the British proposals. Not an inch towards unity, said Craig in Belfast; not an inch from unity, said de Valera in Dublin. The tragedy of their country was incarnate in the stubborn wills of these two Irishmen, and it now only remained to put this rejection and the British reply into formal terms to bring the conference to an end. That was the position when Lloyd George awoke at five on Monday, 5 December 1921, and began to exercise what Asquith once called 'the most resourceful mind in Europe'. In less than twenty-four hours he had completely transformed the situation and had shaken hands with the Irish delegates over a signed treaty which Griffith later declared should end the conflict of centuries.

How was it done? How came it about that the man who scorned to 'negotiate with assassins' had 'shaken hands with murder'? 'Lloyd George', wrote C. P. Scott of the *Manchester Guardian*, 'was

[10] Sir Robert Bruce, *House of Memories*, p. 13.

wonderful in his power of action as in his power of oblivion'. He was Machiavelli's lion and fox. At the climax of negotiations, about 7.30 p.m., he put dramatically the choice of peace or war to the delegates: he had good reason to believe that Griffith would sign— which he did, pledging himself with the words: 'I personally will sign this agreement and recommend it to my countrymen.'

The task of peacemaker was one into which the Prime Minister was free to throw the whole of his rich human nature, his love of liberty, his sympathy for a Celtic people, his belief in the value of the British Empire to the progress of mankind. He put every ounce of energy into the conference. Tenacity, foresight, vigilance, fairness to opponents, patience with opponents and colleagues alike, a mind of the most extraordinary intuitive swiftness, the most unfailing good temper day and night, in hours of intense strain no less than in times of comparative smoothness—these were the shining qualities that brought to an end the deadlock which had baffled all the great statesmen of England.

People and press everywhere welcomed the settlement. John Dove, the editor of the *Round Table*, wrote from Baden on 13 January 1922:

> The feeling about Lloyd George is extraordinary. He may, they even think, be that man of destiny for which the world is longing. 'Is he', said a German guest at the pension to me last night, 'the great and understanding man that all the world believes him? . . . They believe sometimes that he sees beyond the interests of nationality to those of *Mensch*.' [11]

It is a pity that the story cannot continue on the note of pacification. The Treaty ended the rule of Dublin Castle and gave the Free State a parliament, a native army, and fiscal autonomy; gave option to Ulster and to Britain facilities for her navy. British Ministers felt that a basis for future friendly co-operation had been secured and that, given time, economic forces might heal the feud with Ulster.

For a fortnight in January the Treaty was debated in Dublin, and its acceptance was endorsed by a narrow majority of 64 against 57. Griffith became President. Mr. de Valera led the minority, supported by a section of the Irish Republican Army. A fratricidal war followed in June during which Collins was shot, Erskine

---

[11] *Letters of John Dove*, edited by R. H. Brand, p. 173.

Childers executed, and Kevin O'Higgins, Minister for Home Affairs, assassinated. And not in the South only but in the streets of Belfast Catholics and Protestants were being murdered, and in Westminster Sir Henry Wilson was shot by two members of the Irish Republican Army.

On 12 August Arthur Griffith died unexpectedly when leaving for his office, after a short illness in a nursing-home. He was only fifty and at the height of his power. William Cosgrave became head of the Free State Government and declared his intention of supporting the Treaty.

Throughout 1922 there were frequent conferences in London for the settlement of the Irish Constitution and some anxious moments when the law, practice, and constitutional usage of Canada had to be called in evidence. Mr. Churchill, as Colonial Secretary, presided over these meetings. On 19 October Lloyd George ceased to be Prime Minister and he telegraphed to Cosgrave to express his belief that the pledge to pass the Irish Constitution through Parliament would be honoured by his successor. This was done by Bonar Law, and the Constitution came into operation on 6 December 1922, by Proclamation. It lasted until 1937.

FALL OF THE COALITION 1922

As a result of the Coupon Election, the Coalition had been given a majority of nearly 500 (which included 334 Conservatives, 133 Liberal, and 11 Labour Members) over all parties with which to solve the colossal problems left by the war. It might have succeeded had its quality been better and had it possessed inner coherence, but its direction was in the hands of a Prime Minister who, basically a radical and a party in himself, was bound to collide with the Tory machine.

By the end of 1921 Lloyd George was in favour of an early election, and it was widely believed that he would appeal to the country on his return from the conference at Cannes in January and obtain a mandate for the Genoa Conference. Austen Chamberlain, the Conservative leader, regarded his own followers and the National Liberals as 'two wings of one great constitutional and progressive party', but this view was not shared by those who held that with a Conservative majority in the Government there should be a Conservative Prime Minister. He himself had grown to entertain a deep loyalty and admiration for Lloyd George and saw in their continued co-operation the best way of excluding the Socialists from power. But he could not conceal from himself that dislike and distrust of the Premier's methods were on the increase.

Industrial strife was widespread. The war had witnessed the growth of a vast improvised collectivism; the social and economic life of the nation was subjected to control and rationing, the state became the chief importer, manufacturer, and distributor not only of war materials but of domestic commodities. Nearly three million persons were employed in munition factories and nearly five were enlisted in the armed forces. Special Cabinet committees had prepared programmes of decontrol and demobilization in readiness for transition to a peace economy, but when the Armistice came these were swept away by the overwhelming pressure to return to pre-war practice. Plans for orderly reconstruction were scrapped, shipping was derequisitioned, and the national shipyards were sold. Prices were inflated by the sale of enormous quantities of war stores. For most of 1919 there was a boom which lasted into 1920. Deep depression followed. The Government, alarmed and foreseeing a large loss, decided in February 1921 to decontrol the mining industry on 31 March instead of at the end of August as originally intended. The demand of the miners that wages should continue to be fixed by a National Wages Board was opposed by the owners and became the battle-ground for a strike, and it was not until 4 July that the men returned to work, having then concluded the first national agreement between the Miners' Federation and the Mining Association. In July the policy of the Agricultural Act of 1920 was completely reversed: the subsidy, all vestige of control, the Wages Board were all swept away. In August the decontrol of the railways was more peacefully arranged. During 1921 the average weekly number of wholly or partially unemployed drawing benefit was just over two millions; there was therefore vast expenditure for relief, and this entailed severe taxation.

Lloyd George's extraordinary efforts to achieve world recovery and co-operation which culminated at Genoa in May 1922 failed, and his frequent absences from the House of Commons, which success would have condoned, contributed to his undoing. The Coalition and its Chief were persistently assailed by the Independent Liberals or 'Wee Frees'. Lloyd George, said Lord Gladstone, was not as Herbert Fisher had called him, a genius thrown up by a cataclysm, but a genie let out of a bottle by a rash mistake of the Conservative party which was now making desperate efforts to get him back into safe confinement.

At the end of February 1922 Lloyd George wrote to Austen Chamberlain reviewing the political situation and offering to stand down in his favour and to give him loyal support if he would form a homogeneous Government. Chamberlain assured the Prime Minister that his resignation would be a disaster, and nothing came of the suggestion. But the situation was controlled behind the scenes by Sir George Younger, the chairman of the Tory party organization, who saw clearly that a premature dissolution at the instance of Lloyd George would have meant his return to power as leader. Younger was astute enough to avoid such a contingency: when in October he found the time was ripe, the Conservative party freed itself from Lloyd George.

In the autumn, conscious perhaps of his uncertain hold on office, Lloyd George concerned himself with projects for obtaining control of *The Times* which the death of Lord Northcliffe (14 August) brought into the market. One of the financiers consulted was the Welsh coal-owner David (later Lord) Davies who was willing to join in the purchase on condition that Lloyd George severed his connexion with the House of Commons and became Managing Director and Editor of *The Times* under contract for three or five years. Nothing came of this proposal and the property was acquired by John Jacob Astor.

During 1922 the Coalition had grown weaker; numerous by-elections were lost, and it was damaged by the acute friction over Edwin Montagu's departure from the India Office. He had published without Cabinet authority a telegram from the Viceroy, Lord Reading, recommending the evacuation of Constantinople and a strongly pro-Turkish policy, with which he was in full sympathy. Montagu was an able, sensitive, and passionate Minister but personally unpopular, and when he resigned the House cheered. He defended himself in a speech at Cambridge on 12 March in which he described the Prime Minister as an erratic genius who had appealed to a Cabinet responsibility which he himself had destroyed.

With the exception of important financial measures, the Government of India Act of 1919—which pointed 'the way to full responsible government hereafter'—and the Irish Treaty, a settlement unwelcomed by die-hard Tories, the positive achievements of the Coalition were not remarkable. It had to steer a course between reactionaries and revolutionaries in this post-war period. Electioneering promises of radical reform of land, housing, health, and conditions of labour were only partially fulfilled. Two important Ministries were, however, created: the Ministries of Health and of Transport.

In mid-September of 1922 Lloyd George spent a week-end at Chequers with his chief Conservative colleagues, and it was agreed to go to the country as a Coalition Government. On learning this, Sir George Younger was 'frankly appalled' and the Chief Tory Whip, Sir Leslie Wilson, 'very disturbed'. And they did nothing to check the growing resistance of the rank and file to this decision.

The House of Commons had adjourned on 4 August. Before it reassembled on 14 November, the Conservatives had rebelled and Lloyd George had ceased to be Prime Minister. The domestic crisis was precipitated by the sudden fear that the country was being rushed into a new war in the Near East. It is a sorry tale compounded, as Lloyd George wrote, of errors and accidents. The policy was perhaps mainly his, but it was in its early stages endorsed by his colleagues in London and later by his colleagues in Paris.

The history of the Near East from the Armistice to the fall of the Coalition four years later records the rivalry of Italians and Greeks for slices of Asia Minor, the rise of Turkish nationalists into power under the brilliant leadership of Mustapha Kemal Pasha, hopes that the United States might accept mandates for Constantinople and Armenia, and the failure of the Peace Conference to settle promptly on a Near East policy and enforce it.

Lloyd George's extreme hostility to the Turk was curbed by the pro-Turkish section in his Cabinet and by Indian Moslem opinion which he could not ignore. The British Prime Minister had a romantic admiration for ancient Greece, for the Gladstonian tradition, with its concern for minorities, and for Venizelos, 'the greatest statesman Greece had thrown up since the days of Pericles'. The Cretan and the Welshman were Liberals and democrats, and had much besides in common—eloquence, energy, negotiating skill, astuteness—but their mutual admiration proved disastrous for Greece.

During the war the Greeks, despite the efforts of Venizelos, had not done much to help the Allies until in its later phases when they were useful in Macedonia and in the Ukraine. They were rewarded in western Anatolia in May 1919 when they occupied Smyrna with the approval of Clemenceau, Wilson, and Lloyd George. At San Remo in April 1920 Lloyd George, against the advice of Foch and Henry Wilson, listened to the Cretan leader and drafted a treaty which put Smyrna and eastern Thrace under Greek control and internationalized Constantinople and the Straits. These and other provisions emerged in August as the ill-fated Treaty of Sèvres, 'fragile as the porcelain vases', as Poincaré described it. Venizelos brought it in triumph to Athens, but he was repudiated three months later by his own people at a general election. On 17 November 1920 Lloyd George wrote to his friend: 'I was deeply shocked and distressed to see the result of the Greek Elections. It almost makes one despair of Democracy.' Democracy rejected Venizelos as it was to reject Clemenceau, Wilson, Lloyd George himself, and, later, Churchill.

The substitution of King Constantine for Venizelos diminished sympathy for the Greeks in England, but Constantine continued the struggle in Anatolia, with the indirect encouragement of Lloyd George. Throughout 1921 attempts at pacification continued. Curzon vainly tried to compose the differences between the Allies themselves, but the exchange of Briand for Poincaré after Cannes combined with hostility to Lloyd George's pro-German, pro-Russian, pro-Greek policies to make agreement with France impossible. The Greek army, isolated in Anatolia, was deserted by the Powers who (with the half-hearted exception of Britain) made agreements with Kemal and supplied him with guns paid for by Moscow. Gounaris, the Greek Prime Minister, turned to Curzon for help but was repelled. It was at this point, 4 March 1922, that Montagu caused a mild crisis by the unauthorized publication of the pro-Turkish telegram.

In July 1922 the Allies blocked a Greek proposal to seize Constantinople, which would at least have furnished Constantine with 'an invaluable asset in any future negotiations'. This loading of the dice against the Greeks angered Lloyd George, and he spoke out in the House of Commons on 4 August. The speech was read by the Greeks as an encouragement to carry on the struggle, and by the Turkish nationalists as a challenge to fight. A fortnight later the Turks opened an offensive, already planned, and on 9 September they occupied Smyrna and drove the Greeks across the Straits to Europe. For a moment it seemed that Kemal might follow them and set the Balkans ablaze. Lloyd George hastily called for the help of France, Italy, and the British Dominions. Sir Charles Harington, the Allied Commander-in-Chief, was instructed to defend the neutral zones. At this juncture, 12 September, the French and Italians ordered their forces to be withdrawn. 'It must be remembered to the everlasting credit of Mr. Lloyd George that in this apparently desperate isolation he stood firm.'[12]

The outcry in war-weary Britain was immediate and widespread. The Trade Union Congress told the Prime Minister that they had no quarrel with the Turks, no quarrel with the Greeks. Labour was opposed to war in any form against anybody. The Dominions were far from whole-hearted in support of the Prime Minister's belligerence.

The action of the Cabinet did in fact stay the advance of Kemal, who did not press his advantage. An armistice was concluded at Mudania (4–11 October) by General Harington, who interpreted instructions from home in his own sensible way and whose wisdom was matched by Kemal's statesmanship. Friendly relations replaced the quarrel with Greece; Turkey and Britain were reconciled and their friendship endured through the Second World War and still continues. Lloyd George's promptitude prevented war, his desire to deliver Asia Minor from the Turkish yoke was defeated, but the Arab world—Iraq, Arabia, Palestine, and Syria —was set free.

On 14 October he went to Manchester 'to defend our action in the East, which has brought peace to Europe'. 'It is always a mistake to threaten unless you mean it, and it is because not merely we threatened, but because we meant it, and the Turk knew we meant it, that we have peace now.' At the Reform Club in his native city he made the case for the Coalition in modest terms and was not unfriendly to the Independent Liberals, though he could not resist tilting at Lord Gladstone as 'the best living embodiment of the Liberal doctrine that quality is not hereditary'. He spoke of himself as an old actor for whom fashionable circles

[12] G. M. Gathorne-Hardy, *A Short History of International Affairs, 1920–1939*, p. 121.

in London had no further use, but 'I can still go touring the provinces'. He savoured delightedly in prospect the malicious joy of watching his critics tackling the problems they upbraided him for failing to solve. He would welcome freedom, he would love to be free.

At a meeting of Conservative Members of Parliament in the Carlton Club on 19 October, by a vote of 186 to 87, it was resolved that there should be an appeal to the country at once; and that the Conservative party should go to the country under its own leaders, with no understanding with the Liberal party.

When Lloyd George learned that Bonar Law was prepared to form a government he warned the King's secretary that he would be resigning in the course of the day. Lord Balfour, Lord Birkenhead, Austen Chamberlain, Sir Robert Horne, and Sir Laming Worthington-Evans, 'the first-class brains', were among those who remained loyal to Lloyd George and handed in their resignations. They published a manifesto immediately, justifying their action and paying an enthusiastic tribute to the services of the Prime Minister. Before he went to the Palace he had offered to absolve them, but they had determined to stand by him. This moved him deeply, and at dinner that evening he repeatedly returned to the subject.

On 23 October, in the afternoon, Lloyd George's sorrowing secretaries gathered informally in the Cabinet room to say goodbye. He was full of fun, and chaffed them as die-hards who had compassed his downfall. He marched up and down on the far side of the long table, declaring this was the last time he would ever be in the Cabinet room, unless, he said, stopping suddenly, 'I come back as the leader of a deputation to ask some favour of the new Prime Minister'. He then acted a mock conversation with Bonar Law in the merriest of moods:

Mr. Prime Minister, I have come here with my fellow members from Wales to ask . . .
Bonar Law: Pray be seated. (Lloyd George bowed slightly with ironic modesty. His eye fell on the imagined figure of Curzon.)
Lloyd George: I could hardly sit in the presence of the Marquess Curzon of Kedleston. We have come to ask for a grant for Welsh Education and we also wish to approach you on behalf of the refugees from Smyrna . . .[13]

[13] Author's diary.

As he left, at 4 o'clock, Newman, his factotum at No. 10, presented him with a new golf club, a driver. He motored away with his son, Gwilym, to Churt, smiling to the last.

HONOURS AND FUNDS

No attempt to trace the character of Lloyd George as Prime Minister can approach completeness without some discussion of recommendations for honours. 'Service is obligation, obligation implies return.' This principle is inherent in British practice of government, and is common to all parties. Much public service is unpaid in terms of cash and may be recompensed with office, title, or decoration. This doctrine has long been understood and accepted. A system of patronage has grown up by the judicious use of which governments have attracted and rewarded supporters. The fountain of honour, office, and privilege is the Sovereign who normally bestows favours on the advice of the Prime Minister. The pollution of the system has arisen from a combination of the need of political parties for funds with which to conduct their business and the readiness of ambitious persons to satisfy this need in return for some symbol of superiority or mark of distinction. There has thus arisen a 'traffic in honours'.

Objection had been taken to the alleged sale of honours before the war of 1914–18, and in 1917 the question had been brought before the House of Lords. It was laid down, after debate, that the Prime Minister in submitting names for honours should satisfy himself that no pecuniary consideration had influenced the choice and also that, except in the case of honours for members of the royal family, the fighting services, and the civil service, the reasons for their bestowal should be publicly given.

This provision did little to remove the criticism to which the lists issued by Lloyd George were subjected, and the attack came to a head on the publication of the Birthday List in June 1922. The multitude of recipients might be explained by the war, but the principles governing their selection caused disquiet. Conservatives, who had their own party funds, complained of the inclusion of unsuitable members of their own party of whom they knew nothing until the awards appeared in *The Times*. It was alleged that the supporters of the Prime Minister profited out of all proportion to their numbers.

Disturbing features in the honours lists during the years covering Lloyd George's Premiership were the numerous awards to businessmen and to newspaper proprietors and editors whose acceptance of honours might influence the policy of their papers. In these years 'Business' accounted for 26 peerages, 130 baronetcies, and 481 knighthoods, and the 'Press' for 5 peerages, 5 baronetcies, and 37 knighthoods.

During June and July of 1922 the House of Commons clamoured for an inquiry. Lloyd George, in defending himself, reviewed the practice of his predecessors, going back to the days of Pitt who created 140 peers, the vast majority men of no real distinction. 'There is no Prime Minister,' he declared in Parliament (17 July), 'either of today or of the past, who has any knowledge, when names are submitted to him, who has contributed to the party funds, or who has not.' On the system of reward for financial services Lloyd George spoke out firmly and Asquith described the outcry against contributing to party funds as 'vulgar clap-trap', and the disqualification of a man from an honour because of it as 'pure pedantry and folly'. What did most damage to Lloyd George's prestige was not so much any departure from the principles of his predecessors as the deterioration in the quality of recipients and the reputation of some of the go-betweens who acted as links between the Chief Whip and persons considered suitable for inclusion in the lists.

Finally, a Royal Commission of inquiry was announced, and on 29 December 1922, when Lloyd George was no longer Prime Minister, issued a report. It recommended that a committee of not more than three Privy Councillors should assist the Prime Minister. To this body all names included in the honours lists should be submitted, together with a statement of the services the nominees had given, the names and addresses of the original proposers, and an assurance that no payment had been made for the award.

The whole question of party funds, with which the distribution of honours was linked, was a constant source of irritation in the divided Liberal party, and Lloyd George's relations with the party from 1923 onwards were deeply influenced by his control of an enormous sum of money collected in anticipation of future needs and policies. The ways in which it had been obtained, the precise terms of its ownership and control were subjects of constant speculation and innuendo. It was not until 3 December 1927 that Lloyd George published his defence. The Party Fund, he wrote, had been collected by Party Whips, in accordance with the practice of the older parties for over a century. Honours lists had been prepared by the Chief Whips and he did not know which persons in the lists had subscribed. While the National Coalition Liberal party existed, that is, until 1923, its Whips had themselves administered this Fund; afterwards this duty fell to a committee of which three ex-Whips were members. Later, when the Fund had increased enormously owing to the success of the *Daily Chronicle* and other papers which had been bought and, in 1927, resold, the committee was enlarged. He himself, Lloyd George continued, was only consulted on large questions of policy. His part in the administration had been the close attention to the business of the papers acquired and their subsequent sale. Not a penny had been used by him personally. The Fund had been used for financing elections, inquiries into the coal industry, agriculture, and industrial conditions at home and abroad, for propaganda to inform the public of the findings of these investigations, and towards the maintenance of a bureau which looked into the grievances of ex-servicemen.

Such is Lloyd George's defence. The existence of trustees and committees, however, did little to change the fact that anyone wanting help, at least on large questions of policy, had to go to Lloyd George, who had fortified himself with high legal opinion that he could, if he liked, 'gamble the Fund away at Monte Carlo'. So 'Party' Fund was hardly an appropriate name.

On 23 October 1922 Lloyd George left 10 Downing Street and office for the last time. Bonar Law, who became Prime Minister, probably felt much like Lord John Russell in an old *Punch* cartoon, who having been knocking at the Cabinet room suddenly finds it open, and runs round the corner to hide, saying to himself, 'Must I really go in?' Parliament was dissolved on the 26th—the day of the Fascist march on Rome.

Lloyd George's speeches during the election that followed lacked consistency, and this may have been deliberate, allowing him to determine his course when the result of the voting was known. Optimistic one day he was pessimistic the next and on the third he pleaded for a Centre party which would bring together moderate men of progressive outlook from all parties. Writing in his diary on 18 November 1922, Lord Riddell recorded:

The change in the atmosphere since he has been out of office is amazing. Now he is working like a little dynamo to break up the

Conservative Party by bringing the more advanced section to his flag, to join up with the 'Wee Frees', and to detach the more moderate members of the Labour Party—this with the object of forming a Central Party of which he will be leader.[14]

Five years later Lord Beaverbrook referred to him as a 'splendid failure' because he had refused the chance of leading a National or Centre party at this time. Lloyd George replied to a representative of the *Evening Standard* (16 March 1927): 'Failure? Why, the failure would have been if I had accepted the offer and yielded to the temptation. . . . I am at home with Radicals, and nowhere else; and while, in my forty-five years of politics, I can find many mistakes to regret, 1922 was not one of them.'

The Tories were returned with a comfortable majority over all parties combined, and Labour, with 138 members, became the official Opposition. The National Liberals were reduced from 131 to 55, while the Independent Liberals increased their strength from 33 to 60. Over four million Liberal votes were polled, but under a system which left them extremely under-represented.

At the end of November members of both Liberal groups met to consider possibilities of reunion; the two leaders made friendly advances, Asquith wary, Lloyd George cordial. Lloyd George's nature was such that none of the events of the years 1916–22 made the idea of reunion difficult to him. 'I don't mind what anyone was last month, what he said about me or what I thought about him,' he remarked to a friend and assistant, W. McG. Eagar, 'if he is willing to work with me now I will work with him. 'But', he added, speaking of Asquith, 'the old boy is rather different; he can't quite forget; he keeps something in his mind.' One humiliating fact which Asquith found hard to forget was the huge Party Fund of which Lloyd George had control, and which enabled him to keep the Liberal leaders cap in hand on the doorstep.

AMERICAN INTERLUDE

During the months that followed the end of the Coalition Lloyd George's prestige fell many degrees, but it rose again by the efforts he made for the restoration of Europe in a short American tour. He arrived in New York, with his wife and daughter Megan, on 3 October 1923, and sailed for home on 3 November. He spent,

[14] Lord Riddell, *Intimate Diary of the Peace Conference and After*, p. 395.

roughly, a week in Canada and three weeks in the United States, visiting over a score of the chief cities and delivering some eighty speeches of major and minor importance. It was a strenuous month, and it is not surprising that his secretaries found him as hard to manage as a *prima donna*. He was everywhere received with demonstrations of extraordinary warmth and enthusiasm. In Cleveland, Ohio, he addressed an audience that was a world's record. 'Americans have not forgotten', said the *New York Times* (5 October 1923), 'the almost superhuman figure of Mr. Lloyd George, as it seemed to them, looming across the Atlantic in the dark days of the war.' He was still the most interesting public man of his day, versatile, eloquent, buoyant, enormously energetic, with an uncanny ability to read the public mind almost before it had formed itself. His eventual return to power was inevitable, declared the *Ottawa Journal*.

Abraham Lincoln, Lloyd George thought, stood above all men, and he was thrilled to meet his son at a wayside station in Vermont. He visited Lincoln's log-cabin birthplace in Kentucky; he saw the tomb of the martyred President at Springfield, Illinois; and he saw the Gettysburg battlefield. Next to Lincoln, the Sabbath-keeping and theological 'Stonewall' Jackson was his Civil War hero, and he visited the spot not far from Chancellorsville where the great Confederate general fell severely wounded.

At Washington Lloyd George was entertained at luncheon by President Coolidge and met his Cabinet and Chief Justice Taft. He dined with Andrew Mellon. But most moving of all was his last meeting with Woodrow Wilson, now partly paralysed. Wilson spoke kindly of Clemenceau, bitterly of Poincaré, deprecatingly of Coolidge. There was no mention of the League of Nations. A fortnight later, on Armistice Day, Wilson said a few words from the porch of his house to a crowd of ex-servicemen and others, and on 3 February 1924 he died—'this extraordinary mixture of real greatness thwarted by much littleness', as Lloyd George summed him up.

The immediate aim of his mission was to obtain American co-operation in the settlement of a desperate Europe. The situation had steadily worsened since January when the French and Belgians had entered the Ruhr and when an unknown Adolf Hitler was stirring the Munich crowds to protest against the occupation. At Springfield, Illinois (17 October), Lloyd George described the condition of Europe: 'Currency gone; exchange gone; confidence gone and hatreds still left. That is Europe'; and he recalled the watchwords of Lincoln: 'Clemency in the hour of triumph. Reconcile the vanquished.' Unless the mark had value debts could not be collected, and he pleaded that the debtor should be nursed back to health and his credit restored. America had shared the responsibility for victory; her armies had come to Europe to enforce justice, and justice was not an explosion which spent its force on a single outburst, justice was the steadfast will to see right done in the world; force had triumphed over law, not only in Russia and Italy but in France; Germany was being taught to trust again not to justice but to force.

Lloyd George revived an earlier moderate proposal by Charles Evans Hughes: a small body of economic experts, including an American, should be appointed to agree on the amount of Germany's indemnity and on how payment should be made. His mood had changed since December 1918 when he had said: 'We shall search their pockets for it.'

On 10 October President Coolidge astonished the world by repeating the Hughes proposal. The British note of acceptance was sent on 13 October, the American reply on the 15th, and on the 26th both notes were made public. This sudden publicity put pressure on the reluctant and protesting Poincaré. *The Times* on 5 November 1923 made a grudging reference to the part played by Lloyd George in rousing public opinion: 'He probably contributed to its crystallisation in the sense of intervention.' The American correspondent of the *Round Table* was more generous:

Yet, if truth were told, sentiment in this country has been less influenced by those diplomatic accords than by a certain 'discredited' person called David Lloyd George. At every stage of his American visit he has enjoyed a welcome, genuine to its very core. . . . Lord Robert Cecil touched the American intelligence and conscience. Clemenceau made an appeal for sympathy, but Lloyd George will carry away with him a kind of affection which people of one country rarely, if ever, bestow upon the citizen of another.[15]

[15] *Round Table*, xiv (1923–4), 61.

VII

IN OPPOSITION

1923–45

BIDDING FOR POWER 1923–9

BY the autumn of 1923 Lloyd George had come to address himself to two political tasks: the reunion of the Liberal party and the provision for it of dynamic policies. In the following years he filled in his days with journalism, parliamentary activities, the intimate conduct of detailed investigations into domestic social problems, and campaigns in support of the conclusions reached in a series of published reports. They were also years of party bickering and of repeated and dreary attempts at merging the two Liberal camps, at consultation and common parliamentary action.

The retirement of Bonar Law from the Premiership in May of 1923 had released Lloyd George from the personal considerations dictated by their former close companionship. Forbearance had touched the limits of prudence. No pledge had been given which extended to Bonar Law's successors. Baldwin, now Prime Minister, believing that Lloyd George was going Protectionist and about to take Chamberlain and Birkenhead with him, had announced a fortnight before Lloyd George returned from America that in order to conquer unemployment he would need to protect the home market. This entailed an early appeal to the electorate, for Bonar Law had promised that there should be no interference with fiscal policy without a mandate from the nation.

Before leaving the ship on which he returned from the United States Lloyd George declared himself to a group of journalists to be an unswerving Free Trader. At Manchester, on the previous 28 April, he had said: 'If there is going to be a fight about Free Trade, and I believe it, let us clear the decks; let us get rid of the McKenna tariff, the Paris Resolutions, and the Safeguarding of Industries Act. We had each of us his reasons for consenting to these propositions at the time and I am sure neither Mr. Asquith nor I would have done it without adequate cause.' It was in this fiscal field that the restoration of unity was found possible.

Baldwin's willingness 'to take a verdict' was deliberate and as much political as economic. He later said:

> On political grounds the tariff issue had been dead for years, and I felt that it was the one issue which would pull the party together, including the Lloyd George malcontents. Lloyd George was in America. He was on the water when I made the speech and the Liberals did not know what to say. I had information that he was going protectionist and I had to get in quick. I got the Cabinet into line. But for this move Lloyd George would have got Austen Chamberlain with Birkenhead, and there would have been an end to the Tory Party as we know it. Bonar Law had no programme and the only thing was to bring the tariff issue forward.[1]

On 13 November Baldwin told the House that he was going to advise the King to dissolve Parliament, and on the same day the consultation for which Lloyd George had pleaded so often took place. Asquith, Sir John Simon, Sir Alfred Mond, and Lloyd George met and reached a common policy for a united campaign of all Liberals. A manifesto signed by the leaders of both wings was issued. A few days later the resolution by which his portrait had been removed from the National Liberal Club was rescinded and on the 24th he and Asquith spoke on the same platform at Paisley.

The general election followed on 6 December. The Conservatives with 254 Members were still the strongest single party; there were 192 Labour and 149 Liberal Members—the two progressive parties combined could outvote the Government. On 21 January 1924 Baldwin resigned and the first Labour Government took office with Ramsay MacDonald as Premier. Asquith took the view that the experiment could hardly be tried under safer conditions, and Lloyd George declared that if MacDonald was reasonable the Liberals in the House would see him through, but he feared the new Prime Minister's vanity would ruin him.

The nine months during which the experiment lasted did not prove a period of fruitful collaboration between the two progressive parties. There was friction in the constituencies, and in the House the Liberal veterans were more patronizing and more abusive in attack than was necessary. Within the Liberal ranks, too, there was discord. 'The Liberal Party', wrote Austen Chamberlain

---

[1] *Lord Baldwin, A Memoir*, pamphlet published by *The Times* in December 1947, p. 8.

(*Life and Letters*), 'is "visibly" bursting up. It holds constant Party meetings to decide its course; then forty vote with the Government, twenty with us, and the rest (including the leaders) walk out or absent themselves.'

Churchill, who had now dissociated himself from the Liberals, but had not yet rejoined the Conservatives, was at this moment proclaiming that the fiscal question having been decided by the election, no difference of principle separated Liberals from Conservatives and both should unite to combat Socialism. Lloyd George replied at an enthusiastic meeting of the London Liberal Federation and made a fresh confession of his political faith. There were three parties, he said, not one of which commanded a majority. Events had ruled out a Coalition; there might be co-operation, but Labour repudiation made that impossible. The only course left, the one which Labour had chosen, was for the Minority Government to stand on its own feet and wage remorseless war on the other two parties. Liberals should restate their creed. Action was the life of Liberalism. It would break the soil with a plough; Socialism preferred to do it with an earthquake. Liberals and Socialists were both discontented with social conditions, but Socialists and Tories were alike in their contempt for freedom. Liberals would free the nation from the monopolies, privileges, and tyrannies which fettered its great energies.

There followed in the summer and autumn a country-wide Liberal campaign in which Lloyd George took a leading part, the new device of the microphone carrying his words to as many as 50,000 listeners. Welsh Liberals who had been bitterly divided now decided to unite. At a meeting in Llandrindod Wells, on 14 June, Lloyd George spoke to such effect that 'the very thought of schism had come to wear the aspect of sin in his seductive presence'.

July 1924 saw the publication of *Coal and Power*, the first of his notable contributions to Liberal domestic policy. 'When Lloyd George returned to the Liberal Party,' observed Charles Masterman, 'ideas returned to it.' The book was well timed, for it set forth the Liberal answer to a problem the Labour Government proposed to solve by a combination of Socialism and Syndicalism. The book started from the conviction that the function of the state was not itself to undertake creative or productive functions but to provide the conditions in which the enterprise of its citizens could most effectively operate. The state should purchase the royalties and set aside 10 per cent. of the money towards a welfare fund which should include the provision of adequate housing; pits should be amalgamated where efficiency required it, and miners should share in framing a policy for the industry. The Miners' Federation, fearing that any betterment would endanger nationalization, opposed his policy outright.

The book also dealt with the control of electrical energy. Lloyd George proposed that the Electricity Commissioners be empowered to grant to approved bodies, public or private, the right to supply power within substantial defined areas and to acquire generating stations and transmission lines compulsorily. Action on these lines, besides making available cheaper power for industry on a large scale would assist the development of rural indsutries.

Lloyd George might conceivably have achieved this essentially intermediate Liberal plan in the atmosphere of 1919. Now it was too late, and too soon.

FOREIGN AND DOMESTIC AFFAIRS

The first Labour Government was short lived and struck its own death-blow by preferring to resign rather than face an inquiry into its alleged interference with the course of justice in the case of a man named Campbell, then temporary editor of the *Workers' Weekly*. Lloyd George took no public part in the debate, but it was rumoured that behind the scenes there was a plot to restore a Coalition Government based upon a middle party. If so, it came to nothing.

An election followed on 29 October 1924. The campaign was upset by the publication on 24 October of the notorious letter, said to have been written by Zinoviev, President of the Third Communist International, to the British Communist party, describing methods of fostering insurrection within the armed forces as well as in works and factories. Panic spread among moderate voters, who rallied to the Tory banner. When Parliament reassembled, the Liberal group of 158 with its key bargaining position had dwindled to a negligible 42, Labour's 191 had been reduced to 152, while the 258 Conservatives had increased to 415, which gave them a majority of more than 200 over both parties. MacDonald made way for Baldwin, who was thus established as Prime Minister for five years.

It has been suggested by Robert Boothby that 'with Baldwin at his side to manage international and party business' Lloyd George 'might have established a political partnership of at least equal importance with that which he shared before the First World War with Asquith and during it with Bonar Law'. But though their qualities were complementary, Lloyd George always underestimated Baldwin, who, on his part, at this time could barely endure to have 'The Goat' mentioned in his hearing. Lloyd George respected 'the massive and luminous' intellect of Asquith and also the cold and critical intelligence of Bonar Law, but he reckoned Baldwin as of little or no account.

The chairman of the Liberal Parliamentary Party would naturally have been Asquith, but he had been unseated at Paisley and Lloyd George elected to the position. Asquith soon returned to Westminster, but as a member of the House of Lords, having accepted the King's offer of an earldom. The situation for the Liberal party was tragic, and was attributed by Asquithians to Lloyd George's stinginess in allocating the rich resources of the Party Fund. Very tardily he had provided enough money to put only about 300 instead of 500 candidates in the field. But, resilient as ever, Lloyd George proclaimed, 'We are few but we are free', and he continued the campaign to recover power for the Liberal party.

But the old sores festered under the surface unity and set up secondary centres of inflammation. Had he developed into an angel of modesty and rectitude the Asquithians would not have forgiven him for December 1916, or for the Coupon Election two years later. But he grew no wings; he kept control of the Party Fund; he begot new policies and launched them with his own fervour and fuelling; his passion for seeing things done, no matter by whom, continually inspired rumours of coalition with this or that group. Broadly speaking, only Lloyd George's policies were constructive and progressive enough to stir the pulses and capture the imagination of the Liberal rank and file. But it is plain today that he was forcing the pace of progress at a rate too hot for his right-wing colleagues, who were united with the Treasury and the City in hankering after a return to the practice of an almost undiluted *laissez-faire* capitalism.

In the early years of Baldwin's Premiership Lloyd George was active and industrious: he worked hard on his committees of inquiry into land problems; planned an Empire Book; attended meetings of the Liberal Shadow Cabinet; appeared on public platforms with party colleagues; earned a handsome income by writing articles for the home and foreign press; and spoke in the House on all important domestic and international questions.

To turn first to the course of foreign affairs during this period: belief in a League and Covenant which rested neither on force nor on a deep moral revolution was early undermined. When the Anglo-American Guarantee Pact collapsed France felt she had been cheated. Her sense of insecurity was increased by Britain's rejection in 1925 of the proposed Treaty of Mutual Assistance (1923) and of the Geneva Protocol of 1924. The latter had provided for the outlawing of war, compulsory arbitration supported by sanctions, and sanctions against an aggressor. It had been framed in an effort to offset the weakness in the League resulting from the absence of the United States, Russia, and Germany. Lloyd George described the Protocol as a booby-trap for the British, baited with arbitration, and questioned whether under the guise of an arbitration pact it was not a military convention to sustain the *status quo*. He asked if the French would refer the Saar, disarmament, and the evacuation of the Rhineland bridgeheads to arbitration. Taunted with his own Treaty of Versailles he replied in the Commons (18 November 1925) that it should not be operated in a 'pedantic, illiberal, inequitable, oppressive' way, and he referred, more than once, to the covering letter which Clemenceau had sent to the German delegation at Versailles when enclosing a copy of the Treaty, in which he said that it 'creates the machinery for peaceful adjustment of all international problems by discussion and consent, whereby the settlement of 1919 itself can be modified from time to time to suit the new factors and new conditions as they arise'.

Austen Chamberlain, fortunate in the contemporary foreign secretaries of Germany and France, Herr Stresemann and M. Briand, succeeded in bringing about a treaty of mutual guarantee and a series of arbitration treaties at Locarno in October, and they were signed in December by representatives of Great Britain, France, Germany, Italy, Belgium, Poland, and Czechoslovakia. It was, said Chamberlain in Parliament (18 November 1925), 'the real dividing line between the years of war and the years of peace'.

He was complimented on his achievement by Lloyd George, who added in his annoying if realistic fashion that unless its spirit penetrated the armaments question history would regard Locarno as 'slobbering melodrama'. Its value, he urged, was that it was a step, not a goal. The agreement should be carried further, to the Balkans for example, the earthquake region of Europe. That was where the tidal wave of blood came from in the last war. Unless there was a kind of Locarno for the Balkans, Europe would be full of peril.

In February 1926 Germany, according to plan, applied for admission to the League. An extraordinary meeting was called for this sole purpose. It was then that Sir Austen (he had been created Knight of the Garter after Locarno), following a visit to Paris on his way home from a holiday abroad, 'spoilt his own masterpiece' by suggesting the admission of additional authoritative and important members—Poland, Brazil, and Spain were mentioned. This came as a surprise everywhere and caused consternation in Germany where Stresemann had carried the ratification of Locarno against strong opposition. Opinion in Great Britain was deeply stirred. 'On no internal question in recent years', said *The Times* (4 March 1926), 'has there been so emphatic and spontaneous a demonstration of British feeling.' Lloyd George begged the Foreign Secretary to go to Geneva simply to vote for the inclusion of Germany and to keep faith with Locarno. 'There is poison in the loving cup, the poison of suspicion.'

It was Sweden which through her representative, M. Unden, made known her intention to veto any proposal to enlarge the Council except to admit Germany, and so checkmated the intriguers gathered at Geneva. The upshot was the postponement of a decision and the delegates returned home with their task unfulfilled. Lloyd George at once called attention in Parliament 'to the action of representatives of this country at the Conference of the League of Nations' and had no difficulty in showing the widespread opposition to the policy of the Foreign Secretary and its unfortunate effect on the League and in Germany. In September, however, Germany alone was admitted to the League.

Trouble with his throat sent Lloyd George to Madeira for a short holiday with his wife on 4 April 1925, not knowing whether he would be able to return for the Budget due on 28 April. He recovered quickly and was rowed out in a small boat to intercept a

P. & O. liner passing Madeira and was in his place in the House
when his old colleague, Winston Churchill, now Chancellor in the
Conservative Government, made his Budget speech, 'a masterly
performance'. Lloyd George greeted with frank delight the financial provision for the Insurance Scheme and its extension to
widows and orphans and he paid tribute to the part played by the
Chamberlain family in promoting these social measures, recalling the first occasion on which, twenty-five years earlier, he had
spoken to Joseph Chamberlain behind the Speaker's Chair 'and
the subject of our conversation was old age pensions'.

In his Budget speech Churchill announced the decision to
return to the gold standard. Speaking at Wisbech on 10 July
Lloyd George described this action as disastrously premature
and precipitate:

> It has made sterling dearer and thus artificially put up the price of
> British goods in the neutral markets where we were already com-
> peting on very narrow margins with our trade rivals. At this very
> hour coal-owners and miners have been driven to the brink of
> a yawning chasm of strife largely through this deed of egregious
> recklessness by the Chancellor of the Exchequer. . . . There was no
> need to hurry . . . in due time the image of George V could have
> looked that of George Washington straight in the eyes from a level
> platform.[2]

The Budget problem which caused Lloyd George most concern
was unemployment, on the remedy for which expert opinion was
deeply divided. The country's basic industries—coal, iron and
steel, engineering, shipbuilding—seemed incapable of expanding.
The unemployment figure kept obstinately high (in the period
from 1924 to 1929 there were always over a million persons out of
work) and reflected a fall in foreign trade, which was not peculiar
to Britain but was a world phenomenon. The relation between
the return to the gold standard and the misery of the coalfield was
not widely understood. There was the same mystical belief in gold
as in the British Constitution.

Lloyd George prescribed as the radical cure for unemployment
capital development at home and greater mobility of labour. As
for the miners, their standard could only be raised by replacing

[2] Speech by Lloyd George at Wisbech, 10 July 1925; printed in the *Liberal
Magazine*, xxxiii (1925), 477.

old and uneconomic pits by new and profitable ones. He believed that his own orthodoxy while he himself was in office was no reason why his successors should not be heretics. The governments which had been in power since he had been Prime Minister had added nothing to his own panaceas—trade facilities, unemployment insurance, export credits, road schemes—and he told the House (14 May 1925): 'Honestly, if I had been there another three years I should have learned something new. I am sick of this slavish adhesion to the Coalition policy. . . . All you get is this sort of copying of Coalition ideas as if they were copper-plate.'

He appealed in speech after speech for a grave consideration by all parties in the House of the decision to return to the gold standard—a decision which stifled trade, burdened the local authorities, weighed down the suffering manhood and womanhood of the country. His reiterated emphasis that 'all parties' should unite to seek a solution to the country's economic problems made him suspect in quarters hostile to any compromise with coalition or centre parties. To end unemployment he would have brushed aside all sectional considerations, major or minor, as he had done in the critical years of the war. Unemployment, he argued, was a long-term radical evil and politically dangerous. His diagnosis was sound, his warnings justified, but his voice was unheeded.

He appears to have thought that a radical and permanent decline was in process in the nature and amount of British foreign trade, and that Britain ought to trust to her own resources and those in the Empire. These reflections inspired anew his campaign for a better use of the land, his 'old obsession'.

Love of country things was one of Lloyd George's most deeply rooted passions. The boy who had roamed the hill-sides, trespassed and poached, grew to be the statesman who rejoiced in his home at Walton Heath, and later became the enlightened farmer at Churt in Surrey, where he revelled in reclaiming its waste lands. In his youth he had learned to resent landowning as a monopoly associated with the political persecution of tenants and the depredations of sport; in later years in the towns he saw that it enriched landlords at the cost of erecting overcrowded slums. As a Member of Parliament he steadily set his face against concessions to landlords, and in office he had initiated land reforms which were only brought to a standstill by the outbreak of war in 1914.

When himself unemployed, as he said, he resumed the fight for land reform. In June 1923 he had set up two committees of inquiry, first on rural and later on urban land problems, and they issued reports in October and November 1925, the 'Green Book' and the 'Brown Book', as they were usually called. For purpose of propaganda a Land and Nation League was formed, and it conducted campaigns with all the arts of advertisement which ingenuity could devise and money supply.

Liberal opinion coincided fairly closely with the findings of the 'Brown Book'. Local or regional authorities were to be empowered to make the best use of the land in the interests of the community. It must be open to them to acquire land compulsorily for town planning, for housing, for allotments, for arterial roads, for amenities. Land in urban areas should be rated on its land value and the revenue applied to improvements and welfare. Today these notions are commonplaces.

The 'Green Book' was more controversial: the betterment of the soil and country life, and the destruction of land monopoly were to be remedies for unemployment. By the late summer of 1924 Lloyd George had been telling his investigators that he believed landlordism as an institution had failed. Few landlords were able to do the work they ought to do and many had been crippled by taxation since the war. He developed a scheme of 'cultivating ownership'. The state was to take over all land not properly cultivated by its owner and transfer it to tenants, whose property it would remain for life and who could bequeath it to their immediate family so long as they kept it in good heart. This stopped short of complete nationalization, since the state was not to be the cultivator but a sort of landlord.

On 17 September 1925, at an open-air meeting at Killerton Park, Somerset, the home of Sir Francis Dyke Acland, Lloyd George launched the Land Campaign. 'The best exchange for the workless is an exchange of the green doors of the Labour Bureau for the green fields of Britain.' A far-flung crusade followed, and on some days Lloyd George made as many as a dozen speeches on behalf of his rural and urban policies. The interest and the controversy thus aroused led Lord Oxford to summon a three-day convention in February 1926 in London, where he used his reflective, impartial temper to create an atmosphere favourable to its success. Lloyd George showed himself no less anxious to reach a measure of accord with his Liberal critics. But the convention brought about no lasting agreement between the two factions.

GENERAL STRIKE 1926

Meanwhile trouble had long been brewing, perhaps we should say had never ceased to brew, in the mining areas of the country. There had been a threat of a General Strike in the summer of 1925, when the National Wages Agreement of 1924 was terminated and the mine owners were pressing for reductions of wages and a relaxation of the Seven Hours Act. Trouble was only averted by a subsidy from the Exchequer, 'in the form of a subvention in aid of wages', during the nine months between August 1925 and May 1926, and a Royal Commission of inquiry, under Sir Herbert Samuel, was appointed to report in time for agreed terms to be arrived at before the following May.

The official Liberal view was that further inquiry was unnecessary: legislation along the lines laid down in *Coal and Power* would bring peace and prosperity to the industry. The subsidy was a yielding to intimidation. Lloyd George voiced his concern in the House on 6 August 1925. He said the Government was afraid not only of a lock-out of miners but of 'interference with the ordinary course of business by other trade unionists'. 'Democracy is doomed', he exclaimed, 'if it surrenders to the compulsion of a minority. . . . Europe is full of lessons of that kind at the present moment.' But the Government was, in fact, buying time to prepare the national defences against the possible recurrence of this threat.

Events now moved to a crisis. The Samuel Commission reported on 10 March 1926, and recommended some immediate reduction in wages. By 30 April no agreement had been reached. Negotiations between the three parties, the Cabinet, the masters, and the unions, broke down, and on 1 May the Trades Union Council announced that a General Strike would begin at midnight on 3 May. For eight and a half days Britain was the scene of the first serious general strike in history.

On 1 May, in Cambridge, Lloyd George had set forth his own attitude to the crisis quite clearly, and at no time during the General Strike did he depart from it. In his speech, Lloyd George attacked the Government for their dilatory and dawdling methods in the conduct of the dispute, which he described as 'all talking and no tackling'. 'But apart from the merits of the dispute,' he said, 'every citizen will feel it is his duty to support the Government of the day in the maintenance of order and in the organising and facilitating of essential services. The country must come first, always and all the time.' He repudiated any revolutionary intention on the part of the strikers. The people were not 'wild or anarchic'. It was a well-ordered country, a country with a 'deep discipline in the hearts of the people'.

In the Commons, just before midnight on 3 May, Lloyd George pleaded for one more effort for peace: while calling the General Strike a mistake, he said it was not the kind that struck at the root of democratic government, and he bore witness to the loyalty of the Labour leaders to the Constitution. On the 5th he deplored the precipitancy shown in breaking off negotiations and rejected the assumption that the men would throw over the strong discipline of the trade unions and dribble back to work. 'It is this House that will settle this question and I thank God that it is here. . . . Meanwhile, I am entirely with any Government that equips itself with all the necessary powers to preserve law and order and to maintain the essential services of the country.' He accepted the emergency regulations, but pointed out that 'what really matters is the spirit and way in which they are carried out'. He then attacked the *British Gazette* (the improvised Government newspaper, for which Churchill was responsible) for its partisan character and its attacks on trade unionists and the Trade Union Act of 1913. Lloyd George's loyalty was always given to human causes rather than abstract principles, and in spite of the years he spent in close and continuous touch with the governing classes he never identified himself with them.

A speech on 6 May in the House of Commons by Sir John Simon declaring the strike illegal alarmed the unions; thenceforward the constitutional aspect of the struggle stood out more clearly not only in their minds but in everybody's mind. Lord Oxford and Lord Grey publicly identified themselves with the Government by messages in the *British Gazette* on 8 May. They insisted upon the unconditional withdrawal of the strike before negotiations. This did not correspond with Lord Oxford's appeal to keep the door open made in the Upper House on 4 May, and was regarded by Lloyd George as a departure from the 'open door' policy laid down at a meeting of the Liberal Shadow Cabinet of 3 May.

On 10 May the Liberal Shadow Cabinet met once more. Lloyd George did not attend, and wrote to the Chief Whip explaining his reasons. These were: that he was not in agreement with the 'declaration that negotiations for peace should be conditional on an unreserved withdrawal of the General Strike'; neither did he believe in concentrating criticism on the Trades Union Council for their blunder, while abstaining from condemning the Government for breaking off negotiations after the Trades Union Council had accepted a formula, drafted by the Government, and whilst they were actually engaged in pressing its acceptance on the miners. 'I do also think that if we support the Government in an absolute refusal to negotiate until the General Strike is called off, the struggle may be a prolonged one, and the damage to the nation may well be irreparable. I prefer the Liberal policy of trusting to conciliation rather than to force.' This letter was not marked *Private*. Later this omission, and his absence from the meeting, were given a sinister interpretation: he was, it was said, about to make common cause with Labour, and wished to prove his friendliness during the crisis by publishing the letter he had written at this date.

His own explanation of his absence is given by Mrs. Masterman in her biography of her husband. He had brought Masterman back by car from Churt after discussion of a proposed Liberal paper to take the place of the Liberal London dailies which the strike had put out of action. Masterman, on the running-board, referred to seeing him at the Shadow Cabinet. 'No, I'm not going. I'd better not. In my present mood there'd only be a row. I should be sure to say something,' said Lloyd George, and in reply to Masterman's expressed intention of going, added, 'That's all right. You can tell me if anything important turns up.' Thereupon he drove away. 'Neither of us regarded it as a particularly momentous decision,' writes Mrs. Masterman, 'indeed we were rather amused.' Masterman went to the Shadow Cabinet and noted no particular sensation when Lloyd George's letter was read.

Lloyd George was mistaken in his judgement about the duration of the strike: forty-eight hours after his letter was written it was called off unconditionally by the Trades Union Council—a decision described by Baldwin in Parliament on the same day as a victory of the common sense of the best part of the whole of the

United Kingdom. Lord Salisbury, in the Upper House, said that there was no note of triumph in his voice, and hoped there would be no note of triumph anywhere else. These pronouncements truly represented the attitude of the more moderate and responsible members of the Government. The behaviour of the people, certainly, had been marked throughout by common sense, good humour, and an entire absence of panic. The first feeling of relief was followed by many misgivings, but before long, though there were cases of hardship, the great majority of workers were back at their jobs again—all but the miners, who refused to return to the pits for many more weary months.

The threat to the community and to the Constitution had passed. The long-dreaded spectre of a General Strike was laid; what remained was the gaunt and familiar reality of unemployment. Enemies of Lloyd George within the Liberal party and opponents of his attitude during the strike now judged the moment opportune for an attack upon him.

Early in the week of the strike Lloyd George had written his usual fortnightly contribution to the United Feature Syndicate of America; soon after the strike was called off it became available to readers in Great Britain when it was printed in the *Manchester Guardian* (21 May 1926), and its effect upon the mind of Asquith (now Lord Oxford) was an important factor in the final breach between him and its writer. The article had expressed grave concern over the likely effect of the stoppage upon Britain's trade, and described her condition of isolation: 'food distribution and hospital services alone are privileged. The nation is not allowed to work, but neither is it permitted to starve. It is all as if you lived in a nightmare.' Apart from descriptive material there was nothing in the article which he had not said at Cambridge on 1 May and in Parliament just afterwards.

Lord Oxford publicly accused Lloyd George of disloyalty to his country in his account of the strike in the American press, and of disloyalty to his party in absenting himself from the meeting of the Shadow Cabinet on 10 May. The charges brought by less scrupulous Liberals—that Lloyd George's actions had been deliberately calculated to curry favour with Labour, and that he had intrigued with certain of its leaders to desert to it with his money and his friends—were summed up by A. G. Gardiner in the *Birmingham Gazette* for 12 June: 'Under the conviction that the General Strike would be prolonged and that the Government would have to yield, he decided to break with his colleagues.'

In his conciliatory reply, published in *The Times* at the same time as Lord Oxford's attack (26 May), Lloyd George rebutted these accusations and offered to meet his colleagues to discuss their differences. This evoked no response. Instead, twelve prominent members of the party, including Lord Grey and Sir John Simon, published a letter to Lord Oxford expressing their admiration of and unfailing trust in him and associating themselves with his strictures upon Lloyd George.

These rebukes were to Lloyd George as the blast of a trumpet in the ears of a knight of old. He galloped into the lists, the Manchester Reform Club, took up the challenge of his detractors and smote them hip and thigh. Several of them had recently on public platforms lavished fulsome praises upon him; with them, and with their later accusation of instability (which meant, he said, being alive), he made amusing play (*Manchester Guardian*, 7 June 1926). Sir John Simon, for example, had said: 'If at any time my right honourable friend is tempted to repine because he is the target of criticism I think he will always be able to console himself by the reflection that nearly everyone who is criticising him to-day has thanked God for him at some other time.' Lloyd George commented: 'He was one of those who thanked God for me then. He now says that he misled the Deity on that occasion.'

He went on to defend his activities during the strike, reviewed his relations with the Liberal party, in particular the co-operation which resulted in the return of 150 Liberals in the election of 1923, when he had given freely from his Fund towards expenses. His defence lost nothing in the telling, and its reception was enthusiastic.

The dispute which had arisen between Liberal leaders during the General Strike concerned the rank and file chiefly as it affected the fortunes of the party. A letter from Lord Oxford to the Chief Liberal Whip stating that his continued leadership depended upon the assurance that he had their full confidence, evoked from the Liberal Parliamentary Party a resolution deprecating the publicity given to the dispute and appealing for unity. The Liberal and Radical Candidates' Association acted in similar fashion. At their meeting on 11 June the rumour of Lloyd George's treachery to the Liberal party during the strike was tracked to its origin and proved

to have been a malicious invention. A deputation was appointed
to impress upon Lord Oxford their strong desire for unity under
his leadership.

This was the day on which A. G. Gardiner, at Birmingham,
repeated charges of Lloyd George's disloyalty to the party during
the strike and reiterated the ever-recurrent grievance about his
control over the Party Fund:

> When the Conservatives at the Carlton Club meeting rejected
> Mr. Lloyd George and he in due time rejoined the Liberal Party, he
> brought with him a great party fund which he had collected, from
> whom and for what I do not know. That fund remains in his posses-
> sion today. It constitutes a power within the party which is the
> antithesis of all I understand by Liberalism, a source of personal
> influence which can be directed to any occult end, an *imperium in
> imperio*, as sinister and disruptive in its possibilities as it is, I believe,
> unprecedented in the whole history of British political life.[3]

This same 'sinister and disruptive' power was the subject of a
letter published by Lord Gladstone on 11 June: 'Had we been able
in January with pooled resources to go full steam ahead under the
inspiring results of the 1923 election history would have been different. . . . Mr. Lloyd George for nine precious months withheld
the necessary guarantee . . . he is silent about 1924. I give the facts.
They are on record.' To this charge Lloyd George did not reply.

Lloyd George, in discussing the disunity in the party, claimed
to be too radical for the hide-bound and ultra-orthodox:

> There has been a feeling in the party for a long time that the
> 'official gang' were keeping Liberalism from rising to the opportunity
> presented by the problems which arose out of the War. It was felt
> that official Liberalism had allowed Labour to capture the old Ark
> of the Covenant which for over three centuries had been resting in
> the Liberal Temple. . . . The split [in the party] has opened a new
> vision and started a new era in British politics. Liberalism may soon
> again take the lead in the march of progress.[4]

Lloyd George was as mistaken in this prophecy as he had been
about the course of the General Strike. The Liberal Ark could not
rest on the golden quicksand of his private Fund.

During the summer of 1926 Lord Oxford had been recovering

---

[3] Speech by A. G. Gardiner at Birmingham, 11 June 1926.
[4] *Sunday News*, 13 June 1926. See *Liberal Magazine*, 1926, p. 355 *et seq.*

from an illness. In the autumn a chapter in Liberal history came to an end: he gave up the leadership of the party. The process begun in December 1916 had taken ten years to reach its end. Lloyd George had again ousted him from a throne: first the Premiership and now the Leadership of the party. In a letter to J. A. Spender, President of the National Liberal Federation, dated 14 October 1926, Lord Oxford explained his reasons for resigning; in the course of it he says: 'I attach as great importance as anyone to Party Unity, and I have done as much as any man living (often under difficult conditions) to attain and preserve it. But I am satisfied that it cannot be effectively maintained under a system of rival authorities, with separate organisations and separate funds.'

The three years' experiment of Liberal reunion (1923–6) had proved a 'fiction if not a farce'; there were two authorities: the Liberal Central Office very short of money and Lloyd George's rival machine with ample means at its disposal.

To his wife, Lord Oxford wrote: 'The alternatives are to lead a squalid faction fight against Ll. G. in which he would have all the sinews of war; or to accept his money and patch up a hollow and humiliating alliance. I am quite resolved to do neither, so I shall *faire mes paquets* for which I have ample justification on other grounds, age, &c., &c.' And so, Lord Oxford left the field to his rival. But it was a barren triumph and brought the victor no glory.

At the end of 1926 there were conversations which led to considerable gifts from Lloyd George's Fund to the party chest: a conditional offer of money from the Fund was regarded by the Committee empowered to act for the Liberal party as furnishing a basis for negotiations, though an important minority definitely refused to consider a conditional offer. Shortly afterwards Lloyd George himself made an offer which, as far as the income and moneys to be transferred were concerned, was unconditional. He stated that he could not 'during his life-time' part with control over the capital but that he was taking steps to secure the subsequent use of the Fund for the Liberal party, and he retained full liberty at some future unspecified time either to vary or withdraw his offer. He was presumably prepared to risk a good deal on the chance of the Liberal party returning to power, with himself at its head, but he wished in the event of a Liberal defeat to be free for fresh ventures and to be well provided with money for them. After the sale of the *Daily Chronicle* in 1927 he made available the sum of £300,000 together with an annual grant of between £30,000 and £40,000 for the use of Liberal Headquarters.

The official attempt of the Liberal Federation to launch a Million Fund had been wrecked by dissensions among the leaders after the General Strike. Devoted Liberals like Sir Herbert Samuel, Sir Charles Hobhouse, and Mr. Ramsay Muir found it not inconsistent with their principles to accept Lloyd George's offer, but Lord Grey and his friends took the high and dry line and would not condescend to negotiate. To them the existence of the Fund was anathema.

It was [said Lord Grey] a new thing, unprecedented in the politics of this country, that one man should be in possession of an enormous fund at his own disposal for political purposes. It was the Liberal Party today, but it might be the Conservative Party tomorrow or the Labour Party some other day, which might be agitated about the matter, or the fund could be used for an entirely new policy initiated by the person who controlled it. That was a very disturbing element, not merely in the Liberal Party, but in the politics of this country altogether.[5]

Of Lord Grey's speech, Lord Oxford wrote to his friend Mrs. Harrison: 'He certainly told some home truths, but I am not sure that in expression they were sufficiently poignant and compelling to arrest our weaklings who are going a-whoring after Ll. G.'

The Fund, as a controversial topic, faded into the background until after the election of 1929, during and in preparation for which it had been lavishly spent, though the outpouring of treasure did not save the Liberal party from disaster.

Nevertheless, the cycle of uncertainty, relief, uncertainty, relief, repeated itself in the years which followed, and the Lloyd George Fund continued to be a menace to the well-being of Liberalism until the death of its controller. Recent inquiries elicited that all papers relating to the Fund which had been in the possession of the (first) Lord St. Davids, the chairman of the trustees of the Fund, had been efficiently destroyed.

Lloyd George seemed constitutionally unable to perceive that it was impossible to act the wealthy, philanthropic, but despotic and unpredictable sultan towards self-respecting colleagues and yet retain their allegiance. It was their desire to save the party which

[5] Speech by Lord Grey; reported in *The Times*, 14 December 1926.

LLOYD GEORGE, CHURCHILL, AND BALDWIN
outside Westminster Abbey after the Memorial
Service for the Emperor of Japan, 1927

led them to tolerate the situation for as long as they did. If they had refused even to attempt the humiliating compromise the future of Liberalism might have been brighter. If Lloyd George had parted with his treasure, Liberalism might have counted again in the government of the country. But he would not pay the price. So all his clear, practical vision, his cleverness, his riches, his charm, his galaxy of gifts, failed to restore him to power or to the position of trusted leader of a united party.

GENERAL ELECTION 1929

During 1927 and 1928 Lloyd George actively criticized the domestic and foreign policy of Baldwin's administration. At home the unemployment figure continued around a million, huge sums were spent on the payment of insurance benefit, known as 'the dole', and idleness spread demoralization in the depressed areas. The country had not, materially or spiritually, recovered from the shock caused by the General Strike when the Government brought in and carried in July 1927 the Trades Disputes and Trade Unions Bill. This ill-conceived act was repealed by the Labour Government in 1946.

Lloyd George opposed the bill, but accepted the four principles on which Baldwin based it: no General Strike, no intimidation, no coercion to subscribe to political parties, no party politics in the civil service proper. He regarded the measure itself as provocative and mischievous 'of a kind to upset everything' when Capital and Labour should be working together to recover the country's lost trade.

The Government passed its bill by a large majority and, in doing so, closed up the ranks of Labour—its unity impaired by the General Strike—and even did something to bring together the two wings of the Liberal party. Lloyd George seized this opportunity of agreeing with Lord Grey 'with alacrity', as he put it, and they spoke together on the same platform.

New Year's Day, 1928, was spent by Lloyd George on the way to Brazil as the guest of its Government; his sixty-fifth birthday, 17 January, was celebrated on the homeward journey. He had taken the opportunity, at a banquet in his honour at Rio de Janeiro, of pleading with Brazil to withdraw her notice of resignation from the League of Nations. He reached Britain on the 25th, and immediately plunged into public affairs.

Once more he was ready to publish a report. This time it was a 'Yellow Book', entitled *Britain's Industrial Future*. Initiated by leaders of the Liberal Summer School, with Lloyd George's co-operation and support, an Executive Committee and sub-committees which included prominent Liberals and economists had worked upon it under the chairmanship of Walter (later Lord) Layton.

The report took up a position midway between *laissez-faire* and complete nationalization, between individualism run riot and organization for its own sake. It submitted British industry and business, national resources and finance to a critical and constructive examination and made many important suggestions for reform. Among these was the setting up of a Committee of National Development, a Board of National Investment, a Committee of Economic Policy, and an Economic General Staff. A Council of Industry representative of employers, workers, and the Ministry of Labour should be set up to assist the progress of industrial co-operation. Certain enterprises ripe for central or municipal operation should be run by *ad hoc* public boards and subjected to stringent provisions of publicity. The Investment Board should concern itself especially with correcting the faulty balance between investments at home and loans overseas, and with the economic development of India and the tropical colonies.

The bearing of this far-reaching and thorough inquiry upon the Liberal campaign which was to precede the general election of 1929 is plain. Liberals were now provided with a progressive, practical policy on all the burning questions of the day—but they never had the opportunity to put their programme into operation. In subsequent years other parties, rarely with acknowledgement, drew heavily on the ideas of the 'Yellow Book'.

In the field of foreign affairs Lloyd George continued to be interested and critical. He was disquieted by the increase of armaments in Britain and feared that an even greater catastrophe than that of 1914 might overtake Europe. It would be a gross breach of faith if those who enforced the Versailles Treaty did not themselves disarm, as he claimed they had undertaken to do. A League of Nations that excluded from its operations all questions that were inconvenient to the powerful was a sham and a snare. He deplored the Government's technical approach to the problem at Geneva. 'It is not a Disarmament Commission, it is an algebraic farce' vainly in search of an unknown x. Experts should not be permitted to decide; the amount to be spent should be laid down for them and they should be locked up in a room until the various services had agreed on its apportionment.

The Kellogg Pact for the renunciation of war as an instrument of policy, ironic though it appears in retrospect, was signed by a dozen leading countries on 27 August 1928. Lloyd George welcomed the pact, but regretted certain French and British qualifications and the exclusion of Russia. In Parliament on 10 May 1928 he stated: 'I think it is vital, if you are going to condemn war and make war impossible, that somehow or other you should bring Russia within the ambit of some obligation not to make war. You will never get disarmament until you do that.'

In October he condemned the Government's conclusion of a naval agreement with France, submitting that this Anglo-French compromise endangered both the peace of Europe and Britain's good relations with the United States. He deprecated exclusive understandings with any Power, and advocated the founding of British foreign policy on the Covenant of the League and the Kellogg Pact. We had held Germany to all her undertakings, but what about ours, the evacuation of the Rhine and disarmament to the lowest level consistent with safety? To Sir Austen Chamberlain, Foreign Secretary from 1924 to 1929, 'an elegant ditto to Monsieur Briand', and to his bias in favour of France Lloyd George ascribed the delay in the evacuation of the Rhineland and the lack of other gestures of conciliation.

Not only in Parliament and on the platform but in the foreign press he denounced the Government's policy. The Premier, Baldwin, complained that these articles made his task 'incomparably more difficult', and quoted a reference by Lloyd George to the 'scarcely veiled subservience of this country to France'. Lloyd George retorted in *The Times* (24 November 1928) and accused the Prime Minister of unfair selection of sentences 'snipped out by the scissors of malice for partisan purposes'. To Baldwin the fact that a former and possibly future Prime Minister should attack foreign statesmen in foreign newspapers was highly objectionable, but it was not in Lloyd George's nature ever to sit on the penitents' form nor, when he felt it due, to withhold criticism.

Throughout 1928 Lloyd George had been campaigning for the Liberal cause, helping at by-elections, laying bare the defects of the Government. Early in the New Year, to recuperate after influenza, he took a short yachting holiday in the Mediterranean with a family party. On 8 February 1929 he left the south of France for London. The hour had come to weld into one weapon with which to attack the Government all the political and economic thinking which had been put into the 'Brown', the 'Green', and the 'Yellow' books, and into a fourth published in March, the 'Orange Book', *We Can Conquer Unemployment*. This last contained detailed proposals for fulfilling a pledge which he had given to a gathering of prospective Liberal candidates on St. David's Day. If the Liberal party formed the Government after the general election it would, he declared, be ready with schemes of work which would reduce the figures of the workless (now above the million mark) in a single year to normal proportions. 'These plans will not add one penny to national or local taxation.' There would be a stupendous programme of road and bridge building, housing, telephone and electrical development, land drainage and afforestation. A great impetus would be given to trade by the steep rise in purchasing power of the hundreds of thousands set to work. There would be a saving of £30 million in the outgoings of the Unemployment Insurance Fund. The £200 million needed for the road scheme, the main item, was to be raised by a Road Loan, secured upon the increasing income of the Road Fund, none of which would any longer be diverted from its proper use. Motor taxation in 1927–8 had yielded over £25 million, and was increasing yearly by £2 million. It was reasonable to assume that in five years this tax would yield £35 million. In 1928, £57 million of British capital had been sent abroad to develop other countries; this could have been employed at home had opportunity been made. Such, in brief summary, was the policy of productive spending prescribed in the 'Orange Book' and launched by Lloyd George, Herbert Samuel, and other Liberal leaders in a campaign covering the country. Lloyd George's energy and artistry once more cast their old familiar spell over his audiences.

The Liberal programme was immediately attacked from every angle: Labour leaders affirmed that all that was good in it was stolen from them; *The Times* in a leading article (13 March) called the 'Orange Book' rather a vainglorious pamphlet, and feared that over-speedy innovations on the technique of industry would result in chaos; Churchill compared the proposed development of roads to the frenzied enthusiasm with which the railways were promoted in a few years in the first half of the nineteenth century; Neville Chamberlain said Lloyd George knew there was not the remotest chance of his being called upon to fulfil the pledge, while Baldwin was uncommonly caustic and applied to the Liberal leader Carlyle's description of a contemporary: 'He spent his whole life in plastering together the true and the false and therefrom manufacturing the plausible.' 'We are not going to work under a Dictator in this country', he added.

But there were some who thought that Lloyd George with his unrivalled driving force might achieve the impossible, as he had done at the Ministry of Munitions. Others doubted whether Lloyd George had not transcended in his programme the limits, both in extent and speed, of what could be attained. As for Baldwin, he represented those who feared that anything done rapidly would be done badly and had therefore better not be done at all.

To all objectors a reply was forthcoming from two distinguished Cambridge economists, Maynard Keynes and Hubert Henderson, in a pamphlet, *Can Lloyd George do it?*, generally admitted to be the most brilliant piece of election literature produced during the controversy. Subject to certain safeguards, the scheme now received the blessings of *The Economist* (18 May 1929), of Walter Runciman in Parliament (16 April), and, in more qualified fashion, of Lord Grey. A hundred representative business men and industrialists produced a manifesto in support, declaring it to be in their judgement economically and financially sound. Keynes answered queries and met criticisms; challenged about his earlier attitude to the Wizard he replied: 'The difference between me and some other people is that I oppose Mr. Lloyd George when he is wrong and support him when he is right' (*Manchester Guardian*, 29 May).

The General Election of 1929 was at home what the Genoa Conference had been abroad, a supreme effort on the part of Lloyd George. His pledge was the main plank in the Liberal platform; his personality towered above his opponents; his policy was the main target of their attack. It was a Lloyd George campaign, too, in that the treasure of the famous Fund was poured out in hundreds of thousands of pounds for the placing of 512 Liberal candidates in the field, for advertisement and propaganda on the most lavish scale. The methods made familiar by the Land and

Nation League were available—leaflets, pamphlets, posters, portraits. One striking poster depicted GEORGE, white-haired in white armour, on a white charger, slaying the Dragon Unemployment. There were some mistakes. Conservatives had been more skilful in renting poster space. On the way from Churt to London, Lloyd George found his progress to town watched over by innumerable and enormous portraits of Mr. Baldwin with the slogan 'Safety First' smiling at him from all the best sites. He was furious.

Parliament was dissolved on 10 May, polling day was 30 May. What did Lloyd George expect would be the result of what *The Times* called the most baffling political race that had been run within living memory? Broadly speaking, Labour put Peace in the forefront of the programme; Liberals, the Pledge; and the Conservatives, Safety First, with Mr. Baldwin to guarantee it. Nothing could be guessed from the triumphant receptions enjoyed by the party leaders. The electorate included about six million new voters, chiefly women between twenty-one and thirty, enfranchised by the act of 1928.

Lloyd George was so eager to get the results before he reached London from his constituency, Caernarvon Boroughs, where he had been returned with a comfortable majority, that he had messengers with the latest news waiting for him at the stations where the train stopped. Although by the time he reached Euston there were only fifty Liberal seats secured, he had been cheerful and apparently care-free all the way. The results gave Labour 289, Conservatives 260, Liberals 58, others 8. A rise in Liberal representation in Parliament from 43 to 58 was all that the long, arduous, costly preparation had achieved towards the goal of returning Lloyd George to power. It is improbable that he expected more than a party strong enough to give him a good bargaining position, but for 512 candidates to produce only 58 Members must have been a sore disappointment. These few seats had been dearly bought. Such is the British electoral system that the Liberals polled 23 per cent. of the total votes cast but gained only 9·4 per cent. of the seats.

Lloyd George as chairman of the Liberal Parliamentary Party called upon his small band of followers to see that the nation's verdict for peace and disarmament, for the development of the national resources and employment for all was carried out, and he appealed for unity in the party. But on the morrow of the election a leading Liberal and Asquithian started a fresh controversy in *The Times* on Lloyd George—his policies, his methods, and his Fund—thus revealing the fatal disunity within the party.

Lloyd George regarded the position in which he now found himself as 'difficult, hazardous, highly responsible'. He had to pilot the Liberal party with its small—and mutinous—crew of fifty-eight through the cross-currents and shoals of a House of Commons in which the Government was in a minority. He could, at any moment, run down and sink the Labour party by a turn of the wheel, but the power which this gave was really only effective so long as it was withheld, since any impulsive use of it would have enraged the country and involved the Liberal party, as well as the causes of reconstruction and peace-making to which it was committed, in the general shipwreck. The situation tried the skill, the patience, and the temper of the Liberal leader.

ELDER STATESMAN 1929–45

The second Labour Government took office on 8 June 1929, with Ramsay MacDonald as Prime Minister. The prospects for co-operation between parties was assisted by MacDonald's suggestion in the House on 2 July 1929 that, in facing the serious problems of the time, they should consider themselves 'more as a Council of State and less as arrayed regiments facing each other in battle'.

At the end of August Lloyd George set out with his family on a continental motor-tour. His first objective was the battlefields of France. 'It is absolutely necessary for me to get this first-hand knowledge for my *War Memoirs*', he told his secretary, A. J. Sylvester. The party, travelling in three cars, went as far as Innsbruck, then into northern Italy, through the valley of the Piave, to Monte Grappa, where Lloyd George laid a wreath in memory of British and Italian soldiers who had fallen in the war. Returning through Switzerland he was back in London by 23 September.

At this time Lloyd George had two chief aims: to keep the Government in until the promised measure of electoral reform, which would secure fairer representation for the Liberal party, had been passed and, since he had no opportunity of carrying out his own plan for conquering unemployment, to co-operate with and spur the Labour Ministry to act on their own proposals described in *Labour and the Nation*. He failed to achieve either object, and within the Liberal party itself hostility to him persisted. Lord Samuel writes of the parliamentary group: 'Our weekly meetings were not happy occasions.' Finally, in January 1930, the Liberal Council under Lord Grey renounced Lloyd George and all his works.

Great Britain was already feeling the weight and pressure of the world financial crisis foreboded by the crash in Wall Street in October 1929—a financial crisis which was to bring about the fall of the Labour Government in 1931. Through 1930 and 1931 the number of persons registered as unemployed continued to rise alarmingly; meanwhile the Cabinet Committee in charge of unemployment policy faltered and fumbled at its task. Criticisms inside and outside Government circles harassed the Ministry without propelling it to drastic action on unemployment, the subject of its anxious but ineffective preoccupation.

Lloyd George believed that to put Labour out would be to put the Tories in. Baldwin at this time was strongly advocating Tariff Reform; the Liberal leaders, Free Trade. Indeed, a joint Liberal–Labour Free Trade campaign was being planned for the autumn of 1930, Lloyd George and his supporters being convinced that Liberal policies were safer with the existing administration than they would be under a Conservative Government.

Rumour even suggested that the setting up of a Coalition which would include Lloyd George had been discussed by Ministers. The Prime Minister in the first fine careless rapture of victory had, as we have seen, invited Parliament to act as a council of state. Pressed by Lloyd George in the House, he offered in May a committee of inquiry on the unemployment problem comparable to the Committee of Imperial Defence, representative of all parties, with the same access to experts and papers as Ministers—an offer which astounded Winston Churchill, who as 'an old friend of the Prime Minister would advise him to be very careful before inviting Mr. Lloyd George to take charge of the Labour Government' (*The Times*, 29 May).

In any event, this spectacular proposal dwindled to an invitation to a Three-Party Conference, refused by Stanley Baldwin but accepted by Lloyd George, who, in an interview to the *Daily Herald* (17 June 1930) said: 'I can with confidence offer the Labour Government our whole support to secure a sound, dependable majority for emergency measures necessary to wage war on un-employment.' The very next day the leading article in this left-wing journal commented: 'Labour will have no coalition, nor is it possible for Labour to avoid viewing Mr. Lloyd George's new orientation without a certain degree of suspicion.' Frustration may have accounted for an unusual reflection in a speech delivered by Lloyd George in Caernarvon in June 1930. 'If the Parliament fails—and unless some strong and energetic action is taken it must fail—then Parliament itself will be discredited . . . the working population will not believe any longer in the old inadequate wind-mill set up by Simon de Montfort to mill the corn for the people, and they may be incited to do their own milling in their own way' (*The Times*, 13 June).

A Two-Party Conference was, however, set up, in which Lloyd George, Lord Lothian, and Mr. Seebohm Rowntree took part on the one side, and the Prime Minister, the Chancellor of the Ex-chequer (Philip Snowden), and Vernon Hartshorn (soon to replace J. H. Thomas as Lord Privy Seal) on the other. Over the inquiry thus initiated Lloyd George 'took the most enormous pains and entered into the various proposals with keen interest'. On the Liberal side the inquiry resulted in the report, *How to Tackle Unemployment* (October 1930), which brought the proposals of 1929 up to date.

At the beginning of 1931 the auspices for Liberal–Labour co-operation seemed favourable. On 11 February Sir Donald Mac-lean, a prominent Liberal Member, moved and carried, as an Amendment to a Conservative Vote of Censure, the appointment of a small committee to suggest practicable economies. Thus was set up, almost casually, the May Committee (called after its chairman, Sir George May) which was to play an important part in the crisis of August leading to the fall of the Labour Govern-ment. On 12 February Sir Herbert Samuel moved—and his motion was accepted by the Prime Minister and carried without a division—a resolution which, in effect, called on the Government to carry out the common Liberal–Labour plans for curing unem-ployment, and to finance them from private loans, economies in national expenditure, the Road Fund, and the taxation of the in-creased land values resulting from national development.

In the debate which followed Lloyd George insisted that the Government could not plead its minority position as an excuse for inaction; he wanted it put on record that there was a majority for carrying out what was in essence an agreed programme. He then begged the Chancellor of the Exchequer not to be warned off the necessary expenditure by the City of London, which ever since the war had always been wrong in the advice it had given. He recalled the hostility of its 'money barons' in the early days of super-tax and Old Age Pensions when they received him 'with the frigid silence of a row of penguins in the Antarctic'.

Lloyd George's efforts at co-operation went on even until June 1931, but they accomplished nothing and the unemployment figures continued to rise. Winston Churchill's warning found an echo in the hearts of the Labour leaders. Lloyd George's attempts at collaboration failed through fear that association with him meant yielding to his domination.

FRONT OPPOSITION BENCH

At the end of July 1931 Lloyd George had suddenly to undergo a major operation. He made a good recovery and in November went on a voyage to Ceylon, with his wife and Megan, to complete the cure. He returned early in the New Year, and though it was not until the middle of March that he appeared in Parliament or on a public platform he had decisively passed judgement on the financial crisis and the kaleidoscopic changes which during these months had taken place in the political scene.

The May Committee reported on 30 July 1931. A Cabinet Committee was at once appointed to examine its recommendations, which included the making of economies, in particular a reduction in Unemployment Benefit, to meet the prospective deficit in the Budget. On 31 July Parliament adjourned until 20 October, as Members supposed. They were recalled on 8 September, to find Ramsay MacDonald at the head of a National Government in which all but three of the former Labour Ministers had refused to serve. This transformation had been brought about by a phenomenal withdrawal of gold from the Bank of England which had caused great anxiety in the City of London and led to a conflict of views within the Cabinet and to the resignation of the Labour Government on 24 August. The widespread fear that the country was threatened with ruin was confirmed by Philip Snowden, Chancellor of the Exchequer, in a startling and impressive broadcast. The drain of gold was ascribed by financiers to the world slump and to the crises in Austria and Germany. Labour opponents of the National Government referred it to a sinister bankers' ramp engineered to discredit Labour and its policies. False or true, subsequent events gave this charge an appearance of truth, for within two months a new and overwhelmingly Conservative House of Commons had been elected.

Although the new Ministry of 24 August immediately set about planning economies, the drain of capital went on and the Government, set up to save the gold standard, was forced to abandon it. A measure providing for this was rushed through all its stages on 21 September with general approval and without the clamour which would have followed such action by a Labour Government. The National Economy Act was passed on 30 September. It reduced the salaries of practically everyone in the service of the state from Ministers downwards and, besides other economies in Unemployment Benefit, cut the weekly allowance by 10 per cent. It was chiefly objection to this proposal which had caused the resignation of the Labour Ministers.

It might have been thought that the National Government had served its purpose and that a general election would now follow on party lines, but on 8 October Ramsay MacDonald, who, with his supporters, had been expelled from the Labour party, urged the nation to support his Government in an 'unavoidable election' and give it a doctor's mandate to continue its work.

Lloyd George had striven with might and main during the nine years since he left office to restore the prosperity of his country. A trick of fate, his sudden illness, removed him from active public life at the very moment when he would undoubtedly have been invited to play his part once more in the highest counsels of the state. What effect this would have had on the course of events and on the last years of his life can only be surmised; that the effect would have been significant cannot be doubted. As things were, Sir Herbert Samuel had conducted the negotiations leading up to the formation of the first National Government and he, together with Lord Reading, represented the Liberals in the first Cabinet of ten. So far, Lloyd George approved of the steps taken and his son Gwilym accepted a parliamentary secretaryship, but the appeal to the country of the National Government in October in direct contravention of the Prime Minister's pledge broadcast on 25 August and the acquiescence, though unwilling, of the official

Liberal party brought about a complete rupture between the Liberal leader and his colleagues.

Efforts were made to induce him to support the Government. There were pilgrimages to Churt, even the Prime Minister going on one occasion. Winston Churchill stated that 'he had done his best to bring him along', but Lloyd George's hostility to the election was implacable, as he made clear in a letter to his constituency and on 15 October 1931, in a broadcast: the election was 'a tricky attempt to utilise the national emergency to smash the political influence of organised labour', 'a partisan intrigue under the guise of a patriotic appeal'. He appealed to Liberals not to be deluded by the Nationalist label into voting for protectionist candidates; the choice, he said, was often between a food-taxing Tory and a Free Trade Labour candidate. In such a case, since Protection was the impending peril, he would use his vote to avert it. Free Trade was at issue, and he urged Liberals not to walk 'straight into this booby trap' set for them by protectionists merely because it was decorated by the Union Jack.

Lloyd George's own election campaign—he was opposed by a National Conservative—was fought on his behalf by his family and other supporters, but gramophone records made in Churt carried the familiar voice to audiences in Caernarvon Boroughs. Polling took place on 27 October 1931. National Government candidates swept the country: 554 were returned, of whom 471 were Conservatives, 68 Liberals, and 13 Labour. Fifty-two Labour Members and a group of four Welsh Liberals formed the new Opposition. Ramsay MacDonald was therefore Prime Minister in a House of Commons in which the Tories had a majority of three to one over all other Members and made up five-sixths of his own supporters. The Liberal quartet consisted of Lloyd George, *in absentia*, his son Gwilym, his daughter Megan, and a marriage connexion, Major Goronwy Owen. Gwilym and Megan have continued for many years to represent Welsh constituencies, and while they are members of the House the urbanity, wit, and charm of their father will not be forgotten.[6] Telegraphing to his constituency after his own victory, Lloyd George gave thanks that the peaks of Snowdonia remained above the deluge.

On 19 November he left for Ceylon. Before this he had taken

---

[6] Gwilym Lloyd George lost his seat (Pembroke) in the general election, February 1950.

two steps. He had written to Sir Herbert Samuel stating that he was not a candidate for any office in the Liberal Parliamentary Party because he was completely at variance with the disastrous course into which the party had recently been guided, and he referred to the calamitous folly of October which for the time had overwhelmed the causes to which so many millions had rallied hopefully in 1929, but he added that when his health was restored he would gladly co-operate with those who had these causes at heart. He had also removed his personal office from Liberal Headquarters in Abingdon Street to a suite in Thames House, Millbank.

Lloyd George returned from his holiday in the best of health. Three years were to pass before he again took the lead in a new campaign for national reconstruction. During the years 1931-4 he was preoccupied with the writing of his *War Memoirs*. They were ominous years which saw European gangsters consolidate their power. Austria passed through civil war and became subservient to Nazi Germany. Spain was seething with unrest. Japan invaded China and withdrew from the League when that body protested. Russia, on the other hand, having received American recognition in November 1933, entered the League a few months later; Czechoslovakia appeared to be firmly established as a citadel of freedom in the heart of Europe.

From his seat on the Front Opposition Bench—the first time for him to occupy such a position—on the platform, and through the press Lloyd George pronounced judgement on major events. He spoke rarely in Parliament, and usually only on unemployment or disarmament. By June 1932 the continuing world depression had brought industrial production to its lowest point, and the number of industrial and agricultural unemployed to its highest. Between 1929 and 1932 international trade had fallen by one-half, measured in price, and by one-quarter, measured in volume.

Repetition did not stale or enervate Lloyd George's challenges to the Government. He did not deny that financial stability was being achieved, but this counted little with him in the presence of widespread human distress. Capital, unused on deposit, running into hundreds of millions, should be used for rehabilitation. As he had told the Commons (12 July 1932), 'Do not let this country be like that Pompeian slave just discovered in Italy who was found among the ruins clutching the leather bag of his savings. Utilize them!' 'The Empire is not a hollow drum to beat: it is a gigantic estate to be cultivated.'

It was once more an age of European conferences—Geneva, Lausanne, London—but now Lloyd George was a captious spectator. 'We cannot continue these conferences from cloud to cloud, chasing the horizon. The conditions of the world are not such as are propitious to international settlement of our difficulties' (Hansard, 26 July 1933).

By 1934 Lloyd George had before him three examples of nationwide planning, Fascist Italy, Nazi Germany, and Communist Russia, and with them he contrasted the World Economic Conference in London, which had just been adjourned *sine die* having achieved nothing. It was dead, though the Prime Minister, Ramsay MacDonald, was considering the best way of embalming it so as to preserve the appearance of life after the spirit had departed. He had also before him at this time Roosevelt's valiant attempt to raise his own vast country from extreme prostration by means of the New Deal; this had immediately captured the Welshman's imagination.

In the autumn of 1934 Lloyd George set himself to prepare one more programme of reconstruction in consultation with coal, agricultural, and financial experts, many of whom visited him at Churt. For the small area of Great Britain, with two million unemployed and an export trade which had fallen to one-half, Lloyd George announced his programme of a New Deal on 17 January 1935, his seventy-second birthday. Father of the House since the death of T. P. O'Connor, he still had within him the spring of youth. Only Gladstone and Joseph Chamberlain in British political history excelled or rivalled him in the concentrated and continuous exertion required for such a campaign. He had consciously before him the way in which these two gladiators had toured the country and roused thousands who did not read Parliamentary reports.

His gifts for publicity were brought into full play; the expectations of the country were aroused by preliminary trumpetings and a score of journalists gathered in the small city of Bangor for the opening speech. He spoke for no party, but as an Elder Statesman concerned for his country's welfare in its time of tribulation. The prescription was essentially that offered in 1929: a policy which brought together idle hands and idle savings, public works and public money. The old features were repeated in this programme —electrification, housing, the unification of transport services under public control, the reorganization of the iron and steel, coal, and cotton industries, the raising of the school-leaving age —much of it in anticipation of the Labour Government's programme in 1947-8, and only stopping short of complete nationalization. The new features were his emphasis on the unused public savings, on the importance of town and country planning, the need for a statutory National Development Board immune from political intereference, and the need for a small inner Cabinet on War Cabinet lines. There would be two Budgets every year—one for current expenditure and one for capital expenditure.

Other speeches followed, and the interest excited was such that the Prime Minister invited Lloyd George to put his proposals to the Cabinet in writing. In March he submitted a hundred-page memorandum, and from April to June he was cross-examined on it at ten meetings of the Cabinet's sub-committee—a procedure without precedent.

During these months Lloyd George thought it just possible that he might be asked to join a refashioned Cabinet. Baldwin, who became Prime Minister in June 1935, was now believed to be not unwilling to welcome Lloyd George. He moved with his customary circumspection: openly he pointed to the difficulties of co-operation with his old opponent; privately he sent forth scouts to discover the attitude of the Conservative party. The scouts reported that two-thirds were against and one-third in favour of co-operation. There were young Tory Members who welcomed the Bangor programme, but Neville Chamberlain was firmly opposed, and there were others who would have resigned had Lloyd George been included in the Cabinet. Private exchanges, moreover, between Baldwin and Lloyd George came to nought.

His critics were not confined to Whitehall. Waldorf Astor and Seebohm Rowntree, both personal friends and collaborators, challenged his absurdly optimistic estimate of the number of persons who could be settled on the land. They argued that the mechanization of agriculture and the greater yield through fertilizers and other factors precluded there being the least chance of any significant increase in the number of persons engaged in agriculture.

Neville Chamberlain, Chancellor of the Exchequer, had his own policy of recovery: an embargo on foreign lending and the furtherance of a cheap money policy at home; the abandonment of Free Trade in favour of a general tariff and Imperial Preference which was extended to include the Crown Colonies. The total result was a notable recovery of the home market between 1932 and 1937 accompanied, it is true, by much local suffering due to the migration of workers to the Midlands and the London area from Wales and the north-west. But this financial improvement was not in Lloyd George's view a satisfactory substitute for human well-being and the efficient use of national assets. It is possible that had the Lloyd George programme been whole-heartedly applied, the same degree of internal recovery and the same beneficial effects might have been achieved by means of his vigorous and expansionist policy of the New Deal type.

GERMANY

In his comparative leisure at Churt in the early thirties Lloyd George must often have marvelled at the strange course of world events between his own fall from power in England in October 1922 and the rise of Hitler to the Chancellorship of the German Reich in January 1933. What had become of the heroic efforts to pacify and unite Europe he himself had put forth in one conference after another? Where was the general disarmament of Europe on which he had set so much store in his Fontainebleau Memorandum and in the Versailles Treaty? What were the achievements to which the League of Nations could lay claim? The morrow of victory, it has been said, has more perils than its eve, and former allies are a greater problem than former enemies. The first results of the war had been to intensify nationalist passions, dislocate economic life, confuse currencies, pile up debts, put millions out of work. Now, years later, these disorders continued to torture mankind and to lay bare a society which did not possess the moral capital, the political instruments, or the administrative competence to deal with them.

Throughout the twenties Lloyd George had assumed that a quarrel between Germany and France was simply 'undebatable', with the United States 'quite unthinkable'. His own policy towards Germany was one of active conciliation. Europe was exhausted. He was really more eager to see trade restored than reparations paid. France had her devastated regions, Britain her unemployment figures. 'We have never had a great war for forty years after a prolonged war', he told the House of Commons on 27 March 1928. During these same years the British public cherished the Great Illusion of the League as the guarantee of peace.

By the early thirties the facile Utopianism of the post-war years had largely evaporated, and faith in the League was shaken but was far from being destroyed. The fundamental division between the policies of Britain and France had become fixed: security before disarmament, said France; disarmament as a means of security, said Lloyd George. Broadly speaking, Conservative governments in Britain were friendly to France; Liberal and Labour parties were believers in the League, opposed rearmament, resented French militarism, repented the harshness of Versailles towards Germany, and sought to make amends for a treaty which they had never been ready to enforce.

Reparations had been largely taken out of party politics by means of the Dawes and Young Plans, but disarmament remained refractory. Lloyd George had been for years out of office, but he still exerted the Private Member's right to criticize his successors. In speech after speech he proclaimed his disappointment with the failure of the nations to disarm. He joined with Ramsay MacDonald and Baldwin in a huge demonstration in July 1931 in deploring the enormous expenditure on armaments throughout the world, and singled out Britain as having to a considerable extent carried out reductions on land and sea. Other nations had kept Germany to her promise but broken their own. He did not, it is true, go to the disarmament conferences in Geneva himself; had he wished, he could doubtless have been chosen and sent out in some representative capacity. But he continued to declare his belief that Germany's claim to equality of status was well founded, and this was a chief ingredient in his growing sympathy with the former enemy.

It is not easy for the reader today to appreciate the goodwill in Britain towards Germany between the wars. The traditional British treatment of a beaten foe summed up in the words 'fair play' was for a decade in full force. The knowledge we now possess after the proceedings at Nuremberg was not available in the early thirties. The range and power of the demoniacal gifts of Hitler, Goering, Goebbels, and the rest were not suspected; with their avowed opposition to Communism, many in Britain were in complete sympathy. Hitler's emergence was not foreseen nor his right measure taken. He was at first regarded as a passing megalomaniac. No one took him for a political genius or military strategist. It was incredible that the great, educated, scientific German nation would succumb to the hysteria of racial fanaticism and anti-Semitism.

Hitler became Chancellor of the Reich in January 1933, and during the next three years he was visited by eminent politicians and intellectuals from England—Halifax, Eden, Londonderry, Lothian, Allen of Hurtwood, Stamp, Toynbee—bearing in their right hands large olive branches and in their left very small swords. They were variously impressed, but were agreed that what Hitler wanted most of all was the co-operation of Britain in defeating Communism. Lloyd George stated his own views in no ambiguous terms. Speaking at Barmouth in September 1933, he said:

All the trouble that has arisen in Europe and in Germany in particular has come from a flagrant breach of the undertaking to disarm by all the victor nations but one, and the League of Nations' failure to enforce that pledge has destroyed its moral influence. . . . If the Powers succeed in overthrowing Nazism in Germany, Communism will follow.[7]

In 1933 and 1934 Lloyd George believed a genuine peace with Nazi Germany was possible if France could be restrained from the invasion which she was thought to be preparing. Economically Hitler could not afford war, and diplomatically he was not in a position to defy anybody. There was still time for the nations to reach a real understanding 'if we begin at once' (12 August 1934). He deplored the horrible atrocities in Germany, but explained them as the ghastly episodes accompanying revolution.

He was slow to change his mind on these matters. In November 1934 he said in Parliament, after referring to the great military might of Russia:

In a very short time, perhaps in a year, perhaps in two, the Conservative elements in this country will be looking to Germany as the bulwark against Communism in Europe . . . if her defence breaks down against the Communists . . . and Germany is seized by the

---

[7] Speech by Lloyd George at Barmouth, reported in the *Manchester Guardian*, 23 September 1933.

Communists, Europe will follow. . . . Do not let us be in a hurry to condemn Germany. We shall be welcoming Germany as our friend. I beg the Government to consider whether there is not another chance of trying to persuade the Powers in Europe to reconsider their undertaking, their solemn bond, to disarm if Germany did so. We shall not have peace in Europe until we do so.[8]

The Council of Action, founded in the summer of 1935, was a fresh attempt by Lloyd George to get his hands on the levers of power at the next election by means of an organization under his own control. Candidates were asked whether they would pledge themselves to the Council's policy whatever party was in power, even if it meant voting against the Government. The programme included an armistice for five years, a five years' pact of non-aggression during which no military alliances would be entered into, reduced tariffs, abolition of quotas, and sanctions against Italy to include cutting off communications between Italy and Abyssinia. This policy was in harmony with the trend of public opinion as revealed by the Peace Ballot organized by the League of Nations Union at this time.

Baldwin fixed the General Election for November 1935, and the Council of Action was thus early in its life drawn into the campaign along with its founder. Polling took place on 14 November and Baldwin and his Government secured a clear majority of 242. This Parliament was to have a lifetime of ten years, four of them preceding the Second World War. The Opposition was made up of Labour 153, Liberal 16, Independent Liberal (Lloyd George's family party) 4, Independent 1, Communist 1. Sir Herbert Samuel had been defeated, so Sir Archibald Sinclair became Chairman of the Liberals in Parliament at the instance of Lloyd George, who was thus left with leisure to expose the rapidly deteriorating international situation.

From this time onwards, Lloyd George's speeches in Parliament, now very infrequent, dealt almost entirely with foreign affairs, and were directed against the Government's policy of appeasement, at first of Italy and finally of Germany. Lloyd George was never blinded by Mussolini and warned the House that his threats should be taken literally. He recognized and denounced him as the rapacious brigand that he was. The onslaught

[8] Speech by Lloyd George in Parliament, 28 November 1934. Hansard, fifth series, vol. ccxcv.

on weak and defenceless Abyssinia stirred Lloyd George's chival-
rous instincts. To him Abyssinians were the Boers over again,
with the tragic difference that for them no one secured fair play
in defeat or autonomy afterwards.

On the other hand, he was much more tolerant of Hitler, despite
the fact that the Führer was busy tearing up the Treaty of Versailles. Lloyd George discounted the rumours that Germany was
rearming, and he was not opposed to the idea of restoring some of
her colonies. In May of 1935 France concluded a pact of mutual
assistance with Soviet Russia, which was ratified in February
1936. Lloyd George regarded this as provocation for, if not justification of, Hitler's next step, the occupation of the demilitarized
Rhineland; it was a resumption of what had been a part of the
Fatherland and, though a breach of the Treaty, Lloyd George
condoned it. On the day that German troops streamed across
the border Hitler dazzled and fooled his enemies by the spectacular offer of a twenty-five-year pact of peace. In Lloyd George's
view the offer should have been taken seriously.

In the summer of 1936 he still trusted Hitler and saw no reason
why France should not come to terms with Germany. 'She has
everything to gain by it, and she has, in my judgement, nothing to
lose.' This he said in Parliament (27 July 1936) in face of Germany's denunciation of the Locarno Treaty earlier in the year.

In September, in response to a suggestion from Ribbentrop,
Lloyd George arranged to spend three weeks in Germany with the
special object of studying what had been done to deal with unemployment. Naturally, he also wished to meet the Führer. Many
years earlier, Lloyd George had exhorted Parliament to adopt a
programme of road-making, land reclamation, and agricultural
settlement analogous to that which was now being applied by
Hitler, who had also expanded the enormous rearmament programme, and reduced by these measures the number of unemployed to a negligible figure.

Lloyd George, Gwilym and Megan, his doctor, Lord Dawson of
Penn, the interpreter, T. P. Conwell-Evans, and A. J. Sylvester
reached Berchtesgaden on 3 September, and that evening they
dined with the Ribbentrops at the Grand Hotel. Ribbentrop
harped on Russia and the spread of Communism in Spain, France,
and China, and its menace to India. Lloyd George urged that more
perilous than Bolshevism was the growing nationalism and im-

perialism of Russia, and her power as a military state. And the talk ranged on over Europe, past and present.

On the next day (4 September) Lloyd George spent three hours with Hitler at the famous villa and they examined the European situation in the friendliest fashion. Lloyd George could honestly claim to have done his utmost since the Great War to promote good relations with Germany, and Hitler insisted that an understanding between the two countries had been one of his most fervent wishes from his youth upwards.

He agreed that on the co-operation of the two countries the future of civilization depended. The Anglo-German Treaty was a proof of his eagerness to respect British vital interests. At the risk of being regarded as a fanatic he had to warn his people against the Bolshevik danger. The Russian Communistic State and the support it was receiving from sections of the people was a phenomenon which ranked in historical importance with the migrations of peoples or with the Mohammedan invasion of Europe.

Lloyd George urged that everything depended upon a successful outcome of the forthcoming Locarno Conference. An agreement on a basis of equality between England, France, Germany and Italy and also Belgium, which, although not a great power, occupied a key position, would give Europe the protection that she needed.

Hitler agreed that the situation required the re-establishment of Locarno on a new basis. The recognition of German equality was an indispensable condition. The German people were satisfied with the territorial settlement in the West. Russia would endeavour to bring into discussion Eastern problems.

Lloyd George replied that the way to meet this difficulty was to insist that the Conference concerned only the Locarno Powers, its aim being to secure the *status quo* in Western Europe.

Lloyd George asked, 'Would Germany be prepared to agree to an air pact between France, Great Britain and Germany?'

Hitler replied, 'Yes, provided the three powers were able to reach a common defensive position (*Abwehrstellung*), but not otherwise.' He had concluded the Naval Treaty which secured Great Britain's supremacy on the High Seas and the security of Germany in the Baltic. France had not accepted his land armaments proposal and he had accordingly been compelled to establish the security of his own country, as Germany was very vulnerable. To re-arm was not a pleasant task for him. He would have preferred to devote the increased expenditure to the development of his country. Czecho-Slovakia was a positive danger on account of her alliance with Soviet Russia. They had photographic evidence of the military facilities afforded to Russia by Czecho-Slovakia. Clearly a Western bloc would be of paramount importance in pacifying Europe.

Hitler turned to the situation in Spain. If the Left succeeded in Spain, it would not be a victory of the Spanish Government but of anarchic Sovietism. It might spread to France, and Czecho-Slovakia as an ally of Russia would certainly follow. Germany would be an island in a sea of Bolshevism.

'And so would England', Lloyd George interposed. Thanks to Hitler's fourteen years of campaigning and political education, the German people had a new confidence and faith in their future, 'but in Spain the military party had nothing to offer except crude force. The struggle was likely to be a long one and on that account the powers should act with the greatest care and circumspection in preserving strict neutrality.'

At this point there was an adjournment to the great drawing-room for coffee and the talk turned to Hitler's account of his programme of reconstruction, with special reference to the national and regional motor roads and to the Four Year Plan which he was going to announce at Nuremberg in the coming week.[9]

Lloyd George returned from this first conversation much impressed with the Führer's personality. He had been especially struck with an able exposition by Hitler of the system of national finance as applied to public works and to private industries, and did not realize that the consummate actor had delivered this set-piece to eager inquirers on several previous occasions.

Hitler, too, had been deeply thrilled with his visitor but was disappointed when Lloyd George refused his invitation to the Nuremberg Rally.

I have not come to Germany for matters of politics; I wanted to study your social institutions and above all your solution to the unemployment problem, which is threatening us in England also. If I went to Nuremberg, England would be offended.[10]

On the following day Lloyd George and his party took tea with Hitler and Ribbentrop at the villa high up on the hillside in a large reception-room hung with eighteenth-century tapestries and furnished with a round table, a grand piano, and a bust of Wagner. One end of the room had an enormous plate-glass window. On

[9] Author's diary. See also Paul Schmidt, *Statist auf diplomatischer Bühne 1923–1945*, pp. 336–40.
[10] Ibid.

this fine afternoon it was let down into a groove, and the guests enjoyed the fresh air and the view of the Bavarian Alps towards Salzburg. This noble room, which was reached through an arched, crypt-like corridor, gave dignity to the proceedings. With the Führer were his secretary, Meissner, and the rapid interpreter, Dr. Schmidt, deferential, concentrated, impartial; Hitler, when he spoke, addressed Schmidt, not Lloyd George. He gave the impression of complete sincerity and normality; his only gesture was a doubling of his fingers in the palm of his right hand; but when the subject of Russia was broached, his voice became raucous and the fanatic appeared.

Hitler was forty-six, Lloyd George was seventy-three; alike only in their perfect grooming and the brilliance of their blue eyes, these two actors exchanged courtesies at the low, round table. The Führer handed his guest a signed photograph of himself, and expressed his pleasure in meeting 'the man who won the war'. To which Lloyd George replied, with a sob in his throat, how honoured he was to receive the gift 'from the greatest living German'; it would be placed in his little Surrey home next to pictures of Marshal Foch and President Wilson. Lloyd George wondered whether their talks together would influence the Führer's speech at the Nazi party rally at Nuremberg—a rally which it was thought unwise to let Lloyd George attend—and was disappointed that it did not.

Besides seeing Hitler, Lloyd George saw Rudolf Hess, at Munich, and discussed German colonies and raw materials with him; spent some hours cross-examining General Wetzell, Ludendorff's Chief-of-Staff, on the campaigns of the war; and, when German experts or soldiers failed him at meals, cross-examined Lord Dawson and found out from him all he could about vitamins, drugs, wines, and cigars.

The party also inspected a vast work of marsh-reclamation at Emsland, near the Dutch border, where labour battalions were at work digging and trenching drains for miles. Lloyd George was fascinated with this ocular demonstration of his own programme, and the final version of an article for the *Daily Express* which he wrote on the homeward journey was so enthusiastic in praise of Hitler and all his works that the combined pressure of his fellow travellers had to be brought to bear upon him to tone down his superlatives. Despite all protests, he insisted on retaining the sentence: 'The Germans have definitely made up their minds never to quarrel with us again.' This article appeared on 17 September 1936.

Lloyd George returned from Germany having seen what he went out to see—Hitler's programme of reconstruction, and Hitler himself. His critical faculties were in abeyance during the visit. Just as, in the year in which Lloyd George was born, Palmerston had failed to read the character of Bismarck, so now Lloyd George was deceived. Hitler, he insisted, was arming for defence and not for attack; for at least ten years war between Russia and Germany was impracticable; the German army was not in a position to attack anybody, it was formidable only for defence; Hitler and his people admired the British and wanted their friendship, but there was no British leader to exploit this desire; the Germans had made up their minds that they were not going to quarrel with Britain again. Such were the mistaken conclusions he expressed in private letters and gave to the press on his return.

In the winter of 1936, to escape the worst of the weather in England, Lloyd George, as was his custom, went abroad in search of sunshine. He was in Jamaica in December 1936 when Edward VIII, who had succeeded to the throne in the previous January, abdicated in favour of his brother, George VI.

During Lloyd George's Premiership, George V of necessity had seen a great deal of him, and their relationship had been cordial. When, in October 1922, the time came for the King to part with his servant, he wrote in his diary, John Gore reports, after Lloyd George's farewell visit: 'I am sorry he is going, but he will be P.M. again.'

Edward VIII had always been on good terms with Lloyd George, and his investiture as Prince of Wales at Caernarvon Castle, on 13 July 1911, had been due to the initiative of Lloyd George and Bishop Edwards of St. Asaph. This picturesque ceremony had been in abeyance for three centuries. The Prince of Wales was then seventeen. In the next ten years Lloyd George, according to the Prince in *Life* (22 December 1947), 'in no small measure . . . became architect of my career. Concerned over the decline of the British position abroad, he drove me hard.'

Lloyd George, in Jamaica when the crisis came to a head, listened to the broadcast of Edward's abdication on 11 December and was deeply moved. He fancied that the result might have been different had he been at home and able to advise his Sovereign. At Christmas he sent a cable to the ex-King: 'Best Christmas greetings from an old Minister of the Crown who holds you in as high esteem as ever and regards you with deep and loyal affection, deplores the shabby and stupid treatment accorded to you, resents the mean and unchivalrous attacks upon you and regrets the loss sustained by the British Empire of a monarch who sympathised with the lowliest of his subjects.' To which the Duke of Windsor replied on Christmas Day: 'Very touched by your kind telegram and good wishes, which I heartily reciprocate. Cymru am Byth [Wales for Ever]. Edward.'

The reference to 'the lowliest of his subjects' hinted at a base and groundless charge against Baldwin in the American press, but a charge credited by Lloyd George, that the King had been dethroned, in part, because of his public sympathy with the poor and workless.

Meanwhile, Franco's rising against the Spanish Government had taken place; the policy of non-intervention in Spain was being hatched by England and France, and it was to be simultaneously upheld and defied by Germany and Italy and, for opposite reasons, by Russia. Before 1936 ended, the Rome–Berlin Axis and a German–Japanese front against Communism had been proclaimed.

The year 1937 opened with the exchange of British and Italian assurances with regard to each other's rights and interests in the Mediterranean. Lloyd George continued to denounce the Government's tolerance of Italy's infamous deeds in Abyssinia, and its vacillation in Manchuria and Spain. His spirit had chafed for months at the spectacle of the Spanish Nationalist army, an army of the people, valiant and disciplined but utterly unequal in armament to their opponents (even though Russia was giving some material and technical assistance), being deprived of supplies in the name of non-intervention, while the insurgents were being provided by Italy and Germany with all they needed. Moreover, he had come to see the Abyssinian and the Spanish conflicts as rehearsals at key-points for a future war, and he now owned to being disillusioned about Hitler and his intentions.

The Treaty of Non-Intervention had been trampled upon by

Germany for many months. Mussolini and Hitler were both preparing for the hegemony of Europe; they had sized up Britain,
and yet the Government went on with its effort to arrive at terms
with them and persisted in the pretence of non-intervention. He
pleaded with the Government to withdraw the controls, open the
markets, and let the Spaniards fight it out.

By the end of 1937 the three aggressor countries had concluded
firm alliances. The Rome–Berlin Axis and the German–Japanese
front against Communism were already a year old, and now Italy
joined the German–Japanese Anti-Comintern Pact (6 November).
None of these omens nor the withdrawal of the Dictators from the
Non-Intervention Committee abated Neville Chamberlain's blind
and stubborn zeal for appeasement.

In the middle of March Lloyd George spent nearly a week in
Paris, where he met several political leaders and journalists. M.
Paul Mantoux, who had been interpreter at the Peace Conference,
in a letter to the author recalls the visit:

He was as active and brisk as he had been fifteen years before. He
had changed his mind about a great many things, having come to
realize the imminent danger for Britain and France to which German
and Italian intervention in Spain was to serve as a preface and
preparation. Hence his desire to lay a wreath, as a demonstration, on
Marshal Foch's tomb, and another on the tomb of the unknown
soldier under the Arc de Triomphe, both exactly alike. But, on this
occasion as on many others in his life, he spoke and acted as if he had
constantly followed the same line.

When we visited, at the Trianon Palace Hotel in Versailles, the
room where the German delegation, headed by Brockdorff-Rantzau,
had been summoned to receive the terms of peace, Lloyd George said:
'Think now that here we had them like this!' turning his thumb
down, as the Romans did in the circus. The object of his visit to
leading politicians was to try and persuade them that the so-called
non-intervention policy had to be reversed, as fatal consequences
were certain to follow. . . . A luncheon was organized at the Laperouse
restaurant in which fifteen or twenty persons took part, men representing the most varied shades of opinion. . . . There it was that
Lloyd George displayed large maps showing the number of allied
ships which had been sunk in the Mediterranean by enemy torpedoes
in 1914–1918. . . . [He said] 'Now think of a war to be waged with
Germany and Italy, all the Spanish ports being at their disposal as
well as all the Italian bases.' [11]

[11] Letter to the author from M. Paul Mantoux.

Neville Chamberlain had become Prime Minister in May 1937. On 2 May 1938 he asked the House to approve the Anglo-Italian Agreement of April and drew on himself a scathing attack from Lloyd George: Did the Prime Minister really mean in the name of general appeasement to recognize this piratical enterprise in Abyssinia? If a European war broke out, whom would Mussolini sell twenty-four hours afterwards? Lloyd George had no doubt that the two Dictators had a complete understanding; there was nothing in the Rome Pact which bound Italy even to neutrality. If France landed us into war over Czechoslovakia—and the Government had committed themselves to a position where the alternatives were surrender and war—Mussolini would not be likely to remain neutral, his friendship for Hitler had already stood the strain of the unexpected annexation of Austria. The real obstacle to European peace was that the British Government had retreated from one position after another and that the Dictators believed that there was no point at which it would stand. When any strong action was proposed the fatal cry was raised, 'Do you want to go to war?'

But this cry did exactly echo the mood of the nation to whom the thought of another world war was an unbearable nightmare and in preparation for which neither Labour nor Liberals would rearm at all, and Conservatives only half-heartedly. This emotional hostility and unpreparedness in Britain and in France was general and must be remembered in judging Chamberlain.

The Prime Minister was convinced that he could maintain peace and avoid war, and his efforts were blessed by General Smuts and Mackenzie King. He pursued his policy of placation at the expense of Czechoslovakia until it culminated in his visits to Hitler at Berchtesgaden, Godesberg, and the crowning humility of Munich in September. Lloyd George continued to press for a clear statement of British intentions so that the disastrous ambiguity of 1914 might not be repeated. 'They are convinced you won't fight. So am I.' He did this in speeches, in resolutions of the Council of Action, in articles, and on the air. 'We have constantly lowered our flag, and no nation will follow us when it is permanently at half mast,' was the warning he gave (Llandudno, 20 January 1939). He denounced the failure to include Russia in the Munich Conference, and called for an assembly of all the great nations to discuss world peace.

In January 1939 Chamberlain and Halifax visited Rome and toasted the King of Italy as Emperor of Abyssinia; on 28 February the British Government recognized Franco, and on 15 March German troops occupied Czechoslovakia 'which ceased to exist'. It was only at this late hour that the Prime Minister, after many qualifications and hesitations, declared in Parliament (3 April): 'This country has been united from end to end by the conviction that we must now make our position clear and unmistakable whatever may be the result.'

During the summer some Tory and Labour leaders discussed privately the formation of a Cabinet of National Defence in the hope that to announce this would impress and restrain Germany. All sections of the Opposition, it was thought, might work under Halifax, but they would not under Chamberlain. As late as 4 July the Prime Minister wrote to the author: 'I am myself optimistic and believe we shall work through our troubles without a catastrophe.' Nearly a year was to pass before the 'twilight' war ended.

In June there were well-informed anti-Nazi Germans in London whispering secret warnings of Hitler's plans to take Danzig and to redraw the Polish frontier. Nothing, they said, would stop the execution of these plans. There was a last-minute chance that humiliation or war might be averted if Britain were immediately to proclaim her strength and assert her absolute readiness to fight and if this were reinforced by the co-operation of France and Russia.

In August there were feverish negotiations between Berlin and Moscow, and on the 23rd, eleven days before the outbreak of war, the world was shocked to learn that Hitler and Stalin had signed a pact of non-aggression, 'the pact of mutual suspicion', which was to last until the night of 21/22 June 1941, when the world was to be startled again with Hitler's order to the German armed forces to attack Russia 'with all the means at their disposal'.

WAR 1939–45

Britain declared war on Germany on 3 September 1939. On 28 September Germany and Russia announced their partition of Poland. England and France could now have peace if they desired it. Chamberlain replied on 3 October: 'No mere assurances from the present German Government could be accepted by us.' There were press rumours that further proposals would be forthcoming.

Lloyd George urged that these should be considered in secret session; he favoured a conference of Germany, Russia, Italy, the United States, and Great Britain to consider all problems menacing the peace of the world. He secured support for this unpopular view from the central body of the Council of Action and defended it at a meeting of his constituents on 21 October. 'We could be firm at a conference as well as on the field of battle.' France and Britain, he argued, now armed for war, were better equipped for conference than at Munich 'with its unready forces and its shivering diplomats bullied and hectored by the German dictator' (*The Times*, 23 October 1939).

He was much criticized in the House and the country for these 'anxious, almost defeatist' speeches; a prominent London newspaper refused to print an article he wrote in favour of a negotiated peace; he was no longer the war leader of 1916; he was not even the critic inciting the Prime Minister to decisive action; he was nervous of the outcome of the struggle with its unknown terrors and calamities.

In April 1940 supporters and opponents of Lloyd George filled the Caernarvon Pavilion to celebrate his fiftieth year as Member for the Boroughs. His speech was a chain of happy recollections. It was from here he had set forth as a young and ardent Welsh Nationalist, but his projects for uniting the Principality had been rejected by his own people; at the same time his own widening experience convinced him of the indissoluble economic unity of Wales and England. In a broadcast on the eve of St. David's Day, 1936, he had summed up his mature views:

In an age which is threatened with the awful monotony of a spreading standardization, it is no small boon that the people of Wales, by zealously guarding their distinctive spiritual heritage, are able to make their own special contribution to the rich pattern of human life. . . . I myself am not one of those who are convinced that a nation dies with its ancient language. . . . All the same, a nation loses touch with its intellectual past when its life is severed from the language in which for ages its people have given expression to their thoughts.[12]

Nevertheless, in years to come, when out of office, the youthful

---

[12] Speech by Lloyd George broadcast on St. David's Day, 1936.

sentiments would recur in fleeting emotional outbursts against 'dictation from Whitehall'.

Throughout 1940 he wrote weekly articles to the press commenting on the course of the war and criticizing its direction with great freedom. Much of what he wrote was the speculation of a well-informed observer: Will Hitler go through Sweden? When will Italy intervene? Will the Führer invade England? Will he think twice as Napoleon did? Much space went to attacking Neville Chamberlain and his policy. Lloyd George's name carried more weight abroad than at home and there were complaints in Whitehall and in Fleet Street that he had been 'flooding America with defeatist articles'. They were the work, said one critic, of a writer who blended the dignity of an elder statesman and the mischief of a schoolboy with a catapult.

In May it was thought by some that he might again become a war leader. Garvin had an hour's conversation with Lloyd George on 7 May, followed by a small luncheon party at 4 St. James's Square, the object of which was to test his fitness for the highest office. He was, in Garvin's view, still good for six hours a day and it would be six hours of radium.

Lloyd George brought all his evasive technique into play when the question of accepting the Premiership was plainly put to him by his hostess, Lady Astor. He did not disguise his contempt for the Prime Minister, and confessed to great affection for Churchill springing from a friendship of forty years. It was this that made him hesitate to speak in the debate which was to take place on the following day in the Commons. How could he do so without attacking Churchill, as First Lord, for the navy's part in the Norwegian campaign?

He turned, as was now his habit, to past history. A Cabinet like Lord Liverpool's was possible. Clemenceau had waited until France was in the very gravest danger; Reynaud had gone to the top too soon and should have held back. The inference was that Lloyd George preferred to await his country's summons a little longer, and that he expected to receive it as the peril grew. This luncheon party met as the twilight war was drawing to its close and the terrifying reality was about to rain from the skies by night and by day. Before the week was out the Low Countries had fallen to the enemy.

On 7 and 8 May the House of Commons debated the conduct of

the war. On the second day, in what was to prove his last important intervention in a House of Commons debate, Lloyd George arraigned the Government in a sweeping attack of concentrated force. Chamberlain had appealed for sacrifice, and Lloyd George responded in a closing sentence: 'I say solemnly that the Prime Minister should give an example of sacrifice, because there is nothing which can contribute more to victory in this war than that he should sacrifice the seals of office.'

Two days later, 10 May, Neville Chamberlain resigned, and on the evening of the same day Winston Churchill received His Majesty's Commission to form a new Administration. Lloyd George congratulated the country upon Churchill's election 'at this very, very critical and terrible moment'.

He continued his weekly articles in a friendlier tone. He discovered a new cohesion and resolve in the British people and a superior fighting quality in their planes and pilots as the Battle of Britain approached. 'All I say is that the most imperturbable confidence reigns on this side of the water', he wrote on 15 September.

It was natural that Lloyd George's inclusion in the War Cabinet, under Churchill, should be discussed in many circles, and that he should keep everybody guessing about his real intentions. He was now seventy-six and knew it. He sought no departmental responsibility, but thought he could help with food production: 'Food in this War is our weakest flank.' The Prime Minister more than once asked him to join the Cabinet, but the retention of Chamberlain and his opposition to the inclusion of Lloyd George was a major obstacle. Churchill appealed to Chamberlain to lift the ban, and on 6 June he agreed to do so 'in scepticism and dismay'. On this same day Churchill saw Lloyd George and gave him a firm invitation to come in. The Wizard asked for time; the weeks went by and he made no sign. On 30 September Chamberlain resigned, and on 10 November he died. A month later Lothian died in Washington and Lloyd George, had he cared, might have succeeded him as Ambassador.

The Germans went from victory to victory. Holland collapsed, Belgium capitulated, the Bordeaux Government surrendered to Italy without fighting a battle, the Channel ports were overwhelmed and evacuated. Lloyd George, listening daily at Churt to the wireless news of one disaster after another and to the scalding commentary of 'Lord Haw-Haw', grew more and more despondent. He grew critical of Churchill's leadership, and continued to harbour thoughts of a negotiated peace in which he might be called upon to play a part. 'I don't like the look of things,' he kept repeating.

On Sunday, 19 January 1941, he left Churt for Criccieth where his wife, Dame Margaret, was lying dangerously ill. Owing to heavy snowdrifts on the roads he got no farther than a small upland village in Denbighshire; here he had to spend two nights and days while frantic attempts were being made to enable him to proceed by road or rail to Criccieth, forty miles away. Dame Margaret died on Monday morning. Lloyd George reached Criccieth on Tuesday, and on Thursday he saw his wife buried. He was comforted by a message from Mr. and Mrs. Churchill in which Dame Margaret was spoken of as 'that great woman who embodied all that was most strong and true in the British race'. It was a sincere and well-merited tribute to a lady whose innate chivalry and high-mindedness preserved for over half a century her husband's dignity and her own through the chances and changes of his meteoric career.

He remained at Criccieth, where he daily received translations of German and Italian broadcasts of war news, read the newspapers, and secretly cherished the day-dream that he would at some crisis be recalled.

In May the Government gave up two days in the House of Commons to discuss the war situation, and Lloyd George made a speech characteristic of his mood at this time, distributing praise and blame, especially blame. He repeatedly reverted to his own experience in the last war and appealed to the Prime Minister to set up a real War Council who would stand up to him and 'tell him exactly what they think'.

Lloyd George, like the generals, was for fighting this war with the weapons of the last. Churchill did not find this speech of the great war leader of former days particularly exhilarating or helpful at a period of discouragement and disheartenment; he said in Parliament (7 May 1941): 'It was the sort of speech with which, I imagine, the illustrious and venerable Marshal Pétain might well have enlivened the closing days of M. Reynaud's Cabinet.'

Churchill's career had belied the earlier expectations of Lloyd George, who recognized his gifts but thought that defects of judgement, especially on immediate issues, would keep him from the summit. But Lloyd George was fitted to lead in the First World War, and Churchill in the Second. Lloyd George had not Churchill's reckless physical courage, or should one say he showed greater prudence in danger? During the First World War he hurried instantly from Downing Street to the Foreign Office basement at the sound of a siren, and during the Second he built himself at Churt a *de luxe* underground shelter; the military camp at Aldershot was not far away and he feared it might be one of the enemy's targets. Churchill could stand the racket of the warfare in the air better than could Lloyd George, who, it must be remembered, was more than ten years his senior.

In August 1942 the National Eisteddfod was held at Cardigan, and Lloyd George spent three days at Pigeonsford, a few miles away, as the guest of David Owen Evans, Member of Parliament for the county. Megan was with him, and father and daughter were radiantly happy together. Here, in this very Welsh district, moving in and out of two languages, in and out of two cultures, telling tales of old Welsh preachers and deacons, recalling famous scenes and all-night sittings in the House of Commons, he was alert, humorous, and trenchant, with few signs of the approaching octogenarian. He was happier and more vigorous than he had been for a long time at Churt. There he was for ever listening to the news on the radio, English and German, for ever dwelling on reverses and defeats, for ever reverting to parallels with the last war.

At the Eisteddfod he spoke in a crowded cinema for seventeen minutes. He had two pages of notes but he never looked at them, nor did he fail or falter for a word. He spoke with his usual artistry, if with somewhat less than his usual vigour. An interrupter was wittily handled with speed and punch. He was delighted with his reception.

The speech over, returning with his host and the author, he talked freely of the international outlook. He picked out all the blotches on the contemporary map and painted them black. Nothing was fair in the British garden, nor now on the Russian steppe; the odds were in favour of Germany and Japan. 'Russia will be defeated.' He had no faith in Churchill achieving victory:

Winston decided when he became Prime Minister that he would run the War in his own way and alone; I never did that. I relied on the counsel of a group of able men. If I had joined Winston's government two years ago I should have found myself impotent. Beaverbrook professes to stand up to him, but does he really? He mutters an objection and Winston sweeps it aside. And he only talks on the surface with me. He is a bad judge of men: he has moved Wavell and Cunningham and relies far too much on Cherwell and Ismay.[13]

Lloyd George thought the direction of the war was now slack and drifting. He still had a large vision and powerful instincts for original action. At Churt he was lonely, detached, ineffectual; once in control his pessimism would have vanished; but it was in fact too late. The death of Dame Margaret had left its mark, and his periods of energy were fitful and short.

In October, accompanied by Churchill, he presided at a unique ceremony in the Royal Gallery of the House of Lords when peers of the realm and members of the House of Commons met to hear an address from Field-Marshal Smuts. His introductory speech as chairman, most carefully prepared and timed for two minutes took four to deliver, and brought his listeners to the realization for the first time that Lloyd George had become an old man. Smuts spent a week-end at Churt and Mrs. Millin records he asked Lloyd George: 'Why didn't you go into the War Cabinet when they asked you?' 'Because it wasn't a War Cabinet,' he said, 'it was a Churchill Cabinet.'

With the exception of a very short acknowledgement of greetings on his eightieth birthday in January 1943, Lloyd George's last speech in Parliament (11 June 1942) was on Russia. On the announcement of Great Britain's Treaty with the Union of Soviet and Socialist Republics, he said:

As one who has laboured for over twenty years to establish a good understanding between Soviet Russia and this country, I felicitate the Prime Minister and the Foreign Secretary and the Government upon the accomplishment of this Treaty. Had it been a fact some years ago many grave blunders in foreign policy would have been avoided. Not only that: this war could never have occurred.[14]

WALES

On 23 October 1943 David Lloyd George was married to Frances Louise Stevenson at Artington House Register Office, near Guild-

[13] Author's diary.
[14] Hansard, fifth series, vol. ccclxxx, 11 June 1942.

ford, a few miles from his Surrey home. She had joined his staff at the Treasury in 1913 when he was Chancellor of the Exchequer, and had remained on his private staff when he ceased to be Prime Minister.

In August 1939 Lloyd George had bought a small farm of some thirty-seven acres called 'Tŷ Newydd', near his early home at Llanystumdwy. It had first been intended for his daughter Olwen (Lady Carey Evans), but later he decided to live there himself and to experiment with wheat-growing, fruit, and Welsh black cattle. He had the house thoroughly reconditioned and converted into an attractive residence.

In September 1944 he left Churt and motored to Wales, arriving on the 21st with his new wife for their first and last sojourn at Tŷ Newydd. Here he was happy among his own folk. He rose late and retired early. On a fine morning he sauntered to the village, returned for luncheon, rested till four, and after tea withdrew to the study to smoke. An especially good preacher still drew him to a local chapel, and he liked to talk with contemporaries of the days of their youth. He was visibly failing, and let go all thoughts of returning to Churt. His interest in the war declined almost to zero.

The question of the representation of the Boroughs at the next election could not be evaded. Ideally the solution would have been an uncontested election as a mark of gratitude to the most famous Welshman of all time. Soundings were taken among the leaders, but they could not answer for the local associations and no guarantees were forthcoming. The second war had brought a large number of evacuees into the area and a new generation had arisen since the First World War, of which only a minority was thought to be Liberal. At least four speeches were deemed essential if Lloyd George were opposed, and he was unequal to the strain of so many. To be defeated would kill him. So the Prime Minister, his old friend Winston Churchill, a week before Christmas, wrote offering to submit his name to the King for an earldom. He consulted his wife and his brother and next morning a telegram went to the Prime Minister: 'Gratefully accept.' It has been recorded by his brother William that no pressure was put upon him:

'I don't know what to do', he said. 'I never found it so difficult to make up my mind about anything.'

'If you are doubtful about it,' said Mrs. Lloyd George, 'why not send a telegram refusing—that would be an end to the matter.'

After a moment's silence, he said, 'I can't fight another election, but I thought that if I accepted this offer I could say in the House of Lords what I want to say on Peace.' [15]

The thought of being excluded from both Houses was intolerable to him, and he may have pictured himself being carried, as Chatham had been, to speak in the Lords, there to repeat one of his parliamentary triumphs.

There was some momentary friction with the College of Heralds over the precise form of the title. The certificate at Manchester recorded the birth of David Lloyd George, the baptismal certificate at Criccieth said David Lloyd-George; for forty years the two names had been coupled in common usage. The hyphenated form was sanctioned. On New Year's Day, 1945, the Honours List appeared and Llanystumdwy knew and the wide world knew that the Great Commoner was henceforth to be addressed as the Right Honourable Earl Lloyd-George of Dwyfor.

The announcement created no enthusiasm in the Principality; there was some surprise and even disappointment; acceptance of the peerage was attributed to the vagaries of old age, and there was an unfair disposition to blame feminine influence. But of these high and debatable matters the children who gathered at Berea Chapel for their annual party on this memorable day knew nothing, but they noticed with what pathetic difficulty the Grand Old Man—the lean, shrunken frame concealed by the distinguished clothes—spoke a few words to them in Welsh. It was his last speech. On 21 February a bulletin appeared in the press which stated that his physical weakness was causing anxiety to his doctors. During the weeks which followed there were intervals when he revived and seemed his old self; his mind was sometimes cloudy, but often quite clear. He died on Monday evening, 26 March 1945, in the presence of his wife and his two daughters, Olwen and Megan.

At day-break on Good Friday, 30 March, the summits of the Snowden range were veiled in cloud and Criccieth was only faintly visible. At nine o'clock the guns of the anti-tank school at Harlech began their daily practice and boomed across the bay. The day

---

[15] William George, *Atgof a Myfyr*, p. 212.

kept grey throughout, with a keen cold wind blowing. In the late afternoon the sea was shrouded in mist. At midday several planes passed overhead and the villagers asked whether Mr. Churchill had flown to the funeral. In the afternoon, in the presence of thousands of his countrymen singing his favourite hymns, David Lloyd George was buried in a spot chosen by himself high on the bank of the River Dwyfor looking towards the mountains of Snowdonia. On 10 April a Memorial Service was held in Westminster Abbey, shrine of the Commonwealth, where the Unknown Warrior rests.

VIII

THE MAN

SPEAKER AND WRITER

I F courage is the gift especially needed by politicians, the gift of speech, according to Lloyd George, came second: great doers were also great talkers, the strong, silent man was as extinct as the mastodon.

When Lloyd George entered the House of Commons he found there not only Gladstone, Joseph Chamberlain, Lord Randolph Churchill, Goschen, and Balfour among remarkable debaters, but a numerous company of gifted Irishmen such as Healy, Sexton, and Dillon. Of the Irishmen he put Healy first. He was fond of recounting an occasion when the Speaker having ruled that the question of Ireland could not be discussed, Healy succeeded in delivering an ironic speech as a native of Uganda—where a railway was projected—the real subject of which was Ireland.

Celts have practised the art of oratory from the earliest times, with the result that today they are not only good performers but good critics. The standard of public speaking in Wales, as in Ireland, is high, and it was the rich promise of his earliest efforts which first marked out the young Lloyd George as worthy to represent his people in Parliament. He rehearsed his early speeches before a mirror; he tried them out on his friends. He studied the art assiduously by listening to its living practitioners in his own country and reading the recorded speeches of the world's most famous orators.

Lloyd George retained the tone and rhythm and colour of his native speech throughout his life. He was a Welshman in England only less clearly than John Redmond or Tim Healy were Irishmen. The Celtic temperament was unmistakable. Salisbury and Asquith mirrored the mentality and reserve of Englishmen. Baldwin and MacDonald betrayed bardic strains of Highland origin. But these racial or tribal distinctions should not be pressed; Lloyd George transcended them, and was as gladly heard in England as in Wales and in Scotland. To establish immediate affinity with his listeners was natural to him; he developed a diversity of styles—expository, persuasive, humorous, challenging, dramatic, violent

—to suit his audience in Cabinet, in Parliament, on the platform, in church, in the open air, at the microphone. In all these styles he was an artist, and their common foundation was the oratory of the Welsh pulpit.

The great Welsh preachers commanded a wide emotional and dramatic range. They opened their discourse at a quiet, measured pace; as the speaker warmed to his subject the voice rose by imperceptible gradations to higher and higher levels until it passed into a recitative of rhythmic melodious cadences, an ecstasy known in Welsh as *hwyl*.

Lloyd George's early manner was much closer to this Welsh pulpit model than was the conversational idiom of his later years and more responsible utterances. During his campaign against the Boer War, in 1901, Henry Nevinson heard him speak at the Queen's Hall, London, when it was surrounded by a huge and violent mob, making approach dangerous. Lloyd George, he wrote,

was in those days exactly the man for the occasion—courageous, enthusiastic, indifferent to consequences, and convinced of the righteousness of his cause. His eloquence soared ever upward and upward, like an eagle's flight when he rises in vast and spiral curves. It was indeed a superb display of oratorical grandeur such as no Englishman since Gladstone could have attempted. When he concluded, the whole audience rose in an ecstasy of applause, and though I was so torn and battered by the crowd outside that I reached my newspaper office in Fleet Street with the appearance of a shipwrecked sailor, I consoled myself with the thought that we advanced Liberals had gained an ally of incalculable power.[1]

Among his own people the native style lingered on. It was best heard at his annual visit to the National Eisteddfod. For nearly fifty years he rarely missed being present at the Welsh festival of drama, music, and poetry, and he drew multitudes to hear him speak on the day when the winning bard was chaired. The pavilion was always packed with 10,000 or 12,000 men and women, trembling with excitement at the arrival of the national hero. He swept the vast assembly with the all-comprehending glance of the practised orator. When the welcoming din died down his Welsh greeting, *F'annwyl gydwladwyr* (My dear fellow countrymen), evoked a fresh storm of applause, and he would then proceed for twenty

[1] Henry Nevinson, in *Foreign Affairs*, April 1931, p. 460.

minutes, gathering momentum with a succession of short, sharp, vivid sentences, till he reached his peroration. Then he would pause, holding the expectant audience spellbound until he released the crowning phrase and with it the pent-up emotion of the crowd. 'Why should we not sing during the War? The blinds of Britain are not down yet, nor are they likely to be. The honour of Britain is not dead, her might is not broken, her destiny is not fulfilled, her ideals are not shattered by her enemies . . . why should we not sing?' (National Eisteddfod, Aberystwyth, 17 August 1916).

In early childhood Lloyd George learned to speak clearly and correctly, so that all could hear.

We had singing lessons in the village from a farmer's son who was a fine interpreter of tonic sol-fa. He taught us to strike the right tones truly, to enunciate clearly, and to use our voices correctly. 'I can't even understand your words,' he would say, and force us to sing them again and again until every word was intelligible.

You can imagine how valuable such lessons were. We even had competitions. I made my first public appearance at the age of four, when my sucking teeth were coming out. I had to sing a little piece, entitled: 'Remember, child, to tell the truth.' I won a prize.[2]

His tenor voice was admirable; musical, beautifully modulated, and of remarkable carrying power. Lloyd George had not the rich overflowing organ tones of Gladstone, rolling out sentences, clauses, parentheses 'like the Atlantic waves on the Biscayan coast'; its compass was narrower, its quality lighter, it was flexible, caressing, a melodious witchery, mockery, savagery. On the topmost notes his voice became rough and shrill. He played on all the strings of the human heart and matched with each the mobile landscape of his face and bodily posture—the alluring smile, the scowling visage, the thrilling whisper, the eloquent pince-nez dangling from its black silk ribbon, the menacing finger, the arms outstretched to the uttermost. If his voice had not the sonorous rotundity of Gladstone's or the unrelieved pugnacity of Joseph Chamberlain's, he abounded in a sense of fun; his humorous sallies convulsed his audience and there were moments when he reduced them to tears. S. K. Ratcliffe comments: 'It was all done with absolute mastery. Not a paragraph bungled; not a stroke, or a joke, goes awry.' Emotional, dramatic,

---

[2] A. J. Cummings in *News Chronicle*, 1 April 1940.

rhetorical, and never too long, he was always the incomparable actor with a perfect sense of theatre.

If the power of recognizing likeness is the special mark of genius then he had genius, for his most original gift was a command of metaphor. His speeches sparkle with images, 'apples of gold in pictures of silver'. There was at times a meretricious quality about Lloyd George's rhetoric, but the fertility and felicity of his invention were amazing. He spoke to the primitive emotions of the crowd, drawing his images from the elemental forces of nature and the incidents of common life, rarely travelling outside the experience of his audience. Thus, at Versailles in November 1918: 'In the beautiful forests the leaves were falling, but these were not alone. Empires and Kingdoms and Kings and Crowns were falling like withered leaves before a gale.' And at Montreal in October 1923:

I remember just before I started here being in the town of Swansea. The city conferred upon me the same honour that Mr. Mayor conferred upon me to-day in your city, and made me a Freeman. They put the certificate in a casket which was made out of all the metals that were smelted, forged and worked in that city. There was iron, steel, tin, cobalt, nickel; there was gold and there was silver. They were not smelted into one metal. You saw them all there. But they all enclosed my freedom. That is the casket which is the British Empire.[3]

There are few literary references in the speeches of Lloyd George or in the 3,000 pages of his *Memoirs*. The Bible is the only exception; much of it he knew by heart and constantly used. For example: 'Freedom does not descend like manna from Heaven. It has been won step by step, by tramping the wilderness, fighting enemies, crossing Jordan, and clearing Jebusites out of the land.' There are scores of images which light up the commonplace thought: the sunless misery of the slums, the flood of luxury, the pinnacle of sacrifice. Platitudes fall into rhythmic sentences: 'It is a stout heart which endures to the end of a great strain.' And here is a more elaborate example which in the pavilion at Caernarvon brought the audience to its feet.

Yesterday I visited the old village where I was brought up. I wandered through the woods familiar to my boyhood. There I saw

[3] Speech by Lloyd George at Montreal, October 1923; *Slings and Arrows*, p. 280.

a child gathering sticks for firewood, and I thought of the hours which I spent in the same pleasant and profitable occupation, for I also have been something of a 'backwoodsman'. And there was one experience taught me then which is of use to me today. I learnt as a child that it was little use going into the woods after a period of calm and fine weather, for I generally returned empty-handed; but after a great storm I always came back with an armful. We are in for rough weather. We may be even in for a winter of storms which will rock the forest, break many a withered branch, and leave many a rotten tree torn up by the roots. But when the weather clears you may depend upon it that there will be something brought within the reach of the people that will give warmth and glow to their grey lives, something that will help to dispel the hunger, the despair, the oppression and the wrong which now chill so many of their hearths.[4]

Lloyd George made no attempt to conceal the fact that he had prepared a speech; it was due to his audience to have done so and he made no pretence of spontaneity. He could at call make an excellent debating speech and of his gift of repartee there are many examples, but normally he liked to prepare an important speech several days ahead of delivery. When time allowed, he would dictate it to a typist and would then summarize with the aid of keywords to important passages. These notes he would use openly and deliberately, hold up his eye-glasses to read them, let the glasses fall, and then deliver the sentence or the paragraph. If unable to dictate, he would prepare as fully as time allowed and trust to the moment for words to convey his ideas. He took pains with speeches on relatively unimportant occasions, and would spend hours in the preparation of a short address. Presiding at a concert in North Wales, he spoke for a quarter of an hour on Mozart, having read beforehand three voluminous 'Lives' of the composer. He would sometimes speak better when less elaborately prepared, and especially when confronted with an opponent.

Lloyd George coined and memorized striking phrases, lingered over the music of purple passages, and then wrote them down. He was ever on the alert for the right word, and carried a small book in which he noted any thought or phrase which might fit into a speech. There is a characteristic entry on his choice of an interpreter in Riddell's *War Diary*: 'When I speak to a particular man I consider what words will be best suited to appeal to him.

[4] Speech by Lloyd George at Caernarvon, 9 December 1909.

I want the interpreter to use my very words. I don't want him to convey only the sense of what I say. That is not enough.'

The charges brought against Lloyd George of transgressing good taste or of hitting below the belt have occasional justification, but they have been exaggerated. He could quote precedents in the speeches of former Prime Ministers, as, for example, Disraeli's famous description of Gladstone as 'a sophistical rhetorician, inebriated with the exuberance of his own verbosity and gifted with an egotistical imagination that can at all times command an interminable and inconsistent series of arguments to malign an opponent and glorify himself'.

Lloyd George used the language of exaggeration, ridicule, and abuse to cut and smite opponents. A certain bishop, he said, was a third-rate scholar, a fifth-rate preacher, a no-rate theologian, an irate priest. An aloof, cold colleague, much disliked, was compared to the North Pole, often explored and never found. His speeches may lack sustained reflective thought, but they are charged with political wisdom expressed in epigrammatic form.

The characteristics of the public speaker were reproduced when Lloyd George settled down to write. He had in his teens written signed and unsigned letters and articles to the North Wales newspapers, and in his early years in Parliament he continued the practice, as well as writing notes on Welsh questions for the *Manchester Guardian*. When in office, and especially during the war, he wrote many memoranda. Apart from his early correspondence with his Uncle Lloyd, Lloyd George's letters served strictly practical ends and grew fewer as his responsibilities multiplied; he wrote far fewer than Asquith or Baldwin, but he wrote more official memoranda than either. 'Letters are the very devil. They ought to be abolished altogether,' he remarked to Riddell. He preferred direct human contact, heart-to-heart talk, where he could trust his intuitions. When in retirement, after 1922, he was an active commentator on current events in British and foreign newspapers, and earned enormous sums as a journalist. The articles he wrote were acute and fearless criticisms of persons and policies, written rapidly, widely translated (they were published in more than twenty countries), and continued off and on for some twenty years. His main audience was in America. Those articles published abroad often censured the Home Government and were objected

to as disloyal or unfair, and those which attacked foreign statesmen as highly mischievous. Some of them were inspired by such
animosity to France that he and Riddell quarrelled over them
and were estranged for some time.

In August 1922 he announced his intention of writing his
Memoirs by way of reply to the criticisms of his direction of the
war which were constantly appearing in articles, pamphlets, and
books, and of giving the whole of the profits to charities connected
with the relief of the suffering caused by the war. This provision
was especially the wish of Dame Margaret. But the project was
indefinitely postponed, and it was ten years later, when approaching his seventieth birthday and recovering from an illness, that
Lloyd George embarked on the writing of his *War Memoirs*—six
volumes which appeared between 1933 and 1936—his most ambitious book. Two further volumes, *The Truth about the Peace
Treaties*, were published at the end of 1938.

When preparing the *Memoirs*, Lloyd George had the help of a
number of assistants, but he kept control of the material in his
own mind. He accumulated a large collection of official papers,
and these his secretary, A. J. Sylvester, took the precaution of
having indexed by two trained clerks from the Cabinet Office,
Hannen and Ince, in such a way that when Lloyd George came
to write all were in order and immediately available over the wide
range of the six volumes. As this index was on the same plan as
that at the Cabinet Office, discussion with Hankey was facilitated
when he read and 'passed' the volumes on behalf of the then Prime
Minister, Stanley Baldwin.

He did almost all of his writing at Churt, and followed a pattern
of work there. His brain was clearest in the early morning, and he
began to write, propped up in bed, usually around six o'clock,
sometimes earlier, until seven-thirty, when tea and fruit were
brought to him. He then bathed and shaved and read the morning papers, and at breakfast-time he would issue 'orders of the
day'; what he had written would be typed, and he would work
over it until about eleven-thirty when he would perambulate the
farm, returning for lunch at one o'clock. He would sleep for the
whole afternoon, and after tea would work and visit the farm
again. He dined at seven-thirty and went to bed at nine-thirty
with a detective story for a sedative. During the day he would have
managed to examine innumerable papers, documents, and letters

flagged for him by his secretaries. If data were lacking on the subject in hand a secretary would be told off to interview the essential witness, if available, with instructions to return with his *ipsissima verba*. Such was the normal day during the composition of the *War Memoirs* in the thirties.

In his prefaces Lloyd George is at pains to disclaim proficiency as an author; he is an amateur who late in life has set down the facts as he remembers them and has then checked them by an examination of all available evidence, oral and written. The result is a most impressive marshalling of vast material by the one Minister who held office from the beginning of the war through the Peace Conference and beyond. He belongs to the historians who describe events in which they themselves were immersed and many of which they directed.

Many actors in the war had published their recollections of that great drama before he addressed himself to the task. Of these he made the fullest use in defence of himself and in attacking his traducers. As the work proceeded he was able to consult French and German publications. His main sources were the Minutes of the War Cabinet, Imperial Cabinets, and inter-Allied conferences, for which Hankey was responsible, together with other relevant papers from government departments. These formed the framework of his own exposition and comment.

A tone not only of defence but of defiance runs through the work. Lloyd George, like Woodrow Wilson, knew how 'to add sulphur to the ink'. The living, he announces at the outset, have their rights as well as the dead, and through every one of the thousands of pages the author is a pugilist, alert and challenging. The book is the man, and he is a man of action. The style is the man, and the man is not a judge but an advocate. 'I am not writing history as a historian,' he told Herbert Fisher, 'but as a solicitor in possession of the documents.' He fights the war all over again with sustained vigour to the last page of the sixth volume, distributing praise and blame, argument and abuse, mockery and invective, as one who is on trial in a great cause and has been condemned unheard.

When he is describing the merits of friends and the faults of enemies his pen knows no moderation. He has a constant tendency to glaring colours, to strong effects, and will always be striking violent blows. He is not merely exuberant but excessive. There is an overweening confidence about his tone, he expresses himself in trenchant phrases, which are like challenges to an opponent to stand up and deny them . . . we inevitably think of a saying attributed to Lord Melbourne: 'I wish I were as cocksure of anything as Macaulay is of everything.' [5]

This quotation is not from a review of the *War Memoirs*. It is Mark Pattison's estimate of Macaulay as historian, and it is applicable without change to Lloyd George as historian of the First World War.

It is remarkable with what clarity the ever-changing interacting political and military situations are presented, how often he is able in retrospect to justify his policy and to buttress his case with contemporary or subsequent proof. Nor have the critics found it easy to convict him of factual error in a narrative loaded with detail.

John Buchan declared the chief fault of the *Memoirs* to be the monotonous infallibility of their author. Prime Ministers do not readily admit to being wrong. In this as in other ways Baldwin and Attlee are exceptional. Throughout his writings and his speeches it would be hard to find an instance in which Lloyd George admits quite simply, 'I was wrong.' What he said of Churchill in Parliament (9 November 1928) was true of himself: 'Whether the right hon. Gentleman is fighting for the Crescent or the Cross he never appears in a white sheet. He always appears in full panoply.'

As in his speeches, so in his books there are many striking illustrations of an illuminating character. What could be better when dealing with the variability of War Office statistics than 'they were always like desert sands. Any change in the wind either converted humps into hollows or hollows into humps'; or in speaking about the League of Nations, 'that machine which never had a chauffeur but was expected to go of its own volition, through the perfection of its mechanism and the amount of petrol in its tank, with a competing shuffle of feet for the accelerator and a mere scramble of hands for the wheel'. On other pages, it must be admitted, the writing is forced and charged with rhetorical insincerity: 'Every millimetre of the liberated earth was rent deeply by the cruel claws of war and redeemed by the blood of the liberating groups. France . . . was bleeding from every vein, still on her

[in margin: in capable of error]

[5] Mark Pattison, 'Macaulay', *Encyclopaedia Britannica* (1911), xvii. 196.

feet, facing the foe, but staggering.' Moreover, there are pages dis-
figured by cheap sneers and petty vindictiveness and deliberate
suppression. Northcliffe, he asserts, is the mere kettle-drum of Haig
and the mouth-organ of Robertson. Compared with the treatment
meted out to other important figures, the half-page given to Lord
Riddell in the *Peace Treaties* (p. 220) is a passage of perfunctory
acknowledgement, of deliberate under-payment for heavy debts
incurred; his name does not even occur in the exhaustive index to
the *Memoirs*. Notable also is the absence of any mention of William Bullitt and his Russian mission during the Peace Conference.[6]
But these blemishes are forgotten or unnoticed by most readers
when they turn to descriptions of battles and bravery written as
with the pen of an eyewitness.

It is not true, it is far from true, that Lloyd George condemned
every general, admiral, and statesman who took any part in the
war. He presents a list of those whom he has chosen for laudation.
But many readers carry away an impression of posthumous black-
washing by reasons of the merciless portraiture of eminent officers
singled out for attack. He protests that his differences with great
generals were not due to any personal or political motives, but he
devotes so many pages of his *Memoirs* to denouncing Haig, Robertson, Pétain, and Pershing that the cumulative iteration of their
faults and blunders tends to blot out the passages in which Foch,
Plumer, Allenby, Maude, Smuts, and the rest are highly commended.

It was on Haig and Robertson that he concentrated his most
malicious and sustained attack. A critic looking at Augustus
John's savage portrait of Lloyd George observed that had he been
painting Cromwell it would have been all wart. It is rather in this
spirit that the politician turned writer has depicted the British
Commander-in-Chief and the Chief of the Imperial General Staff.

Haig, we are told, ordered many battles but only took part in
two; he was unselfish but self-centred; industrious but uninspired;
painstaking but unimaginative, heavy-footed and narrow; his
judgements were unreliable and warped by his immediate interests; he angrily opposed the formation of a General Reserve and
viciously resisted unity of command; he was a bad chooser of staff;
he preferred gambling with men's lives to admitting an error; he
was a mere name to men in the trenches; even his famous 'Backs-

[6] See *Documents on British Foreign Policy 1919–1939*, First Series, iii. 425.

to-the-Wall' Order of the Day was a mistake; he was ungenerous: his diaries contain no acknowledgement of Lloyd George's work in the production of men and munitions. Nevertheless, he conceded, Haig was admirably adapted to be a second-in-command to a strategist of unchallenged genius.

There are repeated attempts in the *Memoirs* to sum up Sir William Robertson. Thus: he never saw a battle; he was a Westerner; he trusted in attrition; he resisted unity of command; he was Haig's man, supporting him whole-heartedly and allowing his loyalty to dim his vision; he distrusted foreigners; he disliked argument; neither he nor Haig nor Joffre possessed the qualities in which Lloyd George abounded: initiative, resource, pliability, vision, imagination, aptitude to learn from experience, courage and skill to profit by mistakes.

But if a critical biographer were to apply to Lloyd George's conduct the merciless analysis he employs in dealing with these two generals Lloyd George himself would not escape the lash. The French Revolution, he reminds us, was saved by the promptitude with which the generals who failed were removed. He is at pains repeatedly to justify his own failure to remove Haig and Robertson. He praised them publicly, as is the convention; privately he neither trusted nor whole-heartedly co-operated with them, and yet Robertson was not removed until he had been Chief of the General Staff for over two years. Haig, burdened with the long series of defects and defeats, which Lloyd George enumerates, could not be replaced by him from an army counted in millions, and when the war ended he was still at its head. If it be argued that the promotable generals were replicas of Haig, then it may be retorted that the statesmen got the generals they deserved. No one had discouraged professional military ardour more than Lloyd George, who as late as November 1913, in his land campaign, was bewailing the spending of millions on armaments which as Chancellor of the Exchequer he could have used to reduce the burden of local rates.

The conflict between the civilian and military authorities on which the *Memoirs* are a commentary is inherent in the democratic conduct of war. War is an art, and no scientific line can be drawn to delimit the spheres of the statesman and the soldier. The problem is insoluble: the supremacy of one or the other turns on which will is the stronger in any given situation. With reflections on this theme Lloyd George brings his *Memoirs* to a close. It is one element in his greatness that both as Prime Minister clothed with power and as retrospective author in tranquillity he recognized that the greater responsibility rests in the political sphere. His stress on preserving the unity of the home front was more unyielding than his pressure for unity of command in the field. This is where Ludendorff, who lacked political insight, failed. The war was won in spite of collisions with generals, and because of the blunders of the enemy.

STATESMAN AT HOME

No. 10 Downing Street is the Prime Minister's family residence, his workshop, and the meeting-place of the Cabinet. On quitting office he moves out quickly to make room for his impatient successor. When Lloyd George left 10 Downing Street never to return, he found a temporary residence at No. 86 Vincent Square, which was lent to him by Sir Edward Grigg, now Lord Altrincham. Later he moved to No. 10 Cheyne Walk, on the Chelsea Embankment, and afterwards purchased No. 2 Addison Road and named it 'Dwyfor Lodge'. A short time before the Second World War he moved to No. 8 Victoria Road, Kensington, but he disliked the place and spent very little time there. In the early days of the war, until it was blitzed, it was used as an office.

By means of his Fund, Lloyd George kept a large personal office, which was the pivot of his many and varied activities. When he left Downing Street he opened an office at 18 Abingdon Street, from which he moved to a large building at 25 Old Queen Street, the headquarters of the Liberal Coalition party during his Premiership. Later he went to 21 Abingdon Street, the headquarters of the Asquithian Liberals, but he was never happy there. Finally he moved to a magnificent suite of rooms on the sixth floor of Thames House, overlooking the river, where he remained until the early part of the Second World War.

When Prime Minister, Lloyd George made much use of Chequers for relaxation and for the entertainment of colleagues and distinguished visitors; for rest and change of scene there were also available his house at Criccieth and the various country houses usually rented for him by Lord Riddell.

About 1921 he bought a parcel of land at Churt in Surrey, near Hindhead, forty miles from London, and on it built a house where he was to spend most of his later years until the end drew near and he returned to Wales to die. The house, called 'Bron-y-de', stands on top of a knoll: its loggias, a special feature of the house, commanding wide prospects of the surrounding hillocky, heathery country. His visit to Hitler at Berchtesgaden gave him the idea, which he adopted in one of his main rooms, of replacing a wall by an enormous window in which a single pane of glass stretched the whole length of the room. Here for over twenty years the dismissed statesman gathered his books and papers and secretaries, presided over hard-working committees engaged in preparing the 'coloured' books on social problems, welcomed many guests, and wrote most of the million words of his *War Memoirs*.

He set about transforming the original purchase of land and adding to it. He bought several farms, extensive woods and rough ground, including these with his former holding in a ring fence. He ended up with about 750 acres in all, on which he was presently to employ about eighty men and first to lose and then to make money. Experts from the Wye Agricultural College, the East Malling Research Station, and of the Surrey County Council were called in to advise the amateur who had settled in their midst. He grew apples and soft fruit and kept bees; the fruit was marketed in London, the honey sold locally in pots labelled 'From the apiary of the Right Hon. D. Lloyd George, O.M., M.P.'. In the fruit season he would employ several hundred temporary pickers. He gradually developed an economical combination of fruit, poultry, pigs, and vegetables, using the pigs to reclaim land overgrown with young brushwood. He delighted to exhibit and compete with other growers in the local shows.

On this wild, raw estate his gifts of creation ran riot; he was apt to think he knew more of horticulture than his gardeners, and you could never be sure that he did not, for he frequently changed them. Unlike the typical English country gentleman, he was neither antiquary nor sportsman, neither magistrate nor philanthropist.

He was of medium height, with a large head, broad shoulders, deep powerful chest, and short legs. His sparkling blue eyes were his most striking feature, his chin and jaw determined, his voice light and musical. Carefully dressed in homespun, his white locks falling on his flowing cloak, pet dogs at his heels, he delighted to walk his guests over the 'blossoming desert', to expatiate on his

Acme-Planet

MARKET GARDENER, 1943

experiments with this apple or that raspberry, and to argue from his particular demonstration plot to its possible universal imitation all over the country. And so he himself gradually grew and ripened into the Elder Statesman, withdrawn to his rural retreat, hoping to be recalled to Westminster to save his country, a hope that never quite flickered out.

In town or country, in houses big or little, Lloyd George was a gay and genial host with high and low alike, a natural democrat mingling easily with all classes—he was as much at ease with Philip Sassoon and his majestic butler in Park Lane as with a chapel deacon in a Criccieth cottage. The blandishments of Mayfair had failed to seduce him, and of this triumph he boasted to the end of his days. At Churt or Criccieth he soon tired of seclusion and gathered lively company around him. Nothing humdrum or boring was allowed to subdue his happy, fun-loving temperament, and at a ludicrous situation his roguish figure would collapse into a fit of uncontrollable laughter. Children delighted in his company. Few Prime Ministers can have laughed so much and so heartily. His guests never saw him drooping, flat, or stale. He was a good talker and a good listener, eager to learn, interested in everything and everybody, spontaneous, sparkling not with wit but with humour and good-natured chaff. He had much of the fascination of a great actress or clever woman, an expert in amiability, adjusting herself swiftly to her surroundings with the right word and the right look.

He enjoyed other men's stories and told many of his own, polished in the telling, repeated with unquenchable gusto, and illuminated by his surpassing gifts of mimicry. One he liked to tell was 'the Procurator of Judea', by Anatole France—the story of Pontius Pilate, oblivious of the one event in his life which had made him immortal. Of stories about Welsh preachers and illustrations drawn from their sermons there was no end.

He had an insatiable curiosity about public characters, good and bad: gospellers like Spurgeon and Billy Sunday, charlatans like Jabez Balfour and Horatio Bottomley, comic actors like Charlie Chaplin, boxers like Jimmy Wilde—he knew all about them. He was not cynical about great men, and while fond of characterizing them he did so as a rule with a large charity, and in his family circle checked any tendency to denigration. He delighted in fanciful speculation in the manner of Charles Lamb in Hazlitt's essay 'Of persons one would wish to have seen'. What he most liked was to pose questions to his listeners and collect a poll of opinions. Would you rather be a great orator or a millionaire? Was President Wilson a saint or a martyr? Colonel House, a salesman or producer? He would ask his doctor, Lord Dawson of Penn, if he was limited to one drug or to three, which would he choose? He would ask a lady M.P., seasick in the Mediterranean, which would she prefer, to go a voyage by sea with Baldwin or a journey by land with Lenin? Who are the greatest figures in history? Someone would start off and he would label them with a penetrating if not final phrase: Gladstone was much the biggest political figure in our history; he stood for Humanity, Disraeli for Empire; Gladstone had no social consciousness, Disraeli had. Balfour, until he was an Elder Statesman, was only the scent on a pocket-handkerchief—this perhaps reminiscent of 'scented popinjay', the Irish epithet for the Chief Secretary. Bonar Law was always waiting for a course which was inevitable; he had not the gift of wireless speech, his words did not travel. Who were the greatest Welshmen? His list included Llewelyn the Great, Owen Glendower, Henry VII, Elizabeth, Daniel Rowland, Howell Harris, and Robert Owen.

Or he would start a competition in quoting the sayings of famous men and himself bring out Danton's 'Que mon nom soit flétri; que la France soit libre'. The discussions never strayed far from the political field, and rarely did they touch on the arts of painting or sculpture or great music or great poetry. For political talk his appetite was inexhaustible and his comments were his own.

The exercises of religious worship appealed to his emotions and their effect on the people to his strong pragmatic sense; he enjoyed music but did not aspire to any intellectual appreciation of it. On Sundays he returned to the world of his youth, sang hymns, and listened to sermons on the radio. He served on the B.B.C. committee which chose the Welsh preachers. His unfailing recreations were golf, hymn-singing, and sermon-tasting.

Little is recorded and less can be said here of Lloyd George's attitude towards the ultimate questions of life, death, and religious belief. His mind was neither speculative nor devout, and the deep spirituality which is the texture of the finest characters would not be attributed to him at any period of his public life. He told a friend that his notion of Christianity was akin to George Bernard Shaw's in the preface to *Androcles and the Lion*. He respected the religious susceptibilities of his countrymen; for many years he delivered an annual lay sermon at a London Welsh Baptist Chapel couched in language which did not offend his hearers while it preserved his own sincerity. His own religious beliefs may not have been orthodox, but he would have deemed it a tragedy if the world were deprived of the Christian church and the Christian faith. This view, which he always held, is summed up in a speech he delivered in Caernarvon on 23 September 1908.

There is a growing tendency to treat religion as if it were but a stage in the march of humanity towards a higher civilisation—a stage along which the race must pass, but which it must, in spite of the beauty and grandeur of its scenery, leave behind it if it means to reach a more exalted destiny. This is no new attitude on the part of mankind. It has passed through this phase many a time in its history. It sometimes means that the human race is entering upon a dreary march through the parched, arid plains which are stretched between one form of religious thought, which it quits forever, and a purer and nobler faith which is awaiting it at the end of its journey. . . . Human nature in its essence is the same in every age and in every dispensation, and religion provides for the fundamental needs of human life. The joys and perils of life are always the same, and when the wise men who from the altitude of their self-sufficiency shun the churches can think of some more effective agency to guide men and women through the dangerous paths of life, for strengthening their hearts to bear the inevitable sorrows of life—some idea or system or scheme of things that will light up the valley of the shadows, and will swallow death in victory, as the religion of Christ has done in the experience of untold myriads who put their trust in Him, then we, the simple people of the hills, may give up the building of chapels and churches. But until that new ideal is revealed we will go on finding a new pride and a new pleasure in making sacrifices for the old cause that saved our fathers.

At Churt Lloyd George was among his own books and papers. It was part of the early abuse of him, as of Joseph Chamberlain, that he never read a book. Neither statesman was stamped with the trade-mark of Oxford or Cambridge, but both were, in fact, assiduous readers. Lloyd George never thought much of the Welsh University Colleges which were set up in the seventies and eighties.

He was inwardly proud that he had climbed the heights without their aid, and that no one comparable with himself had emerged from their classrooms.

He had early been moved by the humanitarianism of Dickens and Victor Hugo; he read Carlyle's *Sartor Resartus*, Milton's *Areopagitica*, and Charles Reade's *Cloister and the Hearth* many times, and he often returned to the books of Dumas and Stevenson, especially *The Three Musketeers* and *Kidnapped*. He never ceased to be attracted by Napoleon and Lincoln, and was steeped in the literature of the French Revolution and the American Civil War. He had read Gibbon's *Decline and Fall*, and remembered much of Sir Samuel Dill's two books on the Roman Empire in dissolution. For escape he read bloodthirsty tales or novels with happy endings (he also enjoyed Wild West films). In his later years he often dipped into the works of Cicero in the Loeb translation, and perhaps reflected on how he had in himself uneasily united Cicero's love of freedom and the rule of law with Caesar's love of power and popular favour.

His historical outlook showed itself in odd and original ways. The Supreme Council met in Paris in September 1919 to discuss, *inter alia*, the evacuation of the Baltic Provinces by Germany, who apparently could not control her eastern army. The parallel which occurred to Lloyd George must have astonished the Conference: 'In that event the Eastern German forces would be outlawed and would be in much the same situation as were Morgan and Drake in the time of Elizabeth, both of whom had been disavowed by the British Government.' [7]

Gladstone dwelt with Homer, Aristotle, Augustine, Dante, Bishop Butler. Lloyd George did not drink at these springs, and in the accepted sense was not a scholar. 'Brilliant without intellect,' wrote Margot Asquith. Haldane described him as 'an illiterate with an unbalanced mind'—on which the best comment would seem to be Morley's in another context: referring to Lloyd George and Haldane, Morley said: 'This is a fight of the swordfish and the whale, and I put my money on the swordfish.' His mind was formed far more by theology, history, and poetry than by science. His mental processes were intuitive and imaginative rather than logical and scientific. He was not, as Lenin was said to be, 'a very theoretic man'; Haldane complained because he did

[7] *Documents on British Foreign Policy 1919–1939*, First Series, i. 703.

not think in concepts, like a philosopher. He was glued to no economic system, nor had he much interest in abstract ideas or in impersonal history. He had the bias of his upbringing and remained essentially a radical to the end, despite the aberration of the peerage at eighty-one. His sympathy with the under-dog in the mass endured through all changes, and gave a radical consistency to his policies. He believed in private enterprise and in the big business man as essential to industrial progress, but he was also an advocate of planning and not afraid of using the state as an instrument for the execution of the plans. In youth an admirer of Mazzini, in age he followed Cavour—the yeast of the one making the bread of the other.

When he settled at Churt he enjoyed a substantial income— in 1919 Carnegie had endowed him with a life pension of £2,000— and ample domestic comfort. The long third-class night journeys to Criccieth were dim and distant memories. The severe self-discipline of the war had ceased to be necessary. The old Welsh simplicity and frugality dear to Dame Margaret had lost their appeal. She did not spend much time at Churt, preferring the climate of Criccieth. He abounded in hospitality, displaying unaffected kindliness in small matters while in great his generosity found little exercise. In the years of his prosperity he was not given to the financing of men or movements at his own expense, not even in the Principality.

When travelling he demanded luxurious arrangements for himself and his companions. In the twenties and thirties he enjoyed a series of holidays abroad, motoring across Europe, cruising in the Mediterranean in a hired yacht, visiting Brazil and Ceylon. His sudden departures, his lightning reversals of plans, his decision to go east instead of west, his avidity for news at every stage of the journey—these were but the whims of an autocrat who could afford to indulge them and who left all arrangements and accounts to A. J. Sylvester, his indefatigable secretary. His affluent old age contrasted sharply with the modest provision enjoyed by Woodrow Wilson, Clemenceau, and Foch. An illustration he himself once used seems apposite: 'In South Wales there is a river called the Towy. In its lower reaches it meanders through fat pastures—a slow, turgid, muddy stream. In its higher reaches it is a turbulent, violent stream, but the water is clear and bright.'

He not only had no genius for friendship, but he could even say

that he had no time for friendships which were not political. Outside the family circle he had few friends bound to him in a deep
firm sense with hoops of steel; in earlier years D. R. Daniel, Herbert Lewis, Samuel Evans, Llewelyn Williams; in the middle years
Churchill, Masterman, Reading, Riddell, and C. P. Scott were near
to him and might claim the title. Churchill wrote to him as 'My
dear David'. Eric Geddes, Robert Horne, and some others were
welcomed as entertainers and raconteurs. He was always glad to
see Herbert Fisher and Philip Snowden who were neighbours at
Churt. When in office he had, of course, colleagues, supporters,
sycophants, in plenty, and hundreds of acquaintances. 'He does
not understand what friendship means,' summed up F. S. Oliver;
'I neither love nor trust him; nor, mark you, do I hate or distrust
him.'

He displayed different facets of his prismatic self to different
men: Lord Hankey saw the Prime Minister; Lord Lothian, the
statesman; Sir William Sutherland saw the politician and press
manipulator; A. J. Sylvester saw the Chief *en déshabillé*. It will
take ten men to write his *Life*, said Baldwin.

He could be petulant and on occasion ruthless. Delicate understandings might prove evanescent, bargains fragile, and criticisms
of or opposition to him easily be made to wear the guise of disloyalty. Like other men in high places he took credit where none
was due, used men, and parted without tears. Sometimes, but not
often, he went too far and had the grace to retreat. Clemenceau
tells of such an occasion: 'He assailed me with the most violent
reproaches in open session of the Versailles Conference. . . . M.
Sonnino congratulated me on having remained cool and collected,
and Mr. Lloyd George, when the sitting was resumed, proposed
with a smile that the whole of that part of the proceedings should
be expunged from the minutes, to which I nodded assent.'

But what the men who worked with him and for him, especially
through the years of war, recall are not these incidents but the
amazing courage and good temper, 'the shining morning face',
with which day by day he confronted the tremendous responsibilities of his high office. In his prime he was accessible, sympathetic, cheerful in triumph and adversity alike. For half a century
his character was hotly debated, praised, and blamed. Some politicians, he told the students of Edinburgh in a rectorial address (1
March 1923), 'could not walk across a golf course on Sunday with-

out incessant reproach, and others might tee their ball on the church steeple with hardly a murmur'.

There were many occasions in his turbulent career, as during the Boer War, when storms of abuse broke over his head; during the insurance debates and after the Budget of 1909 he was the most vilified man in the kingdom. In later conflicts suffragettes shouted him down, his portrait was removed to the cellar of the National Liberal Club, savage cartoons depicted his infamy, and execrations poured into Downing Street. Margot Asquith headed one of her Lay Sermons with a scriptural text: 'The vile person shall be no more called Liberal . . . the liberal deviseth liberal things; and by liberal things shall he stand.'

He might make use of the rich for his own purposes, especially if they were press magnates, and he might treat his patrons scurvily, but he retained his independence. In a fight he took sides, and if attacked he hit back without mercy. 'He is a man who thrives on fighting,' wrote Clemenceau of him. Reverses roused his combative qualities, he did not cherish animosities for long, and those who hated him politically found it difficult to dislike him personally. To this rule there were, of course, a few exceptions.

When Prime Minister, with a small inner Cabinet and over eighty ministers revolving around him, his methods, which had always been personal, grew more so and there were signs of incipient Caesarism. Those who worked closely with him in Paris detected a growing intolerance of contradiction. Normally his abounding humour kept inflationary tendencies within limits. An extreme self-assertiveness might well be excused. After all, he had broken the bars of birth and circumstance and had done so without the aid of influence or wealth or university in a country where these unlock most doors. It was impossible that Lloyd George should not know that he was a very remarkable man, but he did not parade that knowledge or take undue credit to himself. He had all his life an odd way of judging his achievements as something external to himself, of regarding himself as a performer on a moving stage, and of wondering aloud what he would find were he to return a hundred years hence and what would then be said of him. He had surrounded himself with some of the ablest men of his own time, Milner and Curzon, Churchill and Birkenhead, for example. In one conference after another he had not flinched from pitting himself against the world's outstanding statesmen, and they conceded to him courage, resource, and a flair for leadership. He was himself not afflicted with envy and jealousy, the vices of lesser men.

In later years exclusion from office did not for some time abate his zeal for constructive reforms or his hope of returning to power to carry them through. In the meantime he found an outlet for his critical faculties as historian and journalist. The prospect of office receded, and when the Second World War broke out he was conscious of failing physical powers. Still he cherished a secret hope that the course of events might summon him to share for a second time in the making of peace. But this was not to be, and his fame must be allowed to rest on his earlier achievements.

RETROSPECT

Lloyd George entered Parliament as a young man of twenty-seven, and continued to represent the same constituency for over half a century. Three years were spent as a youthful and often rebellious Private Member when the Liberal party was in power, seventeen as a Cabinet Minister (1906–22), and the whole of the remaining thirty-four in Opposition, eleven before the First World War and twenty-three after. Throughout most of this long period his actions were under minute public scrutiny. He could never for a moment escape public recognition; his most casual utterance attracted the ubiquitous reporter, and he lived daily under the shadow of Parliamentary Questions. Emerging from a remote Welsh village he displayed qualities of political courage and speech and action so remarkable that he attained the loftiest station and the widest fame in the First World War; he was then rejected and excluded from the official direction of affairs for the rest of his life. Posterity will long be engaged in accounting for such dazzling success and such continuous failure. Some attempt at a provisional explanation follows.

Political success depends upon a fortunate conjunction of public events and personal qualities. Lloyd George turned many events into opportunities for his own advancement, but there were other events 'in the nature of things' which defied him. One of these, the eclipse of Liberalism, was proceeding apart from anything he could do to hasten or delay the process. Liberalism was being dissolved from the Right by Baldwin and from the Left by the Labour party on which the Russian Revolution had made a deep

impression. Liberal leaders were anchored to Free Trade and did
not take kindly to planning. Neither Asquith nor Grey betrayed
any live awareness of the new 'economics of plenty' then strug-
gling to displace the old 'economics of scarcity'. When the war
ended Lloyd George might have rejoined the disrupted Liberal
party, gone over to the Tory party, which he would never do,
created a Centre or Coalition party, which he tried and failed to
do, or sat loose from all parties; this in effect is what he finally did
from 1931 onwards.

All are agreed that Lloyd George was not supplanted by superior
men: Bonar Law, Stanley Baldwin, Ramsay MacDonald, and
Neville Chamberlain were his successors. That he was one of the
greatest of British Prime Ministers in war cannot be challenged.
Two hundred years ago Sir Robert Walpole thought the first quali-
fication for that office was the possession of more common sense
than any other man. Today, in a community completely enfranchised, leadership is deemed indispensable, and it was the possession of this gift which raised David Lloyd George to the highest
eminence. Lenin regarded him as the greatest political leader
Britain had known. Leadership is only one sort of greatness, but
the sort essential in war, and in war Lloyd George was at his best—
in Milner's view 'the greatest War Minister since Chatham'. That
he himself held this quality to be necessary we can learn from his
condemnation of those who lacked it. He has drawn a portrait of
his ideal War Minister in order to prove that Asquith fell far short
of the standard and, by implication, that he more nearly reached
it. To the catalogue of qualities he enumerates we may add his
possession of immense self-assurance edged with defiance, and
powers of persuasion, irresistible whether exercised on the few or
on the many. His courage in facing a hostile House of Commons
and his triumphs over it have rarely been paralleled during its
long history. His courage was something personal to himself,
without antecedents or tradition. Churchill's courage grew out
of a distinguished ancestry, a sense of destiny, a study of history,
and it was both grimmer and more serene than the Welshman's,
who had nothing to fall back on but his own pugnacity.

Leadership of the House of Commons in the day-to-day routine
sense was delegated by Lloyd George to subordinate Ministers, to
Bonar Law and then to Austen Chamberlain. He never led a compact party majority in office, nor did he lead a compact party

minority in Opposition. His restless temperament chafed at the divisions and restriction of Whips Offices. He hastened the contemporary transfer of power from Parliament to Cabinet, and while reducing the Cabinet to one-fourth its former size and putting into it the strongest men available he was still big enough to dominate it by initiative, intelligence, and dynamic personal force. The role he did in fact fill was akin to that of dictator to the Coalition; Austen Chamberlain says he went so far as to contemplate a temporary suspension of the Cabinet, leaving Bonar Law to transact business with individual Ministers or groups of Ministers while he himself was at the Paris Conference. This trend towards 'demagogic Caesarism' alarmed some of his colleagues. He out-distanced all competitors in the First World War and raised himself to the stature of Chatham before and Churchill after him. At its close he was the most powerful and most popular statesman in the Empire, the Prime Minister of Europe, his name and figure familiar throughout the world.

Endowed with exceptional vitality, Lloyd George's powers of alternating work with repose were abnormal. He was built for work; when he ceased and sank down into an easy chair his whole frame relaxed; he could sleep at any odd hour in the midst of a raging crisis. His devouring energy, the velocity of his mind and actions bewildered slower-thinking and slower-moving politicians; to those opposed to him he seemed a conjurer who made black appear white and white black. There was something elemental in his strength and self-reliance. He was the artificer of his own destiny and the arbiter of his own conduct. In his forties and fifties his temperament was sanguine, he did not sulk or fret over the past or turn sour. He was untroubled by scepticism or self-criticism, by remorse or conviction of sin. It can also be said of Lloyd George, as Morley said of Gladstone, that he had none of the disastrous self-consciousness that makes a man persist in a foolish thing today because he chanced to say or do a foolish thing yesterday. His buoyancy and courage were contagious, magnifying and diffusing his personal influence from Cabinet to department, permeating Parliament, newspaper offices, and the whole nation.

> A largeness universal, like the sun,
> His liberal eye doth give to everyone,
> Thawing cold fear.

In office he was the fly-wheel of the machinery of government;

out of office he was a wheel which races, grinds no corn, covers no ground. In office his genius had full scope for fruitful and effective use; out of office it spent and wasted itself in a series of brilliant, costly, and barren improvisations.

What was lacking in his splendid endowment? Were there defects of character which diminished or destroyed his immense power for good?

In his early years Lloyd George had to overcome the prejudice felt in England for a foreigner. Welsh Members of Parliament in the eighties, Lord Rendel, then one of them, wrote, were regarded as an inferior category, a cheaper sort of Member. Two eminent journalists, Henry Nevinson and Alfred Spender, have separately recorded their impression that when Lloyd George talked to them he seemed to be translating from Welsh. He always kept the accent and lilt of his native speech. This foreignness together with the speed of his mental processes, his temperamental exuberance, and his preference for very private channels of negotiation contributed to the distrust of him which prevailed and persisted to the end.

For the fact must be faced that he was not universally trusted. This arose in part out of his preference for circuitous methods which he proudly claimed as one of his merits. 'I never believed in costly frontal attacks in war or politics, if there were a way round.' Hesitations and evasions are the stock-in-trade of politicians, and Lloyd George has not escaped the charge, brought even against Mr. Gladstone, of seeking refuge in a haven of ambiguity and leaving a trail of misunderstanding behind him. He was ambidextrous, and like Ehud could steer with either hand as his right hand. Attempts to pin him down to definite statements or promises were apt to be unsuccessful. When asked on a famous occasion what he meant by the control of the coal-mines he proved 'exceedingly amiable, but excessively indefinite'. Margaret Digby in her biography of Sir Horace Plunkett mentions the experience of a deputation from the Irish Convention which waited on Lloyd George in February 1917: 'Afterwards no two delegates were ever agreed on the actual words or even the meaning of the Prime Minister's utterances.' Allied with this was his habit of conveying his wishes to his subordinates by 'subtle indirection' rather than by categorical instruction. Into the winking of authority they had to read a command.

These criticisms must not be magnified. When in the autumn of 1922 the Coalition fell, a dozen Cabinet colleagues remained loyal to Lloyd George and acclaimed his great gifts. In main essentials of foreign policy he had been true to British traditions: the command of the seas, the balance of power in Europe, the maintenance and defence of the Empire; in domestic policy he had been a progressive radical, but revolutionary only in his Budget. In his agricultural policy he might be called an extremist, he certainly was an optimist. Censure must be confined to his methods. Thus a typical Englishman and admiring colleague, Austen Chamberlain, writes to Walter Long in April 1922: 'Even many of those who recognize his great qualities and pay tribute to his great services, dislike his methods and are kept in a perpetual state of uncertainty as to what he will do next.'

It was not, says Harold Nicolson in his life of Curzon, that Lloyd George was consciously evasive or misleading, it was his privacy of method and privacy of aim which undermined confidence. Lloyd George found some colleagues slow and others stupid, and he also fancied he could short-circuit the formal epistolary exchanges of diplomats or the elaborate pronouncements of trade-union negotiators by private interviews or by the use of friends or subordinates as secret instruments. He often did facilitate business by these means, but he paid a price. Agents could not be plenipotentiaries except under a dictatorship, complete secrecy was difficult, gossip created an air of mystery on which supervened suspicion and mistrust. These reprehensible methods have not been entirely abjured by other Prime Ministers, before and since, but one man may steal a horse whereas another may not look over the gate. The opposition he had to surmount in climbing to power was fierce and constant; once on top he was more open and frank, but he did not discard the secretiveness which he had found helpful on the way up.

What is this glittering whirl at the centre of our public life? asked one of Lloyd George's perplexed critics. The answer is that he was a 'sport' in the works of creation. Unlike Chatham, he had no rich Governor of Madras, owner of diamonds and rotten boroughs, for a grandfather; unlike Churchill, he had no Marlborough among his ancestors; he had nobody and nothing. He once told a friend: 'I never had a helping hand stretched out to me from above or heard a voice call, "Climb up here."' Baldwin at the Carlton Club meeting called him a dynamic force. 'A dynamic force is a terrible thing; it may crush you but it is not necessarily right.' It was a destructive force, which had split the Liberal party and might have split the Tory party, but it was also a creative executive force which won the war, by strong and swift decisions, by an ability to work and make the nation work, by resistance or indifference to hampering detail, by sheer personal magnetism. Whatever he may have lacked, in the highest office he had the drive which stretched and strained the powers of his Ministers and secretaries to the utmost and there was no question who was the central animating dynamo. He was best in adversity, 'when the gale ran high'; in a crisis he bent all his strength to face and break it, which was war as well as magnificent.

Sitting with the Prime Minister in the last months of the Coalition Cabinet were two or three mutinous Tories to whom his methods and general behaviour were increasingly distasteful and his dominance intolerable. The chief of these silent critics was Stanley Baldwin who, to his own amazement and that of his colleagues, was shortly to become Chancellor of the Exchequer and, a few months later, Prime Minister and Leader of the Tory party.

The elation of victory in 1918 had been accompanied by a coarsening of morals and manners in all classes. Rapid changes are often accompanied by moral laxity, while established tradition struggles to preserve its standards. None would claim that Lloyd George strove hard to raise the level of political ethics. His constructive strategy was also often spoiled by the tactics with which it was enforced. The House of Commons which sat from 1919 to 1922, Baldwin said, had been filled with hard-faced men who looked as though they had done very well out of the war. Baldwin had been shocked by the Prime Minister's irresponsible and flippant handling of the Coupon Election and the Chanak crisis. To these misdeeds were later added Lloyd George's highly remunerated journalistic adventures and his practice of running down his own country in American newspapers. Baldwin was very well-to-do; Lloyd George was in need of earning a living, but that did not justify an ex-Prime Minister defaming England abroad. It was a view widely shared.

Lloyd George, we have seen, had not only disrupted the Liberal party in 1916 but he had continued to provoke resentment by making the Party Fund a personal fund. His despotic and arbitrary distribution of it was highly offensive to purists and democrats and helped to swell the criticism of his character as a public man. He would have done better for Liberalism and for himself without his Fund. He had been his own Foreign Office, and he could not rest without being his own Party Office. He put his trust in it and became the victim of his own extravagance. For money was not the one thing needful. He commanded advertising experts, special trains, packed halls, responsive newspapers. He piped and the audiences danced, but they did not vote for him.

He was an uncertain asset. Liberals were not prepared to jettison him entirely. The Labour party, steadily growing in power, would have nothing to do with him, fearing that if they did he might become their leader; on his part, he admired Snowden and J. H. Thomas for their political abilities, but with few trade unionists did he feel he could collaborate; he was scornful of Labour intellectuals, calling them 'Professors'—with him, as with Bismarck, a term of contempt. Nor were the Tories ready to take him to their bosom. He was finally reduced to the family party of four. Even on the Continent it came to be well known that his was a solitary voice, still listened to, but with little influence on events.

Distrust is apt to arise beween two men when one is unhurried, shrewd, and suspicious and the other incredibly quick and brilliantly clever. Baldwin liked to compare Lloyd George to the neutron: it is too slim to be confined under pressure in any vessel; it will simply slip through the walls. The difference between the two men went much deeper than party politics. Lord Rosebery, in writing about Napoleon remarked: 'There is one question which English people ask about a great man: Was he a good man?' Baldwin did not shrink from applying this test to statesmen, however exceptional or prodigious their gifts. 'It is better to have second-class brains than second-class characters,' Lord Robert Cecil said. When the turn of the electoral wheel put Baldwin into 10 Downing Street in 1924 his hope was that Lloyd George and his régime would never return there. By 1935 a decade's experience had made Baldwin more tolerant of human and ministerial frailties, and resistance to a *rapprochement* came most firmly from Mrs. Baldwin. Lloyd George would have refused to serve under Ramsay MacDonald, but he cherished hopes of an arrangement which would place him in the same relation to Baldwin as he had assigned to himself in relation to Asquith in December 1916. But there was opposition to him in another powerful quarter and to Churchill, who also was excluded from office because of his intellectual force and dominance.

Associated with Baldwin as colleague and designated successor was Neville Chamberlain. His dislike of Lloyd George dated back to his dismissal from office during the war. Austen, on the other hand, thought his brother wrong in refusing to work in Cabinet with Lloyd George. Neville Chamberlain shared Baldwin's preoccupation with right conduct and carried it further. Quite apart from party differences, Chamberlain's personal hostility was unappeasable. His presence later in Churchill's Cabinet was in Lloyd George's mind sufficient reason for not entering it: 'We should only quarrel,' he said.

Lloyd George in retirement was a dictator *manqué*, but unlike the European dictators there was nothing eccentric, fanatic, or cruel about him. An unchained political genius without responsibility to a government or attachment to a party he had, in the eyes of his inferior successors, as time went on, only a nuisance value, if so much. In the summer of 1935 his Liberal Fund enabled him to launch the revivalist Council of Action as a non-party organization. In October, on the eve of the general election, Neville Chamberlain was writing in his diary: 'Our party is united, Labour is torn with dissensions, Liberals have no distinctive policy, L. G. has ceased to interest.' 'Has ceased to count' would have been more accurate.

The exhaustion caused by the First World War, the desire for a change of leaders and for tranquillity which followed, the reluctance to oppose German breaches of the Treaty or to proclaim British policy in eastern Europe with precision, or to run any risk of a Second World War—all this negation of policy was characteristic of Baldwin and to a lesser extent of Chamberlain. Lloyd George confronted successive governments with positive domestic programmes, with foreign policies at first pacific and later belligerent, but he always failed to commend them to a majority of the electors. He was left more and more alone on his farm.

When Churchill took charge in the Second World War he invited him to join his Government. Lloyd George judged rightly that he could not step twice into the same War Cabinet and control it. He remained outside.

His work was done, and it had been immense and epoch-making. For half a century he had played the hard-hitting political game with zest, accepting its defeats or victories as all falling within the Orders of the Day. The Insurance Acts for which he, mainly, was responsible were the greatest measures of social reform ever placed upon the statute book and made smooth the transition to the Welfare State. It was his social measures which softened the asperities of the post-war world for the rank and file, and laid the foundation of the subsequent structure of social security. These measures, together with the People's Budget, anticipated and prevented revolution by successfully attacking the privileged classes and comforting the poor. There lies his first claim to greatness as a statesman. His second is that more than any other single man he was what Field-Marshal Smuts declared him to be, 'the supreme architect of victory in the First World War'.

In recollection, it is the genial and human warmth he created, his buoyancy, his playful humour, his driving power in the presence of which no one could work hard enough or fast enough or ably enough, which linger in the minds of those who worked most closely with him. He was not content to be, as many politicians are, a voluble prophet of platitudes; he was a great executive. At a crisis of history Lloyd George took hold of flabbiness and muddle; by his own energy he turned flabbiness into resolution, muddle into system and purpose. The last word is with Churchill, his friend and his successor as British War Leader: 'When the English history of the first quarter of the twentieth century is written, it will be seen that the greater part of our fortunes in peace and in war were shaped by this one man.'

BIBLIOGRAPHY

THE books, journals, and documents covering the activities of Lloyd George are legion, and no attempt is made below to do more than mention a minute selection. He left his Parliamentary and other political papers to his second wife. In September 1950 it was announced that they had been acquired by Lord Beaverbrook for presentation to the University of New Brunswick. Valuable general bibliographies are included in:

ARMSTRONG, H. F., and LANGER, W., *Foreign Affairs Bibliography, 1919–1932* (New York: For the Council on Foreign Relations, 1933).

CHAMBERS, F. P., *The War Behind the War, 1914–1918* (London: Faber & Faber, 1939).

ENSOR, R. C. K., *England, 1870–1914* (Oxford: Clarendon Press, 1936).

FREWER, L. B., *Bibliography of Historical Writings, 1940–1945* (Oxford: Blackwell, 1947).

MARRIOTT, SIR J. A. R., *Modern England, 1885–1932* (London: Methuen, 1934).

PROTHERO, G. W., *List of Books Concerning the Great War* (London: H.M. Stationery Office, 1923).

WOOLBERT, R. G., *Foreign Affairs Bibliography, 1932–1942* (New York: For the Council on Foreign Relations, 1945).

I

PUBLISHED OFFICIAL DOCUMENTS

Great Britain

British Documents on the Origins of the War, 1898–1914, edited by G. P. GOOCH and HAROLD TEMPERLEY, 11 vols. (London: H.M. Stationery Office, 1926–38).

Documents on British Foreign Policy, 1919–1939, edited by E. L. WOODWARD and ROHAN BUTLER (London: H.M. Stationery Office, 1946–).

(Hansard) *Parliamentary Debates: Official Report* (London: H.M. Stationery Office).

History of the Great War, Based on Official Documents, by Direction of the Historical Section of the Committee of Imperial Defence. A series of volumes dealing with military, naval, and air operations in all theatres; published by H.M. Stationery Office, Heinemann, Longmans, Macmillan, and Oxford University Press (1920–).

War Cabinet Reports 1917–18, Cmd. 9005, 1918, and Cmd. 325, 1919.

United States

Department of State. *Papers Relating to the Foreign Relations of the United States. The Paris Peace Conference 1919* (Washington: Government Printing Office, 1942–47).

Department of State. *Papers Relating to the Foreign Relations of the United States. Supplements. The World War: 1914, 1915, 1916, 1917, 1918. Russia, 1918*, vols. i, ii, iii, 1919 (Washington: Government Printing Office, 1928–37).

II

PRINTED WORKS

Lloyd George's writings and speeches referred to in the text

In addition to the titles given below, Lloyd George, after he left office, contributed numerous articles to the press of Great Britain and other countries.

Better Times (London: Hodder & Stoughton, 1910).

Coal and Power (London: Hodder & Stoughton, 1924).

The Great Crusade (London: Hodder & Stoughton, 1918).
Extracts from speeches delivered during the war.

Is it Peace? (London: Hodder & Stoughton, 1923).
A collection of articles and addresses commenting on the European situation during 1923.

'National Self-Government for Wales' in *Young Wales* (October 1895).

Slings and Arrows, edited with an introduction by PHILLIP GUEDALLA (London: Cassell, 1929).
Extracts chosen from the speeches.

Some Considerations for the Peace Conference before they Finally Draft their Terms, 25 March 1919 (Fontainebleau Memorandum), Cmd. 1614. Published as Parliamentary Paper, 1922; also published in Cmd. 2169 (1924).

Through Terror to Triumph (London: Hodder & Stoughton, 1915).

The Truth about the Peace Treaties, 2 vols. (London: Gollancz, 1938).
An account of the preparations for and the progress of the Paris Peace Conference, its leading figures, the founding of the new states and the Turkish negotiations (Syria, Palestine, Greece, Asia Minor, Armenia).

The Truth about Reparations and War-Debts (London: Heinemann, 1932). Published also in French and German.
A short topical book in which he pleads that the truest way to honour the sanctity of the Treaty of Versailles would be to cancel future reparation payments from Germany.

War Memoirs, 6 vols. (London: Ivor Nicholson & Watson, 1933–6). Republished, 1938, in 2 vols. by Odhams Press. References are to this edition.
The documented narrative of 'the only official figure who went right through it from the declaration of War to the signing of Peace'.

'Welsh Political Programme' in *Independent Review* (September 1904).

Biographical Studies of Lloyd George

DAVIES, SIR A. T., *The Lloyd George I Knew* (London: Walter, 1948).

DAVIES, W. W., *Lloyd George 1863–1914* (London: Constable, 1939).

Du Parcq, Herbert, *Life of David Lloyd George*, 4 vols. (London: Caxton Publishing Co., 1912).

Edwards, J. H., *David Lloyd George*, 4 vols. 1913, 2 vols. 1930 (London: Waverley Book Co.); also 2 vols. 1929.

Evans, Beriah, *The Life Romance of Lloyd George* (London: At office of *Everyman*, 1916).

A Welsh American edition was published as *Rhamant Bywyd Lloyd George* (Utica, N.Y.: Thomas J. Griffiths, Swyddfa'r Drych, 1916); and there was also a French edition, *La Vie roman de Lloyd George* (Paris: Librairie Delagrave).

Humphreys, E. M., *David Lloyd George* (Llyfrau'r Dryw, Llandebie, Sir Gaerfyrddin, 1943).

A short biography in Welsh by a leading journalist who knew Lloyd George well.

Jones, Jack, *The Man David 1880–1914* (London: Hamish Hamilton, 1944).

An imaginative presentation, based on fact, by the South Wales novelist.

Keynes, J. M., *Essays in Biography* (London: Macmillan, 1933).

Mallet, Sir Charles, *Mr. Lloyd George: A Study* (London: Benn, 1930).

Mills, J. S., *David Lloyd George, War Minister* (London: Waverley Book Co., 1924).

Murray, Basil, *L. G.* (London: Sampson Low, Marston, 1932).

Raymond, E. T., *Mr. Lloyd George* (London: Collins, 1922).

Sidebotham, Herbert, *Pillars of the State* (London: Nisbet, 1921).

Spender, Harold, *The Prime Minister* (London: Hodder & Stoughton, 1920).

Sylvester, A. J., *The Real Lloyd George* (London: Cassell, 1947).

Principal private secretary to Lloyd George 1923–45.

Thomson, Malcolm, with the collaboration of Frances, Countess Lloyd-George of Dwyfor, *David Lloyd George, The Official Biography* (London: Hutchinson, 1948).

West, Gordon, *Lloyd George's Last Fight* (London: Rivers, 1930).

*   *   *   *   *   *

Lloyd George of Dwyfor, Earl, *Dame Margaret: The Life Story of His Mother* (London: Allen and Unwin, 1947).

Diaries, Memoirs, Correspondence, Biographies

Addison, Christopher, *Politics from Within, 1911–1918*, 2 vols. (London: Jenkins, 1924).

—— *Four and a Half Years: a Personal Diary from June 1914 to January 1919*, 2 vols. (London: Hutchinson, 1934).

Allen, B. M., *Sir Robert Morant: A Great Public Servant* (London: Macmillan, 1934).

Arthur, Sir George, *Life of Lord Kitchener*, 3 vols. (London: Macmillan, 1920).

Asquith, *see* OXFORD; SPENDER.

BAKER, R. S., *Woodrow Wilson, Life and Letters*, 8 vols (London: Heinemann, 1928–39).

BAKER, R. S., *Woodrow Wilson and World Settlement*, 3 vols. (London: Heinemann, 1923).

BALFOUR, *see* DUGDALE.

BEAVERBROOK, LORD, *Politicians and the War 1914–1916* (London: vol. i, Thornton Butterworth, 1928; vol. ii, Lane, 1932).

BELL, G. K. A., BISHOP OF CHICHESTER, *Randall Davidson, Archbishop of Canterbury*, 2 vols. (Oxford University Press, 1935).

BERTIE, F. L., VISCOUNT BERTIE OF THAME, *Diary, 1914–1918*, 2 vols. (London: Hodder & Stoughton, 1924).

BETHMANN-HOLLWEG, T. VON, *Reflections on the World War*, translated by GEORGE YOUNG (London: Thornton Butterworth, 1920).

BIRKENHEAD, 1ST EARL OF, *Contemporary Personalities* (London: Cassell, 1924).

BIRKENHEAD, 2ND EARL OF, *Frederick Edwin, Earl of Birkenhead*, 2 vols. (London: Thornton Butterworth, 1933, 1935).

BOOTHBY, ROBERT, *I Fight to Live* (London: Gollancz, 1947).

BRAND, R. H., editor, *The Letters of John Dove* (London: Macmillan, 1938).

BROCKWAY, FENNER, *Socialism over Sixty Years, The Life of Jowett of Bradford* (London: Allen & Unwin, 1946).

BRUCE, SIR ROBERT, *The House of Memories* (Glasgow: Royal Philosophical Society, 1946–7).

BUCHAN, JOHN, LORD TWEEDSMUIR, *The King's Grace, 1910–1935* (London: Hodder & Stoughton, 1935).

CALLWELL, MAJ.-GEN. SIR C. E., *Field-Marshal Sir Henry Wilson: His Life and Diaries*, 2 vols. (London: Cassell, 1927).

CARSON, *see* COLVIN; MARJORIBANKS.

CECIL OF CHELWOOD, 1ST VISCOUNT, *A Great Experiment: An Autobiography* (London: Cape, 1941).

CHAMBERLAIN, SIR AUSTEN, *Down the Years* (London: Cassell, 1935).

—— *Politics from Inside* (London: Cassell, 1936). *See also* PETRIE.

CHAMBERLAIN, JOSEPH, *see* GARVIN.

CHAMBERLAIN, SIR NEVILLE, *see* FEILING.

CHARTERIS, BRIG.-GEN. JOHN, *Field-Marshal Earl Haig* (London: Cassell, 1929).

CHIROL, SIR VALENTINE, *Fifty Years in a Changing World* (London: Cape, 1927).

CHURCHILL, WINSTON, *Great Contemporaries* (London: Thornton Butterworth, 1937).

—— *Thoughts and Adventures* (London: Thornton Butterworth, 1932).

CLARKE, TOM, *My Northcliffe Diary* (London: Gollancz, 1931).

—— *My Lloyd George Diary* (London: Methuen, 1939).

—— *Northcliffe in History* (London: Hutchinson, 1950).

COCKERILL, BRIG.-GEN. SIR GEORGE, *What Fools We Were* (London: Hutchinson, 1944).

COLVIN, IAN, *Life of Lord Carson*, vols. ii, iii (London: Gollancz, 1934, 1936).

CONWELL-EVANS, T. P., *Foreign Politics from a Back Bench, 1904–1918* (Oxford University Press, 1932).

COOPER, DUFF, *Haig*, 2 vols. (London: Faber & Faber, 1935, 1936).

COWDRAY, VISCOUNT, *see* SPENDER.

CURZON, *see* NICOLSON; RONALDSHAY.

D'ABERNON, VISCOUNT, *An Ambassador of Peace*, 3 vols. (London: Hodder & Stoughton, 1929–30).

DANIEL, D. R., Papers in the National Library of Wales.

DARLOW, T. H., *William Robertson Nicoll, Life and Letters* (London: Hodder & Stoughton, 1925).

DAVIDSON, RANDALL, *see* BELL.

DE VALERA, *see* MACMANUS.

DEVONSHIRE, 8TH DUKE OF, *see* HOLLAND.

DIGBY, MARGARET, *Horace Plunkett, An Anglo-American Irishman* (Oxford: Blackwell, 1949).

DONALD, ROBERT, *see* TAYLOR.

DOVE, JOHN, *see* BRAND.

DUGDALE, B. E. C., *Arthur James Balfour, First Earl of Balfour*, 2 vols. (London: Hutchinson, 1936).

EAGAR, W. McG., private diary.

EDWARDS, A. G., ARCHBISHOP OF WALES, *Memories* (London: Murray, 1927).

ELLIS, T. I., *Thomas Edward Ellis, Cofiant*, 2 vols. (Liverpool: Evans, 1944). A biography in Welsh by his son.

ELTON, LORD, *Life of James Ramsay MacDonald, 1866–1919* (London: Collins, 1939).

ESHER, VISCOUNT, *Journal and Letters of Reginald Viscount Esher*, edited by MAURICE V. BRETT, 4 vols. (London: Ivor Nicholson & Watson, 1934–8).

FEILING, KEITH, *Life of Neville Chamberlain* (London: Macmillan, 1946).

FITZROY, SIR ALMERIC, *Memoirs*, 2 vols. (London: Hutchinson, 1926).

FOCH, *see* HART.

GARDINER, A. G., *Life of Sir William Harcourt*, 2 vols. (London: Constable, 1923).

GARVIN, J. L., *Life of Joseph Chamberlain*, 3 vols. (London: Macmillan, 1932–4; 4th volume by Julian Amery, in preparation).

GEORGE, WILLIAM, *Atgof A Myfyr* (Cardiff: Hughes, 1948). 'Recollection and Reflection', in Welsh, by the brother of Lloyd George.

—— *Richard Lloyd, Cricieth* (Cardiff: Western Mail and Echo, 1934). A biography in Welsh by his nephew.

GLADSTONE, *see* MORLEY.

GORE, JOHN, *King George V, A Personal Memoir* (London: John Murray, 1941).

GREY, EDWARD, VISCOUNT GREY OF FALLODON, *Twenty-Five Years, 1892–1916*, 2 vols. (London: Hodder & Stoughton, 1925). *See also* TREVELYAN.

GRIGG, SIR JAMES, *Prejudice and Judgment* (London: Cape, 1948).

GWYNN, DENIS, *Life of John Redmond* (London: Harrap, 1932).

GWYNN, STEPHEN, *John Redmond's Last Years* (London: Arnold, 1919).

HAIG, *see* CHARTERIS; COOPER.

HALDANE, R. B., *Viscount Haldane, An Autobiography* (London: Hodder & Stoughton, 1929). *See also* MAURICE.

HAMILTON, M. A., *Arthur Henderson* (London: Heinemann, 1938).

HAMMOND, J. L., *C. P. Scott of the 'Manchester Guardian'* (London: Bell, 1934).

HARDINGE OF PENSHURST, LORD, *Old Diplomacy* (London: John Murray, 1947).

HARRIS, R. W., *Not so Humdrum; The Autobiography of a Civil Servant* (London: Lane, 1939).

HART, B. H. L., *Foch, the Man of Orleans* (London: Eyre & Spottiswoode, 1931).

HASTINGS, SIR PATRICK, *Autobiography* (London: Heinemann, 1948).

HEALY, T. M., *Letters and Leaders of My Day*, 2 vols. (London: Thornton Butterworth, 1928).

HENDERSON, ARTHUR, *see* HAMILTON.

HENDRICK, B. J., *Life and Letters of Walter H. Page*, 3 vols. (London: Heinemann, 1922–5).

HETHERINGTON, SIR HECTOR, *Life and Letters of Sir Henry Jones* (London: Hodder & Stoughton, 1924).

HOLLAND, BERNARD, *Life of Spencer Compton, Eighth Duke of Devonshire* (London: Longmans, Green, 1911).

HOUSE, E. M., *The Intimate Papers of Colonel House*, arranged as a narrative by CHARLES SEYMOUR, 4 vols. (London: Benn, 1926–8).

HUDSON, SIR ROBERT, *see* SPENDER.

ISAACS, SIR RUFUS, *see* READING.

JONES, SIR HENRY, *see* HETHERINGTON.

KENWORTHY, J. M., *Sailors, Statesmen and Others: An Autobiography* (London: Rich & Cowan, 1933).

KITCHENER, *see* ARTHUR.

LANG, C. G., *see* LOCKHART.

LAW, B., *see* TAYLOR.

LEWIS, SIR HERBERT, Papers in the National Library of Wales.

LLOYD, RICHARD, *see* GEORGE.

LOCKHART, J. G., *Cosmo Gordon Lang* (London: Hodder & Stoughton, 1949).

LONDONDERRY, MARQUESS OF, *Wings of Destiny* (London: Macmillan, 1943).

LUDENDORFF, GENERAL, *My War Memories, 1914–1918*, 2 vols. (London: Hutchinson, 1919).

MACDONALD, RAMSAY, *see* ELTON.

MCKENNA, STEPHEN, *Reginald McKenna, 1863–1943* (London: Eyre & Spottiswoode, 1948).

MACKINTOSH, SIR ALEXANDER, *Echoes of Big Ben: Parliamentary Journalist's Diary from 1881–1940* (London: Jarrolds, 1945).

MACMANUS, M. J., *Eamon de Valera* (Dublin: Talbot Press, 1944).

BIBLIOGRAPHY

MARJORIBANKS, EDWARD, *The Life of Lord Carson*, vol. i (London: Gollancz, 1932).

MASTERMAN, LUCY, *C. F. G. Masterman* (London: Ivor Nicholson & Watson, 1939).

MAURICE, SIR FREDERICK, *Lord Haldane, 1915–1928*, 2 vols. (London: Faber & Faber, 1939).

MIDLETON, EARL OF, *Records and Reactions, 1856–1939* (London: John Murray, 1939).

MILLIN, S. G., *General Smuts*, 2 vols. (London: Faber & Faber, 1936).

MORANT, SIR ROBERT, *see* ALLEN.

MORLEY, JOHN, VISCOUNT MORLEY, *Life of William Ewart Gladstone*, 3 vols. (London: Macmillan, 1903).

MURRAY, A. C., *At Close Quarters* (London: John Murray, 1946).

—— *Master and Brother* (London: John Murray, 1945).

NEVINS, ALLAN, *Henry White, Thirty Years of American Diplomacy* (New York: Harper, 1930).

NICOLL, WILLIAM ROBERTSON, *see* DARLOW.

NICOLSON, HAROLD, *Curzon, the Last Phase 1919–1925* (London: Constable, 1934).

O'HIGGINS, KEVIN, *see* WHITE, T.

OLIVER, F. S., *The Anvil of War; Letters between F. S. Oliver and his Brother, 1914–1918*, edited by STEPHEN GWYNN (London: Macmillan, 1936).

OXFORD AND ASQUITH, EARL OF, *H. H. A., Letters of Earl of Oxford and Asquith to a Friend*, first series, 1915–22, second series, 1922–7 (London: Bles, 1933, 1934).

—— *Memories and Reflections, 1852–1927*, 2 vols. (London: Cassell, 1928).

PAGE, W. H., *see* HENDRICK.

PARES, SIR BERNARD, *My Russian Memoirs* (London: Cape, 1931).

PERSHING, J. J., *My Experiences in the World War* (London: Hodder & Stoughton, 1931).

PETRIE, SIR CHARLES, *Life and Letters of the Right. Hon. Sir Austen Chamberlain*, 2 vols. (London: Cassell, 1939–40).

PLUNKETT, SIR HORACE, *see* DIGBY.

POINCARÉ, RAYMOND, *Memoirs of Raymond Poincaré*, translated and adapted by SIR GEORGE ARTHUR, 4 vols. (London: Heinemann, 1926–30).

READING, 2ND MARQUESS OF, *Rufus Isaacs, First Marquess of Reading*, 2 vols. (London: Hutchinson, 1942, 1945).

REDMOND, JOHN, *see* GWYNN, D.

RENDEL, LORD, *Personal Papers of Lord Rendel*, edited by F. E. HAMER (London: Benn, 1931).

RIDDELL, LORD, *Lord Riddell's Intimate Diary of the Peace Conference and After, 1918–1923* (London: Gollancz, 1933).

—— *Lord Riddell's War Diary 1914–1918* (London: Ivor Nicholson & Watson, 1933).

—— *More Pages from my Diary, 1908–1914* (London: Country Life, 1934).

297

ROBERTSON, SIR WILLIAM, *From Private to Field Marshal* (London: Constable, 1921).

ROBERTSON, SIR WILLIAM, *Soldiers and Statesmen, 1914–1918*, 2 vols. (London: Cassell, 1926).

RONALDSHAY, EARL OF, *The Life of Lord Curzon*, 3 vols. (London: Benn, 1928).

SAMUEL, VISCOUNT, *Memoirs* (London: Cresset Press, 1945).

SCOTT, C. P., *see* HAMMOND.

SHAKESPEARE, SIR GEOFFREY, BT., *Let Candles Be Brought In* (London: Macdonald, 1949).

SNOWDEN, VISCOUNT (PHILIP), *An Autobiography*, 2 vols. (London: Ivor Nicholson & Watson, 1934).

SPENDER, J. A., *Sir Robert Hudson, a Memoir* (London: Cassell, 1930).

—— *Weetman Pearson, First Viscount Cowdray* (London: Cassell, 1930).

—— and CYRIL ASQUITH, *Life of Lord Oxford and Asquith*, 2 vols. (London: Hutchinson, 1932).

STEED, H. W., *Through Thirty Years, 1892–1922*, 2 vols. (London: Heinemann, 1924).

SWINTON, VISCOUNT, *I Remember* (London: Hutchinson, 1948).

TAYLOR, H. A., *Robert Donald* (London: Stanley Paul, 1934).

—— *The Strange Case of Andrew Bonar Law* (London: Stanley Paul, 1934).

TREVELYAN, G. M., *Grey of Fallodon* (London: Longmans, Green, 1937).

WAVELL, LORD, *Generals and Generalship* (New York: Macmillan, 1941).

WEBB, BEATRICE, *Our Partnership* (London: Longmans, Green, 1948).

WHITE, HENRY, *see* NEVINS.

WHITE, T. DE V., *Kevin O'Higgins* (London: Methuen, 1948).

WHITE, W. A., *Woodrow Wilson: The Man, his Times and his Task* (London: Benn, 1926).

WILLIAMS, A. T., *Cheerful Giver: The Life of Harold Williams* (London: Peter Davies, 1935).

WILSON, SIR HENRY, *see* CALLWELL.

WILSON, WOODROW, *see* BAKER; WHITE, W. A.

General Works

ARNDT, H. W., *The Economic Lessons of the Nineteen-Thirties* (Oxford University Press, 1944).

ASTOR, WALDORF, and SEEBOHM ROWNTREE, *The Agricultural Dilemma* (London: King, 1935).

BERRY, W. E., 1ST VISCOUNT CAMROSE, *British Newspapers and Their Controllers* (London: Cassell, 1947).

BIRDSALL, PAUL, *Versailles Twenty Years After* (London: Allen & Unwin, 1941).

BONSAL, STEPHEN, *Unfinished Business* (London: Michael Joseph, 1944).

Carnegie Endowment for International Peace, *Paris Peace Conference: History and Documents* (New York: Columbia University Press, 1938).

BIBLIOGRAPHY

CARR, E. H., *The Twenty Years' Crisis, 1919–1939* (2nd ed.; London: Macmillan, 1946).

CHURCHILL, WINSTON, *The World Crisis*, 2 vols. (London: Odhams Press, 1938; originally published in 6 vols. by Thornton Butterworth, 1923–31).

―― *The Second World War*, vol. i, *The Gathering Storm* (London: Cassell, 1948); vol. ii, *Their Finest Hour* (1949); vol. iii, *The Grand Alliance* (1950).

CLEMENCEAU, GEORGES, *Grandeur and Misery of Victory*, translated by F. M. ATKINSON (London: Harrap, 1930).

CRUTTWELL, C. R. M. F., *A History of the Great War, 1914–1918* (2nd ed.; Oxford: Clarendon Press, 1936).

D'ABERNON, VISCOUNT, *The Eighteenth Decisive Battle of the World, Warsaw, 1920* (London: Hodder & Stoughton, 1931).

DAWES, CHARLES, *A Journal of the Great War* (London: Allen & Unwin, 1930).

FORBES, MAJ.-GEN. A., *History of the Army Ordnance Services*, 3 vols. (London: Medici Society, 1930).

FRASER, LINDLEY, *Germany between Two Wars* (Oxford University Press, 1944).

GATHORNE-HARDY, G. M., *A Short History of International Affairs 1920–1939* (4th ed., revised; Oxford University Press, 1950).

GEORGE, WILLIAM, *Cymru Fydd: Hanes y mudiad cenedlaethol cyntaf* (Liverpool: Evans, 1945).
    A history in Welsh of the first national movement.

GOOCH, G. P., *Recent Revelations of European Diplomacy* (London: Longmans, Green, 1930).

―― *Studies in Diplomacy and Statecraft* (London: Longmans, Green, 1942).

HALÉVY, ELIE, *A History of the English People; Epilogue, 1895–1905, 1905–1915*, 2 vols. (London: Benn & Unwin, 1929; Benn, 1934).

HANKEY, LORD, *Diplomacy by Conference; Studies in Public Affairs 1920–1946* (London: Benn, 1946).

―― *Government Control in War* (Cambridge University Press, 1945).

HARGREAVES, E. L., *The National Debt* (London: Arnold, 1930).

HARRIS, R. W., *National Health Insurance in Great Britain, 1911–1946* (London: Allen & Unwin, 1946).

HART, LIDDELL, *A History of the World War, 1914–1918* (London: Faber & Faber, 1934).

―― *Through the Fog of War* (London: Faber & Faber, 1938).

HUGHES, W. M., *Crusts and Crusades* (Sydney: Angus & Robertson, 1947).

JESSOP, T. E., *The Treaty of Versailles; Was It Just?* (London: Nelson, 1942).

JORDAN, W. M., *Great Britain, France, and the German Problem, 1918–1939* (Oxford University Press, 1943).

KEYNES, J. M., *Economic Consequences of the Peace* (London: Macmillan, 1919).

299

LEVY, HERMANN, *National Health Insurance* (Cambridge University Press, 1944).
    Contains a useful bibliography of this subject.
McCALLUM, R. B., *Public Opinion and the Last Peace* (Oxford University Press, 1944).
    An admirable corrective of much in Keynes's *Economic Consequences of the Peace.*
MACARDLE, DOROTHY, *The Irish Republic* (London: Gollancz, 1937).
McFADYEAN, SIR ANDREW, *Reparation Reviewed* (London: Benn, 1930).
MACHRAY, ROBERT, *Poland 1914–1931* (London: Allen & Unwin, 1932).
MALLET, SIR BERNARD, *British Budgets 1887–1888 to 1912–1913* (London: Macmillan, 1913).
—— and GEORGE, C. O., *British Budgets, 1913–14 to 1920–21* (London: Macmillan, 1929).
MANTEYER, G. DE, *Austria's Peace Offer 1916–1917* (London: Constable, 1921).
MANTOUX, ÉTIENNE, *The Carthaginian Peace or the Economic Consequences of Mr. Keynes* (Oxford University Press, 1946).
MARSTON, F. S., *The Peace Conference of 1919, Organization and Procedure* (Oxford University Press, 1944).
    Contains chronology and bibliography of the Conference.
MAURICE, SIR FREDERICK, *The Intrigues of the War* (London, 1922; reprinted from the *Westminster Gazette*).
MEDLICOTT, W. N., *British Foreign Policy since Versailles* (London: Methuen, 1940).
MERMEIX (*pseud.*), *see* TERRAIL.
MILLS, J. S., *The Genoa Conference*, foreword by LLOYD GEORGE (London: Hutchinson, 1922).
MORGAN, J. H., *Assize of Arms; Being the Story of the Disarmament of Germany and her Rearmament (1919–1939)* (London: Methuen, 1945).
MOWAT, R. B., *A History of European Diplomacy* (London: Edward Arnold, 1927).
NICOLSON, HAROLD, *Peacemaking 1919* (London: Constable, 1933; with new introduction, 1945).
NOEL BAKER, PHILIP, *The Private Manufacture of Armaments*, prefatory note by VISCOUNT CECIL (London: Gollancz, 1936).
O'BRIEN WILLIAM, *The Irish Revolution and How It Came About* (London: Allen & Unwin, 1923).
O'HEGARTY, P. S., *The Victory of Sinn Fein: How It Won It and How It Used It* (Dublin: Talbot Press, January 1925).
OXFORD AND ASQUITH, EARL OF, *Fifty Years of Parliament*, 2 vols. (London: Cassell, 1926).
PAKENHAM, FRANK, *Peace by Ordeal* (London: Cape, 1935).
    An account, from first-hand sources, of the negotiation and signing of the Anglo-Irish Treaty in 1921.
PALLIS, A. A., *Greece's Anatolian Venture and After* (London: Methuen, 1937).

PARES, SIR BERNARD, *A History of Russia* (London: Cape, 1937).

RAPPARD, W. E., *The Quest for Peace since the World War* (Oxford University Press, 1940).

REPINGTON, COLONEL, *The First World War*, 2 vols. (London: Constable, 1920).

SALTER, SIR ARTHUR, *Personality in Politics* (London: Faber & Faber, 1947). [Chapter iii, Lloyd George.]

SEYMOUR, CHARLES, *American Diplomacy During the World War* (Oxford University Press, 1934).

SHOTWELL, J. T., *At the Paris Peace Conference* (London: Macmillan, 1937).

Social Security, edited by WILLIAM A. ROBSON (London: Allen & Unwin, 1943).

SPEARS, E. L., *Prelude to Victory* (London: Cape, 1939).

SPENDER, J. A., *New Lamps and Ancient Lights* (London: Cassell, 1940).

STAMP, JOSIAH, *The Financial Aftermath of War* (London: Benn, 1932).

TARDIEU, ANDRÉ, *The Truth about the Treaty*, introduction by CLEMENCEAU (London: Hodder & Stoughton, 1921).

TEMPERLEY, HAROLD, editor, *A History of the Peace Conference of Paris*, 6 vols. (London: Frowde, Hodder & Stoughton, 1920–4).

TERRAIL, GABRIEL (Mermeix, *pseud.*), *Les Combats des Trois* (Paris: Ollendorff, 1922).

—— *Nivelle et Painlevé* (Paris: Ollendorff, 1919).

VIDLER, A. R., *The Orb and the Cross* (London: S.P.C.K., 1945).
    A discussion of the relation between spiritual and secular power, with special reference to Gladstonian Liberalism.

WHEELER-BENNETT, J. W., *Brest-Litovsk: The Forgotten Peace* (London: Macmillan, 1938).

—— *The Disarmament Deadlock* (London: Routledge, 1934).

—— *Munich: Prologue to Tragedy* (London: Macmillan, 1948).

—— *The Wreck of Reparations; Being the Political Background of the Lausanne Agreement 1932* (London: Allen & Unwin, 1933).

WITHERS, HARTLEY, *War and Lombard Street* (London: Smith, 1915).

WOODWARD, E. L., *Great Britain and the German Navy* (Oxford University Press, 1935).

YOUNG, G. M., *The Government of Britain* (London: Collins, 1941).

ZIMMERN, SIR ALFRED, *Europe in Convalescence* (London: Mills & Boon, 1922).

—— *The League of Nations and the Rule of Law* (2nd ed., revised; London: Macmillan, 1939).

III

PERIODICAL MATERIAL
Articles

AMERY, L. S., 'Henry Wilson', *Blackwood's Magazine* (August 1922).

The Annual Register, A Review of Public Events at Home and Abroad (London: Longmans, Green).

Anonymous, 'Stanley Baldwin, Earl Baldwin of Bewdley, A Memoir', pamphlet published by *The Times*, December 1947.

BEVERIDGE, SIR WILLIAM, 'Sir Hubert Llewellyn Smith', in *Economic Journal* (March 1946).

BINKLEY, R. C., 'Ten Years of Peace Conference History', *Journal of Modern History*, vol. i (Chicago, 1929).

BIRDSALL, PAUL, 'The Second Decade of Peace Conference History', ibid., vol. xi (Chicago, 1939).

BIRKETT, JUSTICE, 'International Legal Theories Evolved at Nuremberg', in *International Affairs* (July 1947).

BLISS, T. H., 'The Evolution of the Unified Command', *Foreign Affairs* (December 1922).

BOWMAN, ISAIAH, 'The Strategy of Territorial Decisions', ibid. (January 1946).

CECIL, ALGERNON, 'Mr. Lloyd George: A Page of History', *Quarterly Review* (October 1922).

CHIROL, VALENTINE, 'Lloyd George's Foreign Policy', *Edinburgh Review* (January 1923).

EDMONDS, BRIG.-GEN. SIR J. E., 'The Fifth Army in March, 1918', *Journal Royal United Service Institution* (February 1937).
    Sir James is the chief compiler of the Official History of the War, 1914–18.

EVANS, B. G., 'Mr. Lloyd George', *Fortnightly Review* (June 1916).

FISHER, H. A. L., 'Lloyd George's Foreign Policy', *Foreign Affairs* (March 1923).

KEYNES, J. M., 'War and the Financial System, August 1914', in *Economic Journal* (September 1914).

MANSERGH, NICHOLAS, 'The Implications of Eire's Relationship with the British Commonwealth of Nations', *International Affairs* (January 1948).

MARKHAM, VIOLET, 'Robert Morant—Some Personal Reminiscences', *Public Administration* (Winter 1950).

MASSINGHAM, H. W., 'The Position of Mr. Lloyd George', *Nation* (6 January 1912).

MILNER, VISCOUNT, 'Report to Cabinet', *New Statesman*, supplement (23 April 1921). Memorandum to the Cabinet by Lord Milner on his visit to France, including the Conference at Doullens, 26 March 1918.

NEVINSON, HENRY, 'Lloyd George: The Leader of British Liberals', in *Foreign Affairs* (April 1931).

RATCLIFFE, S. K., 'Election Rhetoric in Queen's Hall', in *New Statesman* (24 November 1923).

SCHMIDT, WOLFGANG, 'Über den Stil der politischen Rede', *Englishe Kultur* (Marburg, 1936). [Lloyd George's and Baldwin's oratory compared.]

SIDEBOTHAM, HERBERT, 'Mr. Lloyd George: An Appreciation', *Atlantic Monthly* (November 1919).

SPENDER, HAROLD, 'Unemployment Insurance', *Contemporary Review* (January 1909).

BIBLIOGRAPHY

Survey of International Affairs, edited by ARNOLD J. TOYNBEE (Oxford University Press, published annually since 1920).

TEMPERLEY, HAROLD, 'War Guilt in the Peace Treaty', *History* (October 1932).

WEBSTER, SIR CHARLES K., 'Patterns of Peace-making', *Foreign Affairs* (July 1947).

—— 'Peace Making: Vienna, Paris, and Today', *Agenda* (May 1943).

WINDSOR, EDWARD, DUKE OF, in *Life* (New York, 22 December 1947).

Newspapers

The author has relied mainly on the reports of *The Times* and the *Manchester Guardian*, and in Welsh on *Baner ac Amserau Cymru* and *Y Genedl Gymreig* (the files of the latter were consulted at the University College of North Wales, Bangor, by courtesy of the Librarian). There is also useful material in the party publications, for example: *Liberal Magazine*, a monthly issued by the Liberal Publication Department; *Gleanings and Memoranda*, a monthly issued by the National Union of Conservative and Unionist Associations; *Lloyd George Liberal Magazine*, a monthly issued from October 1920 to November 1923.

Many other newspapers have been consulted, among them: *Western Mail, Liverpool Daily Post, News Chronicle, Daily Telegraph, Eye-Witness, Goleuad* (in Welsh), *North Wales Observer and Express*—but to list them all would be impossible; the reader will find specific references in the text.

INDEX

INDEX

Government, May 1915, 59; sets up Ministry of Munitions, with Lloyd George as Minister, May 1915, 61; growing dissension between Asquith and Lloyd George, 1916, 70, 71, 72; denounces proposals for negotiated peace, Oct. 1916, 76; present at conference with the French at Boulogne, Oct. 1916, 77; Cabinet crisis, Nov.–Dec. 1916, 78–80, 83–7; sets up War Committee, Nov. 1915, 80; visits Ireland after Easter Rebellion, May 1916, 81; resigns, Dec. 1916, 86; character as Parliamentarian, 86; dislike of publicity and self-advertisement, 79, 89; Lord Derby proposes him as Ambassador to Paris, 1917, 127; opposes appointment of a generalissimo, 1918, 137; moves appointment of Select Committee to inquire into charges against Lloyd George by Sir Frederick Maurice, May 1918, 149; proposes that Ireland be placed on Dominion basis, Jan. 1920, 189; tentative approaches between Asquith and Lloyd George for reunion of Liberal Party, Nov. 1922, 204; agrees with Lloyd George on policy for Liberal Party in election campaign, Nov. 1923, 208; loses seat in Commons, Oct. 1924, 211; accepts Earldom, 211; renewed tension with Lloyd George, 1924, 211; supports Baldwin Government in General Strike, 1926, 218; final breach with Lloyd George, May 1926, 220–5; resigns leadership of Liberal Party, 1926, 223; his typically English mentality and reserve, 267.

Asquith, Margot (Countess of Oxford and Asquith), 72, 223, 278, 281.
Astor, John Jacob, 196.
Astor, Nancy (Viscountess Astor), 67, 254.
Astor, Waldorf, 94, 239.
Atgof a Myfyr (William George), 260.
Attlee, Clement R., 270.
Austria: Lloyd George's visit to, 1908, 36; Lloyd George proposes attack on, 1917, 116; Charles of, Emperor, 127; Peace overtures by, 1917, 127, 128, 131, 132; Armistice terms for, 156; surrender of, 157; Treaty with, 178; crisis in, 1931, 235; Nazi control of, 237; annexation of, by Germany, 251.
Auxiliaries, in Ireland, 188.

Baden, Prince Max of, 154.
Baghdad, capture of, 1917, 115.

Baker, Ray Stannard, 146, 147, 169.
Baldwin, Lucy (Countess Baldwin of Bewdley), 288.
Baldwin, Stanley (Earl Baldwin of Bewdley), 181, 268, 276, 280, 283; unknown to public when first in office, 89; describes partnership of Lloyd George and Bonar Law, 1916–18, as the most perfect in political history, 96; announces intention to protect home market, 1923, 207; goes to country on Tariff issue, 1923, 208; Prime Minister for second time, 1924, 210; antagonism between Lloyd George and Baldwin, 211, 287, 288; verdict on General Strike, 1926, 219; carries Trades Disputes Act, 1926, 225; complains of Lloyd George's articles in foreign Press, 1928, 227; condemns Liberal programme for 1929 General Election, 229; 'Safety First' slogan for 1929 General Election, 230; advocacy of Tariff Reform, 1930, 232; refuses invitation to Three-Party Conference on unemployment, 1930, 232; negotiates for inclusion of Lloyd George in his Cabinet, 1935, 239; takes part in public demonstration for disarmament, 1931, 241; returned to power in General Election, 1935, 243; charged with forcing abdication of Edward VIII because of latter's public sympathy with poor and workless, 249; Bardic strain in him, 262; as letter writer, 267; share in dissolution of Liberal Party, 282; says House of Commons 'filled with hard-faced men who look as though they had done very well out of the war', 1919, 287.

Balfour, A. J. (Earl of Balfour), 83, 125, 127, 165, 276; introduces Education Bill, 1902, 29; resigns, 1905, 32, 33; member of Buckingham Palace Conference on constitutional issue arising from rejection of Budget by House of Lords, 1910, 39; member of first Coalition Government, 1915, 59; member of Anglo-French conference at Boulogne, Oct. 1916, 77; supports Lloyd George's first attempt at solution of Irish question, 1916, 82; position of, in Cabinet crisis, 1916, 84; present at Buckingham Palace meeting during 1916 Cabinet crisis, 86; supports Lloyd George's efforts to secure all-party backing for second Coalition Government, Dec. 1916, 92; leads mission to

INDEX

Washington to hasten American help, Apr. 1917, 114; views on Germany's first indirect peace advances, Aug. 1917, 129; goes to Paris to discuss use of American troops, May 1918, 147; at Peace Conference, Jan. 1919, 167; his part in Treaties with Austria, Bulgaria, Hungary, and Turkey, 1920, 178; signs Anglo-American Guarantee of French territory, 180, 181; British representative at Washington Conference, Nov. 1921, 183; remains loyal to Lloyd George at the 'Carlton Club Meeting' crisis, Oct. 1922, 200; his powers as a debater, 262.

Balfour Declaration, The, 1917, 126.
Balfour, Jabez, 275.
Balkans: Lloyd George proposes attack via, 1915, 55, 56; Jellicoe urges withdrawal from, 1917, 100; Lloyd George proposes Anglo-Italian campaign in, 1917, 108; Lloyd George urges admission of, to Treaty of Locarno, 1925, 213.
Bangor, 24, 34; Lloyd George opens his 1915, 105; Lloyd George opens his 'New Deal' campaign at, 1935, 238.
Bank Charter Act, suspension of, 1914, 50.
Bank of England, 234; Governor of, 50, 51, 53.
Baring's Bank, 51.
Barisis, junction of French and British armies, 1918, 137.
Barnes, George, 97, 98.
Barthou, representative of Poincaré at Genoa Conference, 1922, 184.
Beauvais, Conference at, 3 Apr. 1918, 140, 145.
Beaverbrook, Lord, 70, 71, 78, 83, 84, 86, 142, 204, 258.
Beer, duty on, 1915, 52.
Beersheba, capture of, 1917, 116.
Belgium: visit of Lloyd George to, 1908, 36; invasion of, 1914, 48; question of the future of, in early peace negotiations, 1917, 129, 130, 131; representation of, at Peace Conference, 1919, 170; signs Treaty of Locarno, Oct. 1925, 212; overrun by Germany, 1940, 254; capitulation of, 1940, 255.
Berchtesgaden, 245, 246, 251, 274.
Berea Chapel, 260.
Bernstorff, Count, 99.
Berthelot, General, 108.
Bethmann-Hollweg, Count von, 98.
Béthune, German attack on, Apr. 1918, 144.

Bevan, Aneurin, 41.
Beveridge, W. H. (Lord Beveridge), 39, 71, 123.
Bible, The, 29, 265.
Birkenhead, Earl of. See Smith, F. E.
Birmingham Gazette, 220.
Birrell, Augustine, 39.
Bismarck, Count Otto von, 248, 288.
Black and Tans, 188.
Bliss, General, 134, 140, 146.
Blockade. See Submarine.
Blockade of Germany, threat to re-impose, 175.
Boer War. See South African War.
Bolsheviks, 105, 106.
Bolshevism, growing fear of, 171, 173, 185. See Communism.
Bonar Law. See Law.
Bonsal, Stephen, 168.
Booth, Charles: Life and Labour of the People in London, 33.
Boothby, Robert, 211.
Botha, Louis, 29, 81, 174.
Bottomley, Horatio, 275.
Bouillon, Franklin, 125.
Boundary Commission, Irish, 192.
Bourbon, Sixte, Prince of, 127.
Bowman, Isaiah, 177.
Bradbury, Sir John (Lord Bradbury), 40, 50, 51.
Braithwaite, William John, 40.
Brazil, proposed admission of, to League of Nations, 213; visit of Lloyd George to, 1928, 225.
Breese, Jones, and Casson, Solicitors, 7, 10.
Brest-Litovsk, Treaty of, 130, 175, 179.
Briand, Aristide, 55, 101, 102, 108, 110, 182, 186, 198, 212, 227.
Britain, Battle of, 255.
Britain's Industrial Future (the 'Yellow Book'), 226.
British Association, 1915 meeting of, 52.
British Communist Party, 210, 243.
British Gazette, 218.
British People, Smuts on character of, 153.
Broadcasting, 91.
Brockdorff-Rantzau, Leader of German delegation to receive peace terms, 1919, 250.
Bron-y-de, 274.
'Brown Book', 216, 228, 274.
Bruce, Sir Robert, 191, 192.
Brusilov, General, 74, 76.
Buchan, John (Lord Tweedsmuir), 53, 270.
Bucharest, Treaty of, 175.

307

INDEX

Cunningham, Sir Andrew (Lord Cunningham), 258.
Curtis, Lionel, 191.
Curzon, Marquess, of Kedleston: member of first Coalition Government, 1915, 59; member of Asquith's War Committee, 80; position of, in Cabinet crisis of 1916, 85; supports second Coalition Government, 1916, 92; member of War Cabinet, 1916, 94, 96; Churchill's opinion of, 97; member of War Policy Committee, 1916, 115; his part in Treaties with Austria, Bulgaria, Hungary, and Turkey, 1920, 178.
Cymro, 19.
Cymru Fu versus Cymru Fydd, 11.
Cymru Fydd, 13.
Cymru Fydd League, 21.
Czar of Russia, 103.
Czarina of Russia, 103.
Czechoslovakia: signs the Treaty of Locarno, 1925, 212; 'firmly established as a citadel of freedom', 237; alliance of, with Soviet Russia, 245, 246; spread of Communism in, 246; British pledge to, 251; German occupation of, 1939, 252.
Czernin, Count, 131, 132.

D'Abernon, Lord, 184.
Daily Chronicle, 47, 61, 203, 223.
Daily Express, 247.
Daily Herald, 232.
Daily Mail, 28.
Daily News, 38.
Daily Telegraph, 86, 130.
Daniel, D. R., 26, 27, 29, 280.
Danton, 276.
Danzig, 171, 252.
Dardanelles: Dardanelles Commission, 56; Churchill's first proposal for attack on, Jan. 1915, 56; failure of bombardment of, Mar. 1915, 57; Cabinet divisions over operations at, 1915, 59; Dardanelles Committee, 1915, 79; proposed internationalization of, 1920, 198.
Davies, David (Lord Davies), 94, 104, 196.
Davies, Sir Joseph, 94.
Davies, J. T., 94.
Davies, Watkin, 24.
Davison, Sir Ronald, 69.
Dawes Plan, 241.
Dawson, Bertrand (Lord Dawson of Penn), 156, 244, 247, 276.
Dawson, Geoffrey, 85.
Death Duties, increase in, in 1909 Budget, 37.

Debts, International. See Reparations.
Defaulting Authorities Act, 1904, 31.
Defence of the Realm (Consolidation) Act, 1915, 65, 69.
Democracy: hope of extension of, throughout Europe after the First World War, unfulfilled, 179.
Democratic Party, in the United States, 164.
Depressed Areas, 1927–8, 225.
Depression of 1920, extent of, 195.
Derby, Earl of, 84, 127, 137, 147.
de Sauvigny, Bertier, 110.
d'Espéry, Franchet, 55, 154.
de Valera, Eamon, 190, 192, 193.
Development Fund, 1909, 37.
Development, National: suggested Committee of, 1928, 226.
— Board, proposed formation of, 1934, 239.
— Hitler's programme of, 246.
Devolution of government, Lloyd George works for, 1895, 22, 24, 25.
Devonport, Viscount, 101, 123.
Digby, Margaret, 285.
Dill, Sir Samuel, 278.
Dillon, John, 262.
Diplomacy: 'open' versus 'secret', 169; post-war changes in methods of, 179, 180.
Disarmament question, after First World War, 167, 168, 170, 171, 182, 183, 184, 185, 212, 213, 226, 227, 241, 243.
Disciples of Christ, Church of the, 2, 6.
Disestablishment, Welsh, 13, 40, 42; the dominant subject of political controversy in Wales since disestablishment of Irish Church in 1869, 11; placed second, after Home Rule for Ireland, on Liberal programme in General Election of 1892, 16; Asquith, as Home Secretary, moves Suspensory Bill, 1893, 17; Gladstone, against the grain, supports, 1893, 18; Asquith introduces Bill for Disestablishment of Church in Wales, 1894, 19; overshadowed by larger issues in 1906, 33.
Disraeli, Benjamin, 125, 267, 276.
Donald, Sir Robert, 61, 83.
Doullens, Conference at, 26 Mar. 1918, 139, 145.
Dove, John, 193.
Duff, Admiral Sir Alexander, 100.
Duma, the, 104.
Dumping, reparations not to be met by, 162.
Du Parcq, H., 8, 25.
Dwyfor: part of Lloyd George's title and his burial place, 260, 261.

INDEX

Apr. 1922, 185; signs Treaty of Locarno, Oct. 1925, 212; effects of absence of, from League of Nations, 212; applies for admission to League of Nations, 213; economic crisis in, 1931, 235; extends Nazi power over Austria, 1934, 237; Lloyd George's policy towards, 1920 and onwards, 240; British goodwill to, between the wars, 241; Lloyd George's belief in, as a bulwark against Communism, 242; inter-war relations of, with France, 242; Lloyd George opposes policy of appeasement, 243; reoccupies Rhineland, May 1935, 244; Lloyd George visits, 1936, 244; post-war remedies in for unemployment, 244; Hitler re-arms, 244, 245; Hitler declares Germany's satisfaction with territorial settlement in West, 245; Hitler would agree to air pact between France, Great Britain, and Germany, 245; Hitler proposes formation of Western bloc, 246; German–Japanese front against Communism proclaimed, 249; Rome–Berlin axis, proclamation of, 249; defies non-intervention in Spain, 249, 250; Anti-Comintern Pact, 1937, 252; occupies Czechoslovakia, 1939, 252; pact of non-agression with Russia, 1939, 252; Great Britain declares war on, 252; attacks Russia, 1941, 252; announces, with Russia, partition of Poland, 1939, 252; disarmament of, *see* Disarmament.

Gettysburg, Lloyd George visits battle-field of, 205.

'Ghent' Scheme of insurance against unemployment, 36.

Gladstone, W. E., 6, 14, 91, 262, 284; replies to a speech by Lloyd George in Commons, 1892, 15; returned to power, 1892, 16, 17; supports Welsh Disestablishment, 1893, 18; endowed with 'an untiring body subject to an unfailing will', 92, 238; crusader for Home Rule, 187; oratorical grandeur of, 263, 264; Disraeli's description of, 267; 'the biggest political figure in our history' (Lloyd George), 276; his scholarship, 278; charged with 'seeking refuge in a haven of ambiguity and leaving a trail of misunderstanding behind him', 285.

Gladstone, Lord, 195, 199, 222.

Gladstonian tradition, Lloyd George's admiration for, 197.

Glasgow Herald, 191.

Glendower, Owen, 276.

'Goat, The' (Baldwin's name for Lloyd George), 134, 211.

Godesberg, Neville Chamberlain visits Hitler at, 251.

Goebbels, Joseph, 241.

Goering, Hermann, 241.

Gold, drain of, 1931, 234, 235.

Gold Standard: Churchill announces return to, 1925, 214; Lloyd George criticizes return to, 1925, 215; abandonment of, 1931, 235.

Goleuad Cymru, 19, 22.

Gore, John, 248.

Gore. *See* Ormsby-Gore.

Goschen, G. J., 262.

Gough, Sir Hubert, 143.

Gounaris (Greek Prime Minister), 198.

Government of India Act, 1919, 196.

Government of Ireland Act, 1914, 159, 187; — 1920, 189.

Graham, Cunninghame, 14.

Great War, Official History of the, 64, 136, 137, 140, 151.

Greece: Lloyd George proposes attack on Central Powers via Salonika, 1915, 55; Sèvres, Treaty of, Aug. 1920, 178, 198; post-war tension with Turkey, 182; post-war policy of, in Near East, 197; Lloyd George's support for, 198; driven out of Smyrna by the Turks, 1922, 199; reconciled with Great Britain after crisis of 1922, 199.

'Green Book', 216, 228.

Greenwood, Sir Hamar (Viscount Greenwood), 189.

Greene, Wilfred (Lord Greene), 40.

Gretton, Sir John (Lord Gretton), 68.

Grey, Sir Edward (Viscount Grey of Fallodon), 46, 50, 77, 83, 185, 225; attitude of, to South African War, 28; supports Lloyd George's proposals for taxation of land values, 1909, 36; uninterested in military operations, 54; his 'failure to unite the Balkan States was the greatest defeat of his diplomacy during the war' (G. M. Trevelyan), 56; member of Asquith's new War Committee, 1915, 80; supports Baldwin Government in General Strike, 1926, 218; condemns Lloyd George's absolute control of political fund, 224; supports Lloyd George's programme for 1929 General Election, 229; Liberal Council, under his leadership, renounce Lloyd George, 1930, 232.

Griffith, Arthur, 190, 191.

Griffith, Ellis, 91.

Griffiths, James, 41.

314

British troops withdrawn from, to
meet German offensive, Mar. 1918,
147; Lloyd George and Clemenceau
embarrassed at Peace Conference by
secret Treaty of London (26 Apr.
1915), 168; post-war territorial settlement with, 172; post-war rivalry with
Greece for territorial gains in Asia
Minor, 197; signs Treaty of Locarno,
212; Lloyd George opposes appeasement of, 1935 onward, 243; partner
in Rome–Berlin axis, 1936, 249;
exchanges assurances with Great
Britain on mutual rights and interests in Mediterranean, 1937, 249;
defies non-intervention in Spain,
1937, 249, 250; invasion of Abyssinia, 1935, 249, 251; joins Anti-
Comintern Pact, Nov. 1937, 250;
Anglo-Italian Agreement, Apr. 1938,
251; Neville Chamberlain and Halifax toast King of Italy as Emperor
of Abyssinia, 1939, 249, 252; Bordeaux Government surrenders to,
1940, 255.

Jackson, Huth, 51.
Jackson, 'Stonewall', 205.
Jamaica, Lloyd George visits, 1936, 248.
Jameson, Dr., 26.
Japan: Lloyd George and Clemenceau
embarrassed at Peace Conference by
secret Treaty with, 168; Anglo-
Japanese Alliance, 1902, superseded
by Four Power Treaty of 1921, 183;
invades China, 1933, 237; German–
Japanese front against Communism
proclaimed, 1936, 249; joins Anti-
Comintern Pact, 1937, 250.
Jellicoe, Sir John (Earl Jellicoe), 99,
100, 118, 138.
Jerusalem, capture of by Allenby,
1917, 116.
Joffre, Marshal, 55, 56, 77, 107, 108,
110.
John, Augustus, 271.
Jones, Sir Henry, 95.
Jones, Thomas: quotations from Diary
of, 200, 245, 246, 258.
Jones, William, 26.
Journal of the Royal United Service
Institution, 151.
Journalism. See Press.
Junkers, 128.
Jutland, Battle of, 27 Apr. 1916, 74.

Kaiser Wilhelm II, 129, 130, 154, 158,
161, 169, 170.
Kellogg Pact, 1928, 227.
Kemal. See Mustapha.

Kemmel Hill, Germans repulsed at,
Apr. 1918, 144.
Kerensky, Alexander, 105.
Kerr, Philip (Marquess of Lothian),
151, 180; in Lloyd George's secretariat, 94; his part in peace negotiations of 1917, 131, 132; Secretary to
Lloyd George at Peace Conference,
166; drafts covering letter in which
revised Treaty of Peace is presented
to Germans, 16 June 1919, 175; mem-
ber of Two-Party Conference to con-
sider unemployment, 1930, 233;
visits Hitler, 242; his death, 1940,
255.
Keynes, John Maynard (Lord Keynes),
172, 177, 229.
Khaki Election, 1900, 28.
King, W. L. Mackenzie, 251.
Kitchener of Khartoum, Viscount, 29,
49, 54, 56, 58, 60, 69, 70, 80, 81, 107.
Knox, Sir Alfred, 104.
Krassin (leader of Russian Trade
Mission), 183.
Kruger, Paul, 26.
Kuhlmann, 129, 130.
Kut-el-Amara, 115.

Labour, Royal Commission on, 33.
— Lloyd George's skill in negotiation
with, 35; direction of, under the
Defence of the Realm Act, 1915, 65;
Treasury Agreement, 1915, 65;
women's labour in First World War,
65, 66; dilution of, in 1915, 65, 67;
resistance of, to Munitions of War
Act 1915–16, 69; unrest in, in First
World War, 64, 68, 69, 123, 124, 142;
post-war unrest in, 195.
Labour and the Nation, 232.
Labour Bureaux, 216.
Labour Exchanges Act, 1909, 39.
Labour, migration of, 1932–7, 240.
Labour Office, International, 179.
Labour Party, 97, 224, 288, 289; Liberal
Government of Jan. 1910, dependent
on support of, 38; Lloyd George
secures support of, for his Government, 1916, 92; opposes holding of
General Election in Dec. 1918, 159;
becomes official Opposition, 1922,
204; first Labour Government, June
1929, 208; defeated Oct. 1924, 210;
claim that Liberal programme of
1929 was stolen from them, 228; co-
operates with Liberal Party on question of unemployment, 1930, 233;
split in, on the formation of National
Government, 1931, 234; expulsion of
Ramsay MacDonald from, 1931, 235;

sions, 1918, 147; Maurice Debate,
May 1918, 147–52; his use of figures
in the Maurice Debate, 151; relations
with Clemenceau, 157, 168, 171, 172;
refuses to accept inclusion in Peace
Treaty of principle of freedom of
seas in war, 156, 157, 169; *The Truth
About the Peace Treaties*, 161, 164,
165, 167, 268, 271; speech at Bristol
on reparations, 11 Dec. 1918, 161,
162, 163, 172, 177; arrival in Paris
for Peace Conference, 11 Jan. 1919,
167; his chief concerns at Peace Conference, 168; Fontainebleau Memorandum, 'Some Considerations for
the Peace Conference Before They
Finally Draft Their Terms, 25 Mar.
1919', 170, 171, 240; his moderation
at Peace Conference attacked by
Northcliffe Press and in House of
Commons, 172, 173; met by the
King on his return from Peace Conference, 29 June 1919, 176; receives
Order of Merit, 5 Aug. 1919, 176;
devotes himself to the settlement of
Europe, 1919–22, 178; 'Prime Minister of Europe', 1919–22, 179; 'brings
into the foreground of international
debate the condition of the poor and
the oppressed', 179, 185; changes in
method of diplomacy effected by,
179, 180; at Conference of Genoa,
Apr. 1922, 186; mutual dislike between him and Poincaré, 184; the
Irish Question, his responsibility for
the settlement of, 1916–21, 70, 81,
82, 186–94; endeavours to secure
control of *The Times*, 1922, 196; his
extreme hostility to Turkey, 197;
his admiration for and support of
Venizelos, 197; encourages Greek
intervention in Anatolia, 1919, 198;
stands firm in Chanak crisis, Oct.
1919, 199; relations with the Independent Liberals, 199; his recommendations for Honours, 201, 202; his control and use of Liberal Party Fund,
201, 202, 203, 204, 211, 221, 222, 223,
224, 229, 231, 273; proposes formation of Centre Party, 1922, 203, 204;
joins in efforts to reunite Liberal
Party, 1922–6, 204, 207, 208, 216, 217;
his American tour, 1923, 204–6; his
opinion of President Wilson, 205;
his work in journalism, 207; his
opinion of Ramsay MacDonald, 208;
restates the Liberal creed, 1924, 209;
publishes *Coal and Power*, 1924, 209;
elected Chairman of Liberal Parliamentary Party, 1924, 211; denounces

return to Gold Standard, 1925, 214,
215; speech on 1925 Budget, 214–15;
campaigns for better use of the
land, 1925, 215, 216; his suggested
remedies for unemployment, 215,
228; Churt, reclamation of land at,
215; his attitude to General Strike,
1926, 217, 218, 219; his disagreement
with Liberal Shadow Cabinet, 1926,
219; his final breach with Asquith,
1926, 220–5; visit to Brazil, 1928, 225;
Mediterranean holiday, 1929, 228;
his supreme effort in 1929 General
Election campaign, 226–30; his difficult situation after 1929 Election,
231; Liberal Council renounce him,
Jan. 1930, 232; undergoes major
operation, 1931, 234; visit to Ceylon,
1931, 234, 236; his absence at critical
moment of formation of National
Government, 1931, 235; final rupture
with Liberal Party, 1931, 236, 237;
political activities confined to unemployment and disarmament, 1931–4,
237; prepares new programme of
reconstruction, 1934, 238; Father of
the House, 238; possibility that he
might join Baldwin's Cabinet, 1935,
239; his attitude towards Germany
in the 1920s, 240; — in the 1930s,
242, 244, 248; forms Council of
Action, 1935, 243; opposes policy of
appeasement to Germany and Italy,
243, 251; condones occupation of the
Rhineland by Hitler, 1936, 244; visit
to Germany, 1936, 245, 246; describes
Hitler as 'the greatest living German', 247; relations with George V
and Edward VIII, 248; his views on
abdication of Edward VIII, 249;
attacks Government for not intervening in Spain, Abyssinia, and
Manchuria, 1937, 249; disillusioned
about Hitler, 249; urges calling of
Conference of Great Britain, Germany, Russia, Italy, and the U.S. to
consider all problems menacing
peace, 1939, 253; celebrates fiftieth
year as Member for Caernarvon
Boroughs, 253; suggestions that he
should become Prime Minister, 1939,
254; invited to join the Cabinet,
1940, 255, 289; suggested as successor to Lord Lothian as Ambassador at Washington, 1940, 255;
favours a negotiated peace at outbreak of Second World War, 253,
256; his pessimism in the Second
World War, 256, 257, 258; last speech
in Parliament, 1942, 258; second

INDEX

MacDonald, Ramsay, 92, 233, 236, 238, 241, 262, 283, 288; Prime Minister, Jan. 1924, 208; defeated in General Election of Oct. 1924, 210; returned to power, 1929, 231; head of National Government, 1931, 234; expelled from Labour Party, 235.
Macedonia, 198.
Mackensen, General, 77.
Mackenzie King. See King.
McKenna, Reginald (Lord McKenna), 53, 60, 61, 80, 85.
McKenna Tariff, 207.
Maclay, Joseph (Lord Maclay), 101.
Maclean, Sir Donald, 233.
Madeira, visit of Lloyd George to, 1925, 213.
Malcolm, Sir Ian, 105.
Mallett, Charles, 49.
Manchester Guardian, 48, 69, 147, 148, 186, 189, 192, 220, 221, 229, 267.
Manchester Reform Club, 221.
Manchuria, Lloyd George denounces British vacillation regarding, 249.
Mandates, question of, at Peace Conference, 170.
Man-power, question of, in First World War, 58, 116, 123, 140–2, 145, 146, 147.
Manteyer, G. de, 127.
Mantoux, Paul, 250.
Marconi Episode, 1912, 27, 41–5.
Marlborough, Duke of, 53, 286.
Marne, first battle of, 1914, 54, 145; second battle of, 1918, 152, 153, 154.
Martial Law, proclamation of, in Ireland, 1920, 189.
Marx's *Capital*, 34.
Massingham, H. W., 38.
Masterman, C. F. G., 36, 40, 209, 219, 280.
Masterman, Mrs., 36, 219.
Matz, Battle of, 9 June 1918, 152.
Maude, General, 115, 271.
Maurice, Sir Frederick, 78, 125, 147–52.
Maurice Debate, May 1918, 147, 152, 160.
Max, Prince, of Baden, 154, 157.
May Committee, Feb. 1931, 233, 234.
May, Sir George, 233.
Medical Inspection of School Children Act, 1907, 39.
Mediterranean, Agreement regarding British and Italian rights in, 1937, 249.
Mediterranean, Lloyd George's holidays in, 24, 228.
Megiddo, Battle of, Sept. 1918, 154.
Meissner, Hitler's Secretary, 247.
Melbourne, Lord, 270.

Melchett, Lord, 208.
Mellon, Andrew, 205.
Memoirs, Lloyd George's. See *War Memoirs*.
Mensdorff, Count Albert, 131.
Mercantile Marine, 156. See Shipbuilding; Submarine.
Merchant Shipping Act, 1906, 35.
Merit, Order of, 176.
Mermeix (Gabriel Terrail), 117, 118.
Mesopotamia, campaign in, of 1918, 136.
Messines, Battle of, June 1917, 121.
Methodist Revival, effect of, in Wales, 3, 4.
Metternich, Count, 46.
Michaelis, German Chancellor, 1917, 128, 129, 130.
Midleton, Earl of, 82, 187, 188.
Military Operations, Director of, 77.
Military Service Bill, 1918, 140.
Mill, John Stuart, 34.
Millerand, President, 182.
Millin, Sarah Gertrude, 258.
Milner, Alfred (Viscount Milner), 96, 97, 123, 147, 149, 156, 174; in charge of negotiations preceding South African War, 27; drafts Bill for purchase of liquor trade, 1915, 68; member of first War Cabinet, 1916, 94; member of mission to Petrograd, Feb. 1917, 104; attends Conference in Rome, Jan. 1916, 108; member of War Policy Committee, May 1917, 115; opposes Flanders offensive, 1917, 119; supports Lloyd George in demanding unity of command, 137, 139, 145; his view that Lloyd George was 'the greatest War Minister since Chatham', 283.
Milne, Sir George (Lord Milne), 108.
Miners' Federation, 195, 210.
Mining Association, 195.
Mining Industry. See Coal.
Misérables, Les (Victor Hugo), 34.
Missions, Foreign, Lloyd George's support of, 10.
Mond, Sir Alfred (Lord Melchett), 208.
Money: Neville Chamberlain's cheap money policy, 1932–7, 240.
Montagu, Edwin (Lord Swaythling), 73, 85, 124, 125, 196, 198.
Morant, Sir Robert, 40.
Morley, John (Viscount Morley), 17, 22, 91, 278, 284.
Motor taxation, yield of, 1927–8, 228.
Moustiques. See Tanks.
Mudania, Armistice at, 1922, 199.
Mudros, Armistice signed at, 1918, 154, 157.

322

INDEX

George's impatience at slow arrival of, 146; — Pershing's opposition to splitting up of Divisions, 146, 147; — first battle of, 153; Navy, 153; Wilson promises pact to aid France if attacked after the war, 175; effects of absence of, from League, 212; Lloyd George's tour in, in 1923, 204–6; Lloyd George's articles in the Press of, 267.

Unity of command in First World War, question of, 98, 101, 106, 107, 108, 110, 111, 113, 135, 137, 139, 140, 145, 147.

Valera, De. *See* De Valera.
Vatican, the, 129.
Venizelos, Eleutherios, 180, 197, 198.
Verdun, Battle of, 1917, 74, 108.
Vereeniging, Peace of, 1902, 29, 174.
Versailles, chosen as meeting-place for Supreme Council, 134.
Versailles, Treaty of, 155, 156, 165, 169, 178, 212, 226, 244, 280; effect of Coupon Election on, 159; relation of, to the Armistice, 166; text of, presented to Germans, 173, 174; revised terms presented, 175; signature of, 175; failure of, 176; judgement on, 177, 178; ratified, 178; French determination to enforce, 178, 182, 184; agencies for execution of, 179; results of, 240.
Vimy Ridge, capture of, 1917, 112.
Viviani, René, 69.
Voluntary Schools Act, 1897, 25, 26, 29.
Votes of Credit, financing First World War with, 51.

Wages Agreement, National, in Coal Industry, 1924, 217.
Wages Board, National, 1921, 195.
Wales: national literature, 3; religion in, 3; class divisions in, 3, 4; culture of, 3, 6, 257; poetry, 3, 6; anglicism in, 4; growth of Liberalism in, 5, 12, 16; religious teaching in, 5; tithe question, 5, 10; growth of nationalism in, 11, 12, 14, 15, 81; National League, 11; Disestablishment question (*see* Disestablishment); Welsh Party, proposed formation of, 12; Liberal Party in, re-unites, 209; migration of labour from, 1932–7, 240; Welsh oratory, qualities of, 263; — Prince of: investiture, 1911, 248.
Wall Street, crash in 1929, 232.
Walpole, Sir Robert, 88, 283.
War Cabinet: formation of, Dec. 1916,

80, 94; Secretariat of, 94; procedure of, 95, 96.
War Committee: formation of, Nov. 1914, 79, 80; superseded by the War Cabinet, 1916, 94.
War Guilt clauses in Peace Treaty, 176.
War Loans, issue of, in First World War, 52.
War Memoirs (Lloyd George), *passim*; writing of begun, 268; criticism of, 269–73.
War Office, its deficiencies at outbreak of First World War, 57, 58, 64.
War, outlawing of, 212.
War Policy Committee, 115, 118, 119.
Washington, George, 214.
Washington, Treaty of, 1921 (Four-Power Treaty), 183.
Wavell, Sir Archibald (Viscount Wavell), 258.
We Can Conquer Unemployment (the 'Orange Book'), 228.
'Wee Frees', 195, 204.
Weimar National Assembly, 175, 178.
Weizmann, Chaim, 126.
Welfare State, the, 39, 290.
Wellington, Duke of, 120.
'Welsh Coercion' Act (Defaulting Authorities Act, 1904), 31.
Welsh Disestablishment. *See* Disestablishment.
Welsh Intermediate Education Act, 1889, 30.
Welsh Land Bill, 1899, 26.
Welsh language, Lloyd George's views on, 253.
Welsh Party, proposed formation of, 12.
Western bloc, Hitler proposes formation of, 246.
'Westerners' versus 'Easterners' in First World War, 55, 75, 102, 108, 115.
Westminster Abbey, memorial service for Lloyd George in, 261.
Westminster Gazette, 25, 149.
Westminster Hall, 88.
Wetzell, General, 143, 247.
Weygand, General, 134, 138.
Wheat, control of, in First World War, 124.
White, William Allen, 163.
Wilde, Jimmy, 275.
Williams, Harold, 104.
Williams, Llewelyn, 23, 280.
Wilson, Sir Henry, 104, 108, 111, 117, 120, 122, 125, 133, 134, 137, 138, 144, 147, 148, 154, 155, 194, 198.
Wilson, Sir Leslie, 197.
Wilson, Woodrow, 114, 118, 133, 146, 154, 167, 169, 173, 174, 178, 179, 205,

329

PRINTED IN
GREAT BRITAIN
AT THE
UNIVERSITY PRESS
OXFORD
BY
CHARLES BATEY
PRINTER
TO THE
UNIVERSITY